Japan and China

Japan and China

Mutual Representations in the Modern Era

Masuda Wataru

Translated by
Joshua A. Fogel

St. Martin's Press
New York

© 2000 Joshua A. Fogel

All rights reserved. No part of this book may be used or
reproduced in any manner whatsoever without written permission
except in the case of brief quotations embodied in critical articles
or reviews. For information, address:

St. Martin's Press, Scholarly and Reference Division,
175 Fifth Avenue, New York, N.Y. 10010

First published in the United States of America in 2000
Printed in Great Britain

Library of Congress Cataloging-in-Publication Data

Masuda, Wataru, 1903-1977.
   Japan and China : mutual representation in the modern era / Masuda Wataru ;
   translated by Joshua A. Fogel.
      p. cm.
   Includes bibliographical references (p.) and index.
   ISBN: 0–312–22840–6 (cloth)
      1. Japan–Intellectual life–1600-1868. 2. Japan–Foreign relations–To 1868. 3.
Europe–Relations–East Asia. 4. East Asia–Relations–Europe. 5. China–History–War
of 1840-1842. I. Title.

DS822.2 . M355 2000
303.48′251052–dc21

                                                                            99-0596782

Contents

Introduction

Masuda Wataru and the Study of Modern China

Joshua A. Fogel

Masuda Wataru, the author of the text that follows was born in a small fishing village in Shimane prefecture in 1903, the only son of a medical doctor.[a] Excelling at school, he entered Tokyo Imperial University's Department of Chinese Literature in 1926. It was not a particularly happy time to study there in the immediate aftermath of the Great Kantō Earthquake, and Masuda frequently made use of the Ueno Library at the time. The Faculty of Letters had been completely destroyed, and lectures were often held in makeshift barracks or in the operating rooms of the Medical School. He especially recalled enjoying the lectures of Shionoya On on the history of Chinese fiction and Taki Seiichi on East Asian art. He also studied with the great poet Satō Haruo and helped with his translations of Chinese fiction.

Upon graduation in 1929, he continued his translation work with Satō. Then, in March of 1931, he decided to go to Shanghai where good fortune enabled him to work and study under the great Chinese writer Lu Xun. Lu lectured Masuda on his own writings, allegedly every day, for three hours from March through December. Masuda later composed a biography of Lu Xun which was published serially in the journal *Kaizō*. He also came to know the Chinese writers Yu Dafu and Zheng Zhenduo at this time, and later Guo Moruo.

Returning to Japan in December of 1931, he communicated with Lu Xun until just before the latter's death in 1936. Masuda spent a great deal of time in the 1930s translating Lu's work, including an edition of his history of Chinese fiction under the title *Shina shōsetsu shi* (History of Chinese Fiction)[b] and, with Satō Haruo, of *Ro Jin senshū* (Selected Works of Lu Xun).[c] In October 1934, together with Takeuchi Yoshimi, Takeda Taijun, and Matsueda Shigeo, he helped organize the Chūgoku bungaku kenkyūkai (Research Group on Chinese Literature). For the next ten years, he wrote regularly for its organ, *Chūgoku bungaku geppō* (Chinese Literature Monthly).

In June of 1936 he traveled again to Shanghai to visit Lu Xun on his deathbed. It was this time that he also secured the rights to publish a translation of Mao Dun's *Zi ye* (Midnight), though he never completed this translation.

After returning to Japan in July, he was asked later in the year by the Kaizōsha publishing house to oversee the planned publication of *Dai Ro Jin zenshū* (The Complete Works of Lu Xun). He agreed, but left Kaizōsha in March of 1939.

Although Masuda did not see military action on the mainland during the Sino-Japanese War, he was active nonetheless. In May 1939, he worked for the Kō-A in or Asian Development Board on a project, which took him to Shanghai and Nanjing, investigating contemporary Chinese culture. From April 1940 to March 1942, he taught Chinese literature at Hōsei University. In November 1942 he went to work for the Dai Tō-A shō (Greater East Asian Ministry) on a project similar to that at the Kō-A in earlier.

After the conclusion of the war, he lectured for a time at Tokyo University in September 1946, taught at Keiō University from April 1947 to March 1949, and worked on and off for the Foreign Ministry. For nearly four years from July 1949 through February 1953, he taught at Shimane University in his home prefecture. The next month he began his longest teaching position at Ōsaka Municipal University which he left fourteen years later in March 1967. Toward the end of this stint, in November 1966, he visited China with a Japanese academic delegation and witnessed the Cultural Revolution in full form.

He began his last teaching position at Kansai University in April 1967 and retired in March 1974. In January of the following year, the Shanghai wenwu chubanshe published *Lu Xun zhi Zengtian She shuxin xuan* (Selection of Letters from Lu Xun to Masuda Wataru). When his old friend and colleague, Takeuchi Yoshimi, died in early 1977, Masuda was asked to give the funeral eulogy. While delivering his speech, Masuda collapsed and died of a heart attack on the cemetery ground.

Although his greatest contribution to scholarship was in the field of modern Chinese fiction, especially through translation – Masuda also translated *Liaozhai zhiyi* (Strange Stories from a Chinese Studio)[d] – still, he will be best remembered for his relationship with and translations of Lu Xun. He later wrote a memoir of his ties to Lu, *Ro Jin no inshō* (Impressions of Lu Xun).[e]

* * *

The volume translated here – *Seigaku tōzen to Chūgoku jijō, 'zassho' sakki* (The Eastern Movement of Western Learning and Conditions in China: Notes on 'Various Books') (Tokyo: Iwanami shoten, 1979) – marked a departure of sorts for Masuda. After many years of collecting books and manuscripts in both China and Japan, he prepared a series of 28 essays serialized in the journal *Shohyō* (issues 19–46 inclusive, May 1972–May 1977). It was the last work he would write, and he may have intended to write more. These represent the first 28 chapters of the volume translated here. The essay on Yamamoto Baigai appeared in *Kansai daigaku nenshi kiyō* (no. 2, December 1976); it was appended to the 28 essays when they were published in 1979.

The sheer love of books, bibliophilia in the best sense of the term, glistens through the pages of this book. Only someone with a lifetime's experience collecting and reading such works would have been prepared to devoted the exhaustive energies needed to write such a work. Anyone who continues to doubt the interrelatedness of Chinese and Japanese culture at the textual level is advised to read this fascinating book.

* * *

In the process of translating this book, I had occasion to call on friends and colleagues to help in their respective areas of expertise, and I would like to thank them here. My UCSB colleagues, Haruko Iwasaki, Kate Saltzman-Li, and especially Luke Roberts, were exceptionally helpful. Luke pondered many a *sōrōbun* passage with me until its meaning became clear. My good friend Zhou Qiqian, of the Institute of Japanese Studies, Tianjin Academy of Social Sciences and one of the Chinese translators of this book, pointed out a number of errors or misprints in the original text. Professor Ōba Osamu of Kansai University enabled me to use the Masuda Collection at his university and provided me with a copy of its invaluable catalogue. As the reader will see, I have significantly added to the footnotes publication information absent in the original work; the aim is to make the book more user-friendly in the West.

Chapter One

The *Wanguo gongfa* and Medical Texts

In his 'On the People's Democratic Dictatorship' (1949), Mao Zedong wrote:

> From the time of China's defeat in the Opium War of 1840, Chinese progressives went through untold hardships in their quest for truth from the Western countries. Hong Xiuquan, Kang Youwei, Yan Fu, and Sun Zhongshan were representative of those who had looked to the West for truth before the Communist Party of China was born. Chinese who then sought progress would read any book containing the new knowledge from the West.

The Yongzheng Emperor (r. 1723–36) of the early Qing dynasty initiated a policy of interdiction against Christianity, but when this ban was removed by virtue of the Tianjin and Beijing Treaties in the late Qing, numerous missionaries came to China. At the same time that they carried on their proselytizing efforts, these missionaries were also involved in enlightenment work through the introduction of Western scholarship. They translated into Chinese a wide array of Western works, and these translations were published for the most part in urban centers such as Shanghai. For concrete data on titles and translators, Liang Qichao (1873–1929) penned the *Xixue shumu biao* (Listing of Western Books, 1896 [3 *juan* with 1 *juan* appended). I have transcribed the entirety of that work in my *Chūgoku bungaku shi kenkyū* (Studies in Chinese Literary History).[a]

With the repeated military defeats from the Opium War on, Chinese were compelled to reflect seriously upon the deficiencies of their country and its culture. At the same time, the outpouring of published [usually classical] Chinese translations of Western academic writings led many to envision on an intellectual plane reform of the state structure. These works of 'enlightenment' [as they became known] formed a bridge linking classical China with the institutional reform of contemporary China.

Such works of 'Western learning' (*xixue*) in literary Chinese published in the late Qing by foreign missionaries were quickly introduced into Japan as well.

1

From the late Tokugawa period into the early Meiji years, a large number of them were reprinted and published in Japan with the appropriate Japanese punctuation for reading classical Chinese texts. Thus, for Japan too, this well became a new source of knowledge opened up by the West; and, it similarly functioned to enlighten Japanese about institutional reform in the late Tokugawa and early Meiji era.

I became especially interested in the phenomenon of the importation and reprinting of these Chinese books in Japan after reading the late Nakayama Kyūshirō's essay 'Kinsei Shina yori Ishin zengo no Nihon ni oyobashitaru shoshu no eikyō' (Various influences from modern China on Japan around the time of the Restoration).[b] I had earlier been concerned with Sino-Japanese relations (especially in the area of culture) and had been collecting out of bibliophilia as many of these reprinted works as I could locate. I have now been buying such works for about 20 or 30 years and wanted to write something about those I have amassed.

The *Wanguo gongfa* (in 4 *juan*) is the Chinese translation by W. A. P. Martin (Ding Weiliang, 1827–1916) of Henry Wheaton's (Huidun, 1785–1848) *Elements of International Law*. Martin was an American missionary who came to China in 1850, became a teacher and later the dean of the Jingshi daxuetang (Metropolitan College, [forerunner of Beijing University]). The original edition of this book in my possession is dated Tongzhi 3 (1864) and reads 'published by the Chongshiguan in the capital' or Beijing. I also have a Japanese reprint (*Bankoku kōhō*) in six stringbound volumes dated Keiō 1 (1865) published by the Shogunate's Kaiseijo, with Japanese reading punctuation and *kana* affixed to personal and place names.[c1] This same edition was reprinted again in the Meiji period [1871], issued by Yorozuya Hyōshirō (Tokyo: Rōsōkan).[d]

In the very last year of the Tokugawa period [Keiō 4] and the first year of Meiji (1868), the *Bankoku kōhō shakugi* (Elements of International Law with Commentary) was published [by Kanaya Sōshirō] in four stringbound volumes [two fascicles] in Kyoto. The first two volumes of this work were a Japanese translation (a mixture of Chinese characters and Japanese syllabaries) by Tsutsumi Kōshishi. Then, in 1876 the *Bankoku kōhō reikan* (Elements of International Law, with Detailed Observations) was published in eight stringbound volumes in Tokyo with 'notes by Takaya Ryūshū, proofread by Nakamura Masanao.' This was a beautifully produced edition [published by Kitabatake Mohee] with large typeface, Japanese reading punctuation, and Chinese notes interspersed throughout the text.

These books are only those editions in my possession. In addition, there is reportedly an 1870 work entitled *Wayaku bankoku kōhō* (Elements of International Law, Japanese Translation), translated and annotated by Shigeno Yasutsugu (1827–1910), published in Kagoshima, but it only covers the first two chapters of the first fascicle of the original work. Also, a Chinese translation with Japanese reading punctuation was issued by Yamada Kin'ichirō in 1886.[e]

Why did the *Wanguo gongfa* enjoy such a warm welcome and become so highly thought of in Japan? From the *bakumatsu* period through the Restoration, Japan found itself suddenly coming into conflict with foreign nations on a whole panoply of fronts. It became a pressing need of the moment that Japanese at that time immediately learn international law, which was the ken of the *Wanguo gongfa*. Since until then knowledge in this area was non-existent, this work in Chinese translation on international law was seen as a uniquely valuable handbook. One story goes that that pioneer mind Sakamoto Ryōma (1835–67) tried to have it reprinted in his own domain of Tosa and strove relentlessly to secure publication funds. Particularly after the Restoration, when the Meiji government transformed national policy and opened its doors, the *Wanguo gongfa* became a virtual classic. In the written curriculum, when university regulations were enacted in third year of Meiji (1870), we find 'Bankoku kōhō' listed. The following year it appears in the curriculum for elementary schools in Kyoto. That it was adopted as a textbook or a reference work in schools elsewhere is well attested by the aforementioned essay by Nakayama Kyūshirō as well as Osatake Takeki, 'Bankoku kōhō shisō no i'nyū' (The introduction of ideas from *Elements of International Law*).[f]

Nowadays when we use terms such as *kenri* (rights) or *gimu* (duties, obligations), they derive, one may argue, from the *Wanguo gongfa*. A glance at its table of contents indicates that the work employs such expressions as *jichi* (autonomy), *jishu* (independence), and *shuken* (sovereignty). When Ōkuma Shigenobu (1838–1922), foreign minister of the [early] Meiji government, entered into disputes with diplomatic officials from England or France, he allegedly would brandish the Chinese translation of *Elements of International Law* freely to cut his way through difficulties. Such stories as this one are described in detail by Osatake in his aforementioned essay, citing a variety of documentary evidence, as well as in: 'Bankoku kōhō to Meiji ishin' (Elements of International Law and the Meiji Restoration) and 'Jōiron to kaikokuron' (Views on expelling the foreigners and opening the country).[g2]

Furthermore, *Gongfa huitong* (10 *juan*), the Chinese translation (also by Martin, in 1880) of *Das moderne Völkerrecht als Rechtsbuch* by the Swiss-born German legal scholar Johann Kaspar Bluntschli (Bulun, 1808–81), was reprinted [in Tokyo] with Japanese reading punctuation accompanying the Chinese text by Kishida Ginkō (1833–1905) in 1881.[h] The edition in my possession was published by Kishida's Rakuzendō in five stringbound volumes. It leads one to believe that even at this time there was a perceived need to know about international law.

Together with the introduction of international law in the *bakumatsu* and Restoration periods, Chinese translations of Western medical texts rendered a great service to Japan. First and foremost, this refers the Chinese-language editions of works by Benjamin Hobson (Hexin, 1816–73).[3] Hobson was an English missionary, sent to China in 1839, who opened a hospital in Hong Kong and later moved it to Guangdong. He subsequently moved to Shanghai where he continued both his missionary and medical work. In 1851 his *Quanti xinlun* (New Essay on the Entire Body) in two *juan* was published in Guangdong; it was a text in human anatomy with numerous illustrations.[i] In the introduction, Hobson wrote: 'I took up medicine when I was a young man,' and when dissecting human bodies, he often knew the various parts upon inspection; now 'I have collected Western medical texts, compared and checked them, cut out the superfluous materials, seized the essentials, written them down, and completed this book.'

I do not have a copy of the 1851 original, but I do possess a copy of the two-volume 1857 'reprint of a Chinese work' (*Shinbon honkoku*) with Japanese readings notations by Mr. Ochi, a doctor from Fushimi. There are as well, I am told, other editions from the second decade of the Meiji period (1877–86), including *Zentai shinron yakkai* (Annotated Translation of *Quanti xinlun*) and *Tsūzoku zentai shinron* (Popular editions of the *Quanti xinlun*).

Three other works by Hobson were published in Shanghai by Renji yiguan (Hospital of Benevolent Giving): *Xiyi lüelun* (Outlines of Western Medicine, 1857); *Fuying xinshuo* (A New Theory of Childbirth and Infant Care, 1858); and *Neike xinshuo* (A New Theory of Internal Medicine, 1858).[j]

Of these three, I have the original three-*juan Xiyi lüelun*; it includes 400 illustrations and detailed information on surgical operations. There is also an appended section concerning medicines. Also, my edition contains the library inscription: 'Hakodate igakujo' (Hakodate Medical Institute). The Japanese woodblock edition of this work is divided into four stringbound volumes, published in 1858 by a Mr. Miyake of the Tōjuen, and issued by 'Yorozuya Hyōshirō of the Rōsōkan.'

While *Xiyi lüelun* deals primarily with surgery, *Neike xinshuo* is, as indicated by its title, concerned with internal medicine. I do not have an original of the latter, but I do have a three-volume edition of it, in which the third volume contains information on drugs and medicines under the heading 'Tōzai honzō rokuyō' (Essentials of medicines, East and West); it was published in 1859 by Tōjuen and issued by the very same Rōsōkan. In the introduction, it reads: '*Neike xinlun* investigates and demonstrates the ways to make use of medicines. All involve the use of European medical texts. I have selected the essential points and translated them into the Chinese language (*Tōbun*).' Although I do not have the original of *Fuying xinshuo*, it concerns gynecology and pediatrics. I do have an 1859 Japanese reprint in three stringbound volumes, 'published by the Tenkōdō of Heian.' At the end is a note titled 'Selecting and Using Medicines.'

These medical texts by Hobson were based on his experiences as a physician (as he notes frequently in his introduction) and were composed as it proved useful in his actual medical treatment of patients. From his style and the content of the material contained therein, it seems clear that he used ideas understandable to Chinese. In all of his works, he listed the names of his Chinese assistants and offered them as co-authored works.

When I was looking through the *Seiyō gakka yakujutsu mokuroku* (Bibliography of Translations of Western Writings) (Sōundō shoten reprint of Kaei 5 edition, 1926) of 'Hotei shujin' who penned a 'preface' dated 1852, I noted that already by that point many translations of Dutch medical texts had been published. The fact that insufficient language skills made these Dutch works still seem strange can be seen in the *Oranda iji mondō* (Questions Concerning Matters of Dutch Medicine) by Sugita Genpaku (1733–1817) and Takebe Seian (1712–82), contained in volume two of *Bunmei genryū sōsho* (Series on the Sources of Civilation).[k] Reprinted only rather late, in the Ansei period (1854–60), perhaps Hobson's medical science which stressed clinical experience did make a major contribution in Japan.[4] I have on occasion seen in second-hand bookstores reprints of Hobson's medical writings bearing the imprints of various medical schools of the early Meiji period.[5]

Chapter Two

Scientific Texts

Hobson's works dealt not only with medicine; his *Bowu xinbian* (New Essay on Scientific Knowledge) was also reprinted. The original text [in three *juan*] which I own states that it is 'the work of the English physician Hobson ... newly engraved for printing in Xianfeng 5 [1855] and published by Mohai shuguan (Large Inkstone Book Store), Shanghai, Zhejiang.'[a] It is divided into three parts. The first has sections on 'topology' (*diqi lun*), 'heat' (*re lun*), 'water' (*shuizhi lun*), 'light' (*guang lun*), and 'electricity' (*dianqi lun*); as a whole, it is a kind of explanation of physics.

The second part covers universal astronomy, with detailed discussions under such entries as 'outlines of astronomy' (*tianwen lüelun*), 'days and nights' (*zhouye lun*), 'Earth is a planet too' (*Diqiu yi xingxing lun*), 'the orbit of the moon is not a perfect circle' (*yuelun yuanque lun*), 'lunar eclipses follow fixed patterns' (*yueshi dingli lun*), 'Mercury' (*Shuixing lun*), 'Earth' (*Diqiu lun*), 'tides accompany [phases of] the moon' (*chaoxun suiyue lun*), 'Venus' (*Jinxing lun*), 'Mars' (*Huoxing lun*), 'Jupiter' (*Muxing lun*), 'Saturn' (*Tuxing lun*), and 'comets' (*huixing lun*).

The third part, entitled 'Outlines of Birds and Beasts' (*niaoshou lüelun*), offers explanations for a wide variety of animals and birds; it begins with illustrations of 'viviparous sorts' (of beasts), 'oviparous sorts' (of birds), 'varieties with scales,' and 'varieties of insects.' Beautiful illustrations are inserted not only in the third section but throughout the entire work.

The Kaiseijo, the center for Western learning in the *bakumatsu* period, reprinted this work (including the illustrations) with Japanese reading punctuation. In the first part, the Dutch pronunciation of words was affixed next to the technical terms. The date of the Japanese reprint is not noted, but in a publication advertisement of 'Yorozuya Hyōshirō of the Rōsōkan' at the end of this volume, this work is listed together with *Xiyi lüelun*, *Neike xinshuo*, and *Fuying xinshuo*; the very last line of the advertisement reads: 'Autumn, *kōshi* year of the Genji reign period' or 1864. Thus, it was obviously reprinted some time before this date, probably during the Bunkyū period (1861–64). The

Japanese reprint edition of *Bowu xinbian* (J. *Hakubutsu shinpen*) in three volumes which I own is imprinted in red on the first page of each volume: 'Hitotsubashi gakumonjo' (Hitotsubashi Institute). It remains unclear if the Kaiseijo was known by this name or whether this was the library imprint of the Institute of Tokugawa Yoshinobu (1837–1913, last shōgun of the Tokugawa Shogunate) from the collateral Hitotsubashi family.

The *Hakubutsu shinpen yakkai* (Annotated Translation of the *Bowu xinbian* [Tokyo: Kariganeya Seikichi]) in five stingbound volumes contains a preface dated Keiō 4 or 1868. This work is a 'translation' with a mixture of Chinese characters and Japanese syllabaries. In the directions to the reader at the beginning of the text, it reads: 'We have not changed the original at all and have made it possible to read through it.' This quasi-translation into Japanese also includes the illustrations just as they were in the original. The translator is listed as 'Ōmori Hiroya.'[b]

From the *bakumatsu* period into the early Meiji years, this work was warmly welcomed in Japan as a text conveying scientific knowledge that had developed in the West. The repeated reprintings of it in the Meiji period provide evidence for this claim, as do the numerous editions of it published; in addition to a *yakkai*, there were *chūkai* (commentary), *engi* (expansion [into a popular edition]), *kōgi* (exposition), and hyōchū (annotations) on the *Hakubutsu shinpen*. This is discussed in detail in Ozawa Saburō, 'Shina zairyū Yasokyō senkyōshi no Nihon bunka ni oyoboseru eikyō' (The influence exerted on Japanese culture by Christian missionaries living in China).[c]

Tan tian (Outlines of Astronomy) in eighteen *juan* and three stringbound volumes is a work of astronomy by John F. W. Herschel (Houshile, 1792–1871), head of the British astronomical association (as noted in the introduction). The translation was by Alexander Wylie (Weilieyali, 1815–87), an English missionary living in Shanghai since 1847, and Li Shanlan (1810–82). The original edition which I possess contains the information that it was 'printed on movable type by Mohai in the eighth lunar month of Xianfeng *jiwei*' or 1859.[d] It is probably not a complete translation inasmuch as it reads at the beginning: 'The original work by the Englishman Herschel was translated orally by the Englishman Wylie and abridged and revised by Li Shanlan from Haining.' Still, in eighteen *juan*, it is a major piece of work.

Illustrations are inserted here and there in the text. In his *Xixue shumu biao*, Liang Qichao called it a 'most detailed and fine' work. In 1861, just two years after its publication in Shanghai, it appeared in a Japanese edition with reading punctuation by Fukuda Izumi of Naniwa (Ōsaka). The Japanese edition retained the title [*Dan ten* in Japanese] and transcribed the introductory materials by Li Shanlan and by Wylie. It then continued: 'Fukuda Izumi, master of heaven's nature (*shitensei*)' included an 'introduction to the reprinted *Tan tian*,' penned 'at the Juntendō in Naniwa.' I am not sure what the term *shitensei* meant, but it would seem to imply a specialist in astronomy. He did revise *juan* eight through sixteen for the reprinting of the Shanghai edition at his own discretion.

Wylie and Wang Tao (1828–97) were the translators of the *Zhongxue qianshuo* (A Simple Theory of Dynamics).[e] It is mentioned in the *Xixue jicun* (Compilation on Western Learning), put together by Wang Tao, though I do not own a copy of it. I do, however, have the Japanese reprint in one stringbound volume: *Jūgaku sensetsu*. On the inside of the cover it reads: 'Fourth month, Xianfeng 8 [1858], printed by the Mohai shuguan in Shanghai.' This would indicate that the reprint was based on this 1858 edition. The original preface is missing in this edition, and there is a 'postface' by the punctuator. Also, the words, 'Spring, Ansei *kōshin*' year (1860), are added which would mean that the reprinted edition was published in Japan two years after the original in Shanghai. All of this indicates just how assiduous men of that time were in acquiring knowledge of various sorts. The content of this book concerns dynamics, ordinarily translated now as *lixue* in Chinese, not *zhongxue*. There is a 'summary' at both the beginning and the end of this work. It is divided into sections entitled 'levers' (*gan*), 'wheels and axles' (*lunzhu*), 'pulleys' (*huache*), 'inclined planes' (*xiemian*), and 'spiral screws' (*luoxuan*), with illustrations and explanations added. On the last page, it reads: 'Sixth month, Man'en 1 [1860, same as Ansei *kōshin*], reprinted by Kimura Junyū, Den'yō, with reading punctuation by Arai Kōri, Den'in.... Published by the Kōkaen.' It would appear that the punctuator and the printer were men who lived near Ōsaka.[1]

Furthermore, Wylie continued the translation work on Euclid's *Geometry* [in Chinese *Jihe yuanben* (Elements of Geometry)], which the Italian missionary Matteo Ricci (1552–1610) and Xu Guangqi (1562–1633) had together translated (from Latin) through *juan* 6 in 1603.[f] Wylie and Li Shanlan jointly translated (from the English) from *juan* 7 through 15, and in 1865 Zeng Guofan (1811–72) had it printed in eight stringbound volumes in Nanjing. I own a copy of this edition. However, inasmuch as a Japanese reprint never appeared, I have digressed from the main theme here. Nonetheless, the terms presently in use [in Japanese] – for example, decimal point (*ten*), plane (*men*), line (*sen*), right angle (*chokkaku*), acute angle (*eikaku*), obtuse angle (*donkaku*), rectangle (*kukei*), parallel lines (*heikōsen*), diagonal line *taikakusen*), base (*teihen*), cube (*rippōtai*), volume (*taiseki*), and ratio (*hirei*) – were already all to be found in the Chinese translation of Euclid. Perhaps this book did find its way to Japan. First and foremost, we borrowed and continue to use to this day the Chinese term of Ming dynasty vintage for 'geometry' itself: *jihe* in Chinese, *kika* in Japanese.[2]

As for books of this 'enlightenment' genre which cover the entire area of science, there is the seven-*juan Gewu rumen* (Introduction to Science) by W. A. P. Martin, translator of *Wanguo gongfa*. Although I do not have an original edition, I do own a Japanese reprint by Motoyama Zenkichi in seven volumes, dated Meiji 2 or 1869.[g] The two prefaces in the original, by Xu Jiyu (1795–1873) and by Dong Xun (1807–92), dated Tongzhi 7 or 1868, were transcribed into the reprinted edition. Thus, the Japanese reprint appeared in the year following the initial Chinese publication of this work, which would seem to indicate the perceived utility of this work in Japan at the time. According to these prefaces, Martin was a man of 'wide learning and phenomenal memory ... who came to China many years ago and excels in the writing of Chinese.' He 'sums up [the areas of] Western knowledge to be learned' and wrote this work in a question and answer style to facilitate easy understanding.

The Japanese reprint with reading punctuation is divided into seven volumes with illustrations in each: (1) the study of water; (2) the study of gas; (3) the study of fire; (4) the study of electricity; (5) dynamics; (6) chemistry; and (7) the study of calculation. The last of these involved the calculations in surveying techniques and was subdivided into 'calculating in the study of water,' 'calculating in the study of gas,' 'calculating in the study of light,' and 'calculating in dynamics.' According to the introductory notes, this book 'was arranged so that it will be easy to understand and indeed be quite useful.' Also, it notes that the Chinese prose of the text was embellished by Li Guanghu and Cui Shiyuan.

The *Gewu tanyuan* (In Search of the Roots of Science), 'published from movable type in Guangxu 2' or 1876, was a work in three *juan* by the English missionary Alexander Williamson (Weilianchen, 1829–90) who came to Shanghai in 1855. The first *juan* is an explanation of science, covering such subjects as nature, matter, the state of Earth, and the atmosphere, as well as such medically-related items as physiognomy, the head, the throat, the stomach, the intestines, the bones, and the muscles. The second *juan* is pure Christian propaganda: 'there is only one God' (*Shangdi weiyi*), 'God is supreme' (*Shangdi zhida*), 'God is omnipotent' (*Shangdi quanneng*), 'God is omniscient and all-loving' *(Shangdi quanzhi quanren)*. He entwines 'God' into a discussion of physics and nature. The third *juan* looks at elementary substances, geology, human creation, God as the master of human affairs, and finally resurrection after death. This work was clearly 'searching out the roots of science' for the purposes of religious proselytizing.

In Meiji 11 (1878), *Gewu tanyuan* (J. *Kakubutsu tangen*) was reprinted in Japanese 'with reading punctuation provided by Kumano Yo and proofread by Okuno Masatsuna.'[h] According to a preface by Shigeno Seisai, Kumano was a Confucian scholar, although Okuno was one of those pioneer Christians to take baptism quite early together with Uemura Masahisa and others in 1873.[3] In the first preface, Kumano wrote: 'From the immensity of heaven, earth, the sun, and the moon to the birds, beasts, fishes, and insects to the least blade of grass, everything, as this work will argue, is God's design in creation. ... This is a book which everyone should read.' This perspective that explains all creatures as the creative design of God would indicate that it appeared just after the relinquishing of the ban on Christianity. It also seems that such a theory provided a new and stimulating explanation even to Confucian scholars.

I also have a copy of a punctuated, Japanese reprint in three stringbound volumes of *Zhiwuxue* (Botany) or *Shokubutsugaku* in Japanese, 'compiled and translated by Williamson, transcribed by Li Shanlan.' On the title page, the publication year and place of the original are given: 'First printed by the Mohai shuguan in Xianfeng *dingsi* year [1857].' There is, however, no preface to the Japanese reprinting, and thus we do not know when it appeared. Some argue that it was 1867, but I believe my edition was printed later.

Chapter Three

The *Zhihuan qimeng* and Related Texts

I own a work entitled *Honkoku chikan keimō* (Introduction into the Circle of Knowledge, [Japanese] Reprint), dated Keiō 3 (1867) and published with appropriate Japanese punctuation added by the Kaibutsusha in Edo.[a] My copy also bears a red seal which reads 'Seal of the Library of the Domainal School,' though which 'school' is not made clear. The work is a sort of small encyclopedia, divided into 200 entries, explaining the basics of Western learning. The entire work is only 100 pages, and each page carries the English text on top with Chinese translation on the bottom. The preface is in English and is signed 'J. L.' These were the initials of James Legge (1815–97), the famous British missionary who lived in Hong Kong and used the Chinese name Liyage. Legge is well known as the translator of such Chinese classical texts as *Shujing* (Classic of History), *Shijing* (Classic of Poetry), *Chunqiu Zuoshi zhuan* (The Spring and Autumn Annals with the Commentary of Mr. Zuo [Qiuming]), and *Liji* (Book of Rites). Legge began his work in Hong Kong, but was later recalled to his native Scotland. He was much helped in his translation work by Wang Tao. Legge translated into Chinese the text in my Japanese edition of *Zhihuan qimeng*, by a Mr. Baker, under the Chinese title *Zhihuan qimeng shuke chubu* (Elementary School Lessons of the Circle of Knowledge), which carried the English title of *Graduated Reading: Comprising a Circle of Knowledge in 200 Lessons, Gradation 1.*[b] It initially appeared in 1856, was reprinted in 1864, and the Japanese edition retains the bilingual layout of the original, just adding reading punctuation for Japanese readers. The punctuator is given in a colophon: Yanagawa Shunsan (1832–70).

A postface to the original edition also appears, with Japanese punctuation, in the reprinted edition. The author of the postface, Ren Ruitu, dated it winter 1856, and hence it appeared with the first edition. In the text of the postface, Ren notes: 'Mr. Legge is a Christian missionary and teacher at the Anglo-Chinese Academy.... I am deeply grateful for living as a guest teacher with him since 1854.' This would indicate that Ren also taught at the Anglo-Chinese Academy. After praising Legge's personal and studious qualities, Ren continues: 'Herein is translated in one volume *A Circle of Knowledge* to be bestowed on students.' This book was thus originally intended as a textbook at the Anglo-Chinese Academy, combining lessons in English with introductions to Western learning and Christian teachings. As for the content of the book, Ren notes: 'You will find everything here, from the functions of the nature of God to the myriad things that [He] creates in astronomy, geography, people's affairs, clothing and food, instruments, and all the many animals that fly and swim beneath the surface.'

What Ren refers to as 'functions of the nature of God' occupy the last nine lessons or *ke* (numbers 192–200) of the work; the remainder of the text is divided into 24 sections or *bumen*, each with several lessons. Sections bear such names as: 'Shenti lun' (On the human body), 'Yinshi lun' (On drink and food), 'Jusuo lun' (On residences), 'Jiaoxue lun' (On education), 'Shengwu buru leilun' (On ways of rearing living things), 'Feiqin lun' (On birds), 'Caomu lun' (On vegetation), 'Di lun' (On the earth), 'Zhu wuzhi ti lun' (On the essence of various substances), 'Tianqi zhutian lun' (On various weather patterns), 'Diqiu fenyu lun' (On the regions of the world), 'Rensheng huiju tongju dengshi lun' (On various matters concerning human beings' capacity to live together), 'Guozheng lun' (On national government), 'Da Bulidian yiwai bieguo lun' (On Great Britain and other countries), 'Tongshang maoyi lun' (On commerce and trade), 'Wuzhi ji yidong deng lun' (On substances and movement and like matters), 'Wuguan lun' (On the five organs of the senses), and 'Shangdi tiyong lun' (On the essence and the functions of God). Altogether there are 200 'lessons.' He used the term *lun* with each of these entries, and it carries the Chinese sense of an explanation [herein rendered 'On' in English]. The section originally entitled 'Human Beings' was rendered 'Renlei lun' in Chinese; the section 'The Body and Its Parts' was translated as 'Shenti lun.' Also, the Chinese version is less a direct word-for-word translation than an explanatory translation; for example, the section originally entitled 'The Mechanical Powers' was rendered 'Jieli jiangqi lun.'

The Japanese punctuator of the text, Yanagawa Shunsan, was a scholar of Western learning in the *bakumatsu* period who died in the third year of the Meiji era (1870). He served as head of the Kaiseijo and was said to be conversant in Dutch, French, English, and German. He appears as a character at the very beginning of *Nagori no yume* (Lingering Dreams)[c] by Imaizumi Mine (1858– 1937), the daughter of Katsuragawa Hoshū (1822–81), a physician to the family of the shōgun and a scholar of Dutch learning. Osatake Tateki's study, *Shinbun zasshi no sōshisha Yanagawa Shunsan* (Yanagawa Shunsan, Initiator of Newspapers and Magazines),[d] provides a great deal of detail concerning Yanagawa; he offers a high assessment, apparently sufficient to warrant such a title to his book, of the accomplishments of Yanagawa in initiating publication of *Seiyō zasshi* (Western Miscellany) in 1867 and *Chūgai shinbun* (News of Home and Abroad) in 1868. We should note to be precise that, even before he began issuing this newspaper and magazine in Japan, already during the Bunkyū reign period (1861–64) *Batabiya shinbun* (Batavia News) was translating into

Japanese articles from Dutch newspapers in the Dutch colony of Batavia; also, the Shanghai serial edited from 1857 by Alexander Wylie, *Liuhe congtan* (Stories from Around the World), was being reprinted with reading punctuation in Japan.

In the opening paragraph of his work *Nihon shinbun rekishi* (History of Japanese Newspapers),[e] Koike Yōjirō states: 'The first newspapers in Japan appeared in the autumn of 1863. They were *Batabiya shinbun* and *Rikugō sōdan* (Ch. *Liuhe congtan*), published by Yorozuya Hyōshirō from a store with its main office in Edo.'[f] We see in an advertisement at the back of a Japanese reprint edition of the *Bowu xinbian* (J. *Hakubutsu shinpen*) that, during the Bunkyū years, Yorozuya was also reprinting under official auspices: *Zhongwai xinbao* (News from Home and Abroad), published in Ningbo from 1858; *Zhongwai zazhi* (Miscellany from Home and Abroad), published in Shanghai from 1862; and *Xianggang xinwen* (News of Hong Kong), published in Hong Kong from 1861. Because of the Japanese government's ban on anything having to do with Christianity, the reprinted editions eliminated all articles concerned with it. I have in my collection the reprint edition of *Liuhe congtan* (volumes 1–13), *Zhongwai xinbao* (issues 1–8), and *Zhongwai zazhi* (issues 1–7); although not every issue is complete, it still provides concrete material for one aspect of the history of Sino-Japanese cultural relations. They also played the important roles of providing Japanese in the *bakumatsu* period with news from abroad, while serving as an intermediary in disseminating knowledge. For example, Hashimoto Sanai (1834–59) copied out the following articles from the *Liuhe congtan* even before the Japanese reprint edition appeared: 'Taixi jinshi jiyao' (Record of recent events in the West), 'Yindu jinshi' (Recent events in India), 'Jinling jinshi' (Recent events in Nanjing [i.e., news of the Taiping Rebellion]), 'Yuesheng jinshi shulü' (Outline of recent events in Guangdong [i.e., reports of the Opium War]).[1]

In Osatake's book on Yanagawa, he cites a portion of a letter Yanagawa wrote to Katsuragawa which concerns the Japanese reprinting of the *Zhihuan qimeng*. He notes that, although he tried to reprint the first edition of the text, his friend Narushima Ryūhoku (1837–84, an official of the shogunal government and, after the Restoration, a newspaper reporter and head of the *Chōya shinbun* [News of the Entire Nation])[2] owned a copy of the second Chinese printing which had emended various errors in the original; he thus thought it better to use this edition for the Japanese reprint. He then quickly added the necessary Japanese reading punctuation to the text and forwarded the work to Katsuragawa, imploring 'earnestly the help of your good offices.' We thus learn that this book was published with Japanese punctuation by Yanagawa on the basis of the second Chinese edition and with the efforts of Katsuragawa. (A note at the end reads: 'Issued by Yamatoya Kihee').

Yanagawa had many works concerning Western learning to his credit, including *Furansu bunten* (A Grammar of French), *Igirisu nichiyō tsūgo* (Everyday Colloquial English), and *Yōgaku benran* (A Manual of Western

Learning). It seems he was reasonably capable at Kanbun as well, for Osatake cites in his biography of Yanagawa from many instances where Yanagawa translated Japanese popular songs into literary Chinese; and, in addition to his punctuating of the *Zhihuan qimeng*, Yanagawa also participated in work on a complete Japanese translation in twenty stringbound volumes of the *Gewu rumen* mentioned earlier. The translation work that went into this last effort, entitled *Kakubutsu nyūmon wage*, was divided among several men, and Yanagawa had responsibility for the section on the 'study of water' (two volumes).

Among the terms used in the translations by Yanagawa and the other early Meiji period scholars of Western learning, we owe them a particular debt of gratitude today for the convenient usage to which the particle *teki* (Ch. *de*) was added to nouns to transform them into adjectives and adverbs.

Ōtsuki Fumihiko (1847–1928) has written that the men who translated many texts in the early Meiji years included:

> Yanagawa Shunsan, Katsuragawa Hoshū, Kurosawa Magoshirō, Mitsukuri Keigo [d. 1871], Kumazawa Zen'an [1845–1906], and even myself. Odd as it might seem, this group in general enjoyed reading Chinese novels, such as *Shuihu zhuan* (Water Margin) and *Jinpingmei* (Plum in the Golden Vase). One day we got together and began chatting, and someone mentioned inadvertently the following. It was fine to translate 'system' as *soshiki*, but it was difficult to translate the term 'systematic.' The suffix 'tic' sounded similar to the character *teki* (*de*) as used in [vernacular Chinese] fiction; so why not render 'systematic' as *soshiki teki*? Everyone thought it was a brilliant idea and agreed to give it a try. Eventually, we paid someone to write out the expression *soshiki teki* clearly and bring it to the authorities. 'Have you put this into use?' 'Yes.' 'This is rather extraordinary, isn't it?' 'Not that I am aware, no.' We joked with these sorts of comic play-acting, but very often we were only able to escape difficult [translation] points with this character *teki*. Ultimately, it moved from pure invention to fact, and it was used later without a second thought, as people picked up on this usage.[3]

The text *Keimō chie no tamaki* (The Guide to Knowledge Forms a Circle) in three stringbound volumes was first published in 1872. I have a copy of the fourth printing [by Izumiya Kichibee] from 1874. It is a mixed *kana*-character Japanese translation of the *Zhihuan qimeng* with illustrations added at certain points. The translator's name is given as Oto Shigeru, but this is in fact Uryū Tora. In the preface by Osa Sanshū, an assistant director in the Ministry of Education, at the beginning of the first volume, it is pointed out that 'Uryū and I live in the same residence, and we have discussed educational systems.... On one occasion, he pointed out to me the *Keimō chie no tamaki* which has a description [of educational institutions]. When it was lamented that there were no good books for elementary school pupils, ... I suggested that this book was just what was now needed, and we should quickly reprint it for the benefit of all elementary school students in Japan.' Thus, he continued: 'The benefits of opening [areas of] learning and generating knowledge will by no means be limited to elementary school students.' An official at that time in the Ministry of Education, Uryū seems to have translated this work simply as part of an effort to diffuse the rudiments of Western learning, for which *Zhihuan qimeng* seemed to him to have value. However, the translated text ended with lesson 192, eliminating the last lessons of the original work which dealt with Christianity; the Japanese edition also added a lesson (number 144), 'On Japan,' and where the lesson in the original on 'Currency' explained Chinese and British monetary currencies, the Japanese edition dealt with that of Japan. Apparently the Japanese edition was well received, as it went into its fifth printing in 1876.

In his essay, 'Chikan keimō to Yasokyō' (*Zhihuan qimeng* and Christianity),[g] Ozawa Saburō collects and examines the various Japanese editions (including translations) of the *Zhihuan qimeng*. His analysis points out several Japanese editions of this work in addition to that of Yanagawa: a Kanbun edition without the English, one with Japanese reading punctuation, printed in 1870 by the Numazu School; a similar edition printed in Kagoshima prefecture; and a third edition (no firm publication information) without English text, with reading punctuation, reprinted on the basis of the first edition.

In addition to the Uryū edition, Ozawa points out two other Japanese translations of the text: that of Hirose and Nagata, published by the Ishikawa Prefectural School Library in 1873; and an edition with the English text only, published by the Kōgyokujuku Library.

Ozawa's study of the 'dissemination of Japanese editions' indicates that the *Zhihuan qimeng* was being used in the domains of Tanabe, Tokushima, Fukui, Nobeoka, and Nagoya; and the *Keimō chie no tamaki* was being used as an elementary school textbook in Saitama prefecture, Tokyo women's schools, and in Kyoto prefecture. As an introduction to the basics of Western learning, or as a textbook for learning English, this book certainly played a major role in opening up new cultural vistas in Japan of the early Meiji period.

Chapter Four

Geography Texts

Yanagawa Shunsan also wrote a work in one stringbound volume entitled *Yokohama hanjō ki* (Chronicle of the Prosperity of Yokohama). On the title page, it reads: 'Proofread by 'Kikka senkaku' (Hermit of the Haze), printed by the Bakuten Bookstore.' There are also introductory poems by 'Taihei isshi' (Retiree in Peace) and 'Nishikitani rōjin' (Old Man of the Gilded Valley). When we move into the actual work itself, it reads at the start: 'Written by the Old Man of the Gilded Valley and proofread by the Retiree in Peace.' Apparently, because it was a comic work, he used *kana* in it. Although the date of publication is no where to be found, it seems to have been written in the Bunkyū period. According to Osatake, this volume, as well as such works as *Tenshōsha kaiwa* (Conversations at the Tenkōsha),[1] which was a record of friendly chats at the Yanagawa mansion, were part of a group that was given the name 'Kikka rōshin rokurokubu shū' (New collection 66 of the Tower of Haze), all generally from the Bunkyū era. In his chronological biography of Yanagawa, Osatake thus claims *Tenshōsha kaiwa* to be a work of Bunkyū 1 (1861).

Yokohama hanjō ki was written in literary Chinese, but unlike ordinary Kanbun, Yanagawa mixed in character usage typical of China's great novels [written in the vernacular]. Thus, one finds here and there expressions such as *neige* (that), *buhaole* (no longer any good), *nandao ... bucheng* (Is it possible? Do you mean to say?), and *na huar* (that story), all colloquial Chinese usages. He also used the expression *huaqi* (the stars and stripes), which from the late Qing period had become a [kind of] pronoun for the United States. He even went so far as to use the Chinese character *de* in the manner he and his associates had derived its usage from Chinese novels.

In a section of *Yokohama hanjō ki* entitled 'Imported Publications' (*hakurai shoseki*), the text reads:

> Recently, Americans and Englishmen have been diligently perfecting their knowledge of Chinese learning, and in Hong Kong and Shanghai they have been publishing numerous works in Chinese.... Although nothing further

16

need be said about the writings of [Robert] Morrison [Molisong, 1782–1834] and Lin Zexu [1785–1850],[2] a recently published bibliography listed the following: in the field of mathematics, *Tan tian*, *Shuxue qimeng* (Introduction to Mathematics), *Daishuxue* (Algebra), *Dai wei ji shiji* (Elements of Analytical Geometry and Differential and Integral Calculus, [by Elias Loomis, 1811–89]), and *Jihe yuanben*; in the field of chemistry, *Bowu xinbian*, *Zhongxue canshuo*, *Gewu qiongli wenda* (Questions concerning Experimental Chemistry), and *Zhihuan qimeng*; in the field of medicine, *Quanti xinlun*, *Neike xinshuo*, *Xiyi lüelun*, and *Fuying xinshuo*; in the fields of geography and history, *Yinghuan zhi lüe* (Brief Survey of the Maritime Circuit), *Dili quanzhi* (Complete Gazetteer of Geography), *Diqiu shuolüe* (Summary of Theories of the Earth), *Wanguo gangjian lu* (Chronological Narrative of the Countries of the World), *Da Yingguo shi* (History of Great Britain), and *Lianbang zhi lüe* (Brief Survey of the United States of America); and under the category of newspapers and magazines, *Xiaer guanzhen* (Rarities from Near and Far), *Liuhe congtan*, *Zhongwai xinbao*, and *Shanghai xinwen*.[a]

All of this would indicate a wide variety of books, newspapers, and magazines being imported from China. At the very end of the work, though, it reads: 'The old man [i.e., the author] has yet to examine many of these, and for a time I made mental notes of what I heard, listening to those who had actually seen them.' Yanagawa's 'mental notes' indicate that these books and serial publications from China were topics of conversation among those men who sought this new (i.e., Western) knowledge.

The *Kunyu wanguo quantu* (Atlas of the Nations of the Earth) by Matteo Ricci, who came to China in 1583 (during the Wanli reign at the end of the Ming dynasty), and the *Zhifang waiji* (Chronicles of Foreign Lands [in 6 *juan*, by Yang Tingyun])[b] by Giulio Aleni (Airulüe, 1582–1649), an Italian missionary who came to China slightly later than Ricci, helped to expand Chinese knowledge of world geography. During the Edo period, these books came to Japan where they had a similar effect. However, because they were included in the late Ming collection edited by Li Zhizao, *Tianxue chuhan* (Early Writings on Christianity), they fell within the interdiction of the Kan'ei reign period. As Kondō Seizai (1771–1829) noted in the first section, entitled 'Kinsho' (Banned books), of his *Kōsho koji* (Background to My Favorite Books):[3] 'In the fifth year of the Kyōhō reign period (1720), the ban was loosened for items unrelated to heresy.' In a section of this work entitled 'Among Banned Books, Those Published Earlier in Nagasaki Under the Relaxed Ban,' he mentions the *Zhifang waiji* and notes: 'In Kyōhō 16 [1731], it was contained within the *Huang Ming zhifang ditu* (World Atlas of the August Ming Dynasty), which was brought by sea from China, having been requested for purchase.' Apparently, the purchase went through and it entered Japan.

Probably because the work was written by a missionary and had originally fallen within the category of 'banned books,' the ban on its sale was loosened but no reprint appeared. They merely loosened the 'ban,' for permission, it would seem, did not extend to reprinting and wide dissemination. Although no reprint edition came out, the *Zhifang waiji* in manuscript seems to have circulated rather extensively and to have been widely read. As a result, knowledge of world geography was introduced to many Japanese at the time. A scholar of this subject, the late Ayusawa Shintarō claimed to have had eight manuscript editions of the *Zhifang waiji* (J. *Shokuhō gaiki*) from the Bunka (1804–17), Bunsei (1818–30), and Tenpō (1830–44) eras.[4] I have examined the four manuscript editions of the text I own, and I think we can safely say that it circulated in manuscript quite widely in its day.

Although the date recorded in Aleni's preface to the *Zhifang waiji* is Tianqi 3 (1623), the book seems not have found its way into many Japanese hands until the late Edo period. By the same token, in the *bakumatsu* period, scholars of Dutch learning directly consulted geographies written in Dutch in order to write their own new world geography books. Such works would include: *Kon'yo zushiki* (Annotated Maps of the World) (3 volumes, 1845) by Mitsukuri Shōgo (1821–46); the same work with further annotations (4 volumes, 1846); and *Hakkō tsūshi* (Comprehensive Gazetteer of the Entire World) (6 volumes, 1851–56) by Mitsukuri Genpo (1799–1863). Genpo's work only covered 'Yōroppa bu' (Section on Europe), as the volume planned for Asia (in one fascicle) was not published. There was a work by the Englishman Colton (Geertun) 'translated by Sawa Ginjirō and printed by Tezuka Ritsu' in 1862: *Bankoku zushi* (Illustrated Gazetteer of the Nations of the World [printed by Shundairō in one stringbound volume]). I own a copy of each of these works. (I bought them in order to determine how they were handled in China). There were in addition numerous world geographies based on works in European languages that were published around this time. (For details see the work by Ayusawa and Ōkubo cited in note 4 to this chapter).

Among these books, the *Dili quanzhi* is a work by the Christian missionary William Muirhead (Muweilian, 1822–1900) who lived in Shanghai at the end of the Qing period. It was reprinted in Japan at the time and conveyed a highly systematic understanding of world geography and topography. Although I do not have a copy of the original,[c] I own a reprint edition with Japanese reading punctuation 'first published in Ansei 6 (1859), printed by Sōkairō (House of Exhilaration).' (I have heard as well of an 1858 'first publication' by the same printer).

It is divided into fifteen volumes, five in the first half and ten in the second. The first half is divided into the following four sections: 'Yaxiya zhi' (Gazetteer of Asia), 'Ouluoba zhi' (Gazetteer of Europe), 'Afeilijia zhi' (Gazetteer of Africa), and 'Dayang qundao zhi' (Gazetteer of the [Pacific] Ocean Archipelago). The latter half is sub-divided into ten parts: 'Dizhi lun' (Geology), 'Dishi lun' (Topography), 'Shui lun' (Water), 'Qi lun' (Atmosphere), 'Guang lun' (Light), 'Caomu zonglun' (Plants, Overall Account), 'Shengwu zonglun' (Living Creatures, Overall Account), 'Renlei zonglun' (Human Beings,

Overall Account), 'Diwen zonglun' (Physiography), and 'Dishi lun' (Historical Geography). At the end of my copy of the work, there is a note that reads: 'Yamashiroya Sahee, Hakkō shorin, Number 2 Nihonbashi Street,' but it is unclear whether this was the original publisher or not.

There is also a preface at the beginning of the work, dated 'Ninth [lunar] month, fall, Ansei 5 [1858],' by Shionoya Tōin (Seikō, 1809–67). Shionoya was a Kangaku scholar, who was also much concerned with foreign affairs and an avid supporter of national defense. He particularly devoted his attention to collecting information about the Opium War in China, so as to warn Japanese of the dangers to their country. His works in this vein include: *Ahen ibun* (Reports on Opium), *Kakka ron* (On Ineffectuality), *Chūkai shigi* (Personal Views of Maritime Planning).

In his preface, Tōin compares the *Dili quanzhi* to the *Haiguo tuzhi* (Illustrated Gazetteers of Sea Kingdoms, by Wei Yuan [1794–1856]) and the *Yinghuan zhi lüe* (by Xu Jiyu, (1795–1873), both of which were reprinted in Japan, as I shall discuss later. 'The [*Haiguo*] *tuzhi* is absorbed in detail,' he notes, 'while the [*Yinghuan*] *zhi lüe* stresses facts. Neither one has yet to exhaust [knowledge of] geography.' The *Dili quanzhi* had 'many errors in its chronicling of Japan,' but 'that was probably due to the fact that grasping everything in simple terms by reading through materials in just a few days so as to elucidate the general contours of Japan and discuss its geography must have been the only available shortcut.' At the end of the preface, he notes: 'Recently, Mr. Senshū Iwase put money into reprinting this work, and he asked me for a few words. I was inclined to reject the idea, but could not.' In other words, Iwase invested his own money in reprinting the *Dili quanzhi* and requested that Tōin pen this preface.

The 'Mr. Senshū Iwase' mentioned in Tōin's preface was Iwase Higo no kami (Tadanori, 1818–61), an administrator in the foreign office in the *bakumatsu* period. Senshū was his style. He had long been concerned with foreign affairs and in the *bakumatsu* period was particularly attentive to plans for the opening of Japan to foreign interaction; he was well known as the man who brought about a shift in shogunal foreign policy from exclusion to openness. In *Bakumatsu seijika* (Politicians of the Late Edo Period),[d] Fukuchi Ōchi (Gen'ichirō, 1841–1906) mentions Iwase as one of the 'three outstanding men of the *bakumatsu* period.' When Iwase and other officials of the *bakufu* entered into point-by-point deliberations with Townsend Harris over the text of a commercial treaty that Harris, the American envoy, had drafted, Fukuchi notes: 'Iwase was an exceedingly astute man. Not only did he often attack first and compel Harris to defend himself; but, years later when I was in the United States, I learned directly from Harris of many treaty stipulations which had to be altered when Iwase refuted his arguments, and I came to understand just how talented Iwase had been.'[5]

Thus, Iwase saw that the anti-treaty group of the time did not know of the conditions overseas, just holding obstinately to an exclusion policy of keeping Japan cut off from the outside. He deplored this situation (as we can see from his letters), and it would seem he was trying to enlighten his countrymen by having this book reprinted in Japan. Here, political and diplomatic considerations appear to have been behind the reprinting of this work.

In the second part of his *Keigaku shibun shū* (Collection of Poetry and Prose by [Hashimoto] Keigaku [Sanai]),[e] there is a poem by Hashimoto (1834–59) entitled 'After Reading the *Dili quanzhi*.' On the basis of poems written at about the same time, it seems that the poem was written in the twelfth month of 1858, when Hashimoto was living in confinement. Because Tōin's preface to the edition of *Dili quanzhi* reprinted by Iwase is dated 'ninth [lunar] month, fall, Ansei 5 [1858],' Hashimoto may have read a text Iwase reprinted and presented to him. (I have heard that there may be an 1857 edition of the *Dili quanzhi* as well).

In order to do something in a forceful manner that would reform the shogunate, Iwase tried to go beyond Hotta Masayoshi (1810–64), a member of the shogunal Council of Elders, and Ii Naosuke (1815–60), chief minister to the shōgun, directly to the daimyō of Fukui domain and member of the Tokugawa family, Matsudaira Shungaku (Yoshinaga, 1828–90). In this connection, he became closely acquainted with Hashimoto, who was an associate of Shungaku's.[6] Also, Hashimoto and Iwase were linked as advocates of opening Japan to foreign contacts and trade. And, thus, the anti-Tokugawa Hashimoto received a wide array of reports about internal shogunal business from Iwase. More than twenty letters from Iwase to Hashimoto that are contained in the *Hashimoto Keigaku zenshū* are ample testimony to this connection between them. Furthermore, their close ties in activities surrounding national affairs are detailed in a volume by Nakane Yukie (1807–77), *Sakumu kiji* (Diary of Recent Dreams).[f] Nakane and Hashimoto were Shungaku's two righthand men and were thoroughly up on all his secret doings of the time.

In a letter to Hashimoto, dated 4/20/1858, Iwase writes: 'I have in my possession the *Xiaer guanzhen*. If you would like to look at it, please let me know when I can make it available to you.' *Xiaer guanzhen* was a Chinese-language, monthly news report published (beginning in 1853) in Hong Kong by foreign missionaries. According to Ge Gongzhen's (1890–1935) *Zhongguo baoxue shi* (History of the Press in China)[g], it continued publishing until 1856. Unlike *Liuhe congtan*, though, it was not reprinted in Japan and seems to have circulated in manuscript copies. (I have a copy of the third issue). About fifteen years ago, I caught sight on a booklist from a used-book store of a more or less complete set of these, albeit with the dates slightly off. Yoshida Shōin (1830–59) and others of his day read this journal, as we can see from a letter Shōin wrote on 9/2/1857 to Nagahara Takeshi: 'Although difficult to come by, I have received the *Xiaer guanzhen*.'[7] Also, in his 'Batsu Isabo yugen' (Afterward to *Aesop's Fables*), Shōin noted having read in the *Xiaer guanzhen* about the fable of the horse and the tiger.[8]

Not only was Iwase an administrator in the foreign office; he was also much interested in events overseas, and he collected this sort of journal to read through.[9] Where he noted in the letter cited above that he 'could make it available to' Hashimoto, he was effectively offering it to Hashimoto's lord, Matsudaira Shungaku, at the latter's convenience and asking him to examine it.

Furthermore, William Muirhead, the author of the *Dili quanzhi*, was on many occasions visited by Takasugi Shinsaku (1839–67), who traveled to Shanghai in 1862 aboard the shogunate's trade ship, the *Senzaimaru*. Takasugi described doing so in his *Yū-Shin goroku* (Five Diaries of a Trip to China).[h] In the diary entry for the morning of 5/23/1862, he notes that he and Godai Saisuke (1835–85, later Tomoatsu, the first president of the Ōsaka Chamber of Commerce) 'visited the Englishman Muirhead. Muirhead is a Christian missionary who carries on his missionary work among the people of Shanghai. The churches within the city fall within Muirhead's jurisdiction. We proceeded to his place of residence, ... and asked for a copy of the book *Lianbang zhi lüe* and other works before leaving.' They again visited him on the morning of the 25th, but on this occasion Takasugi noted that Muirhead was not in. On the 27th, Takasugi and Nakamuda Kuranosuke (later vice-admiral in the Japanese navy, head of the Naval Staff College, and Chief of the Naval General Staff) 'went to Muirhead's [home]. We asked to see such writings as *Shanghai xinbao* (Shanghai News), *Shuxue qimeng*, and *Daishuxue*, and then returned.' The last two works, mentioned immediately above, were works by Alexander Wylie and Li Shanlan. On 6/26, Takasugi and Nakamuda again visited Muirhead, but he was not at home.

In his *Nakamuda Kuranosuke den* (Biography of Nakamuda Kuranosuke),[i] Nakamura Kōya frequently cites Nakamuda's own notes of this trip to China. In Nakamura's section entitled 'Shanhai tokō' (Crossing to Shanghai), he writes that when Nakamuda 'visited the Englishman Muirhead on 6/12, he borrowed a four-volume work on the Long-Haired Bandits [Taiping rebels].... He spent the entire next day copying (the borrowed work) into his diary.' At this time, a group of Taipings were holed up on the outskirts of Shanghai, and reports about them were circulating furiously within the city. On 5/27 as well, Takasugi and Nakamuda visited Muirhead, and Takasugi purchased *Shanghai xinbao* (which carried news stories about the Taiping rebels), *Shuxue qimeng*, and *Daishuxue* from him. Nakamuda also requested several books, and as a return gift for receiving on the earlier occasion (5/25) Muirhead's work, Nakamuda gave him a folding fan and a color woodblock print. Nakamuda fails to note specifically which of Muirhead's works he had received on that earlier occasion, but we can see in Nakamuda's *Shanhai tokō kiji* (Diary of the Crossing to Shanghai), where he records the maps and booklists he sought in Shanghai, Muirhead's *Dili quanzhi* and *Da Yingguo shi*. Thus, it would seem as though he was given works of this sort, which had already been reprinted in Japan in 1861. Perhaps Takasugi's reference to 'other works' when he asked Muirhead for '*Lianbang zhi lüe* and other works' included the *Dili quanzhi*.

Needless to say, it would have been unthinkable for the visits paid by Takasugi, Godai, and Nakamuda to Muirhead who resided at a Christian Church to have been in search of Christianity itself. The national interdiction on Christianity was still in effect. On this same voyage to Shanghai was Nōtomi Kaijirō (1838–1912). In his *Shanhai zakki* (Notes on Shanghai),[10] he wrote that on two occasions they were visited at their lodgings by some Chinese students who wanted to present them with a Bible, and both times the entire Japanese group sent them away. This tends to indicate as well the strength of the anti-Christian ban. Churches often had printing presses on their premises and, while they printed religious materials for missionary activities, introductory works of Western scholarship and learning written by missionaries as well as various newspapers and magazines (with missionary phrases included here and there) were also published. Thus, in their search for the 'new' learning (as well as intelligence reports), Takasugi and his fellow travelers had no choice but to go and come at churches frequently.

Chapter Five

The *Haiguo tuzhi* and *Shengwu ji* by Wei Yuan

In Japan, the most stimulating and influential Chinese-language work in the field of world geography and topography was doubtless the *Haiguo tuzhi* (Illustrated Gazetteer of the Sea Kingdoms). That is to say, the *Haiguo tuzhi* was not simply a work that conveyed knowledge of geography and topography. It was also a study of defensive military strategy and tactics in the face of the foreign powers then exerting considerable military pressure on East Asia, including gunboats and artillery. Wei Yuan (1794–1856) wrote the *Haiguo tuzhi* from an indignation borne of China's defeat in the Opium War and with that experience as an object lesson. Because of the concrete quality of their arguments concerning naval defenses, the *Haiguo tuzhi* and the *Shengwu ji* (Record of August [Manchu] Military Achievements), written at about the same time, were packed with suggestions for Japan at that time. This was a time when naval defense was being actively debated in Japan, spurred by the arrival of vessels, commanded by Admiral Matthew Perry (1794–1858) and Admiral E. V. Putiatin (1804–83), along the Japanese coast and by the stringent diplomatic posture assumed by Townsend Harris (1804–78).[1]

The *Shengwu ji* was, for the most part, a chronicle to that point in time of the Qing dynasty's 'august' (*sheng*) military victories in which the rebellions of border peoples, gangs of pirates, and rebellious religious insurgents had been suppressed. Although it did not concern the geography or topography of foreign nations, Wei Yuan did insert an appendix entitled 'Wushi yuji' (Personal notes on military matters) after his recounting of the military victories. The material found in this section on strategy and tactics, based on the historical facts described, proved useful as a reference for naval defense in Japan at that time. Thus, it was this section of the *Shengwu ji* (three editions, see below) that was reprinted in Japan with reading punctuation. (One tiny portion of the original text, without Japanese reading punctuation, was also reprinted as part of a longer series).

Similarly, what many critics and analysts in Japan raised for discussion in the *Haiguo tuzhi* was not the portions of the text dealing with the geographical or topographical information recorded for the various continents and countries of the world, but the very first *juan* of the text entitled 'Chouhai pian' (Coastal defense preparations), namely that part of the text which analyzed coastal defense strategies and the like. This portion of the original was first reprinted in Japan in Kaei 7 or 1854. Thereafter, a number of different men successively reprinted the main part of the text on geography; these reprintings appeared for each section on a given continent or country either with Japanese reading punctuation added to the Kanbun text or with a mixture of *kana* inserted into the text. Hence, the conditions in the countries of the world were ultimately conveyed to Japan at the same time [as in China].

In the section on 'source materials' in his *Edo jidai ni okeru Tōsen mochiwatarisho no kenkyū* (A Study of the Books Brought on Chinese Vessels in the Edo Period),[a] Professor Ōba Osamu collected, primarily for the *bakumatsu* period, the ledgers of the Nagasaki Commercial Hall in which were recorded the titles of Chinese texts and the numbers of copies transported to Nagasaki, as well as such information as the purchase prices and the bidding prices of these texts. In comparison to other works, there are an extraordinary number of entries concerning the *Haiguo tuzhi* and the *Shengwu ji*. In all likelihood, this would indicate that members of the shogunal Council of Elders were buying up the available copies, but in addition the *Haiguo tuzhi* also made its way into the Momijiyama gakumonjo (Momijiyama Institute) and Shōheizaka gakumonjo (Shōheizaka Institute), facts which would indicate that this work was considered to be highly important at the time in Japan.

Each time the *Shengwu ji* and the *Haiguo tuzhi* were imported to Japan, the price shot way up. Professor Ōba's investigation indicates that, in the first year of the Kōka reign period or 1844, when *Shengwu ji* first appeared in Japan, Abe Ise no kami (Abe Masahiro, 1819–62) of the Council of Elders purchased it for 25 *monme*; in the sixth lunar month of Ansei 6 or 1859, Motoya Keitarō made a successful bid for 160.3 *monme*. The *Haiguo tuzhi* was first imported to Japan in Kaei 4 or 1851 and fetched a price of 130 *monme*, but a record of a bid for the seventh month of Ansei 6 (1859) indicated that Motoya Keitarō successfully bid the high price of 436 *monme* to obtain this work. These points provide evidence to show that people in Japan vied to get their hands on these books to read them.

Biographies of the author of these two works, Wei Yuan (Wei Moshen), can be found in the *Qing shi gao* (Draft History of the Qing Dynasty) (*liezhuan* [biographies] 273, 'wenyuan' 3) and *Qing shi liezhuan* (Biographies in Qing History) (*juan* 69, 'Rulin,' *xia* 2). He was well known as a scholar and author. In addition, in his *Qingdai puxue dashi liezhuan* (Biographies of Great Teachers of Pure Scholarship in the Qing Period),[b] Zhi Weicheng (1899–1928) includes Wei among his 'biographies of historians,' and perhaps on the basis of his writings he deserves to be recognized as a historian. When Wei passed the *juren* or second stage of the imperial civil service examinations [in 1822], the Daoguang Emperor saw his examination paper and praised it highly. This high evaluation is recorded in both the *Qing shi gao* and the *Qing shi liezhuan*. His name was thus well known from early in his career. Later, Wei was invited by He Changling (1785–1848), provincial administration commissioner of Jiangsu, to edit the *Huangchao jingshi wenbian* (Collected Writings on Statecraft of the August Dynasty), a collection of essays by men who had served state and society under the Qing dynasty. Wei actually wrote the introduction to this multi-volume work in He's stead. He then proceeded to write the *Shengwu ji* and *Haiguo tuzhi*, which only increased his fame.

In recent years, many scholars have discussed Wei as a thinker. After the founding of the People's Republic of China in 1949, Hou Wailu published his *Zhongguo zaoqi qimeng sixiang shi* (A History of Early Enlightenment Thought in China),[2] and in it he regarded Wei as an enlightenment thinker of the late Qing period. In other words, he was arguing that Wei's political thought had played a progressive role, and, drawing on Wei's writings, Hou explained that Wei was among the earliest of 'reform-minded' (*bianfa, weixin*) thinkers.

Similarly, in an essay entitled 'Wei Yuan de sixiang' (Wei Yuan's thought),[3] Feng Youlan analyzed Wei ideas from the perspective of their class basis. Feng argued that, although Wei came from a landlord household that lacked even power in decline, his stress on the economic power of merchants reflected the beginning of the decay of Chinese feudalism and the fact that capitalism was beginning to emerge in China. Both Hou and Feng reserved esteem for Wei's knowledge not because it was based on a set of fixed writings but because of its basis in his own genuine changing experiences. They both saw him as an advocate of 'reform' who placed emphasis on the notion of *bian* (change, transformation) and adopted historical and political positions different from all traditional Chinese thought in feudal society. Hence, they argued that Wei was a progressive intellectual who appeared at a time of great change in Chinese history.[c]

Furthermore, one finds in Shi Jun's *Zhongguo jindai sixiang shi cankao ziliao jianbian* (Volume of Reference Materials on Modern Chinese Intellectual History)[d] reference documents for the history of modern Chinese thought, including: the introduction and first *juan* ('Chouhai pian') of *Haiguo tuzhi*; the introduction to *Shengwu ji*; and Wei's introduction to the *Huangchao jingshi wenbian*.[4] Also, the *Zhongguo zhexue shi ziliao xuanji, jindai zhi bu* (Selected Materials from the History of Chinese Philosophy, Modern),[e] put out by the Philosophy Institute of the Chinese Academy of Sciences, contains reference documents for the history of modern Chinese philosphy and it includes: the introductions to the *Huangchao jingshi wenbian* and the *Haiguo tuzhi*, as well as the section entitled 'Mogu' (Reading notes) from Wei's *Guweitang neiji* (Inner Works from the Hall of Ancient Subtlety).

In his 'Lun Zhongguo xueshu sixiang zhi bianqian dashi' (On overall conditions surrounding modern Chinese scholarly thought),[f] Liang Qichao (1873–1929) noted: 'Wei wrote fondly of the art of statecraft and wrote the *Haiguo tuzhi* to encourage a conception of foreigners among the [Chinese] people. Although today this work has only the value of wastepaper, in Japan it exerted influence on [Sakuma] Shōzan [1811–64], Yoshida Shōin [1830–59],

Saigō Takamori [1827–77], and others, and hence played an indirect role in the Meiji Restoration.' I have no material on the connection by which Saigō Takamori came to have a copy of the *Haiguo tuzhi*,[5] but we learn from the writings of Sakuma Shōzan and Yoshida Shōin that the two of them read both *Haiguo tuzhi* and *Shengwu ji* and something of the stimulation these works provided them with. Yet, whether these works actually played a role, however indirect, in the Meiji Restoration remains dubious.

In his *Seiken roku* (Reflections on My Errors),[g] Sakuma Shōzan chronicles his reflections and feelings during a seven-month stint in jail where he was thrown in the fourth month of 1854. Written in Kanbun, he touches on Wei Yuan and Wei's writings:

> At the time that my former lord [Sanada Kōkan, daimyō of Matsushiro] Shinshū assumed office in the government and took charge of coastal defense matters, rumors were rife of the English invasion of China. Greatly lamenting the events of the time, I submitted to the throne a plan for coastal defense in the eleventh lunar month of Tenpō 13 [December 1842–January 1843] in a memorial.[6] Later, I saw the *Shengwu ji* of the Chinese writer Wei Yuan, a work he too had written out of sorrow over events of that time. The preface to his work was composed in the seventh month of the same year [August–September 1842], a mere four months before my own memorial. Thus, without any consultation, our two views were often in complete agreement. Ah! Isn't it strange indeed that Wei Yuan and I, born in different places and ignorant even of each other's names, wrote of our views in sadness with the times during the same year and that those view should be in such accord? We really must be called comrades from separate lands.

What is clear here is that, although Shōzan and Wei Yuan were born in different countries, they were developing and expressing similar ideas at the same time. Thus, even if Wei perhaps served as some sort of stimulus to Shōzan, however well-disposed he may have been to Wei in spirit, we can see that Shōzan was not influenced by *Shengwu ji*. Hence, their difference of opinion over coastal defences is clear.

> However, Wei ... argues that the best method for coastal defense is to strengthen fortified towns and clear the fields and thereby cut off the enemy's landing from sea. My view, though, is that, through education in military techniques involving guns and warships, we establish a plan of attack whereby the enemy is intercepted, destroyed, and hence its fate is sealed before it ever reaches our shores. This is a point of difference between Wei and myself.

Yet, we could point to instances as well where their opinions were the same:

> In the winter of Kaei 2 (1849–50), I came to Edo.... During the time I was there, I first obtained Wei's book and read it. He argued [in this book] that,

26

in the cause of mastering the enemy, it would be useful to establish schools in his country primarily for the translation of foreign writings and foreign histories and to promote a clear understanding of conditions among the enemy nations [just as I had argued]. In this, too, his opinion concurred with my own.

In this instance concerning what Shōzan referred to as 'Mr. Wei's work' (*Gi shi no sho*), the words cited correspond to a section of Wei's 'Wushi yuji' (*juan* 12 of *Shengwu ji*).

Shōzan was also reading *Haiguo tuzhi* and had the following to say:

The main requirements for maritime defense are guns and warships, and guns are the more important item. Wei included a section on guns in his *Haiguo tuzhi*. It is altogether inaccurate and unfounded, like the doings of a child at play. Without personally engaging in the study of a subject, its essentials cannot be learned. Although a man of considerable talent and intellect, Wei was inattentive to this fact. I have profound pity for Wei that, in the world of today, he, ignorant of artillery, should have perpetuated these errors and mistakes.

Perhaps it was because Shōzan was himself knowledgeable in artillery and prided himself in knowing how to produce it, that he pointed out Wei Yuan's lack of knowledge in this area.

If we were to look only at the *Seiken roku* (I have only this text before me right now, as I do not have a copy of Shōzan's collected works), it would certainly seem as though he was not influenced to any great measure by Wei Yuan. At least insofar as matters of coastal defense are concerned, Shōzan as artillery specialist, prior to reading Wei Yuan, seems to have concocted his own ideas. How then did Shōzan's disciple, Yoshida Shōin, approach Wei Yuan? We move next to consider this question on the basis of a text known as *Shōin sensei icho* (Posthumous Works of Yoshida Shōin).[h]

Chapter Six

Yoshida Shōin and Wei Yuan

Sakuma Shōzan's *Seiken roku* carries an introduction by Katsu Kaishū (1823–99) which argues as follows. After it was completed, the *Seiken roku* was stored at the bottom of a bamboo basket when Shōzan, after meeting with misfortune, was thrown in jail. (Shōzan was arrested for his alleged connections with the activities of Yoshida Shōin; the latter was apprehended for trying to stow away on an American ship in 1854 after the arrival of Commodore Perry's warships). Shōzan's son Kaku (or Kakujirō) was also implicated, but he managed to preserve the manuscript even during his peregrinations and in times of great danger. During that time he carried the text with him and showed it to Kaishū, asking for help in getting it published. Kaishū's younger sister was Shōzan's legal wife; as Kaishū put it in his preface, he 'was related to the esteemed Shōzan by marriage.' Through this link, Kaishū supplied the necessary funds, and in the early Meiji era it was first published.

In this preface, Kaishū praises Shōzan as a pioneer in 'calling for enlightenment and progress,' but, when he stripped away the formalities, he offered this criticism of Shōzan: 'His learning was broad, and he did have a fair number of views of his own. However, his boasting often caused problems.'[1] Perhaps because they were in-laws, Kaishū felt he ought to speak of Shōzan with reservation, but one can clearly see a tendency toward bragging and exaggeration in Shōzan's words about *Shengwu ji* and *Haiguo tuzhi*.

Shōin assiduously studied the works of Wei Yuan. While he referred to Japan's more prominent analysts of coastal defense of the time as mimics of Wei Yuan, he also severely cross-examined Wei Yuan's work.

In his 1850 work *Seiyū nikki* (Diary of a Journey to the West) (in *Yoshida Shōin zenshū* [Collected Works of Yoshida Shōin; hereafter, *YSZ*]),[a] a diary account of a trip to Kyūshū, Shōin noted that, on the fifteenth day of the ninth month of that year, he traveled to Hirado to visit Hayama Sanai, a local Confucian teacher, and borrowed from him the *Seibu ki furoku* (*Shengwu ji* with Appendices) in four stringbound volumes (*YSZ*, 9:36). This edition of Wei's work was a Japanese woodblock reprint. I own a copy of it, but it does not give

28

the name of the reprinter. Because it is a woodblock printed edition, there are no Japanese reading punctuation inserted into the text. It would seem that Shōin's first contact with the *Shengwu ji* was the appendix portion of this reprint edition. For, from that day forward, he spent practically every single day covetously reading the *Seibu ki furoku* and copying out excerpts.

Shōin's diary entry for the sixteenth, the day after he borrowed *Seibu ki furoku* from Hayama, reads in part as follow: 'I returned to Hayama's and read the *Shengwu ji.*' On the seventeenth as well, he wrote: 'I went to Hayama's and read the *Seibu ki furoku,*' and he copied out by hand the sentences from the text, 'its marvelous words,' that were of interest to him. On the eighteenth he was again reading the same work and excerpting its 'marvelous words,' and on the nineteenth he was doing the same (*YSZ*, 9:36–39).

From the 21st, he borrowed the *Ahen ibun* (Reports on Opium), compiled by Shionoya Tōin, and was meticulously copying out its book list and excerpting from it as well (*YSZ*, 9:39–41). It would seem that he had taken a brief respite from his reading and copying from the *Seibu ki furoku*, but on the 24th and 25th he was again reading and excerpting as well from the *Shengwu ji* (*YSZ*, 9:42–44). From the 26th, Shōin borrowed the second part of the *Keisei bunpen shō* (Selections from the *Huangchao jingshi wenbian*) (a Japanese reprint edition to be discussed below) and began copying out its lists of books and excerpting it as well (*YSZ*, 9:44–45). For the 28th, he noted in his diary: 'I have finished reading the seven stringbound volumes of the *Ahen ibun*' (*YSZ*, 9:47). The *Ahen ibun* was circulated in manuscript, and I have yet to see a copy, but from Shōin's detailed table of contents and excerpts one can get a general picture of the work.[2]

When Shōin finished reading the *Ahen ibun*, he returned once again to *Seibu ki furoku*, as his diary reads for the twelfth day of the tenth month of 1850: 'I read the *Shengwu ji* at Hayama's' (*YSZ*, 9:55). On the same day, he noted: 'I asked if Master Issai had copied out any excerpts, and Gaiken [Hayama's style] responded that he knew of none, but that [Issai] left numerous stickers and the like inserted into the margins of every book he read, and with the various slips placed here and there he indicated important points in the text. I thus learned a great deal in examining Gaiken's books' (*YSZ*, 9:55–56). We thus learn that Satō Issai (1772–1859), Confucian official for the Tokugawa Shogunate and teacher at the Shōheikō (informal name of the Shōheizaka gakumonjo, the official academy of the Tokugawa regime), carefully read the *Shengwu ji*, making interlinear notations and inserting slips of paper along the way.

On the sixteenth of the month, Shōin noted: 'I read the *Shengwu ji* at Hayama's' (*YSZ*, 9:57), though precisely when he completed it remains unclear. On this day he borrowed the *Sentetsu sōdan* (Collection of Biographical Notes on Wise Men of the Past)[b] and began copying out excerpts from it. While in Nagasaki during this same trip, Shōin also had occasion to borrow two works by Takano Chōei (1804–50), *Yume monogatari* (Story of a Dream) and *In'yū roku* (Record of Hiding Gloom) which concerned the Opium War, as well as the *Haiguo wenjian lu* (Record of Things Seen and Heard Among the Maritime

29

Kingdoms) by Chen Lunjiong (fl. 1730) of the Qing dynasty.[c] And, as had become his standard practice, Shōin copied out the table of contents and excerpts from the text. Although Chen's work was never reprinted [in Japan], according to Ōba Osamu's work cited above, it was imported to Japan in roughly similar numbers as the *Haiguo tuzhi*; and it too provided Shōin with knowledge of foreign lands. I now have in my possession only a portion of the text, two stringbound volumes (second edition, dated Daoguang 3 or 1823): one of essays and one of maps.

In a letter (dated the eighth month of 1851) from Edo to his uncle (and teacher from youth), Mr. Tamaki (Bunnoshin), Shōin wrote: 'On the morning of the 23rd of the eighth month, I met Yamaga [Bansuke],[d] and in the evening we read and studied the *Shengwu ji* together until nightfall when I returned home' (*YSZ*, 7:80). That he met other interested men with whom he read the *Shengwu ji* together indicates that he was continuing his study of this text. In a letter to his elder brother (dated the twelfth month [24th day] of 1854), Shōin indicated that the *Shinron* (New Theses) by Aizawa Seishisai (1782–1863) and Shionoya Tōin's *Chūkai shigi* (Personal Views on the 'Chouhai' Chapter [Wei Yuan's first chapter in the *Haiguo tuzhi*]) were then quite popular: 'these men both ask why warships need be constructed, but neither knows how to do so' (*YSZ*, 7:310).

He was criticizing the fact that arguments and points of view were by themselves of no practical utility. He then proceeded to mention that he had read Tōin's memorial and that it proposed a plan to purchase warships and artillery from the Dutch. Shōin continued in a deprecatory tone: '"The construction of ships is not the same thing as the purchase of ships, nor is the building of artillery the same as buying it"; one can find these points made in the *Shengwu ji* of Wei Yuan of China. . . . People who today make plans to purchase such things are all mimicking Wei Yuan' (*YSZ*, 7:310). In any event, this sort of criticism on the part of Shōin reveals just how widely read and studied Wei Yuan was at that time. Hence, be it in the area of political programs or ideas of military strategy, we can see the considerable influence Wei exerted on Shōin in matters of maritime defense from the latter's assiduous daily reading schedule.

There are points, however, where he opposed points that Wei had written. In an essay written by Shōin in Kanbun, entitled 'Kōin Rondon hyōban ki o yomu' (Reading an account of the fame of London in the *kōin* year [1854]),[e] he had the following to say:

Wei Yuan of China often writes about conditions in foreign lands.[3] However, inasmuch as Russia, the United States, and France all despise Great Britain, it would be fine, argues Wei, to accept their naval and infantry support. To substantiate this point clearly, he quotes from sources both ancient and modern. Yet, as far as I can tell, such a view is biased, only looking at one side of the picture [*YSZ*, 2:333–34].

Shōin then goes on to develop his own understanding. It is the way barbarians usually do things, he argues, that they look only after profit and ignore righteousness; if it is beneficial to them, they will forge alliances even with their enemies, and if their allies cause them harm, they become enemies.

> As I was reading this account [cited above], I learned that, once Russia and Turkey commenced hostilities, Britain and France joined to help Turkey. The fact that Russia and Britain hate one another is just as Wei Yuan supposes, but the union of France and Britain indicates that Wei strikes wide of the mark here. Furthermore, who knows where the United States will fall on this matter? [*YSZ*, 2:334]

Thus, Shōin here noted points where Wei's analysis of international conditions of the time went astray.

In another essay by Shōin entitled 'Chūkai hen o yomu' (Reading [Wei Yuan's] 'Chouhai pian'), he raised his most basic doubts about Wei's ideas. This essay was composed in literary Chinese on [the fourth day of] the fifth month of Ansei 2 or 1855.[f] Shōin had great praise for Wei, noting that the sections 'Yi shou' (Discussion of defense), 'Yi zhan' (Discussion of war), and 'Yi kuan' (Discussion of treaties) from the 'Chouhai pian' clearly hit the mark, and that if the Qing government would put these measures into effect, not only would it be able to control the British, but Russia and France could also be kept at bay. His 'only doubts' run as follows:

> This book was published in Daoguang 27 [1847], at a time when he did not know that only three or four years later the popular uprising in Guangxi [namely, the Taiping Rebellion] would erupt and spread disorder over eight provinces and misfortunes would continue for a decade, and Beijing would come to a standstill under perilous conditions. It is not the barbarians but the Chinese people who need to be apprehensive about the [future of the] Qing. Why is it that Wei Moshen mentions not a word about this? [*YSZ*, 2:322]

In addition to raising doubts about the absence of evident concern in Wei's book for domestic conditions then pregnant with upheaval and chaos, there is a sense of rebuke in Shōin's style as well. Shōin was himself deeply concerned at the time with the Taiping Rebellion, and, at 25 years of age in 1855 while in Noyama Prison, he translated into Japanese a lively report of the Taiping Rebellion (both the uprising and its background) by a Chinese who had come to Japan aboard one of Perry's vessels, entitling it: *Shinkoku Kanpō ran ki* (Record of the Uprising in China during the Xianfeng Reign).[g] Although Shōin noted in his own preface, 'I do not know the name of the author of this work, and it has no title' (*YSZ*, 2:99), from the manuscripts in my possession, I have done a fairly detailed investigation of the author of the manuscript Shōin had and its transmission. I have also done some work on the quality of Shōin's translation in relation to the original.[4]

Shōin's note that 'this book was published in Daoguang 27 [1847]' refers to the fact that the *Haiguo tuzhi* which had been imported to Japan at the time was published that same year in a 60-*juan* edition (of which I have a photolithographic copy). Inasmuch as the original publication of the *Haiguo tuzhi* came out in 50 *juan* in 1842, this was an enlarged edition. A 100-*juan* edition, with added front and back matter, appeared in 1852.[5]

On [the 22nd day of] the eleventh month of 1854, Shōin wrote to his older brother: 'A few days ago, I copied out one *juan* of the *Haiguo tuzhi* so that you could make use of it' (*YSZ*, 7:265). He then continued: 'Lin Zexu and Wei Yuan are really men of will, and they were quite capable at reading books written in horizontal [Western] script. I have exhorted [our own Japanese] men of will [to study] books in horizontal script, for I would like to see them write such fine works. What is your opinion?' (*YSZ*, 7:266). While admiring the *Haiguo tuzhi* as a 'fine work,' Shōin was also encouraging interested Japanese men of spirit to study Western works, and it was his earnest desire that the latter might write such works. However, Shōin was incorrect in assuming that Lin Zexu and Wei Yuan were fluent in horizontal script. On the frontispiece to each of the sections on India, Europe, and the United States in the *Haiguo tuzhi*, the following notation appears: 'Originally written by a European, translated by Lin Zexu of Houguan, and edited by Wei Yuan of Shaoyang.' There are as well *juan* that read simply: 'Edited by Wei Yuan of Shaoyang.' These notes would seem to indicate that Lin and Wei read foreign languages.

The basis of the *Haiguo tuzhi* was the *Sizhou zhi* (Gazetteer of Four Continents) which was translated by Lin Zexu. In his introduction to the 60-*juan* edition of the *Haiguo tuzhi*, Wei explained something of his sources: 'First is the *Sizhou zhi* of the Western barbarians translated by former Liang-Guang Governor-General Lin Zexu; and second are the various historical records, the gazetteers of islands from the Ming dynasty forward, and recent barbarian maps and writings.' Thus, we know that the note in the text – 'Originally written by a European, translated by Lin Zexu of Houguan, and edited by Wei Yuan of Shaoyang' – refers to the *Sizhou zhi*. The *Sizhou zhi* is now included in the 'Zaibu bian' (Second Supplement) to the *Xiaofang huzhai yudi congchao* (Collection of Documents on World Geography).[h] Although this last work is primarily a collection of excerpts, I have long thought of trying to check or compare the portions of the *Haiguo tuzhi* translated by Lin Zexu, but I have still been unsuccessful in getting my hands on this section of the *Xiaofang huzhai yudi congchao*. Thus, there is nothing at this point that I can say with surety about the relationship of the *Haiguo tuzhi* to the *Sizhou zhi*.

I think it is correct to say, though, that Lin Zexu did not directly translate the work in question but ordered someone with a knowledge of foreign language(s) to translate it and affixed his name only. The writings of high Chinese officials while in office often took this form, and I think that this case in particular exemplifies a kind of 'report on conditions' which Lin collected from his interactions with foreign powers as a Chinese official of highest diplomatic and military responsibility. Wei Yuan touches on this briefly in the *Shengwu ji* (*juan* 10, 'Daoguang yangsao zhengfu ji' [Record of the pacification of the foreign vessels in the Daoguang reign], part 1): 'Since coming to Guangdong last year, Lin Zexu has employed someone every day to investigate Western affairs, translate Western books, and purchase Western newspapers as well.'

It would thus seem as well that the note 'edited by Wei Yuan' referred to the 'recent barbarian maps and writings' mentioned in the preface, and these 'barbarian maps and writings' were used as source materials by Wei Yuan's close associates. An examination of the chronological biographies of Lin and Wei or of any of their writings reveals not a trace of evidence that either of them ever studied a European language. Thus, Shōin's note that this work took much of its material from 'writings in horizontal script' is due to the fact that 'how this book [namely, the *Haiguo tuzhi*] differs from the works about maritime nations of men of the past, the older works are all Chinese discussing the West, while this is Westerners discussing the West.'

Chapter Seven

The Opium War and the 'Daoguang yangsao zhengfu ji'

As noted in his diary, cited earlier, Shōin spent nearly every day copying out excerpts and studying in great detail the *Shengwu ji*, but absent from mention in his diary, it seems, was the 'Daoguang yangsao zhengfu ji,' which appeared in *juan* 10 of the text. This is apparently due to the fact that Shōin's study of the *Shengwu ji* was based on the Japanese edition of Wei Yuan's work which only reprinted the 'Wushi yuji' portion of this *juan*. But, it seems that, even if he had been able to examine the original edition of the *Shengwu ji*, that too did not include the 'Daoguang yangsao zhengfu ji' section at the end of *juan* 10 – namely, a section discussing the Opium War.

The story becomes rather complicated at this point, but that final portion of *juan* 10 dealing with the Opium War was apparently first introduced in the third revised edition of the text in 1846. Yet, in the 'Sibu beiyao' edition (in my possession) of the *Shengwu ji* in six stringbound volumes,[1] it reads: 'based on the original woodblock edition by the Hall of Ancient Subtlety.' In a note following the table of contents, there is a discussion of the places in the text revised with each edition of the work, and it claims that 'this is the third revised edition of the text.' Despite the Daoguang 26 (1846) date given, the 'Daoguang yangsao zhengfu ji,' a treatment of the Opium War, is missing. In another printing of the third revised edition of the *Shengwu ji*, published in 1936 by 'Shijie shuju,' we find this section included. It is not precisely clear what edition of the text the 'Shijie shuju' printing was based on, but, inasmuch as 'Shenbaoguan' in Shanghai published this work at the end of the Qing period, this was probably the edition used. Although I do not now have a copy of the 'Shenbaoguan' edition, I do have at hand a pamphlet, entitled *Shenbaoguan shumu*, which describes the books published by them. Since it carries a preface dated Guangxu 5 (1877), the Shenbaoguan publication of the *Shengwu ji* must predate this. In an addendum to this pamphlet there is an explanatory note concerning the *Shengwu ji*; it says that the *Shengwu ji* 'has been handed down by men for the past 30 or more years, but because portions of the text were avoided, ultimately two portions [namely, parts one and two] entitled 'Daoguang yangsao

34

zhengfu ji' were forcibly excised.' Yet, this pamphlet goes on, 'we are now reprinting them on the basis of the original edition of the work.' Thus, so too was the 'original woodblock edition by the Hall of Ancient Subtlety' upon which the 'Sibu beiyao' edition was based, though it would seem that 'Daoguang yangsao zhengfu ji' has been excised from editions now in circulation.

At the time, discussing a topic such as the Opium War in which China had just sustained a crushing defeat called China's face into question, and perhaps for that reason this section was avoided.[2] Who it was that actually 'forcibly excised' this section from the text remains unknown. If, however, this section of *Shengwu ji* made its way to Japan, it would certainly have been quickly reprinted as a didactic piece of source material on an urgent issue at hand. Though, were it reprinted for dissemination in Japan, it would still have had to get bureaucratic approval prior to publication, and it is impossible to say what might have happened at this point. At least, it appears certain that the text circulated in manuscript form, but there is no trace of it now. Incidentally, the *Ahen shimatsu* (The Opium [War] from Beginning to End) by Saitō Chikudō (1815–52) was banned for publication and circulated in manuscript. I have a manuscript edition of this work dated Kaei 3 (1850), though it was not published until 1937.[a]

Neither coastal defense policies during the *sakoku* period nor the military exploits of the Qing regime are of engrossing interest to us now. However, the Opium War is a major issue in world history, or at least in East Asian history. In China, the period following defeat in the Opium War is considered the dawn of 'modernity,' and for Japan as well the Opium War marked a major shift in the direction our history would take. American envoy Townsend Harris, who pressured Japan into signing a commercial treaty, gave a major address before an assemblage of shogunal leaders at the residence of Hotta Masayoshi in October of 1857. He argued that, with Great Britain's relentless pressures forcing a surrender on the Qing, the English would be coming with their opium next to Japan; if they were prevented from doing so, he noted hearing from the British governor-general of Hong Kong, then they might turn their warships docked in Hong Kong on Japan.

The stunned shogunate had no choice but to open Japanese ports, setting the direction for subsequent Japanese history, and Harris's threatening speech at the Hotta residence was widely disseminated in manuscript as 'Amerika shisetsu mōshitateru sho' (Declaration of the American envoy). I have several different editions of this work. It appears as well in a number of works: *Sanjūnen shi* (Thirty-Year History) by Kimura Kaishū (1830–1901), battleship commander and head of the department of the navy in the *bakumatsu* period; Katsu Kaishū, *Kaikoku kigen* (Origins of the Opening of the Country); in summary form in Naitō Chisō (1826–1902), *Kaikoku kigen Ansei kiji* (Account from the Ansei Period on the Origins of the Opening of the Country); quoted in Ōkuma Shigenobu (1838–1922), *Kaikoku taisei shi* (History of General Trends Since the Opening of the Country); and more recently mentioned in Yoshino Maho, ed., *Kaei Meiji nenkan roku* (Account of the Years from Kaei to Meiji).[b] There is no lack of access to a published text. Harris's speech and the shogunate's response were undoubtedly a major shock, especially to the anti-foreign (*jōi*) group. One of the manuscript editions in my collection was an item sent by Umeda Unpin (1815–59) to his comrades in Totsukawa, Yamato (in 1881 a man by the name of Tamada Onkichi from the village of Yamazaki in Totsukawa copied out this text).

In his *Bakufu suibō ron* (The Decline and Fall of the [Tokugawa] Shogunate),[c] Fukuchi Gen'ichirō (1841–1906) wrote:

> On [October] 26th, [Harris] proceeded to the residence of Minister Hotta. In his speech lasting roughly six hours, he spoke of the drawbacks to keeping the country closed and of the necessity of opening it up.... He drew references to examples from as far away as the West and as near as Qing China. He spoke with the fluid eloquence of a rushing stream. Minister Hotta, of course, paid heed to this practical discourse on politics; although the shogunate's finest man, this was the first time he had his umbilical cord severed. The effect on his frame of mind was remarkable, as if with his spirits crushed and his soul excised he were being awakened in a daze from illusion.... It is clear that the spirit he showed in later drafting a national plan for the opening of the country and facing all manner of obstacles owed its origin to the harsh criticism of Harris's speech.

Also, in *Sakumu kiji*, Nakane Yukie (1807–77) noted: 'The story was later told by people who gathered there at the time' that Minister Hotta 'was disconcerted and, wincing,' he could only 'let out a great sigh,' having effectively lost all powers of speech. To use contemporary language, this speech by Townsend Harris was truly 'a decisive moment in the history' of Japan, and from that point forward Japan had become firm in its determination to step ahead into a new era.

The Opium War was a major event of unprecedented proportions for China, and chroniclings of it are numerous.[3] Among such documents, Wei Yuan's 'Daoguang yangsao zhengfu ji' was transcribed as the first item in *Zhongguo jindai shi ziliao xuanji* (Selected Materials on Modern Chinese History),[d] surely because it was so suited to the theme of this volume. As described in the 'publication information' included in this work, it was a collection published first in 1940 in Yan'an and reprinted for use in the various base areas thereafter; Rong Mengyuan later made some revision in the contents in re-editing the work for subsequent republication.

In mentioning the Opium War, I have for some time wanted to check certain historical facts on the basis of Wei's piece and Liang Tingnan's (1796–1861) *Yifen wen ji* (Reports of Barbarian Portents). It is also necessary to make simultaneous use of *Yapian zhanzheng shishi kao* (A Study of the Historical Facts of the Opium War) of Yao Weiyuan who verifies and revises the deficiencies and errors in Wei's work by comparison with many other historical texts, such as the *Chouban yiwu shimo* (The Management of Barbarian Affairs from Beginning to End).ᵉ In his own preface, Yao notes with perhaps a touch too much praise: 'The "Daoguang yangsao zhengfu ji" is a first-class work recording the historical facts of the Opium War. Reports that later circulated about the Opium War were generally recastings or copies of this work.'⁴

The totality of the actual facts themselves concerning the Opium War is overwhelming, and it seems meaningless to try to use this alone as a way to understand the history of cultural relations. Yet, if we look primarily at the records and writings of the time and those that were reprinted in Japan, then perhaps this is the best framework for analysis. Before examining the Japanese reprintings and translations of *Shengwu ji* and *Haiguo tuzhi* (both were written, as well as reprinted and translated, out of concern for the Opium War), we need first look at the contemporary reports passed to the shogunate by the Dutch, reporting the concrete details of the Opium War, the importation to Japan of Chinese chronicles, as well as the reprintings in Japan and the writings of Japanese about the war (including novels).

While reports about the war with and defeat by a 'foreign barbarian' of a neighboring country were vague, they seemed to have caused a startling shock generally for many Japanese then living in the dream world of *sakoku*. Reflecting this image of things, even novels based on the war were published, and I have collected several such works myself.

Chapter Eight

The *Ahen fūsetsugaki*

There were a number of written reports and various accounts concerning the Opium War that circulated in Japan at the time, and I would now like to take a look at some of the more important of the historical materials I have acquired. Generally speaking, there were two sorts of contemporaneous reports: those conveyed as part of overseas intelligence which the shogunate obtained, via the Nagasaki Administrator (*bugyō*), from the director (or 'Captain')[a] of the Dutch trading factory at the island of Deshima, near Nagasaki; and those conveyed piecemeal from Chinese merchant vessels that called at the port of Nagasaki. In his preface to the *Ahen ibun*, the editor Shionoya Tōin wrote: 'I worked to compile news from the documents and detailed records of the Chinese merchants and Dutch residents here. They have filled to overflowing the box in which I keep them, and it is sufficient to make me realize the great quantity of detail here.'[1]

Among them, the reports from the Captain offered considerably detailed information, based largely on foreign newpapers, and he was in a position to amass a wide range of accounts and reports. In this connection, we have the following note by Fukuchi Gen'ichirō, which appears in his *Shinbunshi jitsureki* (A Career in Newspapers).[b]

When I was fifteen or sixteen [Japanese style], I was still in my hometown of Nagasaki, studying Dutch with my teacher Namura Hanamichi. While I was practicing at being an interpreter, every time Dutch ships arrived in port, they produced documents entitled *fūsetsugaki* which reported to the Nagasaki Administrator on conditions overseas. The shogunate at the time considered this one indication of the loyalty of the Dutch. Mr. Namura received these documents from the Captain of the Dutch factory and assisted in their translation into Japanese. He always had me prepare the actual transcription of the text. When I once asked how the Captain, who lived in Deshima, gained knowledge of the information contained in the *fūsetsugaki*, my teacher replied: 'In the countries of the West, they speak much of the news and publish it every day. The newpapers reveal information not only of one's own country but of other countries as well. The Captain reads these newspapers, and he writes down the more prominent information from them to present to the Administrator.'

When Dutch arrived at port, they apparently brought with them various foreign newspapers for the factory at Deshima and the Captain gathered his information from the reports received. In special cases, it would seem, reports were assembled and dispatched by the Dutch governor-general in Batavia and then these were presented to the Japanese. The *fūsetsugaki*, written annually for presentation to the Japanese on the order of the governor-general in Batavia, contained all manner of information.

Among related works in my possession is a three-stringbound-volume manuscript entitled *Ahen fūsetsugaki* (Reports about Opium). It is a detailed, year-by-year chronicle that frequently repeats information concerning the importation of opium to China from some 300 years before, its prohibition, its illicit sale, severe punishments surrounding it, and the like; then, it concerns the sending of Lin Zexu to Guangdong and his efforts to maintain strict control over opium, his incineration of the opium of the English merchants, the resultant commotion (from war to diplomacy), the nature of the war in its different locales; and, finally, from the negotiations to the peace treaty and disturbances following the incident. Information was drawn from Guangdong, Hong Kong, Macao, Xiamen (Amoy), Shanghai, Singapore, and elsewhere.

This *fūsetsugaki* manuscript (dating to the late Edo period) is written with tiny characters on roughly 80 pages of Mino paper [*Minogami*, a kind of Japanese paper], folded in half, and bound into three stringbound volumes. The material contained in it brought together translations from the Dutch documents presented to the Nagasaki Administrator, covering four occasions. A preface at the beginning of the first volume reads: 'Written here are the remarkable incidents which arose in China [lit., Tōkoku] due to the [Chinese] prohibition imposed on the sale of opium by the English and others from 1838 to 1840 according to the Dutch calender.' At the beginning of the second half of the first volume, there is another preface which reads: 'Chronicled here is the prohibition imposed on the sale of opium in China by the English and others from 1840 to 1841 according to the Dutch calender.'

Volumes two and three similarly carry prefaces 'chronicling the exceptional events' that transpired, respectively, from 1841 through the fourth month of 1842 and from the fifth month of 1842 through 1843. The passage of the events are then recounted in a kind of itemization.

At the end of the translated text presented first, there is the following note: 'As stated by the governor-general in Jakarta [i.e., Batavia, Asian headquarters of the Dutch East India Company], the materials immediately preceding are presented as instructed. The Captain.'c Concerning the translations presented by the Captain, the next line reads: 'As to the foregoing report, the Japanese translation is presented along with the original text,' and it is dated to what corresponds to the seventh month of 1840. The signatures of the interpreters who provided the translation are also given: Nakayama Sakusaburō (1785–1844) and Ishibashi Jojūrō.

As this passage indicates, in the name of the Dutch governor-general in Batavia, the information was sent to the Captain in Deshima and then he presented it to the Nagasaki Administrator. We know also of special reports (*betsudan fūsetsugaki* [additional reports]) prepared by the governor-general in Batavia. Beyond the *fūsetsugaki*, there are also many documents which were referred to as *Jagatara no kashirayaku no mono kara mōshitsukete kita kara* (Inasmuch as instruction from the governor-general in Jakarta have arrived); sometimes, in place of *kashirayaku no mono* (governor-general), this kind of document might read *totokushoku no mono* (military commissioner).

At the time, Holland enjoyed preferential treatment as the only Western country allowed to carry on trade with Japan, but in compensation the Dutch were obliged to present these reports on foreign affairs. This arrangement was said to have derived originally from the shogunate's policy of preventing the intrusion of Christianity into Japan. According to section eight of the 'Oranda koku bu' (Section of Holland) in the *Tsūkō ichiran* (Survey of Foreign Relations) of Hayashi Fukusai (1800–59),[d] *kan* 246: 'In the Kaei era [1848–54], every year when the [Dutch] ships arrived at port, the Captain, as he was obliged, presented his report on the black ships under restraint and on observations concerning views on the various disorders overseas. Thereafter, it became the practice that these documents were presented from the ships when they entered port.'

Below this entry a note goes on to explain: 'These were called *fūsetsugaki*. Many of these annual *fūsetsugaki* are included in such works as *Ka-i hentai* (The Transformation from the Civilized to the Barbarian), compiled by Hayashi Shunsai [1618–80].[e] Its principal purpose arose with the matters involving the Christian southern barbarians.' Yet, there were *fūsetsugaki* whose aim was to illuminate Japan, then under the *sakoku* policy, about the Opium War.

Itazawa Takeo's article in this connection, 'Oranda *fūsetsugaki* no kenkyū' (Studies of the Dutch *fūsetsugaki*),[f] mentions nothing of the *Ahen fūsetsugaki*. Itazawa has also written: *Oranda fūsetsugaki no kenkyū, Oranda fūsetsugaki no kaidai* (A Study and Explanation of the Dutch *fūsetsugaki*).[g] In the latter piece, he put together 158 of these Dutch *fūsetsugaki* covering the period from 1644 (Shōhō 1) to 1745 (Enkyō 2) with appended materials and annotations. Since he included nothing after 1745, the *Ahen fūsetsugaki* of the Tenpō period were not included in his collection, and these *fūsetsugaki* have been published nowhere else.

Now, let us return to the story of the *Ahen fūsetsugaki*. At the end of the translated text of the report of the second batch of them (1840–1841), the interpeter added this postscript: 'Last year when [the documents] about to be presented arrived, the ships turned around and did not follow the established procedures. The Japanese translation was prepared in the tenor of the materials

40

brought during the years in question.' In other words, with the translation still incomplete, the reports seem to have been delivered hurriedly in midstream. 'The final items will be delivered very soon.' It remains unclear whether the ships withdrew without having arriving at Nagasaki or, if they in fact did arrive but the presentation of the *fūsetsugaki* was forgotten amid the confusion. In any event, the previous year's material was brought back and delivered as that year's. In the end the translator appended the following justification:

> In the matter of the presentation of the Japanese translation of the *betsudan fūsetsugaki*, in due time it was pressed for. Although we worked on it diligently day and night, and there were documents which we copied out into Dutch from the record of daily events of the aforementioned Englishman, it was still different from the customary materials translated into Japanese. When we reported on it secretly, it was only among a small group of people and was not released. Thus, maximum discussion of this could not make much headway at all. When about half of it was completed, we delivered it first, and that left the remaining portion.

This note is dated the 'seventh month, year of the tiger.' It goes on: 'Seals of the overseer, the senior and the junior translators,' but the names of these three individuals were omitted from this manuscript.

I cannot say if the foregoing applied only to the *fūsetsugaki*, but, as can be seen in the quotation above, it had to be reported on in secret. Thus, because it was apportioned to a small number of people and not released, the translation did move ahead rapidly. Was this due to official secretiveness or were they additionally wary of the considerable impact that would be exerted on the general populace by this affair?

The subsequent sections were similarly presented in the 'seventh month, year of the tiger,' and in the postscript it reads: 'The earlier material was already delivered, and the final item was translated into Japanese and presented,' and the official titles of those responsible for the translation are given as 'overseer, senior translator, office of document translation, and junior translator.' And, finally, it reads: 'Presented according to the instruction stated above from the governor-general of Jakarta,' and signed: 'Notetaker Captain.' The next line reads: 'Translation and original of the text presented together as above,' and it is signed 'seal of the senior translator,' though the senior translator's name is omitted. Although no date is given (it may have been omitted from the manuscript), from the content it was clearly brought aboard the ships that entered port in the year after the year of the tiger, corresponding to the translated reports of 1843 or Tenpō 14.

This three-volume manuscript is an extremely detailed transcription of reports. As can be seen, however, from the translation office's efforts not to allow any leaks in the process, this manuscript was probably delivered to either the Nagasaki Administrator or to the Tokugawa shogunate and then later copied by people in their service. Thus, the Japanese authorities had concrete, detailed reports from the beginning of the Opium War, through its course of development, and the consequences of its conclusion.

I also have in my collection a manuscript in one stringbound volume which is a record of the Opium War entitled *Kanton nikki* (Canton Diary). It is identical in content to the *Ahen fūsetsugaki*, with the minor caveat that the copyist was a different person and hence there are a few differences in characters. For example, the *Ahen fūsetsugaki* notes only 'shinko ryō Kapitan' (the two Captains, old and new) and omits their names, but the *Kanton nikki* inserts the two Captains names. Also, where the *Ahen fūsetsugaki* notes only 'overseer, senior translator, office of document translation, and junior translator' for the official titles of those responsible for preparing the translation, the *Kanton nikki* lists in a row the names of thirteen individuals. However, the *Kanton nikki* only contains about half of the volume of records found in the *Ahen fūsetsugaki*, ending with the translated texts through the seventh month of 1842 and not covering the final peace talks.

Chapter Nine

The Influence of the Opium War on Japan

The Second Opium War developed as a joint Anglo-French military force invaded Tianjin and Beijing, and as a result the Chinese signed the Treaty of Tianjin (1858) and the Convention of Beijing (1860) with England and France. These supplied the legal basis to spur on the latters' policies for the colonization of China. This development transpired with the eruption of the 'Arrow Incident' in October 1856, or the ninth lunar month of the third year of Ansei, according to the Japanese calendar. As a result of this incident, the British military forces burned the Guangzhou (Canton) market area to the ground. Information regarding all of these 'incidents' was conveyed to Japan in concrete detail in documents submitted to the shogunate which were based on direct conversations between Opperhoofd (Captain) Donker Curtius and the overseeing officials under the command of the Nagasaki Administrator, Nagamochi Kōjirō, and an assistant overseer.

It was similar to the transmission of an explanation of incidents conveyed by the British authorities stationed in Hong Kong, and at this time many members of the British Parliament were opposed to their government's hardline stance. Richard Cobden (1804–65), William Gladstone (1809–98), and other influential politicial figures fiercely attacked their government's policies, and the issue became entangled in the events leading to the dissolution of the House of Commons. At this time (1857), Karl Marx (1818–83) was living in London and he took up the issue himself. He published two articles in the *New York Daily Tribune* which scathingly exposed and attacked Britain's China policies (March 15, 1857 [no. 4970] and April 10, 1857 [no. 4984], both unsigned).[a] What caught the eye of the Japanese, though, was the latter half of the conversations with the Captain, inasmuch as these included instructions from the Dutch government, where an important recommendation was offered to the Japanese government.

The Captain pointed out that, while the British had become caught up in the attack on and destruction of Guangzhou, the shogunate's inclination to self-conceit and condescension toward foreign nations was readily apparent in the diplomatic correspondence; this was due either to Japan's dissatisfaction with the other party or to its being completely out of line with commonly accepted diplomatic knowledge at the time, being mired in details and causing delays in negotiations. As the Guangzhou case indicated, trivial events could clearly give rise to grave matters. Although the Dutch did not actually say 'Your country is as weak as China,' if the peace were broken, the shogunate was not as well prepared militarily as the Europeans. Thus, the Dutch warned that, 'in this matter concerning China, we should like your candid judgment and disposition insofar at they concern matters of foreign nations with nothing overlooked.'

It was just at this time that Townsend Harris (1804–78) arrived aboard ship and, through face-to-face meetings with the shogunal Council of Elders (Rōjū) and an audience with the shōgun, he persistently demanded that he be allowed to present his credentials to the *bakufu*. However, unable to come to a decision about public opinion easily, the *bakufu* was embarrassed by this treatment and tried simply to gloss over the matter through procrastination and the like. Thus, the authorities received something of a shock from the recommendation of the Dutch Captain, apparently sufficient to make them reconsider matters.

Among the senior members of the Council of Elders, Hotta Masayoshi, who was now employed full-time by the Office of Foreign Affairs, circulated a report of the Captain's conversation to 'the members of the Hyōjōsho [high ranking shogunal officials], the office of maritime defense, the Nagasaki magistracy, the Shimoda magistracy, and the Hakodate magistracy' to which he attached his own 'opinions' as follows: 'Should there once be the sound of a single cannon-shot, then it will already be too late to turn back.... It is evident that the policy we have pursued so far cannot long be maintained. Therefore while we are still in safety we must make a long-term plan, devising means whereby the laws so far in force may soon be revised and the *bakufu*'s actions may thereafter be guided.' He went on to order an evaluation of the Dutch recommendation, saying: 'With these objects in mind, you are accordingly to give full and careful consideration to the question of future *bakufu* policy and after investigation are to submit an early report.'[b]

In my manuscript edition of the work that excerpts this document, it reads: 'On the 24th day of the second lunar month of Ansei 4 [1857], the lord of Sakura [namely, Hotta Masayoshi] delivered this document in person. The original was sent to the Hyōjōsho, and a copy went to the overseer.' The very fact that this document was 'delivered in person' by Japan's highest diplomatic official would seem to indicate the gravity of the matter.

In their joint 'Letter Presenting Discussions on the Matter of Your Note [namely, Hotta's position piece] Concerning the Matter of the British Burning of Guangdong,' Matsudaira Chikanao (Kawachi no kami), Kawaji Toshiakira (1801–68, Saemon no jō), and Mizuno Tadanori (1810–68, Chikugo no kami) reported the same views of the 'discussants': 'It is difficult to foresee what shall come in the wake of [the despoilation of] Canton,' and thus 'we must make a long-term plan, devising means whereby the laws so far in force may soon be revised and the bakufu's actions may thereafter be guided.' Later, Japanese foreign policy underwent a rapid transformation with the 'devising [of] means whereby the laws so far in force may soon be revised' (namely, from a policy of exclusion to one of peaceful diplomatic intercourse), Harris's audience with the shogun, his presentation of credentials to the *bakufu*, his speech to shogunal leaders at Hotta's residence, and his conversations (negotiations over the concrete details of the texts of treaties) with important *bakufu* officials (Inoue Kiyonao [1809–67, Shinano no kami] and Iwase Tadanori [1818–61, Higo no kami]).

I also have a manuscript copy of a text in three stringbound volumes entitled *Amerika shisetsu taiwasho* (Text of Conversations with the American Envoy). It notes that on the sixth day of the eleventh lunar month of Ansei 4, such important shogunal officials as Toki Yorimune (Tanba no kami), Kawaji Toshiakira, Udono Chōei, Inoue Kiyonao, and Nagai Naomune (1816–63, Genba no kami) 'had a variety of questions to raise about certain items which they wished to examine among those discussed at the home of Bichū no kami [Hotta Masayoshi] the other day [Ansei 4/10/26]. Upon receiving word from Bichū no kami, they discussed it in great detail.' They then set out for Harris's lodgings at the Bansho shirabesho (Office for the Investigation of Barbarian Books), and at the time of the conclusion of the treaty, they questioned him about conditions in foreign lands; they listened to his answers in the greatest detail.

Later, from the eleventh day of the twelfth lunar month of that year until the twelfth day of the first month of the following year, Inoue and Iwase as representatives of Japan met with Harris on thirteen occasions to examine in the finest detail and go over questions and answers one by one concerning the draft of the treaty proposed by Harris. A detailed record of these meetings, the *Amerika shisetsu taiwasho*, was compiled as a documentary report and signed by Inoue and Iwase. Reports on conversations with the aforementioned Captain Donker Curtius and other documents from the same time period are collected in a manuscript edition in my possession (twelve stringbound volumes on Mino paper, edited and a clean copy made in what appears to be the early Meiji period).[c] It carries the title *Gaii chinsetsu zakki* (Collection of Strange Ideas of the Foreign Barbarians), although it ought to be called 'A Collection of Documents on Foreign Relations of the Late Edo Period.' In particular, the Captain's conversations have been cited in a number of works now, such as volume 15 of the *Bakumatsu gaikoku kankei monjo* (Documents Concerning Foreign Relations in the Late Edo Period), and *Bakumatsu ishin gaikō shiryō shūsei* (Compilation of Historical Materials on Foreign Affairs in the Late Edo and Meiji Restoration Eras).[d]

Also, in the *Ishin shiryō kōyō* (Essentials of the Historical Materials on the Meiji Restoration),[e] one finds an item dated Ansei 4/2/24: 'The shogunate has learned a lesson from the disputes between China and Britain in Guangdong and has laid out the essentials for reforms in the apparatus of diplomacy. Orders went out to the members of the Office of Evaluation, the naval defense office, the

Nagasaki magistracy, the Shimoda magistracy, and the Hakodate magistracy to review these [reform ideas] closely.' It then proceeds to cite numerous documents (manuscripts, largely). The traumatic conversations of the Captain apparently circulated rather widely at the time.

Hotta Masayoshi attached his own 'opinions' to Captain Curtius's conversations, and I first saw this document in two works: Naitō Chisō, *Kaikoku kigen Ansei kiji* and Kimura Kaishū, *Sanjū nen shi,* both cited earlier. The former, in particular, after mention of the Captain's conversations and Hotta's 'opinions,' goes on to say: 'Here was a proposal for trade and peace negotiations, and opinions among shogunal officials were fixed.' Despite the regularized nature of opinions at the *bakufu,* public opinion among influential members of the populace at large was by no means uniform. Within many domains, the uproar continued with countless views being expressed on the exclusion policy. Be that as it may, the shogunate had taken the decisive step toward reform in the world of foreign affairs. Thus, the burning of Guangzhou to the ground by the British military as a result of the Arrow Incident, which precipitated the Second Opium War, eventually drove Japanese history to a new stage.

Among the works written about the Opium War (the first one) from the perspective of China as the victimized country and then conveyed to Japan where it was widely read in manuscript form was the *Yifei fanjing lu* (A Record of the Invasion of the Barbarians, J. Ihi hankyō roku).[f] It is still unknown who wrote it and the route by which it made its way to Japan. While this work was indeed well known in Japan as a text describing the events of the Opium War, it did not circulate widely in China. The 'Yapian zhanzheng shumu jieti' (Annotated Bibliography of Works on the Opium War)[g] is a compilation with explanatory notes of numerous historical materials concerning the Opium War that are extant within and without China. At the mention of the title *Yifei fanjing lu* in this bibliography, however, it is listed only as a work presently being searched for. For, although only the name was known in China of this work that circulated in Japan, the work itself could not then be found in its native land. Perhaps, it was never published in China, but made its way overseas only in manuscript form.[1]

Although manuscripts of the work were made in Japan as well, Katsura Isoo (Koson, 1868–1938) notes in his *Kanseki kaidai* (Explanations for Chinese-Language Texts)[h] a text by the name of *Ihi hankyō bunkenroku* (A Record of Observations about the Invasion of the Barbarians, Ch. Yifei fanjing wenjianlu)[i]: 'This work chronicles the circumstances surrounding the British invasion of the southern border of China during the Daoguang reign period, hence its title. Its author does not make his identity clear.' The following words are further appended at the very end of the Japanese reprint: 'Fourth year of the Ansei reign in Japan, woodblock print edition in the collection of the Meirindō.' By the same token, though, Kasai Sukeji (b. 1905), in his *Kinsei hankō ni okeru shuppansho no kenkyū* (Studies of Published Works in the Domainal Schools in the Early Modern Period),[j] mentions an *Ihi hankyō kenbunroku* (Ch. Yifei fanjing jianwenlu) as a publication of the Meirindō from the domain of Takanabe in Kyūshū, and notes: 'Written by domainal lord Akitsuki Taneki published in Ansei 4.' As concerns its contents, Kasai writes: 'It describes events concerning diplomacy with various foreign countries in the Kaei and Ansei periods prior to the Meiji Restoration. It also compiles various diplomatic documents, and is thus a work intended to teach students knowledge and the circumstances appertaining at the time in foreign lands.'

Although both of these works were published in six fascicles in Ansei 4 at the Meirindō (note the slightly different titles), in the annotations offered by each we can see that they are entirely different in content. Furthermore, where the *Kanseki kaidai* says that the 'author [of *Ihi hankyō bunkenroku*] does not make his identity clear,' the *Kinsei hankō ni okeru shuppansho no kenkyū* mentions that the *Ihi hankyō kenbunroku* was: 'Written by domainal lord Akitsuki Taneki.'

The *Itsuzon shomoku* (Listing of Lost Books)[k] is a listing with annotations of old Chinese texts lost in China but still extant in Japan. It carries the following notation: 'The *Yifei fanjing lu* in three volumes and the *Ihi hankyō bunkenroku* in three volumes.' Noting that 'no author's name is given,' it says they were both in published and manuscript editions, 'a woodblock printing from the Ansei period and manuscript copies from the Edo period.' It goes on to offer the explanation that these works 'chronicle events concerning the eruption of the Opium War. Many manuscript copies came to Japan, and woodblock printings have recently circulated somewhat.' However, it is incorrect in saying 'the eruption of the Opium War,' for the work lacks material about the start of the war and describes events from the British military's abrupt call for the surrender of the Dinghai magistrate through to the peace treaty negotiations. It would seem that the annotator had not read the text here closely. .

In the section entitled 'zasshi' (various histories) in the *Naikaku bunko tosho dainibu Kansho mokuroku* (Bibliography of Chinese-language Books in Section Two of the Naikaku bunko),[l] there is an entry which reads: *Ihi hankyō roku*, published in Ansei 4, six stringbound volumes.[2] However, in the section entitled 'zasshi rui' (varieties of histories) in the *Seikadō bunko Kanseki bunrui mokuroku* (Catalogued Bibliography of Chinese-language Texts in the Seikadō Library),[m] there is also an entry for the *Ihi hankyō roku* which reads in fine print: 'Three volumes, appended is the *Ihi hankyō kenbunroku* in three volumes. . . . Author's name missing, manuscript.' The number of volumes would thus be six. This work was originally from the collection of Nakamura Keiu (1832–91). Although a manuscript, had this been copied from a woodblock printed edition of the work, then perhaps: there was the three-volume chronicle of the Opium War, *Yifei fanjing lu*, which came to Japan from China; and Akitsuki Taneki wrote 'appendices' to this work and compiled a collection on diplomacy and foreign relations with foreign lands in the years of the Kaei and Ansei reign periods, which was called the *Hankyō kenbunroku* in three volumes; and these two works (each with two different editions) were combined into one six-volume work.

Chapter Ten

The *Yifei fanjing lu* and the *Ahen shimatsu*

Of the two manuscript editions of the *Yifei fanjing lu* in my possession, one is in four stringbound volumes and one is in two. Although they are the same in content, the four-volume edition is missing some of the material found at the end of the two-volume text. The two-volume text is written on thin paper in small characters close to one another; although only half as many volumes, it actually has somewhat more material contained within it. Because these were manuscripts that were not originally separated into *juan*, they have now become the basis, respectively, for the Iwanami bunko reprint edition in five volumes and the Sonkeikaku bunko reprint edition in three volumes.

My two editions of the original have Japanese reading punctuation inserted into the text, lines beside the names of places, people, and the like, and notes indicating where incorrectly transcribed characters appear in the text. The four-volume edition has the library seal of the Meimeidō, although I do not know to whom the seal belonged. Two red seals are stamped in the two-volume edition: 'Library of the Seinokan' and 'Seal of the Fukuyama Military School.' The reference here is to the library of the former Bingo Fukuyama domainal school, the Seinokan. For a time toward the end of the Edo period, daimyō Abe Masahiro (1819–62) was the leader of the shogunal Council of Elders. Since he was as well mindful of and in actual charge of foreign relations, such books were perhaps collected at the domainal school by the vassals. As with the four-volume edition, so too the two-volume edition of this work contains reading punctuation, lines beside the names of people, places, and bureaucratic offices, and corrected inaccurately transcribed characters. In addition, there are many declensional syllabaries (*okurigana*) added to the text of the two-volume edition, and the latter's explanations are much more detailed, with more inaccuracies and omissions noted.

Furthermore, in the two-volume edition, there are explanatory notes added in the blank spaces beside and above the words in the text that seem difficult to understand. It gives the appearance that it was rigorously read in detail. It would seem that the scholars – perhaps the Confucian scholars of the domainal school or the military officials for coastal defense – read the work carefully and added notes where appropriate. However, there are a fair number of erroneous or simply undependable notes, such as explaining: the Chinese term *maomei* (ignorant, rash) as *shi o okashite* (defy death); the Chinese expression *matou* (wharf, jetty) as *shijō* (market); and the Chinese term *zhongtang* (large scroll hung in a reception room; also an unofficial reference to a grand secretary) as *kenrei* (prefectural ordinance).

The *Yifei fanjing lu* does not describe the changing circumstances in the Opium War on the basis of any chronological order; it has neither preface nor afterward, and the name of its compiler is absent. It simply begins in the seventh month of 1840 with a list of the names of the leaders of the British land and sea assaults and the demand for surrender that they sent to the magistrate at Dinghai. After that it is primarily a compendium of documents and reports from the time of the war – such as directives of the highest governmental authorities, reports from local officials, memorials to the Daoguang Emperor from various responsible officials, imperial edicts, promulgations from officials to the general populace as well as those from the British military to local officials, dispatches from influential Chinese, documents exchanged between the British military and the Chinese, and the text by knowledgeable Chinese entitled 'Pingyi xiance' (Plan to pacify the barbarians). Among them we find mixed in the depositions of British captives, a biography of Chen Huacheng who fought valiantly to the death as a Chinese military leader, as well as a record of the atrocities committed by soldiers of the British navy. However, primary among them remain the public pronouncements and reports, and from them one can glean the concrete circumstances of the war and the changes over time. It concludes with the text of the peace treaty of 1842, but this portion is missing from the four-volume edition of this work in my possession.

Although the reports of the Dutch Captain may have been known by one group of the authorities and other concerned parties, the general intelligent public, it seems, was able to get a rather detailed description of the Opium War that had erupted in their neighboring land through the *Yifei fanjing lu* and its successive transcriptions. In an 1853 (Kaei 6) letter to Nagahara Takeshi, Yoshida Shōin (1830–59) wrote: 'I have heard that you are engaged in a comparative textual reading of the *Fanjing lu*, and I would like to join your group. I hope you will accept me.' This would indicate the enthusiastic, academic pose taken by some Japanese as they tried to study the Opium War through group reading of texts.

In this connection, Shōin had at the age of sixteen in 1846 (Kyōka 3) copied out the text of a report on foreign relations of the time entitled *Waiyi xiao shi* (Short History of the Foreign Barbarians).[1] In it he transcribed reports (perhaps from the lower Yangzi region) concerning the Opium War brought by British ships that called at the port of Nagasaki in 1841 (Tenpō 12). These were quite vague and contained a large number of incorrect characters and clerical errors.

I also have a copy of an anti-Christian tract written by Aizawa Seishisai (1782–1836), *Sokuja manroku* (Full Record of Putting a Stop to Wickedness) (manuscript copy [in one stringbound volume] completed in 1852), in which the author cites the *Shengwu ji* and, when touching on the Opium War, occasionally cites the *Yifei fanjing lu*. Earlier yet, at the very beginning of his *Shin-Ei sen ki* (Record of the Sino-British War) (four stringbound volumes in manuscript, preface dated 1849, to be discussed more fully below), Nagayama Nuki (or Kan) notes: 'I have recently read books on the British bandits, *Shinpan* and *Hankyō*.' These last two are references to *Shinpan jiryaku* (Summary Account of the Invasion) and *Yifei fanjing lu*.

Similarly, in the 'introductory remarks' (*reigen*) to his *Kaigai shinwa* (New Stories from Overseas) (published in five stringbound volumes, to be discussed in more detail below)[2] to Mineta Fūkō's (1817–83) treatment of the Opium War (preface dated 1849), he also notes: 'The reports in this work are based on the *Yifei fanjing lu*.' It would thus seem that the *Yifei fanjing lu* was widely disseminated, although I still have no hard historical material to date precisely when this work actually came to Japan from China. In the *Iwase bunko tosho mokuroku* (List of Books in the Iwase Collection),[a] there is an entry dated 1848 (Kaei 1) for a manuscript edition of the *Yifei fanjing lu* in one stringbound volume. That may mean that the book initially came to Japan in the preceding Kōka period (1844–48). If that is the case, that would place it just after the ratification of the peace treaty (the Treaty of Nanjing).

As I noted earlier, though, this book strangely begins with the British demands for surrender conveyed to the magistrate of Dinghai. Perhaps an earlier section of the text (dealing with events in the Opium War before that) has since been lost.

One work, compiled concisely in Japan, which deals with the Opium War from its eruption through the small commotion following the conclusion of the peace treaty and which concludes with the author's own views appended is the *Ahen shimatsu* (The Opium [War] from Beginning to End) (original in Kanbun, one stringbound volume) by Saitō Kaoru (1815–52, also known as Chikudō and Shitoku). In an afterward to this work, dated the sixth month of Kōka 1 (1844), Saitō Setsudō (1797–1865, Masanori) writes: 'This chronicling of the events is far better than reading the reports (*fūsetsugaku*) of the Chinese and Dutch. The writing is far clearer as well.'

The next postface, dated the ninth month of the same year, is signed Heikei (Sakuma Shōzan, 1811–64), and it reads in part:

> There is no greater danger to the realm to be feared more at present than the foreign bandits. Nothing is more important than our making military preparations and coming to an understanding of them.... However, people today are confused about this and few know that this is something to be overcome. By himself Shitoku has worked hard in this cause to compose his *Ahen shimatsu* to provide the material to know them. The breadth of his knowledge is such that he is not just a gifted writer.

He thus saw this book as a valuable piece of work to come to understand 'them' (foreign countries) and to encourage Japan toward military preparedness.

There is also an appended afterward, dated to the next year (1845), by Kanda Mitsuru which notes: 'How well [are described] the affairs of foreigners!' And, from the same year, there is an afterward by Murase Shū which reads: 'Border defenses must also be attended to.'

All of these authors saw the Opium War as a mirror of sorts, encouraging Japan strongly to make defensive preparations. With these events of the time as its background, the *Ahen shimatsu* seems to have been circulated widely.

In a preface (dated Kaei 6 or 1853) to Saitō Chikudō's *Tokushi zeigi* (Superfluous Words upon Reading History),[b] Asaka Gonsai (1791–1860) notes: 'When he was a student [at the Shōheikō, the shogunal school in Edo], he wrote the *Ahen shimatsu* in one stringbound volume, and it won him a high reputation for his talents.' He goes on to mention that Chikudō died at the young age of 37, leaving over twenty written works. The creator, he notes, provided him with an abundance of talent but was stingy in his allocation of years. Shinozaki Shōchiku, in an 1844 postface to *Chikudō bunshō* (Selections from the Prose Writings of [Saitō] Chikudō),[c] writes: 'Shitoku's writing and his intelligence are widely known and each of his prose and poetic writings have stunned men. This great admiration is enough to inspire jealousy.' In any event, the facts that he was a highly talented man and that he had a wealth of ability as a writer may have been sufficient to make this book known at the time.

According to the *Chikudō Saitō kun nenpu* (Chronological Biography of Saitō Chikudō) (written by Saitō Daizaburō and included at the front of the *Chikudō bunshō*), the *Ahen shimatsu* was a work written in 1843 (Tenpō 14) when Chikudō was 28 years of age and a student at the Shōheikō. The next year he became the headmaster at the Shōheikō. As can be seen from the many afterwards cited above, already from these years the *Ahen shimatsu* seems to have been a well known work, widely distributed, and it would seem a work that slightly predated the coming to Japan of the *Yifei fanjing lu*. For this reason, the first part of the *Ahen shimatsu* (in Kanbun) on the whole corresponds to the *Ahen fūsetsugaki* (in Japanese) of the Tenpō period, introduced earlier. Possibly, it was written on the basis either of the *Ahen fūsetsugaki* or a similar work (such as the reports of the Captain). One sees in the section at the end of which Chikudō appended his own views that he wrote in a highly deprecatory fashion of China and was apparently taking sides with the British.

I have three different editions of the *Ahen shimatsu*. One is the aforementioned manuscript (ten sheets of Mino paper, with two pages of postfaces); another is a printed edition dated 1937 with Ise Saisuke from Sendai listed as 'editor, publisher, and printer.' In the text of the latter, there is in addition to the afterward by Saitō Setsudō (Seiken) a 'Seiken yūshiki' (Additional words from Seiken) and it reads: 'It was circulated but prohibited from being published, [so] people copied it out and placed it on their shelves.' We thus learn that this work was banned from printing at the time, and only in

1937 did Mr. Ise, an apparent admirer of Chikudō's, also from Sendai, manage to have the work published. Ise actually printed ten of Chikudō's works, including *Chikudō bunshō* and *Chikudō shishō* (Selections from the Poetic Writings of [Saitō] Chikudō).[d]

The third edition of the *Ahen shimatsu* in my possession is a manuscript edition with Japanese syllabaries inserted into the text, an effective Japanese translation of the Kanbun original. There are lines drawn along the sides of the names of countries, place names, and personal names, and the owner of this edition was quite an enthusiastic reader. He wrote at the end on the last page: 'Borrowed from Mr. Kubō in the third month of Kaei 3 [1850] and copied by hand.' It is signed 'Takemura Shōrei.' The fact that this work was circulated in manuscript, as was the original Kanbun in manuscript form, indicates well the great concern of Japanese intellectuals about the Opium War.

According to his chronological biography, Chikudō was born in Tōda, Mutsu domain in the year of Bunka 12 (1815) and died in Edo at the age of 37 in Kaei 5 (1852). He studied at the Shōheikō, served as the headmaster there, and was a scholar of Chinese learning (Kangakusha). However, we find in his 'Yaku Yōsho gi' (Ideas for translating Western works) (contained in the first volume of *Chikudō bunshō*) the following lines: 'We must not sever ties with Holland; we must read and study Western books'; and 'those who call themselves Confucian scholars have not observed Western learning in breadth. As a rule, they try to ban it as heterodoxy.' These citations would tend to indicate that he was preparing translations of Western works with the aim of learning about foreign lands.

This orientation in his thought appears in his *Ban shi* (History of Foreign Lands) (one stringbound volume). At the end of the introductory remarks to this work, he signed the pretentious name 'Bō Yōshi' (he who has vast knowledge of the West). In his preface (dated 1851) to this work, Sakaya Yutaka writes: 'Japanese translators have not written general accounts of the major events [in the West],' and 'this made Saitō Chikudō angry, do extensive reading in history, and gather together [information concerning] these major events. On that basis he wrote a historical chronicle tracing the history from past to present of the ups and downs which would be clear at a glance.' It is from this note that we learn Chikudō to be the author of the work. Written in the spring of 1851, it circulated in manuscript of which one such copy is now in my library.

Later, in 1882, Takenaka Kuniyoshi transcribed the *Ban shi* in six stringbound volumes into volume five of his edited work *Tenkōrō sōsho* (Collection from the Tower of Heavenly Fragrance); this information can be gleaned from Hamano Tomosaburō, *Nihon sōsho mokuroku* (List of Book Collections in Japan).[e] I have not seen this last publication, but the *Nihon sōsho mokuroku* incorrectly gives the author as 'Saitō Setsudō.'[3] I would like now to examine the *Ban shi*, for it enables us to glimpse another side of Saitō Chikudō, author of the *Ahen shimatsu*.

Chapter Eleven

On Saitō Chikudō's *Ban shi* and Other Writings

The preface by Sakaya appears at the very beginning of the *Ban shi*. It indicates what provided the motive for Chikudō to write this work in the first place:

> Scholars at present are discussing the skill of Westerners in military tactics and the relative strengths of their materiel. On this basis they are establishing national defense policies as the most important task. Often, however, they are ignorant of the reasons for victories or defeats, successes or failures, and they express their opinions on the basis of thin air. However skillful they may elaborate such a point of view, however brilliant their argumentation, they are, figuratively speaking, searching about in a dark room, with no necessity that they will gain their objective. Indeed, it is dangerous. We have no recorded histories for foreign lands, because Japanese translators have not written general accounts of the major events [in the West]. This made Saitō Chikudō angry, do extensive reading in history, and gather together [information concerning] these major events. On that basis he wrote a historical chronicle tracing the history from past to present of the ups and downs which would be clear at a glance.

In other words, people at the time considered it urgent to discuss and debate Western military tactics and weaponry and to consider a wide range of defense policies. He pointed out that, because Japanese did not know what had occurred in the histories of the countries of the West, they were spinning many fanciful, imaginary theories. This situation enraged Chikudō, so he went foraging among the histories of Western lands and wrote up [his research].

Sakaya goes on to say: 'He planned this piece of work (*Ban shi*) and established his principal points of view. He discussed the times and the most efficacious timing for implementing policy. Thus, his views were well founded, offered clear examples, and illuminated that which had been little known.'

If we argue that the *Ban shi* was written to try and point up what were the bases to the generally vacuous positions being taken on foreign affairs at the

53

time as well as to match his own insatiable curiosity, then the writing of the *Ahen shimatsu* was based on similar premises.

In the 'introductory comments' to the *Ban shi*, Chikudō notes:

> When you look through the affairs of foreign countries and various books, you see that there are as yet no unified chronicles [in Japanese]. There is thus no way to think about major trends in their histories. This has always deeply troubled me, so I did extensive reading in Western history, taking notes and copying out material here and there, and in a chronological form I have now enabled men to gain an outline view at a glance.... Inasmuch as I have not obtained every single book on Western history, I cannot claim to have gained full detail of its long past. For the time being, let us divide [this history] into three eras: antiquity (*taiko*), the new world (*shin sekai*), and 'revolution' (*kakumei*). From revolution to the present, there has not yet been another change in period. Thus, we can stop there. As yet I do not know Western theories on the subject.

The 'introductory comments' conclude with: 'Kaei shingai [4 or 1851], early spring; signed: one who has vast knowledge of the West.'

The opening sentences (of the main body of the work) read in general as follows. In the *taiko* period of high antiquity, we find Adam and Eve in a paradise known as Eden.[a] At the time, the climate there was conciliatory and there were no illnesses. There were four rivers: the Andes, the Tigris, the Indus, and the Euphrates. There were numerous fish everywhere; and there were numerous trees in the water where one could relax and lots of fruit and grains for consumption. Birds and beasts formed groups, but they did not harm people. Adam, however, eventually became very proud in his heart and did not obey heaven's teachings. As a result, the earth's vapors changed, the five grains did not ripen, and the birds and beasts harmed people. Thereupon, men began to labor in the fields, and women began to bear children. The concerns of livelihood commenced.

To this section a 'viewpoint' (*ron*) is attached:

> In the theories of Westerners, heaven and earth are not self-generating. There is an entity which must give birth to them, and it is called the Creator. After heaven and earth were formed, He produced Adam and Eve and warned them against eating the fruit. They did not obey and were visited with limitless retribution. The Creator had mercy on them, and he vowed that one born of human beings would expiate their sins, and over 3000 years later was one who was born to Judea, the founder of their faith, and he was crucified.

He then cites from a critique of these ideas by Arai Hakuseki (1657–1725), who wrote to the effect (in Chikudō's words): 'Although the exaggerations and falsehoods of this theory are those of a mere child, it clearly lacks the basis sufficient for belief.'

The next portion returns to the main text and describes as follows. Adam's eldest son Cain succeeded him and administered government far and wide, as towns and cities came into existence. People all lived to the old age of several hundred years. The descendants of Cain divided into four generations; allotted to each era was one of four metals (gold, silver, copper, and iron), and machines of many kinds came into existence in this period. The *taiko* universe lasted from Adam for 1650 years. In the era of his descendents, the Seruteito (the Celts?) (implying the 'iron age'), there was a great flood. At that time, Noah, the son of Lamech, was a man of sagely morality.[b] He gained forewarning of the great flood and helped construct a large box like a boat. Thenceforth, the 'new world' began.

The flood was brought under control, and once again the world returned to its former state of peace, but this was the 'second world' or 'new world,' Chikudō argued. Noah had three sons, all men of sagely morality:[c] 'each became the founder of a state in the West.' Later, Noah's descendant Nimrod became the king of Babylonia; his was the first of the great Western kingdoms, and he remained in power for 63 years. Thereafter, the lineage of kings continued with Persia, Greece, and Rome, and they are 'referred to as the four great Western kingdoms.' (Another 'viewpoint' is inserted at ths point).

Next, we enter the era of 'revolution.' What is indicated by the term 'revolution' here is the epoch of the birth of Christ. When the daughter of Judea, Saint Mary (Santa Maria), was sixteen, it was revealed to her by God in a dream that she would be blessed with a sagely son; the era began when she gave birth to this son without a father. Yet, insofar as he was the 'founder of a religion,' it is strange that he did not earn the reputation of Jesus or Christ. There are no subsequent epochs in the West, argues Chikudō, and as such on that basis he explains the rise and fall of the states of Europe in chronicle form. He touches as well on the Mongols and the Turks, and he concludes in 1840 with the ceremony by which the king of France enacted the reburial of Napoleon.

The passages summarized and quoted above were all written in Kanbun, and in my manuscript edition the 'ancient' and 'new world' sections fill roughly ten pages. The section from 'revolution' forward, however, occupies some 60 pages. And, here and there Chikudō inserted his own evaluations in the form of 'viewpoints' into the text, each roughly half a page in length.

Chikudō did not read original texts in Dutch directly and then proceed to write the *Ban shi*. He wrote, it would seem, on the basis of translated works. This can be gleaned from the last entry in his 'introductory comments': 'I have still not had time to study how to read Western languages and thereupon try to put things in order.'

He does not specify which variety of translations he used for writing, but his 'introductory comments' note: 'I did extensive reading in Western history, taking notes and copying out material here and there.' This comment would seem to indicate that he took information from a wide variety of translated works. From what I have seen, he put into Kanbun but otherwise took unchanged at least the portions 'antiquity' and 'new world' from the first volume of a work entitled *Seiyō zakki* (Chronicles of the West) (published in four stringbound volumes, with a preface dated Kyōwa 1 [1801] by Harimaya Shōgorō). The latter work, 'newly carved for a woodblock printing in Kaei 1 [1848],' was written in Japanese by Yamamura Shōei (1770–1807), a scholar of Dutch Learning who edited and enlarged Arai Hakuseki's *Sairan igen* (Varying Words Observed [in one stringbound volume]); I have an incomplete edition of this work which circulated in manuscript as *Zōtei sairan igen* (Varying Words Observed, Edited and Enlarged).

In the volume *Sakoku jidai Nihonjin no kaigai chishiki: sekai chiri, Seiyō shi ni kansuru bunken kaidai* (The Overseas Knowledge of the Japanese During the Period of the Exclusion Policy: Explanation of Documents Concerning World Geography and Western History),[d] Ōkubo Toshiaki argues that Chikudō's work was written in Kanbun but was structurally almost identical to two works written in Japanese: *Yōgai tsūran* (Overall View of the West) in three stringbound volumes (by Muze Kōshi, preface dated Kōka 5 [1848]); and *Seiyō shōshi* (A Short History of the West), a manuscript in three stringbound volumes (by Nagayama Nuki, preface dated Kaei 2 [1849]). A comparison of Chikudō's *Ban shi* with the *Yōgai tsūran*, in particular, reveals almost parallel sentences, which leads Ōkubo to conclude that 'although perhaps unsuccessful as a Kanbun translation it was not that far off'; and, hence, 'this author of the *Yōgai tsūran*, 'Muze Kōshi,' may be none other than Saitō Chikudō himself.' Inasmuch as I do not own a copy of the *Yōgai tsūran*, I cannot make the comparison nor offer an opinion on the matter, but I present Ōkubo's views by way of a precaution.[e]

Chikudō's interest in learning about the world overseas was built upon curiosity. The last volume of *Chikudō shishō* (published by Ise Saisuke of Sendai in 1893) includes eight items under the title 'Ryūkyū chikushi' (Songs of the Ryūkyūs), ten under the title 'Ezo chikushi' (Songs of Hokkaidō), and four under 'Oranda chikushi' (Songs of Holland). One of the 'Oranda chikushi' reads as follows: 'The bluish lapis of the tower matches the colorful pendant-like moon in the evening; and not using the silvery candlelight at the banquet, this poem moves along sideways to convey its clarity.'

In a preface (dated 1888) to the *Chikudō shishō*, Ōnuma Chinzan (1818–91) notes: 'Shitoku [i.e., Chikudō] knew a great deal about the affairs of foreign countries, and thus wrote these poetic songs. He was very clear about what was being sung, and they may be superior to those of You Tong [1618–1704].' Thus, it would seem that Chikudō's knowledge of foreign lands was considerable, which is praised here with examples from his songs about foreign lands, but these songs probably were written in imitation of the You Tong's *Waiguo zhuzhi ci* (Songs and Prose Poems of Foreign Lands) (reprinted with Japanese reading punctuation by Okuda Mototsugu, Tenmei 6 [1786]).[f]

Furthermore, in his preface (dated 1882) to *Chikudō shishō*, Ono Kozan (1814–1910) praises Chikudō's poetry: 'Ancient in flavor and modern in style, he conveys his intentions throughout.' In particular, 'one can see his mental powers and his scholarship at their best when it comes to songs of events in the countries of the West.' By 'songs of events in the countries of the West,' he may have also been referring to the thirteen poetic songs entitled 'Gaikoku eishi' (Historical poems of foreign lands), contained in *Chikudō shishō*. He wrote poems: to Noah's ark; to the unification of Western lands by the kings of Babylonia; to Alexander the Great for spreading his boundaries to the three continents of Europe, Africa, and Asia; to Alexander again for taking as his teacher the sagely Aristotle; and to Aristotle who, being coldly treated by Alexander's descendants, committed suicide by drowning like Qu Yuan (the origins of this apocryphal tale are unknown). He also wrote poems to Columbus for sailing to the American continent with the help of the queen of Spain and to Peter the Great of Russia for traveling incognito through a number of countries, studying ship-building technology there, and returning home to encourage navigation vigorously and raise national prestige. He also wrote poems concerning a number of anecdotes and stories about Napoleon and about the great achievements of George Washington in attainment of American independence. Such deep-felt interest in the events of foreign lands make it only natural that Chikudō would be profoundly concerned by the Opium War and national defense issues, and that he would investigate these matters and compile a book on the subject.

There are also poems in *Chikudō shishō* written for Chen Huacheng and for Liu Guobiao. These also belong in the category of 'historical poems.' At the time of the Opium War, Chen Huacheng was the aged provincial military commander guarding the Wusong fortress which was strategic to the defense of Shanghai. Though the great majority of the garrison troops had fled midway, Chen was greatly praised for his bravery in fighting to the bitter end and dying on the field of action. Liu Guobiao, Chen's commandant and close associate, was a military *jinshi*. At the time of Chen's bold battle, Liu carried Chen's corpse on his back away from the fray and hid it in a clump of reedy grass, protecting it from the enemy. He also wrote a record of Chen's martyrdom in which he described for all the conditions prevailing at the end.

Scholars from Shanghai and its environs collected poems written to commemorate the brave actions of these two men in a work entitled *Biaozhong chongyi ji* (Collection of Demonstrated Devotion and Revered Righteousness); an edition in three stringbound volumes, including an appendix, was reprinted with Japanese reading punctuation in 1851 ('printed,' according to the text itself, 'by Takishirō' (Tower of Bountiful Determination), and Chikudō contributed a preface to this Japanese edition (which would have circulated under the title *Hyōchū sūgi shū*).[g] In his preface, he wrote: 'Matsuura Shijū prepared a woodblock printing of this for me, so I would have it in my library.' Either the Japanese punctuator of this preface was not clear about it or perhaps it was Chikudō who was vague on the subject, but the relationship between this Matsuura and Chikudō remains unknown. Perhaps there is some connection with the *Ahen shimatsu* which was reprinted for

Chikudō so that the students in his private academy (at that time in Shitaya, Edo) would be able to read it.

We have been looking at the second volume of the *Chikudō shishō*, but in the first volume we find a regulated verse entitled 'A Poem Chronicling News of the English Barbarians' Invasion of China' as well as a long poem entitled 'A Poem in Commemoration of the Fiftieth Anniversary of the Death of Hayashi Shihei' (1738–93). The former reads: 'The lands across the seas are vague and distant/ Suddenly we have heard that the might of the Western barbarians has come galloping.' The latter poem also deals with the issue of the Opium War: 'Recently, the extraordinarily violent English bandits ... have encroached upon nearly all of Europe and are now moving south, seeking to gobble up China'; and 'Although victory or defeat remains undecided, the noxious vapors remain foul/ Everyone in the two capitals [Beijing and Nanjing?] and thirteen provinces remains confused.'

These poems were from the time of the Opium War that he 'suddenly heard' of and in which 'victory and defeat remain[ed] undecided.' We thus know that they were composed before the *Ahen shimatsu* which he wrote after the conclusion of the peace negotiations.

In his 'A Poem Chronicling News of the English Barbarians' Invasion of China,' he wrote of one who 'unknitted [her] arched eyebrows to become the commander of a great army'; and, in his commemorative poem for the fiftieth anniversary of the death of Hayashi Shihei, Chikudō wrote of a 'woman general who took troops under her command and crossed the sea.' It seems he meant that the commander of the invading British armed forces was a woman. This story was undoubtedly based on a rumor circulating at the time, perhaps brought on Chinese ships, but it was incorporated as well into the *Ahen shimatsu*. In this latter work, we read of the (Chinese) capture of a 'brave and superb' woman chieftain who, it turns out, is the third British princess (*kōshu*). The English have three princesses: the eldest is known as *kinshu*; the second is known as the *fushō* (perhaps on the Tokugawa pattern of an assistant [*fu*] to the *shōgun*) who remains at home; and the third princess is known as the *senshō* (commander of a naval vessel), and she is the one presently being held captive. 'She has bright eyes and beautiful eyebrows. Her hair is jet black, and her skin tone is like snow. She is only eighteen years of age' (Japanese-style).

While recognizing that 'she may not actually be the younger sister of the king of England,' Chikudō notes that 'a barbarian official [of England] immediately sent a communication demanding the return of the princess. If complied with, he promised to offer up all lands seized, but if she were killed, he vowed to raise an army and take revenge.' Thus, we are told, the Qing government dispatched two specially deputed officials, Yilibu (Elipoo, d. 1843) and Qishan (d. 1854), to hold negotiations with barbarian officials. When agreement was reached on her return, and they memorialized the throne for permission to do so, but, prior to the arrival of permission, they boldly went ahead and set her free on the fifth day of the second month of Daoguang 21 (1841).

Although the *Ahen shimatsu* chronicled in considerable detail the events of the war in a month-by-month, year-by-year fashion, as the above anecdote demonstrates, unreliable stories were also mixed into the account. Perhaps, when trying to describe such major occurrences of a distant country and a culturally more familiar one in which 'everyone in the two capitals and thirteen provinces remains confused,' it is to be expected that such stories as these seemed to be half-truths. This particular story was subsequently incorporated into novels, such as the *Shin-Ei kinsei dan* (Recent Tales of China and England),[h] and with such egregious elements included. Here we read that, in order to save the captive princess, peace negotiations were held, the English army gained control over her, and took her back to England.

Fiction was not the only outlet for this story of a British princess being taken prisoner. One finds it as well in a history of the Qing dynasty written in the second decade of the Meiji period (1877–86) by a Japanese scholar of Chinese studies. Before we move on to a discussion of this work, we should touch on a similarly detailed chronicle as the *Ahen shimatsu*, the *Kairiku senbō roku* (Account of Military Defenses on Sea and Land) by Satō Nobuhiro (1769–1850).

Chapter Twelve

Satō Nobuhiro's *Kairiku senbō roku* and *Son-Ka zateki ron*

There is a 'work entitled *Kairiku senbō roku* (An Account of Military Defenses on Sea and Land) by Satō Chin'en' mentioned in Katsu Kaishū's *Kaikoku kigen* (Origins of the Opening of the Country; preface dated 1891, copyrighted by the Imperial Household Ministry) as an 'outline of the uprising in China.' In it as well the story of the capture of the English princess is recorded. I have not seen an original edition (or even a manuscript copy) of this work and know of it only through Katsu's work. The author, Satō Chin'en is best known as Satō Nobuhiro (1769–1850), Chin'en being his style. In the *bakumatsu* years, a variety of fragmentary news about the Opium War circulated in Japan, but Satō's work was probably noted in the *Kaikoku kigen* because it was seen as a relatively coherent chronicle of information and perhaps a representative work.

The chronicle begins: 'In the seventeenth year of the Daoguang reign period [1837], the English transported 27,000 chests of opium [to China]. . . . Huang Juewen, a civil official of Shandong province, memorialized requesting that it be banned.' Lin Zexu (1785–1850) henceforth proceeded to his new appointment in Guangdong, had the English opium brought before him, and burned it entirely. It goes on to note that in the end war broke out between the two countries, and it records the movements in the battle situations by month and year. It concludes that in Daoguang 22 or 1842 a 'peace treaty was concluded' in Nanjing and a celebration banquet was held aboard an English vessel to commemorate the conclusion of the peace negotiations.

There is no mention in the *Kairiku senbō roku* as to when it recorded these events, and thus we do not know precisely when it was written. It occasionally makes use of the same phraseology as does the *Ahen shimatsu* – for example, both works in describing the tale of the English princess's fighting refer to her as 'brave and superb' (*gyōyō zetsurin*) – but one is in Japanese and the other in Kanbun, and there is a difference in the manner in which the same sorts of things are expressed in the respective texts. Although we do not know which of the two was composed first, possibly Satō wrote his work with the *Ahen shimatsu* as a

60

referent. His work merely notes: 'This woman general was the younger sister of the English king, and she docked at Ningbo.'

Early in the text, it mentions that 'Huang Juewen, a civil official from Shandong province, memorialized' the throne to ban opium; the *Ahen shimatsu* reads that 'Huang Juezhi, a civil official from Shandong, memorialized.' This would seem merely to be a copyist's error as the characters *wen* and *zhi* are similar. However, both *wen* and *zhi* are errors; it should be Huang Juezi (1793–1853, *jinshi* of 1823). Inasmuch as Huang hailed from Guangxi province, it is interesting that the text mentions Shandong.' Reference to him as 'a civil official from Shandong' probably indicates the time when he served as the presiding official at the Shandong provincial examinations in 1837. Yet, the appointment as provincial examiner was a temporary post, and were the text to mention the name of his position it should have referred to him as *honglu si qing* or 'Chief Minister of the Court of State Ceremonials.'[1]

In terms of size, the *Kairiku senbō roku* is a slightly longer work; that is, when comparing the aforementioned Japanese edition of the *Ahen shimatsu* with it, not comparing the Kanbun text of the latter with the Japanese *Kairiku senbō roku*. Satō's work, of necessity, combines pieces from the Dutch *fūsetsugaki* or official 'reports' as well as Qing government sources, and there is no uniformity in style or prose through the text; indeed, there is a manufactured quality about the work. For example, there are occasional conflicting ways of writing the same term: Shanghai is occasionally produces in *kana* as 'Sanhai' and sometimes in Chinese characters; the Yangzi River (Yangzijiang) is rendered both in Chinese characters and sometimes phonetically in *kana* as 'Yassekian.' 'Yassekian' may be an error on the part of the original Dutch translator, but it remains unclear how such an error arose. In other Dutch *fūsetsugaki*, we find it rendered 'Yansēkian,' but from that point forward it would seem that 'Yangzijiang' is rendered phonetically (in the local dialect). Perhaps, the *Kairiku senbō roku* mistakenly transcribed a *kana* syllabary *n* as a *tsu*.

Furthermore, the *Kairiku senbō roku* notes that 'the Dutch for Zhenjiang fu' is 'Shinkyanfuoi.' This is merely [a Japanese rendition of] the Chinese pronunciation of Zhenjiang fu, though 'Dutch' should probably be altered to 'Dutch pronunciation.' Yet, in saying that it is 'the Dutch for' the Chinese term, this indicates that they used as a historical resource the *fūsetsugaki* which were translated from the Dutch.

By the same token, though, in describing Chen Huacheng, the text reads: 'The English heard of his renown and did not recklessly approach Shanghai. Hence the English had the expression, "Do not fear a million troops in Jiangnan, Fear only Chen Huacheng in Wusong."' Elsewhere it notes: 'When the English attacked Dinghai [a second time] they exchanged the princess for land returned to the Qing.' The latter instance would indicate literal use having been made of reports from the Qing. Later in the text, we read: 'Imperial Commissioner Yuqian [1793–1841] died a martyr and lost the territory under his command, and the English acquired the walled city of "Teinhei."' Earlier the text used the

Chinese characters for Dinghai, and here only a short while later it employs *kana* 'Teinhei' (*hei* is the local pronunciation for standard Chinese *hai*). This would seem to indicate the use of the historical sources as raw resources. Also, the placename Ciqi appears in Chinese characters and sometimes it is rendered – apparently phonetically – as 'Tsēkē.'

This point would indicate that the content itself, irrespective of whether it is accurate (this being a problem, in any event, of the sources upon which it is based), is at least related overall to the Kanbun text in descriptive phrasing, though one may say that the *Ahen shimatsu* is better composed.

Satō Nobuhiro was a vigorous scholar of astounding breadth. From the years of the Tenmei reign (1781–89) through the early years of the Kaei period (1848–54) (it is generally held that he died in 1850 at the age of 81, but there are other theories), he published an extraordinary number of works: 205 different pieces in all, filling 563 traditional volumes, remain extant.[2] Numerous works are extensions or rewritings of others, and hence there is much reduplication of content. There are other works he claimed as his own that are of dubious authenticity. Some seriously doubt that such a massive number of writings could have been the work of his brush alone.[3]

Shionoya Tōin wrote in a preface to Satō's *Keizai yōroku* (The Essence of Economics):

> The venerable Satō Yūzai [a style of his] handed down to us works of many sorts. He made a particularly detailed study of mathematics, did penetrating research in agricultural administration, water utilization, military systems, and artillery. As a young man, he travelled about the realm and tried to examine things closely in person. Later, he was invited by several feudal lords to help plan their domainal affairs. He was always a man for results, never for empty chatter.

He seems to have been quite a specialist in matters concerning agriculture, as indicated by such works as *Keizai yōroku*.

As the basis for agricultural management, he studied the 'Yu gong' (Tribute of [King] Yu), a chapter from the ancient Chinese text, *Shu jing* (Classic of Documents), and he penned a two-volume work in literary Chinese entitled *U kō shūran* (Collected Views on the 'Yu gong') (with an explanatory preface dated Bunsei 12 [1829]). He prepared this work by putting together the commentaries by past Chinese scholars concerning the phraseology of the 'Yu gong.' Inasmuch as there were many such works in China before Satō's, there is no doubt that he made use of them and copied material directly from them.

In his work, *Suitō hiroku* (Confidential Memoir on Social Control), he also offered his own distinctive methods for ploughing the land and utilizing water resources, and he made a study of the qualities of the soil. His principal attention was focused on raising production and enabling the smooth circulation of produce. To do so, he proposed an administrative reform program which called for the division of all domestic administration into six bureaus or *fu*, each with its own responsibilities. He proposed as well a social plan which would set up at various locales elementary schools, benificent societies, clinics, orphanages, factories for itinerant children, and other educational facilities.

In his *Bukka yoron* (My Views on Commodity Prices), he stressed a financial policy in which the government supervised merchants and took control over commodity prices. In addition, he wrote pieces on astronomy and calendrical science and on artillery strategy, but these were probably the result of his use of Western scientific techniques based in Dutch Learning.

As concerned financial policy, he referred frequently to King Yu, Yi Yin, and Guang Zhong, from citations in the Chinese classics, and he demonstrated enthusiasm for Western astronomy as it was transmitted more recently from Holland; furthermore, in 1805 he copied out by hand in Nagasaki the *Rangaku daidō hen* (On the Great Way of Dutch Learning) by Shiba Kōkan (1738–1818). A copy of the latter replete with his 'genuine autograph' was anastatically printed in 1920 by the *Hōkō gikai*. I own a copy of this work, and on it one can already see explanatory charts for Copernicus's heliocentric theory and sunspots. Apparently these were the sources by which he acquired such knowledge, and he would often make public his knowledge of Western astronomy – the sun at the center nurturing all things and forming the basis for agricultural administration – in such works as *Tenchū ki* (Record of the Pillar of Heaven) and *Yōzō kaiku ron* (Essays on Creation and Cultivation).

This formed one part of Satō's research in Dutch Learning. Either by virtue of his studying with the specialist in Dutch Learning, Udagawa Kaien (Genzui, 1755–97), or by making use of Yamamura Shōei's (1770–1807) work *Seiyō zakki*, he wrote the *Seiyō rekkoku shiryaku* (A Brief History of the Western Powers) (preface dated Bunka 5 [1808] in Japanese; my edition is a manuscript edition in three stringbound volumes, dated Tenpō 8 [1837], and bearing the inscription 'Matsuura Library'). Inasmuch as Ōkubo Toshiaki has given a detailed explanation of the formation and content of the *Seiyō rekkoku shiryaku* in his *Sakoku jidai Nihonjin no kaigai chishiki*, I shall not do so here, but I should just say at this point that it is of epochal importance if only because it was the earliest comprehensive history of the West written by a Japanese, earlier even than the *Ban shi* of Saitō Chikudō.

In the *Son-Ka zateki ron* (On Preserving China and Crushing the Barbarians) (*kan* 1), Satō wrote: 'Since I have no knowledge of Dutch Learning, I cannot read Dutch books.' Yet, in his own introductory remarks to the *Seiyō rekkoku shiryaku*, he noted: 'I once studied under [the Dutch Learning scholar] Udagawa Kaien, and together with the late [scholar of Dutch Learning] Mr. Yamamura Shōei, I learned of various histories of the West.' Thus, the *Seiyō rekkoku shiryaku* was clearly written after Satō learned of the contents of various Dutch and Japanese works on Western history from Udagawa and Yamamura. However, just as Saitō Chikudō, author of the *Ahen shimatsu*, wrote the *Ban shi*, Satō wrote the *Kairiku senbō roku* and *Son-Ka zateki ron* (see below) on the basis of reports about the Opium War, and he wrote the *Seiyō rekkoku shiryaku* [i.e., each wrote works on East Asia and on the West]. In short, he had acquired a fair amount of information about conditions in Western lands at that time, and he keenly felt that the Western powers – with a mighty naval force of artillery and gunboats (as proven by the Opium War) were gradually invading East Asia.

Satō's work, *Son-Ka zateki ron* in five *kan*, carries an introduction dated Kaei 2 or 1849. It was said to be only rarely circulated in manuscript form, and I have not seen a manuscript of it. It is, though, included both in the last volume (of three) of *Satō Nobuhiro kagaku zenshū* (Collected Works of Satō Nobuhiro and His Family), and in the first volume of *Satō Nobuhiro bugaku shū* (Satō Nobuhiro's Compendium on Japanese Military Science).[a] In explanatory texts appended to each of these two collections, it is hypothesized that the *Son-Ka zateki ron* was the ultimate result, first, of Satō's response to an inquiry of the lord of the Tsu domain in Ise, Tōdō Izumi no kami, to propose a plan for coastal defense, which he subsequently revised and wrote up. The form of the text is questions and answers, though in content the prose style is distinctively Satō's.

The title of the work simply means 'enable the [Central] Efflorescence to continue its existence and crush the barbarians.' China had been defeated in the Opium War, he noted at the end of the work, and:

> It brought grave pain to the hearts and minds of the Qing dynasty's sovereign and subjects and afflicted their thoughts, while they offered alms for the poor and mourned the dead, with all classes suffering equally in these regards. When they have trained troops for a number of years, then they can raise a righteous army of revenge, subjegate the English barbarians, and finally eliminate without remnant all of them from East Asia. This should long serve as a western wall for our land [Japan]. Such was my principal aim in writing *Son-Ka zateki ron*.

The fourth and fifth volumes of this work are largely comprised of a chronicle of the Opium War, and they discuss the events of the war from the outset, the peace negotiations, Canton residents after the conclusion of the peace treaty, and the anti-English movement of the masses at Dinghai. At the very end of this account, though, he wrote: 'The foregoing text is based on reports acquired from Dutch vessels that have entered port this year.' By 'this year,' he probably meant Kaei 2 (1849), the year of the introduction, which may mean that it was actually written earlier.

In the fourth volume of *Son-Ka zateki ron*, there is a section, almost identical to its presentation in *Kairiku senbō roku*, describing the capture of the English king's younger sister.

> They had among them a woman general who was brave and superb, who could bring down four or five men and fight off seven or eight swords. The Chinese came forward and bowed to her one after the next, until finally she was captured alive.... She was the younger sister of the English king and

was imprisoned at Ningbo. Details of these events can be found in [my] *Suiriku senpō roku* (An Account of Military Strategies on Sea and Land).

He had written the *Suiriku senpō roku* prior to this and therein clarified the point here made.

Furthermore, in his *Bōkai yoron* (My Views on Naval Defenses) (published in Kōka 4 [1847], included in *Satō Nobuhiro kagaku zenshū*) as well, he touches on the events of the Opium War, and notes: 'The details of this military confrontation can be found in my *Suiriku senpō roku.*' In the 'list of works' used for the *Bōkai yoron*, he lists the *Suiriku senpō roku* (in seven volumes) and adds his own explanation:

Because there have been no military conflicts between the Japanese and the Western barbarians, we do not know who is superior. From the eleventh year of the Tenpō reign [1840], however, the Chinese engaged them several dozen times and incurred great defeats every time, incapable of being their match. In the final analysis, they paid them tribute, ceded land, begged for peace, and just barely eluded ultimate disaster. I have chronicled the numerous Chinese and English strategies at land and sea [in the battles of the Opium War] and detailed them here.

The *Suiriku senpō roku* was not transcribed into the *Satō Nobuhiro kagaku zenshū*, perhaps because 'the author compiled this collection by his own hand, and certain military texts were left out of it.' Yet, among the works 'left out of . . . this collection,' the author lists the *Suiriku senpō roku*, printed in eight stringbound volumes. 'Printed' here probably indicates woodblock printing.[4]

Although not in the *Kairiku senbō roku*, in the *Son-Ka zateki ron* we find, after the story of the capture of the king's sister, a comment that begins 'Chin'en shi iwaku' (Mr. Chin'en remarks). He conceded that 'this princess was an extraordinary curiosity,' but he condemned the fact that the Chinese did not use such a hostage to good advantage during the peace talks, and that the 'base official' Yilibu, not even waiting for his sovereign's orders, unilaterallly released her.

One work by Satō that has been praised to the sky, especially during the war, was *Udai kondō hisaku* (A Confidential Plan for World Unification). The expression 'udai kondō' carries the meaning of 'world unity.' In a piece entitled *Kondō tairon* (Greater Treatise on Unity) which serves effectively as an introduction to this work, he argued that: 'Our great and glorious land was the first created in the world and the foundation for all countries of the world. Thus, to govern this foundation well, we must make all of the rest of the world into our districts and prefectures and the sovereigns of all these lands into our servants.' In this way he developed his views on a 'secret' plan for world unification.

In order to attain world unification, he argued: 'The very first thing we must do is annex the land of China (*Shina koku*). . . . Therefore, this work will initially detail a plan for how we should take China.' And, he proceeded to a discussion of a concrete plan for the invasion of the Chinese mainland. Modeling his plan on the proven example of the Qing which had arisen in Manchuria and rapidly swept down to consolidate its control over China, Satō's first premise was a Japanese invasion of Manchuria. A naval force was to set out with alacrity from Aomori, and an attack force would hit Heilongjiang (in northern Manchuria) from the northern reaches of Sakhalin; similarly, naval forces were to assemble and set sail from Nuttari (along the coast in Echigo) and Kanazawa, cross the sea, and seize by storm various prefectures along the southern coastal region of Manchuria. A separate army was to land on the Korean peninsula, link up with other forces in Liaoyang, and attack Beijing. In addition, a march was to commence from the ports of Kyūshū and lay siege to Jiangnan and Zhejiang. A self-acknowledged expert on military tactics and strategy, he vigorously developed these wild notions for this process of invasion and conquest on paper with great detail giving it plausibility.

This fantasy invasion of the mainland was consistent with the idea of *hakkō ichiu* ['the whole world under one roof,' a common expression during the years of World War Two, used as justification for Japan's imperialist adventures], and Satō was loudly praised during the war years by one group of scholars affiliated with the Kōdō (Imperial Way) party as a sublime, pioneer 'thinker.' The explanatory essays appended to *Satō Nobuhiro shū* (Writings of Satō Nobuhiro),[b] is probably representative of this tendency.

By chance, I happened across a book some years ago in a used book store entitled *Satō Nobuhiro no shisō* (The Thought of Satō Nobuhiro) by Nakajima Kurō.[c] It bears a private library seal that reads: 'Tokyo Preventive Detention Center.' According to the *Kōjien* dictionary, 'preventive detention' means: 'A measure, for the purpose of preventing crime, to continue the confinement of someone who after the completion of a term of imprisonment has shown no sign of repentance. During the Pacific War, it was used for thought criminals.'[d] During the Shōwa period, though, in the place that these 'thought criminals' would have read such a book, they were not likely to do anything with the thought of Satō Nobuhiro. It stands as a monument to the circumstances surrounding political thought during the war years.

The major idea of the *Udai kondō hisaku* was, as we noted with reference to *Son-Ka zateki ron*, that once the Chinese, having been defeated in the Opium War, 'had trained troops for a number of years, then they can raise a righteous army of revenge, subjugate the English barbarians, and finally eliminate without remnant all of them from East Asia. This should long serve as a *western wall for our land*' [emphasis Masuda's]. Thus, the idea that the first step in the process toward world unification was the conquest of China would seem to have retrogressed rather dramatically here where the emphasis is on *son-Ka* or aiding China's existence and the expection is for China 'long serving as the western wall for' Japan.

At the very end of the *Udai kondō hisaku*, the date Bunsei 6 or 1823 is given, and the *Son-Ka zateki ron* was written in Kaei 2 or 1849. In that period of 26 years, the real historical experiences of the Opium War would seem to have caused a major and sudden turnabout in Satō's divinely-inspired delusions about the conquest of China. The transformation was doubtless the result of the changing temporal background, as the lessons of the Opium War and the arrival in Japan of foreign gunboats during the Kōka and Kaei periods (1844–54) led Japanese to be startlingly awakened to reality from the peaceful slumber and foolish dreams of the Bunka and Bunsei reign periods (1804–30).

Chapter Thirteen

Strange Tales of the Opium War

Stories of the capture of the English king's sister were, needless to say, based on information emanating from the Qing side in the conflict. However, the exact foundation for such stories (be they written documents or in the form of *fūsetsugaki*) I have yet to determine. Thus, they may be based upon reports of the time, and these reports may have come from essays of writers of the late-Qing period. In the *Qingchao shiliao* (Historical Materials on the Qing Dynasty), which comprises volume four of the *Qingchao yeshi daguan* (Overviews of Unofficial Histories of the Qing Dynasty),[a] there is a section entitled 'Ying nü beiqin' (English woman captured). It reads in part as follows:

> The Chusan Archipelago is the doorway onto the coast of Zhejiang province. In the twentieth year of the Daoguang reign [1840], English troops seized it [Chusan]. A warship took refuge in the port and raced eventually as far as Yuyao county. It became stuck in the sand there and was unable to continue. The local militia was called together, attacked it, and captured one English woman. Upon questioning, it was learned that she was the third sister of the King of England.

The author of the text goes on at this point to add his own view; namely, had the officials on the scene at the time used her as a means of attaining peace, insured that she was well treated even as she was losing face, and thereafter made use of her (as a hostage) in the transactions of the peace talks, then the Chinese would probably not have invited losses such as local sovereignty in the aftermath, but the local officials did not take such considerations into account. This position is precisely the same that we saw articlulated in 'Chin'en shi iwaku' in the *Son-Ka zateki ron*.

The *Qingchao yeshi daguan* cites numerous historical materials and anecdotes as well as incidental jottings. It was compiled in the Republican period, and many references are given at the beginning of each of the volumes. Each and every note is not, however, clearly cited with a reference. Thus, we cannot say for certain upon what source this story is based. Perhaps works that collected such tales came to Japan at the same time, for both the *Ahen shimatsu* and the *Kairiku senbō roku* (as well as the *Son-Ka zateki ron*) are based on such works.

The story of the capture in Yuyao of a princess in the English military seems to have become a subject of discussion early on in Qing circles. We find it even in the *Zhong-Xi jishi* (Accounts of China and the West) by Xia Xie (1799–1875) which is cited often as a historical document on the Opium War.[b] The *Zhong-Xi jishi* in 24 *juan* was apparently compiled over a fairly long period of time; my edition of this text is a woodblock printing, designated a 'definitive edition' (*dingben*) and dated Tongzhi 7 (1868); it carries an 'initial preface' (*yuanxu*) dated Daoguang 30 (1850), a 'secondary preface' (*cixu*) dated Xianfeng 9 (1859), and an explanatory preface (third in order) to the *dingben* dated Tongzhi 4 (1865).

As the 'initial preface' notes, 'I have excerpted here [materials from] the Peking Gazette and other official dispatches. I have also consulted the newspapers, transcribed material, and placed it here.' The work was thus composed by gathering together evidence from a variety of intelligence sources, and while limited its overall historical value is still quite high. The author Xia Xie was an official – he subsequently became a county administrative clerk in Jiangxi – who at the time probably found it convenient to collect these sorts of information. In his explanatory preface to the 'definitive edition,' he mentions the *Haiguo tuzhi* of Wei Yuan and notes that he is 'the same year as Wei Moshen.' This would mean that he and Wei were contemporaries who had passed the provincial examinations and become *juren* in 'the same year.' As had been the case with Wei, he put this work together, because he 'was filled with anger as he glared with great fury' on the English invasion of China.

In *juan* five of the *Zhong-Xi jishi*, we read the following passage:

> During the time that Bremer [Bomai, commander-in-chief of the English naval unit that invaded Dinghai] held control over Dinghai, he put a ceasefire into effect, and Western vessels were permitted to sail about and enjoy themselves. Coming to Yuyao, one such pleasure party encountered local people, was enticed by the large five-masted ships, and ran aground on a sandbar. They [i.e., the locals] seized several white barbarians, among whom was one barbarian woman who was exceedingly decked out in dress and make-up. It was reported that she was a Western princess. Imperial Commissioner Yilibu heard this report and issued a written appeal to Yuyao county. He formed a welcoming committee and escorted it as it entered Guangdong.

We have here a 'barbarian woman' who is 'reported' to be a foreign princess. The text only notes that Imperial Commissioner Yilibu 'escorted' the party to Guangdong, though it says not a word to the effect that she was the commander of the English navy there or in what manner she had conducted a battle. Furthermore, it does note that the commander of the naval forces at the time was

Bremer. Thus, it would seem that there were rumors at the time of the capture of a princess, and gradually these were padded with exaggeration.

In fact, this 'barbarian woman' was the wife of Lieutenant Douglas, captain of the *Kite*, an armed English freighter, and details of her capture can be found in Duncan MacPherson's book, *Two Years in China*.[c] Also, the story of the English vessel running aground, as well as tales of raids on them by local Chinese militias and their seizing of prisoners from among the passengers, have been examined in considerable detail in the aforementioned *Yapian zhanzheng shishi kao* by Yao Weiyuan, as well as in the *Chouban yiwu shimo* and works by foreigners.

During the second decade of the Meiji period (1877–87), a number of histories of the Qing dynasty were written in literary Chinese by Japanese scholars of Chinese culture or Kangakusha, such as: *Shinshi ran'yō* (An Overview of the History of the Qing) in six volumes by Masuda Mitsugu (Gakuyō, fl. 1877) and *Shinchō shiryaku* (Brief History of the Qing Dynasty) in 12 volumes by Satō Sozai (Bokuzan, 1801–91).[d] Where they described the Opium War, just as in Saitō Chikudō's *Ahen shimatsu*, they wrote as well of the live capturing of a English princess.

The style of the *Shinshi ran'yō* is less one ordered by a rigid chronology than it is one in which the years give order to the events. The author first names a time period and then records the events that took place during the years of that period. Under Daoguang 20 in volume four, the text first lists Chen Huacheng becoming military commander of Jiangnan, and then under this heading it offers a detailed description of Chen Huacheng's efforts to defend the coastline. Next, it lists: 'The English besieged Ningbo, and General [sic.] Yilibu battled them there, capturing a female chief.' Under this heading, the text describes in considerable detail the circumstances leading up to the capture of this female chief.

> An English vessel became stuck in the sand [at Yuyao, and] the local militia gathered and attacked it. A female chief stepped forward bravely to launch the battle and killed several people with her bare hands. One of the local militiamen brandishing a spear attacked her from behind and wounded the female chief. Thereupon the assembled group [of militiamen] took her prisoner, along with over twenty others. The female chief was the third daughter of the king of her country. . . .
>
> The English commander presented a document to the Yuyao provincial magistrate. It said that, if the princess was returned, he would obey the order to return the invaded and occupied terrain [to the Chinese] and leave Guangdong. She was not returned. Ultimately, he went to the imperial capital to sue for peace. The emperor ordered Imperial Commissioner Qishan to proceed to Guangdong and bring the matter to deliberations.

At the very end of the *Ahen shimatsu*, Yilibu and Qishan enter into negotiations with 'barbarian officials' (*bankan*), memorialize for the release of the princess, and await orders, but before their orders arrive they go ahead and release her.

70

Although this portion of the story is different (from that given in the *Shinshi ran'yō* account), the general point is virtually the same.

In the *Shinchō shiryaku*, the general story of the capture of the king's younger sister in battle is taken over directly in large measure, with a few differences in character usage, from the appropriate chapter of the *Ahen shimatsu*. Inasmuch as the *Shinchō shiryaku* lists the names of cited texts right at the beginning and among them is Saitō Chikudō's *Ahen shimatsu*, the author clearly made use of it. In the margin to the text, one finds the following notation: 'It was said that the capture of the princess may have been an erroneous story.' This too, it would seem, was taken directly from a line in the *Ahen shimatsu* that goes against the thrust of the main body of the text: 'It was said that perhaps she was not really the younger sister of the English king.'

In addition to the printed works already mentioned, I also have in my possession a manuscript entitled *Kanshi enryaku* (Brief History of China), written in Kanbun, which gives an outline account of Chinese history. My edition is missing the first and second stringbound volumes, and I thus have only volumes three (on the Tang and Song) and four (on the Yuan, Ming, and Qing). At the very end of the fourth volume, the text concludes: 'The son of the Emperor's younger brother Prince Chun, Zaitian [1871–1908], inherited the throne, and changed the reign period name to Guangxu.'

It is thus a history of China through the Guangxu Emperor's accession to the throne (in 1875). It is written in brush on ruled-line paper on which is printed 'Tōkyō shihan gakkō' (Tokyo Normal School); reading punctuation and suffixed syllabaries needed to read a Kanbun text in Japanese have been added in red; and simple headings giving an overview of the content have been placed in the margins. Here and there through the text, labels have been pasted in and removed and the text emended, indicating that it was a rough draft. With every era, the name of the emperor is given first and then follows a simple chronicle not so much of the most important events that transpired under that emperor, but of topical pieces.

The pattern then is one in which events are detailed within the reign of a given emperor. For example, at the end of the 'Chronicle of the Qing,' the text reads: 'Emperor Xuanzong, Mianning, changed the era name to Daoguang.' The text then immediately follows with: 'Wei Yuan was a drafter in the secretariat. The emperor saw his examination paper and endorsed it with great praise.' In the margin beside the text at this point is the heading, 'Praise for Wei Yuan.' Within the Daoguang section of the text can be found another marginal heading which reads 'Capture of Beautiful Woman.' The main text here reads:

> The English attacked and took Ningbo. General [sic.] Yilibu went to offer assistance. By chance, while withdrawing, a English vessel ran aground in the sand. Local militiaman Shen Zhen and others captured a female chief of theirs, and they requested the return of the English princess. An order went out to Imperial Commissioner Qishan to proceed to Guangdong,

consult with Yilibu, and have the princess returned. The English had not yet retreated, and two officials were cashiered while the peace talks broke down.

This portion of the work is almost identical to the record given in the *Ahen shimatsu*, though the latter does not explicitly name the local militiaman Shen Zhen. Nor is this name to be found in either the *Shinshi ran'yō* or the *Shinchō shiryaku*. Hence the text must have been based on some other source.

As noted above, I have only the third and fourth volumes of this work, and since I have not seen the first volume, I cannot say who the author of the *Kanshi enryaku* was. It ends with the accession of the Guangxu Emperor in 1875. According to Ishii Kendō's *Meiji jibutsu kigen* (The Origin of Things in the Meiji Era),[e] the Tokyo Normal School was founded in the aftermath of the Shōheikō; it in was placed a 'Compilation Office' (*henseikyoku*) where textbooks were to be edited. Perhaps this work was a draft of just such a textbook done at Tokyo Normal. It too would then be a work of roughly the second decade of the Meiji period.

In the third decade of the Meiji period (1887–97), the tale of the capture of the English king's younger sister apparently ceased to be believed. I have a work in one stringbound volume entitled *Shin-Ei ahen no sōran* (The Sino-English Opium Disturbance) (edited and published in Tokyo by Shimizu Ichijirō), printed on movable type in 1888 with a thick cardboard cover.[f] It is taken almost entirely (over 99%) from *Kaigai shinwa* (New Stories from Overseas) (five volumes, woodblock printed [see Chapter Fourteen]) by Mineta Fūkō (1817–83) which it rewrote in novel form on the basis of the *Yifei fanjing lu*. Inasmuch as the story of the capture of the sister of the English king is absent from both *Kaigai shinwa* and *Yifei fangjing lu*, it does not appear in *Shin-Ei ahen no sōran* either.

The *Ei-Shin ahen sen shi* (History of the Sino-English Opium War)[g] by Matsui Kōkichi (Hakken, 1866–1937) is a work of history, not of fiction. It has links as well with material based on English sources, and reads at one point:

> The Queen originally had no younger sister. Had she had one, there would have been no reason for her to go recklessly into battle and be taken prisoner.... Some among our Kangakusha [such as Satō Sozai] have believed this story, and in works by them on the history of the Qing they have quite clearly recounted it. Thus, I offer a description of this tale in its simplest details, with a smile on my face.

With this, he then introduced and translated into Japanese Saitō Chikudō's *Ahen shimatsu*. Afterward, he concluded: 'Although I have rewritten Saitō Kaoru's *Ahen shimatsu* from Kanbun into Japanese, there are now a variety of other books that describe these events at great length. Many even insert a diagram of the scene of the capture. In the final analysis, the story has no basis in truth; it is completely false.'[1]

Matsui Hakken noted that 'many [works] even insert a diagram of the scene of the capture,' and in the novelistic account entitled *Shin-Ei kinsei dan* (Recent Tales of China and England)[h] by Hayano Kei (woodblock printing, five *kan* in one stringbound volume), where the author recounts the story of the battle with the king's sister, one finds a double-page chart entitled 'Depiction of Chen Huacheng's Capture of the Princess General' inserted into the text at that point. Of course, the appearance of Chen Huacheng at this juncture is pure fiction, but it recounts how Chen led an ambush attack on the princess at Yuyao, the two fought, the planks of her ship were destroyed, and both of them fell overboard. Soldiers fell upon her and took her captive. They sent her to Shanghai under a guard of several hundred troops, and she was placed in prison. Since this was a novel, the author, having located the story probably in the *Ahen shimatsu*, took it and made it even more interesting, recasting it in a dramatic form.

The *Kaigai shinwa shūi* (Gleanings from the New Stories from Overseas)[i] in five stringbound volumes is a similar sort of fictional account which describes the heroic battles of the valiant princess who 'could undergo countless miraculous changes and just for fun cleverly transform herself into a spring iris or flutter in the autumn breeze.... In the end, she was taken prisoner by the Qing military.' A two-page insert, entitled 'Diagram of the Woman Warrior Putting Up a Valiant Fight,' is also to be found in this text.

The 'introductory notes' to the *Kaigai shinwa shūi* read (in part): 'Although the events depicted in *Kaigai shinwa*, written by Mr. Mineta Fūkō, were all taken from such works as the *Yifei fanjing lu* and the *Shinpan jiryaku* and reorganized, there were still to be sure omissions of various and sundry import. He thus wrote this work after gathering up such omissions.' This might lead us to the

From the *Kaigai shinwa shūi* (Kansai University Library)

73

conclusion that inasmuch as the *Kaigai shinwa shūi* was a novelistic account full of happy news, it took the shocking story of the princess's capture, which is missing from *Kaigai shinwa*, probably from *Ahen shimatsu*.

In this connection, Samura Hachirō, in his *Kokusho kaidai* (Descriptions of Japanese Books),[j] mentions only the *Kaigai shinwa shūi* in his discussion of novelistic treatments of the Opium War published in Japan at that time. He argues: 'It chronicled the arrival on Chinese soil of the English and French and facts surrounding the opening of various relations. However, in his *Kaigai shinwa*, Mineta Fūkō wrote a full account of Sino-English relations using the *Yifei fanjing lu* and the *Shinpan jiryaku*, and this work was thus an effort to gather together that which had been left out of his account. The [*Kaigai shinwa*] *shūi* was published in 1849.' This was a perfunctory explanation, to say the least, especially the first half which makes no sense. The latter half was taken directly from the 'introductory notes.'

The *Kaigai yowa* (Additional Stories from Overseas) in five stringbound, woodblock-printed volumes (by 'Suimu chijin' [Crazy man in a drunken sleep], Kaei 4 [1851]) is written in a mixture of Chinese characters and *katakana* syllabaries, though without diagrams. Transposed into *hiragana* syllabaries and with the addition of diagrams at the beginning of the text and interspersed within, as its compiler apparently saw in other works, it was retitled *Kaigai jitsuroku* (True Stories from Overseas), five woodblock-printed *kan* in one stringbound volume (with a preface by the lay monk Baikon dated Ansei 2 [1855]).[k] On the frontispiece to this work is a diagram entitled 'Atai, Younger Sister of the King of England.' The name Atai is appended here, and she is given as the commander-in-chief of the English military. 'I am Atai,' it reads, 'the second ruler of England in the Atlantic Ocean. I received orders to correct the treacherous crimes being committed in Guangdong recently and then return home.' The fiction grows more and more curious. In the end, this Commander Atai together with Vice-Commander Elliott (a real historical personage) are taken alive by Lin Zexu, but both are forgiven by the Daoguang Emperor and enabled to return to their home country.

The text concludes that England 'struck the deep sympathies of the Daoguang Emperor and became an eternal dependency of the Qing. Year after year the English brought tribute to China, and they were invigorated by the great majesty of China far and near. The reign of the Qing dynasty remained its essence for many, many years.'

The theme that runs through these fictional accounts is that, in the final analysis, the barbarian bandits were no match for the Chinese.

Chapter Fourteen

The *Kaigai shinwa* by Mineta Fūkō and Other Works

As noted earlier, I have in my collection of books a number of novelistic accounts of the Opium War that appeared in the *bakumatsu* period. These include: *Kaigai shinwa* (New Stories from Overseas); *Kaigai shinwa shūi* (Gleanings from the New Stories from Overseas); *Kaigai yowa* (Additional Stories from Overseas); *Kaigai jitsuroku* (Veritable Records from Overseas), which is a rendering of the *katakana* text of the *Kaigai yowa* into *hiragana* and with the addition of illustrations; and *Shin-Ei kinsei dan* (Recent Tales of China and England). All were published in the Kaei reign period (1848–54); only the retitled edition of the *Kaigai jitsuroku* appeared later in Ansei 2 (1855).[a] Inasmuch as publication of the *Ahen shimatsu* was not permitted until the Shōwa period, it seems that these novelistic treatments of the Opium War were not widely published at the time of their composition.

Mineta Fūkō (1817–83), the author of *Kaigai shinwa*, the first of these to be published, was thrown in prison on the charge of having published this work without having secured official consent. Even after he was released, he was deprived of the right to reside in Edo, Kyoto, or Ōsaka – known as the *santo kamae* or 'triurban banishment' – and this treatment would seem to have influenced subsequent events as well. *Shin-Ei kinsei dan* has imprinted on its inside front cover: 'Restricted to a binding in 200 copies, forbidden to sell or distribute.'

On the inside cover of the *Kaigai shinwa shūi* as well, it reads: 'Forbidden from sale.' My edition of the *Kaigai yowa* has a blank inside cover, but at the very end it carries the sycophantish line: 'This is but a dream concocted in amused intoxication during the tedium of these rainy months.' It is signed: 'Suimu chijin' (Crazy man in a drunken sleep). The *Kaigai jitsuroku* which rewrites the *Kaigai yowa* in *hiragana* does, in fact, carry the note inside its front cover that the book is 'forbidden from sale.'

To explain the structure and shape of the first of these works, the *Kaigai shinwa*, we need first to describe the general form this novelistic account took, because the other works all follow the form set down by it. So, let me now touch on the person of the author, Mineta Fūkō, and the punishment meted out to him.

The *Kaigai shinwa* is printed on Mino paper in five stringbound volumes. The 'introductory remarks' at the beginning read:

Events recorded in this account are based upon the *Yifei fanjing lu* [J. *Ihi hankyōroku*]. However, the latter work is organized into a variety of sections by the memorials, political essays, and observations on the battles of the valiant warriors from the various provinces [of China]. Accordingly, the sequence of dates and times are based on the *Shinpan jiryaku*, and there are still a number of mistakes which have been corrected by reference to other works.

Later, it goes on and mentions several works upon which it is based:

The events chronicled in the *Yifei fanjing lu* commence with the British barbarians' invasion of Dinghai county on the second day of the seventh lunar month of Daoguang 20 [1840]. From it one learns of the widespread poison of opium, of Lin Zexu's operation strictly to ban it in Guangzhou, and thus ultimately of the root cause of the barbarian invasion. For a time now, I have been compiling a list of the various incidents related to uprisings, based on such works as the [*Huangchao*] *Jingshi wenbian* (Collected Essays on Statecraft [of the August Dynasty]), the *Yinyou lu* (Chronicle of Furtive Gloom), the *Zhapu jiyong* (Zhapu Collection), and the *Qing wu ji* [sic., *Shengwu ji*].

Generally, though, what afforded it great interest as a work to be read in its day were the reports on battles drawn from the *Yifei fanjing lu* and the anecdotal sections also found in that work.

Further in the 'introductory remarks' to the text, we find: 'The style of this work employs the conventional phraseology of military texts, such as the [*Genji*] *seisui ki* (Account of the Rise and Fall of Genji) and *Taihei ki* (Account of an Era of Great Peace), long in use in our country from time immemorial, for even children-warriors could memorize them with but a single reading.' It was written in a simple style, interesting to read, and had Japanese syllabaries attached to all Chinese characters.

In addition, to assist readers' comprehension of the material, there was included in the first volume of the work a summary entitled 'Ingirisu kokki ryaku' (Outline Account of England). Though brief, it touches on English geography, history, products, trade, schools, customs, and military preparedness (namely, warships and guns). It concludes: 'Warriors who have set their wills on maritime defense cannot belittle them as barbarians from a far-off secluded area in the West.'

Next, the text discusses 'Yochi ryakuzu' or 'Sketch Map of the World,' and on it the English-held lands are indicated in red. These are followed by 'Shinkoku ryakuzu' (Sketch map of China), and on this the names of Chinese prefectures and counties that have 'come under barbarian invasion' are indicated with red dots. This is followed by 'Eishō jūsō zu' (Picture of English commander in barbarian garb), 'Hosotsu gunsō zenmen' (Frontal view of a foot soldier in military garb), 'Hosotsu gunsō sokumen' (Side view of a foot soldier in military garb), 'Eikoku taigunsen zu' (Picture of a great English warship), and 'Jōkisen zu' (Picture of a steamship). From that point the main text commences with 'Ahen enryūdoku, fuku Kō Shakushi jōsho ji' (The spread of opium-smoking, Huang Juezi's memorial to the throne). The fifth volume of the text ends with 'Ryōgun waboku, fuku wayaku jōmoku' (Reconciliation between the two armies, articles of the peace treaty). Here and there within the main body of the text are double-paged charts and pictures to enhance the reader's appreciation.

Books that came out after *Kaigai shinwa* and made good reading out of stories from the Opium War all inherited the pattern set by *Kaigai shinwa*. Only *Kaigai shinwa shūi* was woodblock-printed and composed in *katakana*, without frontispiece pictures or inserts. The *Kaigai jitsuroku* which rewrote it with *hiragana* did, though, follow the pattern of the *Kaigai shinwa*.

The author of the *Kaigai shinwa*, Mineta Fūkō, was punished for allegedly publishing this work without the prior approval of the Gakumonjo. Mineta was summoned and interrogated by the Edo Administrator, Tōyama Saemon no jō. His engraved woodblocks were incinerated, he was ordered to print no more copies of it, and he was imprisoned. As for information on this incident and the manner in which it was sanctioned, the correspondence between the Nishimaru steward (*rusui*), Tsutsui Kii no kami, and Edo Administrator Tōyama cites the *Kaihan shishin* (Guide to Publishing), and it appears in *Hikka shi* (History of Censorship) by Miyatake Gaikotsu (1867–1955).[b] The charge against Mineta for which he was punished was failure to have his work inspected by the Gakumonjo, but in a letter from Tsutsui to Tōyama, we find the following:

> Insofar as I have noted that the *Kaigai shinwa* is all a rewriting of the *Yifei fanjing lu* into a *kana* text, although the author recounts heretical and falacious ideas in place of the facts, as concerns differences with the aforementioned ordinary works [the text earlier mentioned Confucian, Buddhist, Shintō, medical, and poetic texts], this sort of work ought not be published in a mixed Sino-Japanese style. And, after carefully coming to a decision on the basis of consultation and deliberation, this work need be detained from publication.

Such was the ruling on the basis of consultation and deliberation of the Shogunate. Although it is not too clear, it would seem that the author, in touching on the state of affairs at the time, was concerned with the influence this work would have on people's minds. Miyatake Gaikotsu writes: 'Because of the aforementioned points, the author Mineta Ugorō [Fūkō] received a sentence of imprisonment, and the case was settled in the tenth lunar month of Kaei 3 [1850].' In the margin, one find the notation: 'In a manuscript work entitled *Shinai torishimari ruishū* (Collection on City Management), this matter is also described. At the end of this work, it goes further to note that the woodblock printer Kuma Gorō had surrepticiously reissued this work [by Mineta] and was punished for his actions.' Such actions would seem to endorse the notion that the demand for this work was not inconsiderable.

For information on Mineta Fūkō, we find mention in volume four [of five] of the *Jijitsu bunpen* (Collection of Factual Essays) by Gokyū Hisabumi (or Sessō, 1823–86) of a piece entitled 'Fūkō Mineta ō juhimei' (Epitaph for the Venerable Mineta Fūkō) which reveals Mineta as a man with quite an accomplished career.[c] Furthermore, in *Kinsei Kangakusha denki chosaku dai jiten* (Encyclopedia of Biographies and Writings by Early Modern Sinologists)[d] by Seki Giichirō and Seki Yoshinao, there is a short biography and brief mention of some of his writings, including *Satō Issai to sono monjin* (Satō Issai and His Disciples) and *Fūkō ibun* (The Posthumous Writings of [Mineta] Fūkō).

However, there is a more detailed biography of Mineta to be found in a work by one of his disciples, Akashi Kichigorō, *Mineta Fūkō*.[e] While this book is not completely based upon a close investigation of historical documents, it is the work of a disciple, someone who knew Mineta personally, and it does incorporate memoirs and similar writings concerning Mineta. Hence, it does convey well the man's personality and appearance, indeed better than historical documents might be able to do.

As noted earlier, Miyatake Gaikotsu simply states that Mineta 'received a sentence of imprisonment, and the case was settled.' According to Akashi's *Mineta Fūkō*, though, we find:

> *Sensei* spent two full years in prison.... Eventually, in the spring of Kaei 4 [1851], he was pardoned and was completely cleared of all charges once again. At the time of his release, however, he was ordered into *santo kamae*, a form of detention. He was thoroughly unhappy with the shogunate's ordinance [against him], in which his slightest movement could incur its displeasure and harm be likely to afflict him.... Around 1881 or 1882, in order to control more tightly the stalwarts advocating popular rights, the government at that time similarly put into effect a series of laws and ordinances concerning assembly and the preservation of peace.

Santo kamae was a law which deprived one of the right to reside in the three cities of Edo, Kyoto, or Ōsaka for a period, following release from prison, of three years.

Though this is not spelled out in the *Hikka shi*, at the point in *Mineta Fūkō* where it is elucidated the text goes on to note that, at the same time that Mineta was thrown in prison, the artist who at Mineta's request drew the illustrations for *Kaigai shinwa* was implicated and also went to prison. This artist, we are told, died in prison. Mineta was deeply troubled over his artist's death in prison, precisely because he had landed there on Mineta's behalf. As the author of *Mineta Fūkō* relates it: 'Over the next few years, we were told this story by *sensei* from time to time, and every time all of the disciples quietly cried, and their tears dampened their sleeves.'

From our perspective on the matter today, the penalty he suffered seems unimaginably harsh. In the war fought between Great Britain and Qing China, sad misfortunes were suffered as far away as a single Japanese commoner, one illustration artist. By the same token, though, this fact has much to say about the extraordinary wariness, perhaps the tension, felt by the shogunal authorities in the face of the Opium War.

So, because of the *santo kamae*, Mineta left Edo, traveled to Bōsō [present-day southern Chiba prefecture], and made it his place of residence. Thereafter, he did educational work in various places in Bōsō and was much admired by local residents. In 1883 at the age of 76, he died in Isumi-gun in Chiba prefecture. Akashi Kichigorō, author of *Mineta Fūkō*, was one of those he taught during these last years, and the volume *Mineta Fūkō* was written primary to exalt the honor and deeds of Mineta as an educator.

For generations the Mineta family served as retainers to the Makino family, feudal lords of the Tanabe domain in Tango [in present-day northern Kyoto prefecture]. Fūkō was the second son of Mineta Noritoshi, and he was born on the daimyō's estate at a time when his father was in service in Edo. Thus, it may have been precisely because he was born into a samurai family that he later became entangled in the public order regulations. Fūkō himself left the following notes concerning his career (all taken from *Mineta Fūkō*):

Kaei 2 [1849], twelfth lunar month. On the publication of the *Kaigai shinwa*, the Edo Administator, Tōyama Saemon no jō, called for the carrying out of an investigation. During the examination, I was compelled to remain under my parents' responsibility.

Kaei 3 [1850], tenth lunar month, second day. Concerning the aforementioned matter, it was ordered that I be placed under house arrest by a communiqué of Councillor of State Toda Yamashiro no kami.

Kaei 4 [1851], first lunar month, thirteenth day. I was ordered released from house arrest.

Kaei 4, fourth lunar month, thirteenth day. Several years after having departed, my conduct remained dissipated and would not change, and I was permitted to present a request for separation from my family and disinheritance.

Ansei 2 [1855], first lunar month, eighteenth day. The separation has been allowed me to reform the depths of my heart and mind.

The *santo kamae* may have been part of his request for separation, but after it was approved, he again served in Tanabe domain and became an investigating official in the area of 'military reforms.' By 'military' what was meant was, of course, primarily coastal defense, for he had earlier acquired a fair amount of knowledge in this area.

In *Mineta Fūkō* Akashi cites a Kanbun text entitled *Fūkō Gyochō Mineta shun shōden* (Brief Biography of the Great Mineta Fūkō) by Ono Kozan. In part that citation reads as follows: 'In his youth, Shitoku [Mineta Fūkō's style] studied swordsmanship, read works on military strategy, ... and early in life acquired a mind indignantly concerned with maritime defense. Be it the production of cannons and great warships or theories of offensive and defensive military tactics, he was able to explain them quite clearly. He was in effect much like the Dutch Learning scholars.'

Early on Mineta studied under Satō Issai, though later he studied with Hayashi Fukusai (or Hayashi Akira, 1800–59, *daigaku no kami* [head of the shogunal college in Edo]); later, at the time of the Perry's mission to Japan, he represented the shogunate in diplomatic negotiations with Perry). That Mineta was a fine scholar of Chinese learning is evidenced by the fact that he filled in for Fukusai as lecturer and frequently was compensated by a variety of domainal lords with gold as his lecture fees (according to conversations with Mineta as recorded in *Mineta Fūkō*).

He studied Chinese-style poetry (*Kanshi*) with Yanagawa Seigan (1789–1858), and he was considered – together with Ōnuma Chinzan (1818–91), Ono Kozan, and Tōyama Unjo (1810–63) – one of the 'four masters of Seigan's school.' In *Mineta Fūkō*, Akashi cited numerous poems either written by Yanagawa Seigan and his other disciples to harmonize with Mineta's poetry or poems they wrote for him. All of this would indicate that he was undoubtedly a fine poet in *Kanshi* as well.

For a three-year period, from the first lunar month of Tenpō 10 (1839) through the twelfth lunar month of Tenpō 12 (1842), Akashi tells us that Mineta studied Dutch Learning with Mitsukuri Genpo (1700–1863), and that by this time he had already devoted 'concerted attention to [matters of] coastal defense' and was well versed in conditions overseas.

Thus, Mineta produced the *Kaigai shinwa* as a rewriting in the same genre and straightforward language of military tales such as the *Yifei fanjing lu*. This, it would seem, he did to enlighten his countrymen by giving utterance to his 'devoted attention to coastal defense.' He included a long poem at the start of *Kaigai shinwa* which effectively tells Japanese to look upon the defeat of the Chinese as a harbinger of what is to come in Japan. 'That heaven has presented us with this foretelling is not without significance. It records these things out of solicitude, out of innermost sincerity. Alas, the essential matters for a maritime nation require knowing these things. They depend on preparedness, strict discipline, and waiting.' Perhaps such writing did in fact move the hearts and minds of men and may have been understood by the shogunal authorities as a sort of implicit criticism.

Chapter Fifteen

On the *Shin Ei sen ki*, the Japanese Edition of the *Shengwu ji*, and Nagai Kafū's *Shitaya sōwa*

Though not a fictionalized account, one chronicle written in a combination of Japanese syllabaries and Chinese characters that traces the Opium War from its start through the concluding negotiations is Nagayama Nuki's *Shin Ei sen ki* (Account of the War between China and Britain) (manuscript edition in four stringbound volumes). The work was apparently not published but circulated in manuscript form, and manuscript editions are now quite rare. The copy in my possession bears a stamp reading 'seal of Imazeki Tenpō.'

Imazeki Tenpō (1884–1970), who passed away a few years ago, was well known as a Chinese-style poet. In addition, many years ago he published a translation of Chinese dramatic works – *Shina gikyoku shū* (Collection of Chinese Dramas) – and among his other writings are *Kindai Shina no gakugei* (Belles-lettres in Modern China) and *Tōyō garon shūsei* (Collections of Essays on East Asian Painting). When I was a high school student, I particularly remember reading his *Shina jinbun kōwa* (Essays on Chinese Humanities)[a] and learning a great deal from it as a kind of introductory text. I had the opportunity only twice to meet Mr. Imazeki, both times at the home of friends, and he once wrote an introduction to a work of mine.

Shin Ei sen ki carries a preface at the very beginning, dated Kaei 1 (1848), by Asakawa Dōsai (1814–57), and it reads in part: 'Recently, Nagayama, style Ho, wrote the *Shin Ei sen ki*, and it chronicles the history of [the Opium War], altogether coming to two volumes (*kan*). Its aim is to make known the integrity of loyal ministers and righteous men, the crimes of corrupt and thieving officials, and the conditions surrounding the cruelty and craftiness of the British barbarians. It is an attempt to ring a tocsin and issue a warning.'

Next is the author's own preface to his work, dated Kaei 2 (1849):

The British have already seized Hong Kong, and wouldn't their occupation of the ports of Guangzhou, Xiamen, Ningbo, Fuzhou, and Shanghai be but lands of the skin of oxen [Masuda himself has no idea what this means – JAF]? I have read Western books, and I know that their rapacious greed is not satiated. At first, they came, humbly asking to engage in commerce, and once they had attained that end, they constructed forts and placed troops in them, waiting to take advantage of a breach. As can be seen in their annexations of the lands of the South Seas, every one of [the Western powers] follows this plan, and they are thus truly to be simultaneously feared and detested.... Alas, China has already negotiated a peace settlement and obstructed their wicked avarice but a bit. Who knows how this may be used in the future? I am afraid that their violent blaze has not burnt out.

His tone was such that this should serve as a warning in Japan as well. We know from Asakawa's remarks in his preface – 'It is an attempt to ring a tocsin and issue a warning' – that this was Nagayama's reason for composing the *Shin Ei sen ki*.

At the end of the text, we find a postface by Tōjō Kindai (Nobuyasu, 1795– 1878), dated Kaei 2. In it are the following remarks: 'My friend Nagayama Ho had studied the scholarship in the writings [*ōbun*, lit. 'horizontal writings'] from the Far West (*kyokusei*), and well does he know the circumstances prevailing between the Chinese and the barbarians. Thus, relying on documents from the 1840 war between China and Great Britain, he has evaluated what it can teach us.' Thus, as he notes earlier: 'Recently, everyone has been asking questions about coastal defense policies. Though this is correct, those who know something about these matters do not speak and those who speak do not know. There are no realistic proposals [lit., those with their feet on the ground] at all.... ' The implication seems to be that, by studying the horizontal writings of the Far West and this learning about conditions prevailing between China and Britain, Nagayama's book did have its feet on the ground.

Nagayama also wrote two works entitled *Kaibō shigi* (My Views on Coastal Defense) and *Kaibō shigi hoi* (More of My Views on Coastal Defense); these are said to be transcribed in *Kaibō shiryō sōsho* (Collection of Historical Documents on Coastal Defense), but I have not seen them personally. Nonetheless, this book seems to have been written as a reference for maritime defense policy. Yet, while Tōjō's mention of his study of Western writings was meant to add force apparently to the content of his work, an examination of the *Shin Ei sen ki* now reveals nary a single citation to a historical document from the West.

For example, he did not translated the Dutch (or English) documents that Bremer sent to the county magistrate at Dinghai. He simply translated from the *Yifei fanjing lu*, added *kana* syllabaries where appropriate, and wrote it down (as his own work). At another point, he inserted Bremer's letters as they were in literary Chinese, precisely as they were to be found in *Yifei fanjing lu*.

In his own preface, Nagayama noted:

I have read the British barbarians' writings in the *Shinpan jiryaku* and the *Yifei fanjing lu*, which chronicle in general the afflictions surrounding the

Chinese state. However, the documents of the officialdom at the time record only conversations among contemporaries and the general situation in their own estimations. Thus, the sequence of events are all in a jumble, and it is difficult to make sense of them. I have accordingly noted the dates of events and written in Japanese.

The *Kaigai shinwa* also claimed to be 'based upon the *Yifei fanjing lu*,' though 'the sequence of dates and times are based on the *Shinpan jiryaku*.' Both works relied upon the *Yifei fanjing lu* and the *Shinpan jiryaku*, and both described the events of the Opium War. Within his work, Nagayama inserted a 'Karinsen zu' (Picture of a steamship), an 'Enkai zu' (Map of the coast), and a 'Teikai ken zu' (Map of Dinghai county), all in color.

Among Nagayama's other works in my possession are a one-stringbound-volume work entitled *Hōka shuchi* (Essentials of Artillery) (published [by the Eikadō] in Ansei 3 [1856]) and a four-stringbound-volume work entitled *Jūsen kidan* (Chronicle of Armed Warfare) (published [by Yamatoya Kihee in Edo] in Bunkyū 3 [1863]). They appear to be texts for students of guns and their use. The latter work, *Jūsen kidan*, contains a preface by Ōnuma Chinzan. It cites extensively from Japanese war accounts and miscellaneous notes and provides a study of Japanese wars that were fought with the use of guns. The former work, *Hōka shuchi*, describes in great detail, with the inclusion of diagrams, the way to mix gunpowder, as well as the casting and installation of cannons. In a translation from Dutch writings, the text notes: 'Each and every item herein has been excerpted from Western books, and although not a single guess has been added to it, naturally this work – responding to the urgent needs of the times – eliminated superfluous verbiage, shortened the wording, and thus will be all the more useful.'

Nagayama used the pen name of Choen, and he was said to have been a Confucian scholar, but a detailed biography of him is not available. In Kure Shūzō's *Mitsukuri Genpo*,[b] when describing Western histories written in the late Edo period, he mentions three works: Satō Nobuhiro's *Seiyō rekkoku shiryaku*, Saitō Chikudō's *Ban shi* – both mentioned above – and Nagayama's *Seiyō shō shi* (Short History of the West). Of the last of these, he notes: 'A work in three thin stringbound volumes, the first two are a general survey history of Western lands, and the last is an account of the European nations' invasion of the East.' He then goes on to say something about its author Nagayama: 'His given name is Nuki and his style is Shiichi. He is a grandson of Katayama Kenzan [1730–82] and a nephew of Asakawa Zen'an [1781–1849], according to the *Shoga kaisui* (Elegance and Luxuriance in Painting) which was published in Ansei 6 [1859].' I noted above the preface by Asakawa Dōsai for the *Shin Ei sen ki*; Dōsai was the adopted son of Zen'an, and there certainly may have been a relationship between Zen'an and Nagayama. Furthermore, Zen'an was the biological son of Katayama Kenzan, and if Nagayama was Kenzan's grandson, then he may have been the son of Zen'an's brother or sister.

I touched earlier on the Japanese reprinting of Wei Yuan's *Shengwu ji* (Record of August [Manchu] Military Achievements), which was a partial reprinting in any event. I now have three editions of it among my books. The first of these appears in a woodblock work in five stringbound volumes, bearing the title *Tazan no ishi* (Food for Thought). The first two volumes of this work comprise the *Shengwu ji*. In the first volume we find the sections: 'Guochao fusui Xizang ji' (Account of the Dynasty's Pacification of Tibet) (in two parts), 'Xizang houji' (Further Account of Tibet), 'Kuoerke fuji' (Supplementary Account of the Gurkhas), and 'Fulu Aomen yuebao' (Supplementary Monthly Report on Macao). In volume two we find: 'Kangxi Qianlong Eluosi mengpin ji' (Account of the Russian Embassies to the Kangxi and Qianlong Courts), 'Qianglong zheng Miandian ji' (Account of Qianlong's Expedition against Burma), 'Ru Mian lucheng' (Route of Entry into Burma), 'Qianlong zhengfu Annan ji' (Account of Qianlong's Conquest of Vietnam), and 'Jiaqing dongnan jinghai ji' (Account of the Pacification of the Southeast Coast during the Jiaqing Reign).

Tazan no ishi is a woodblock edition and bears no punctuation marks; nor does it have any prefaces, and thus the name of the publisher remains unclear, and the year of publication is not recorded. However, in a letter to his elder brother, dated Ansei 1 (1854), eleventh lunar month, 27th day, Yoshida Shōin (1830–59) wrote: 'I saw a copy of both *Tazan no ishi* and of *Chigaku seisō* (Principles of Geography) on sale in the market.'[1] This leads me to believe that *Tazan no ishi* was published probably in the Kaei reign period.

Looking at the various works that are included in *Tazan no ishi*, it would appear as though they were edited so as to contribute to knowledge about coastal defense; all are works that inform about conditions in foreign countries. In addition to *Shengwu ji*, the *Hai lu* (Record of the Sea) of Yang Bingnan (1765–1821) can be found in the third volume; *Hongmaofan Yingjili kaolüe* (A Study of England of the Red-Haired Barbarians) of Wang Wentai, *Dang kou ji* (An Account of the Destruction of the Rebels) of Jiao Xun (1763–1820), and *Pao kao* (A Study of Artillery) of Xu Kun can be found in volume four; and volume five contains *Diqiu tu shuo* (Explanations of Maps of the World), translated by Jiang Youren (pen name of Michael Benoist), with a preface by Ruan Yuan.

One further reprint is entitled the *Seibu ki furoku* (*Shengwu ji* with Appendices). It is comprised of four woodblock-printed, stringbound volumes and lacks punctuation. The volumes correspond to the last four *juan* of the original edition (of the *Shengwu ji*, volumes 11–14). Volume 11 of the text bears the title 'Buji yoki (heisei heishō)' (Notes on Military Affairs [Military Systems, Military Provisioning]); volume 12 is 'Buji yoki (shōko, kōshō)' (Notes on Military Affairs [Historical Records, Corroborating Evidence]); volume 13 is 'Buji yoki (jikō, zatsujutsu)' (Notes on Military Affairs [Successes, Various Accounts]); and volume 14 is 'Buji yoki (gibu gohen)' (Notes on Military Affairs [Five Essays on the Military]). Regarding its composition, the text carries only the phrase 'Seibu ki jo' (Introduction to the *Shengwu ji*) of Wei Yuan; there is neither a preface by the reprinter nor a date of publication given, though it appears to be a work of the Kaei period. My copy of the work has a stamp on it reading: 'Stamp of the Library Collection of the Meirinkan of Suō' [in present-day eastern Yamaguchi prefecture].

There is another Japanese reprint work in three stringbound volumes entitled *Seibu ki saiyō* (The Essentials of the *Shengwu ji*).[c] A newer edition of it was printed in Kaei 3 (1850) with the note: 'Library of Sekiyōrō.' This person, unlike those in the previous two cases, punctuated the text and signed his name as: 'Edited by Washizu Kan of Owari' [in present-day western Aichi prefecture], and before Wei Yuan's original preface to the *Shengwu ji* in the first volume of the work, Washizu inserted his own preface under the name 'Sekiyōrō mujindokoro' (Pavillion of the Setting Sun, where there is no one present). It is thus known that it was he, Washizu Kan (Kidō, 1825–82), who provided the punctuation and published the text.

In content, he added punctuation solely to 'Buji yoki (gibu gohen),' which comprised the fourth stringbound volume of the aforementioned woodblock-printed work *Seibu ki furoku*, and divided the text into three stringbound volumes: the first includes 'Jōshu hen' (On City Garrisoning) and 'Suishu hen' (On the Protection of Waterways); the second includes 'Bōbyō hen' (On Defending the Fields), 'Gunsei hen' (On Military Administration), and 'Guncho hen' (On Military Provisioning); and the third continues the last of these, 'Guncho hen.' In a preface at the beginning of the text, we find: 'Sunzi offered an inferior plan for a fire attack, but nowadays we must not ignore the fire attack as a technique for defending against the British barbarians.' He then went on to add:

> I recently borrowed the *Shengwu ji* from an esteemed individual and read it. Altogether it has fourteen *juan* and is the work of the Chinese Wei Yuan.... In all probability Wei Yuan himself encountered the opium calamity (*ahen no hen*) of the *renyin* year [1842] of the Daoguang reign, and hence gained access to understanding the successes and failures of Chinese military administration as well as the situation surrounding the British barbarians' invasion. He used the opportunity to prepare a detailed depiction of the circumstances. Thus, for policies concerning coastal defense, there is nothing better than this work. I have accordingly excerpted from it and printed it with woodblocks. I have entitled it *Seibu ki saiyō* and offer it to the public.

In other words, he is saying here that it is the work of Wei Yuan who personally experienced the Opium War and that it is the best reference work for coastal defense policy which was then being widely debated. However, an incident arose whereby the *Seibu ki saiyō* was at first unable, it would seem, to gain official approval for publication, was suppressed, and then came out in a woodblock edition. In the *Hikka shi* of Miyatake Gaikotsu as well, the *Seibu ki saiyō* is listed as one of twelve 'works whose date of publication is uncertain.... They were

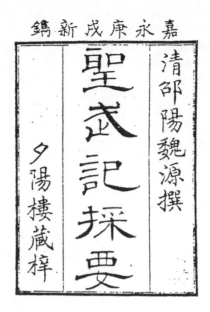

Cover of the *Seibu ki saiyō* (Kansai University Library)

suppressed works and are either not yet out or, if they did appear, the date of publication remains unclear.'

In the first volume [of five] of the *Ishin shiryō kōyō* (Essentials of the Historical Materials on the Meiji Restoration),[d] we see for the fifth month of Kaei 3 (1851): 'The shogunate admonished several persons in the office of coastal defense and warned them against the disclosure of affairs of state. Subsequently, it banned the spread of false reports concerning coastal defense matters around the city.' It would seem that the suppression of the *Seibu ki saiyō* was a result of its confrontation with shogunal policy.

The *Shitaya sōwa* (Collected Stories of Shitaya)[e] by Nagai Kafū (1879–1959) is a work describing the Chinese-style poets who lived in the Shitaya area of Edo at the end of the Tokugawa period. In it he offers a detailed portrayal of Washizu Kidō.

Despairing over military preparedness along the coast, Washizu Kidō published a work entitled *Seibu ki saiyō*. This work is comprised of selected excerpts from the fourteen *juan* of the *Shengwu ji* by Wei Yuan, a drafter in the Grand Secretariat, of Daoguang 26 [1846]. I have searched the used book stores of the city for Washizu's *Saiyō*, but have been unable to obtain it. I have thus looked through the original, *Shengwu ji*.... The *Shengwu ji* was first completed in Daoguang 22 [1842], but two years later he replenished it, and subsequent to that he revised it further in Daoguang 26. That corresponds to the third year of the Kōka reign in our [country]. At that time it was the freshest of all the new books that came [to Japan from China] by ship.

In this way, he describes the *Shengwu ji*, and then he goes on to depict the ban enacted by the shogunate on Washizu's *Seibu ki saiyō*.

Washizu's publication of his selection of excepts from the *Shengwu ji* incurred the displeasure of the shogunal authorities. In May of that year, the *bakufu* ultimately banned indiscriminate discussion by the public of coastal defense for the troubling effects it had on people's minds. In order to avoid interrogation at the office of the Edo Magistrate, Washizu left Edo for Bōshū, and for a time he remained in hiding at the Tōyō gyosha of Suzuki Shōtō.

Kafū goes on to note that he 'obtained several volumes of the *Unko shinbun ki* (Account of the Newspapers of Unko), a work personally compiled by a man by the name of Kanamori Shintoku, in the used books stores of the city.' Among these volumes, he claimed to have discovered an article concerning Washizu, and he introduced the article. In general, it contained the following information.

The case of the *Seibu ki saiyō* was summoned before the office of the northern urban magistracy on the seventeenth day of the twelfth lunar month of the previous year (Kaei 3). It was published by its author, a masterless samurai by the name of Washizu Ikutarō (Kidō's pen name) who lived at the Shōgen Temple in Teramachi, Ushigome-dōri. The woodblock printing was carried out at the home of Nakajirō in Shōei-chō, Kanda. As the aforementioned text gradually became more problematic and the investigation became more severe, Ikutarō did not pay Nakajirō the printing costs, left the woodblocks in his care, and fled. Nakajirō thus took the woodblock printed texts to the authorities. After an investigation, Ikutarō's actions were not at all understood. At the end of last year, Nakajirō was officially summoned three times, and this spring as well he has been summoned three times. Today (fourteenth day of the second lunar month) the case was resolved with 'a correctional fine of three *kan* being imposed on the woodblock printer Nakajirō.' As Washizu concealed his actions so that a full investigation could not be carried out, only the woodblock printer came under repeated inquiry, and in the final analysis the matter came to an end with the imposition of a fine.

Why did Nagai Kafū undertake such a thorough investigation of his own and write in such detail about Washizu's case? Kafū's mother, Tsune, was the eldest daughter of Washizu, and thus Washizu was Kafū's maternal grandfather. Also, Kafū's father, Nagai Nogihara, was a disciple of Washizu.

In the third year of the Keiō era (1867), Washizu became the educational superintendent of Owari domain and served in the educational administration there. At the same time, he assisted the former daimyō Tokugawa Yoshikatsu and planned on behalf of the Meiji Restoration. In the Meiji period, he worked as a magistrate in a prefecture in the northern part of Honshū, and later he changed fields to the juridical profession and became a judge. He also became a member of the Gakushikai. These matters are detailed in Kafū's book.

Shitaya sōwa appeared in a reprint edition as well.[f] In it Washizu's literary Chinese preface to the *Seibu ki saiyō* is rendered in a mixed character and *katakana* syllabary form; also mention is made of Mineta Fūkō's *Kaigai shinwa* and the calamities that befell the author, neither of which were to be found in the original edition of Kafū's work.

Chapter Sixteen

The *Unnan shinwa* and Novelizations of the Taiping Rebellion

We have seen to this point a number of fictionalized treatments in late-Edo Japan of the Opium War, and I have inserted commentary into the discussion, but one work which I did not bring up at that time and which is also concerned with the Opium War I would now like to add. This work did not deal with the Opium War as its main or central theme, but was written as a daily chronicle of the subsequent anti-Qing revolution known as the 'Taiping Heavenly Kingdom' (or Taiping Rebellion). It was a piece of fiction in which the story line went as follows: Seeing that the ferocity of the Taiping military force would not in the end succumb to the Qing armies alone, the British – the Qing dynasty's trading partner ever since the Opium War – dispatch a great armed force to aid the Qing court 'unaware as it is of their [i.e., British] ulterior motives,' and the joint Qing-British army destroys the Taipings.

The text is in one stringbound volume, entitled *Unnan shinwa* (New Stories from Yunnan), printed on half-sized Mino paper. At the very beginning is a color-printed map of Qing China, and throughout the text lightly colored illustrations have been inserted. To the side of the book's title on the cover – *Unnan shinwa* – is added in small characters: 'Ichimei haiya no hanashi' (The Story of an Ashman). Also, on the inside of the front cover, we find the subtitle, 'Ichimei Tōdo haiya no hanashi' (The Story of an Ashman from China), with woodblocks newly cut in Kaei 7 (1854).[a]

The reason for this expression 'haiya no hanashi' is apparently that in reports of the time it was circulated that the leader of the Taiping movement was a lime merchant by the name of Zhu Hua (or Zhu Yuanye, Zhu Tiande). Stories of how this lime merchant was a descendent of the Ming court and was leading an immense peasant military force against the Qing to restore the Ming dynasty spread as far as Japan. In the text of the *Unnan shinwa*, the expression 'haiya no hanashi' appears nowhere, but we know this information from reports of this sort then current.

In the initial section of this work, the author chronicles how the Chinese lost the Opium War, the decline of the nation's fortunes, and the spreading dominance of traitors and villainous officials selfishly running rampant and causing the peasants untold misery. At this point, the peasant masses rise in rebellion against the officialdom, taking as their leader one whom villagers had for successive generations revered, the lineal descendent of the Ming dynasty, Zhu 彪 (?, a *kana* pronunication of 'Gin' is given in the text for this character, though it appears to be in error). With this beginning, Zhu ? is eventually named as the King of the Chinese province of Yunnan. In addition, two groups of bandits offer him their support, and gradually the strength of the rebels grows great.

The Qing then raises a large army and attacks them, but is routed. Taking advantage of his victory, the army of the King of Yunnan attacks and conquers the two provinces of Guangxi and Guizhou. He then enters Sichuan and after that Jiangxi, but where he aims there is no enemy to be found. 'A number of years pass, and the six provinces of Yunnan, Guizhou, Guangxi, Sichuan, Huguang, and Jiangxi – all the land for several thousand *li* – falls under the jurisdiction of the King of Yunnan.' At that point, 'he sets forth to attack the city of Nanjing.'

At this time, 'England, having fought China in Daoguang 21 [1841] and defeated her handily, ended up occupying the strategic ports in Fujian, Ningbo, Jiangzhe, and Guangdong, seized several pieces of terrain, and engaged in trade. Now, however, [England] saw that the army of the Later Ming (Hou-Ming) was winning successive victories, and that the Qing was at the end of its tether. . . . Though their alterior motives remained concealed,' England brought help to the Qing, 'which arrived [in the form of] over 70 warships and over 80,000 mounted troops, calling them all reinforcements.'

> Be that as it may, the army of the King of Yunnan took Nanjing. Suddenly having brought the panic-stricken British force to its knees, he cut them down right there. Without taking so much as a brief pause, he continued the onslaught. . . . And so, the enemy, abandoning several thousand artillery pieces and without a leg to stand on, was attacked and scattered. Unable to endure in Fujian as well, they set off at once for a port city from which to try to withdraw to their home country. In no time at all, however, they found they could not get there, as Fan Wenhu [lit., Fan, the literary tiger], the fierce commander of the Later Ming, aligned several thousand warships at the harbor and attacked with fire the British warships there. As a result the British war fleet, renowned as a castle town at sea, was all but completely decimated, and the remaining few vessels scurried home [to Britain] in defeat.

At this point the novel comes to an end.

At the end of the work, there is an appendix by the author, and it reads:

> The foregoing work, *Unnan shinwa*, I initially wrote and published in one stringbound volume. It covers the attack on the Qing dynasty by the rising

of the last descendent of the Ming emperors, the assistance rendered the Qing by a large army commanded by the British barbarians, and through the crushing defeat of both the Qing and the British forces at Nanjing. Who shall attain that eternal victory, the Qing or the Ming? On this, I have written in detail for subsequent publication and prepared a summary here. By Master Wen Haotang.

'Master Wen Haotang' was the pen name of the author of this work, but whether the subsequent publication mentioned here ever appeared is unknown. It would seem, though, that since the Taipings entered Nanjing in March 1853 and this work was published in 1854, that only reports (unreliable at best), roughly through the period that the Taiping army had brought down the city of Nanjing, reached Japan at the time. He apparently stopped at that point with plans to write a second part.

In this novel, the author wrote that the British aided the Qing military and engaged the Taiping forces in the field. There may have been reports to this effect, but at the time reports of entirely the opposite sort were also being circulated. I have several manuscript works that chronicle the rumors and forms of responses at the time of Admiral Perry's arrival in Japan in 1853. Amid the three sorts of such documents, one reads: 'Reports have it that a Ming descendent had risen in rebellion in China and is in the midst of a battle with the Qing. The English are helping the Ming in major military engagements, while the United States is about to lay hands on Japan.' This was conveyed by one Higuchi Tatarō, the police chief with the receiving party for the American minister at Uraga. This should be sufficient to indicate the many and varied rumors and conjectures that caused considerable agitation, especially spurred by the arrival of American warships at this time in Japan.

In addition to the *Unnan shinwa*, a number of other fictional accounts, dating from the late-Edo period, treat the theme of the Taiping Rebellion. However, in none of these do we encounter either the name of the movement, 'Taiping Heavenly Kingdom' (Taiping tianguo) or the name of its leader, Hong Xiuquan (sometimes given with a different final character). The leader's surname is always given as Zhu, that of the emperors of the Ming dynasty. Accordingly, these accounts never mention the fact that Christianity formed the framework for this rebellious group. All of these novelizations recount that a Mr. Zhu, last descendent of the Ming house, rose in rebellion, unfurled his anti-Qing banner, and set off with his rebel forces to restore the Ming dynasty; and they confronted and engaged the Qing military in various places. These accounts are military tales first and foremost, stories centering on battles fought.

The fictional accounts seem to have been based for the most part on reports conveyed by Chinese vessels from Fujian and elsewhere, or from Korea, to Nagasaki during the Kaei period. I have in my possession a number of manuscript reports of this sort under the title, *Shinchō jōran fūsetsugaki* (Reports on the Uprising in China [all in one stringbound volume]): two are dated the

91

second lunar month of Kaei 6 (1853), two are dated the fourth lunar month of that year, and one is dated the sixth month of the same year. The last of these is an item in which a Sō family retainer from the domain of Tsushima reports to the shogunate on what he has heard from Korean interpreters. It is a generally accurate, though somewhat simplified, report in which a number of other accounts were transcribed. The others, however, are little more than tales of rumor, full of strange exaggerations; they are consistent in one area, as noted above, that all name a Mr. Zhu, last descendent of the Ming dynasty, as the leader who is the head of a rebellious band intent on restoring the Ming. Only the report from the sixth month gives the leader as someone 'surnamed Hong,' but it too says that he sought a revived Ming dynasty.

The Taiping armed forces took Nanjing in March of 1853, though none of the reports in my possession make any mention of the establishment of a capital city at Nanjing. It would thus appear that these reports are based on subsequent information, though Mr. Zhu of the Later Ming takes Nanjing in the *Unnan shinwa*, and the other novelizations also touch on this theme.

These fictional accounts all mention a Mr. Zhu of the Later Ming who rises in rebellion and engages the Qing military in battle, but the layout of the plot line, the development of the plot, and the characters who appear in the story are all based on arbitrary structures with little relationship at best to historical fact. Yet, we find recorded in most of these fictional accounts that a general with the robust-sounding name of Hong Wulong (lit. Hong, the martial dragon) led the armies of the Later Ming to victory against the Qing. This must have been drawn from the aforementioned report in which the leader is given as 'surnamed Hong'; it was adopted and tailored with the fierce given name of Wulong. In this instance, though, a Mr. Zhu (here with the given name Tiande), descendent of the Ming, is the leader, the emperor, and Hong Wulong is the name of the general who assists him. There is one further character, a woman by the name of Li Boyu who can perform sorcery. She too is a courageous general for the forces of the Later Ming who crushingly defeat the Qing armies. In addition to Commander-in-Chief Zhu, both Hong Wulong and Li Boyu appear in such fictional accounts as *Shin Min gundan* (Military Tales of the Qing vs. Ming), *Dattan shōhai ki* (Chronicle of the Battles with the Tatars), *Gaihō taihei ki* (Chronicle of Peace against the Foreigners), and all appear to have been based on the same source.

Let us now turn to the publication data on the fictional accounts in my possession. Aside from the *Unnan shinwa* (1853), we have the *Shin Min gundan* (five stringbound volumes on Mino paper, preface dated 1854 [published by the Aoe juku]),[b] *Dattan shōhai ki* (five stringbound volumes on Mino paper [published by the Bokuteisha]; no date of publication given, though it appears to be the latter portion of some work), *Shinsetsu Min Shin kassen ki* (New Account of the Battle between the Ming and Qing) (five stringbound volumes on Mino paper, published 1854), *Gaihō taihei ki* ([by Hanjōken shujin], five stringbound volumes on Mino paper, preface dated 1854), *Man-Shin kiji* (Chronicle of the

Manchus) (five stringbound volumes on Mino paper, preface by 'Mumei Sannin' [Anonymous Good-for-Nothing], undated), and *Shin zoku ibun* (Reports of the Bandits of the Qing Period) (undated, with a postscript by Aoe Sannin [in five stringbound volumes]).^c

All of these works follow a pattern familiar from the fictionalized tales concerning the Opium War. At the beginning we find maps and portraits of the principal personages of the story; double-paged charts are inserted here and there in the texts; and *hiragana* syllabaries are attached to the Chinese characters. Let us look among these at the 'introductory remarks' at the very beginning of *Shin Min gundan* in which we find the following:

> This work is based on written reports coming out of China. They speak of a Mr. Zhu, given name Hua, style Yuanhua, a lime merchant from Sichuan, who took the reign name of Tiande, and amassed an army in the locales of Guangdong province. An enchantress, surnamed Li, from Zhejiang province joined him at the head of the troops.
>
> From intelligence gathered from the Sō domain [of Tsushima, we know that] Commander-in-Chief Zhu has given himself the imperial title of the Tiande Emperor, and assisting him is one Hong Wulong who has a fort in Langshan, Guangzhou....
>
> We have chronicled the public order and the rebellions of the three reigns of Qianlong, Jiaqing, and Daoguang prior to the [rise of the] lime merchant, and thus the rebellion of Mr. Zhu did not just happen over night.

In fact, the above line – 'We have chronicled the public order and the rebellions of the three reigns' – was not composed 'prior to the [rise of the] lime merchant.' In the third volume of this work, the Opium War of the Daoguang reign is described in a completely separate section, entitled 'Shin Ei kassen no koto' (On the Sino-British War), from its eruption through the peace negotiations.

The *Dattan shōhai ki*, just as was the case with the *Unnan shinwa*, describes how the Qing military sought help from the British, and not just the British military forces stationed at ports along the coast, but reinforcements arrived from Great Britain as well, all of whom were defeated and dispersed.

Furthermore, it seems that while Hong Wulong and Li Boyu were characters concocted by Japanese novelists, a certain measure of authenticity appears to have been derived from the 'reports' of the second lunar month of 1853, conveyed on Chinese trading ships that came to Nagasaki. In those documents, one finds statements such as: 'The bandits' fort was known as Langshan'; and 'Among the leaders of these bandits there is one woman and one person from Shamian who practices sorcery.'

At the very end of the *Shin Min gundan*, Zhu Yuanhua attacks and captures Nanjing with Generalissimo Hong Wulong and second-in-command Li Boyu. He makes it his royal capital and takes the name of the Tiande Emperor. It then ends: 'He transformed the customs and clothing of the Manchu Qing dynasty, and returned to the regime of the Ming.... [Thus,] in one fell swoop, China was divided in two, and the chaos among the people disappeared.' This is then followed by a paragraph which serves as a publication advertisement:

> After this, the Tatars also rose in rebellion in the north, descended on the cities of Manchuria, the former homeland of the great Qing, attacking as far as Ningguta and the Amur River which fell under the control of the Tiande Emperor. Once again Great Britain came to the aid of the Qing, and although they fought, they succumbed to the Later Ming through the wisdom of Wulong and fear of the sorcery of Li Boyu. The Qing leader at the time was [the] Xianfeng [Emperor], and he himself picked up a battle ax and several times fought great battles, but in the end it was useless, and the imperial capital at Beijing fell. A variety of interesting reports and strange ideas, tales of loyal ministers and chaste women, and the efficaciousness of the deities – all these have never leaked out of China till now. They are recorded and published here as a sequel.

So, acting in concert with the Tiande Army in Nanjing, the Tatars in the north (Mongolia?) arose in rebellion and attacked Manchuria, homeland of the Qing, and England surrendered to the Later Ming. This too seems to have been taken directly from the report submitted at Nagasaki in 1853 (in Kanbun):

> Zhu Yuanhua was installed as their new king. The British barbarians in the various ports again submitted to them. In the eighth lunar month of the fall, the Qing ruler Xianfeng personally led an expedition, but it failed to overcome them. The Tatars then rose again in the north, declared their support for Mr. Zhu, descended on the former homeland of the Qing, and seized it. They advanced as far as Ninggudao [as recorded in *Shinchō jōran fūsetsugaki*].

The *Dattan shōhai ki* conveys the gist of this Kanbun report, with a bit of exaggeration here and there and the addition of some complexity to the story. Conjecturing from what was appended to the end of *Shin Min gundan*, this text may in fact be its sequel.

At the end of the 'introductory remarks' at the start of the *Shin Min gundan*, it reads 'by Aoe Shujin,' and on the inside front cover is the line, 'Collection of the Aoe Academy.' Also, in the final remarks at the end of the work, there is the preliminary announcement of a sequel to be published, and the *Dattan shōhai ki* was written as if to continue this work. Hence, the *Dattan shōhai ki* may be seen as a continuation of the *Shin Min gundan*, though at the very end of the 'postscript' to the aforementioned *Shin zoku ibun* too we find the phrase, 'by Aoe Sannin.' Thus, *Shin zoku ibun* is doubtless the second sequel to *Shin Min gundan*. Only the identity of this Aoe Shujin (or Aoe Sannin) remains unclear to us, though I shall offer some conjectures about him.

Unlike the other novels described above, the *Shin zoku ibun* ends with the ultimate victory and pacification by the Qing military over the Taipings. Mr. Zhu's base at Nanjing finally falls in a ferocious attack by the Qing forces, and 'the Qing dynasty once again attains peace.' There is a table of contents at the very beginning of this work, and a note just after it reads: 'The Later Ming lasted for about five years from the rebellion of Zhu Tiande [the emperor] until its destruction. The Qing dynasty pacified it.' So saying, the text then continues:

> However, a band of ruffians known as the Small Sword Society (Xiaodaohui) still runs rampant over various parts of the terrain of that country [*hido*, i.e., China]. Though many of them have been pursued and captured, they have not been completely suppressed as yet. Thus, when we hear that peace and tranquillity do not reign within the four seas, might this not be attributed to the weakness of Chinese officials? Furthermore, the bravery and magnanimity of these bandits are still not known in great detail. The feelings and customs of people from overseas we can only read about in books. Having never been to China, neither I nor others are in any position to observe it in depth. We can only offer evaluations. By Aoe Sannin.

Mention of about five years passing from the rise of the Taipings to their collapse is way off; in fact, about fifteen years passed before the Taipings were put down. The late Kaei or early Ansei years, when this novel seems to have been written, corresponds to the early period of the establishment of a capital in Nanjing by the Taipings.

The author notes that the Small Sword Society ran rampant over portions of Chinese terrain, and this point we find in none of the other novels.

The Small Sword Society is usually considered a branch of the Heaven and Earth Society (or Triads), an anti-Qing organization that lay dormant among the people from the fall of the Ming dynasty forward. Though it did not profess belief in Christianity, it did make common cause with the Taipings in a shared opposition to the Qing dynasty. It is thought that early in the period of the Taiping uprising, the Taiping military absorbed this anti-Qing organizational affiliate of the Heaven and Earth Society, and when the Taipings invaded Zhejiang and Jiangsu, the Small Sword Society – having gathered in Shanghai from a variety of localities in Guangdong, Fujian, and Zhejiang – coalesced with secret societies of the same place. Shortly after the Taipings seized Nanjing, the Small Swords responded by occupying the county seat at Shanghai; it was the eighth lunar month of 1853.[1] Their leader was Liu Lichuan, a man from Chaozhou, Guangdong province. They planned to link up with and assist the Taipings in Nanjing, but a secret messenger of theirs was captured en route and never reached his destination; the army of occupation was isolated, and seventeen months later it collapsed. This rebellion of the Small Sword Society in league with the anti-Qing revolution of the Taiping rebels was felt in the local areas closest to them,[2] and apparently a great shock was felt back in Japan at the time as well. The *Man-Shin kiji*, which I shall discuss in the next chapter, carries the subtitle, 'Shōtōkai hanashi' (Story of the Small Sword Society).

There is a detailed description of the Small Swords' occupation of the city of Shanghai in the *Tongzhi Shanghai xian zhi* (County Gazetteer of Shanghai of the

Tongzhi Period) (*juan* eleven, a section entitled 'Lidai bingshi' [Military Affairs through the Ages]). An accurate portrayal as well is the account of an eyewitness, Huang Quan, who put his observations together in 'Xiaolin xiao shi' (A Short History of Xiaolin).[d]

Among recent works that I have seen, I think one well-done essay is that of Xu Weinan, 'Shanghai Xiaodaohui luanshi de shimo' (A Full History of the Small Sword Society Uprising in Shanghai).[3] Also Jian Youwen has translated, for the same issue of the journal, *Yi jing*, in which Xu's essay appears, two contemporaneous accounts from the *North China Herald*: Matthew T. Yates (Yan Matai), 'Xiaodaohui zhanju Shanghai muji ji' (Eyewitness Account of the Small Sword Society's Occupation of Shanghai) (September 10, 1853); and Issachar J. Roberts (Luo Xiaoquan), 'Xiaodaohui shouling Liu Lichuan fangwen ji' (Account of a Visit with Liu Lichuan, Leader of the Small Sword Society) (October 1, 1853).

Chapter Seventeen

The Small Sword Society and the Novel *Man-Shin kiji*

Information concerning the uprising of the Small Sword Society seems to have reached Japan via Chinese ships that docked at the port of Nagasaki. The third volume of *Kaei Meiji nenkan roku* (Annual Records for the Kaei through Meiji Periods) (compiled by Yoshino Maho, 1820–70)[a] carries such an account.

In the seventh intercalary month of the first year of the Ansei reign period (also Kaei 7, or 1854), we read the following entry: 'Vessels from China have entered the port of Nagasaki, and they tell of a rebellious state of affairs in that country.' The names of Hong Xiuquan and Yang Xiuqing, two leaders of the Taiping revolution, are clearly cited in this report; and there are further points as well that cannot be found in the various reports of Kaei 6 (1853) recorded in *Shinchō jōran fūsetsugaki*. Thus, in comparing the later report with the information conveyed in the earlier reports, the later one is considerable more accurate and, indeed, more objective. There are, however, points at which it accepted hearsay as fact, such as when it is noted: 'The two bandits Hong and Yang have together produced a wooden figure which they call the Tiande [Heavenly Morality] Emperor. They greatly revere it, and troops in the field make their decisions about advancing or retreating on the basis of divine revelations received after praying to this wooden figure. In the final analysis, they do believe in sorcery.' Aside from exceptions of this sort, *Kaei Meiji nenkan roku* is on the whole quite detailed and realistic in outlook.

Let me now quote from it at length:

You have requested of me that I report on the recent situation in the rebellion presently going on in China. From the 30th year of the Daoguang reign [1850], it has become particularly severe with bandit groups of good-for-nothing hooligans massing in Guangxi and Guangdong. Two men by the names of Hong Xiuquan and Yang Xiuqing are the ringleaders; the numbers of their accomplices are rising, and they have many followers. They divide the work, each of them pursuing the rebellion with some 2000–5000 men. In addition, they have attacked government offices and plundered walled cities, used artillery and land mines, and are quite adept in the employment of military strategy. Crowds of people are coming together talking about these things.

All of these men have full heads of hair, and they wear pieces of red cloth around their heads. Thus, the government troops have taken to calling them Red Turbaned Bandits as well as Long-Haired Bandits.

During the second or third lunar month of last year, bandit strength was immense in three separate places in the Jiangnan region: Yangzhou, Zhenjiang, and Nanjing. With 40,000–50,000 men they seized these three cities, and the number of local officials there who died in battle was numerous. In due time, they trained and sent troops to the neighboring counties, while an imperial commissioner departed from the capital [for the trouble areas]. Around the tenth month of the year, Yangzhou was speedily recovered, and the bandit remnants escaped to Zhenjiang and Nanjing. Defending themselves staunchly, they were surrounded by the government's troops. There was no passageway between the two cities for them, and thus cut off they withdrew. Nanjing is where [Emperor] Taizu of the Ming dynasty built his capital. Excellent as a strategic stronghold, it will probably not be defeated too quickly....

There is another group of bandits as well there [i.e., China] and they go by the name of the Small Sword Society. They originated in Fujian [province], and concealing themselves under the guise of ordinary common folk, they travel about the land to promote their activities. At a signal they come together at a designated place and go to plunder the wealth of the people. Members of the group know one another as each carries a small sword concealed on his person. Wherever they happen to meet, they check one another's identity with these small swords. However, they do not have the desire to slaughter [the populations of] walled cities nor to occupy provincial towns. They merely steal valuables, and then immediately disperse all over.

From the Jiajing and Daoguang eras, these [bandit] groups were in these parts [of China], and I have learned that gradually they spread out later. Recently, many more joined, and in the eighth month of last year some 3000 [bandit troops] attacked Shanghai county. They intimidated the government forces and killed the county magistrate there....

> Intercalary seventh month
> Shipowner Wang, Jiang Xingqin [yu]
> Yang Shaotang [tang], representative of twelve

At the very end of this report is an 'enclosure' noting: 'The areas affected by these rebellions are Guangxi, Guangdong, Jiangnan, Yangzhou, Zhenjiang, Nanjing, Fujian, Shanghai, Hunan, Hubei, Wuchang, Jiujiang, Manzhou [sic.], and Suzhou.' The last sentence reads: 'The foregoing is a Japanese translation of the observations of the Chinese who have recently come to Japan.' Thus, we know it was a current report conveyed to Japan by a Chinese vessel, submitted by the shipowner's representative to the office of the Nagasaki Administrator, and translated by the official Japanese interpeters.

Japanese novelizations based on material concerning the Small Sword Society were clearly based on this sort of report conveyed to Nagasaki from China. In particular, the news that Nanjing had been occupied by anti-government forces and that now the Shanghai county seat (separate from the foreign concession area in the city) was also occupied seems to have served up a major shock to the Japanese at the time. Although novels quickly took up this theme from the news, since the authors had no means at their disposal to learn of the actual, concrete goings-on, they turned the stories into military chronicles centering on the fighting, works of pure fiction.

On the inside of the cover of the *Man-Shin kiji* (Chronicle of the Manchus), (five stringbound volumes on Mino paper, preface by 'Mumei Sannin' [lit., Anonymous Good-for-Nothing], undated), the title of the work is written in large characters down the center.[b] To the right it reads 'The Story of the Small Sword Society,' and to the left it reads 'printed by the Kinseikaku.' Because there is no colophon, can cannot say with certainty what sort of bookshop the Kinseikaku was. It may have been a disguise taken from name of Jin Shengtan, compiler of the *Shuihu zhuan* (Water Margin). The protagonist of this Japanese novel bears the name of Hong Xiuquan, something unique to this novel. At the time, the final character of the name of leader of the Taipings, Hong Xiuquan, was written sometimes as 全 and sometimes as 泉 (both pronounced *quan* in the second tone). Even in contemporary Chinese documents concerning the Taipings, we often see his name rendered in the non-standard manner with 泉. This was particularly true of official documents, such as Wang Xianqian's *Xianfeng donghua lu* (Records from within the Eastern Flowery Gate of the Xianfeng Period). Perhaps, because he was considered a rebellious bandit by the Qing dynasty, people specifically sought to avoid using his real name.

In the *Man-Shin kiji*, Hong Xiuquan is portrayed as the leader of the Small Swords; this is, of course, inaccurate, as Liu Lichuan was the actual leader of the Small Sword Society. By the same token, though, co-conspirator Yang Xiurong (who appears in the novel as the fictive younger brother of Hong Xiuquan's father) seems in fact to be a slight transformation of the name Yang Xiuqing (who was the real force behind the Taipings, second-in-command to Hong Xiuquan; he later fought with Hong for leadership of the Taiping movement and was killed).

All this notwithstanding, the novel is entirely fictional in content. The author explained his aim in his own autobiographical preface:

> In the middle of the tenth lunar month on a lonely rainy day, a man stopped by for a short while under the eaves of my thatched hut to avoid the rainfall. I summoned him inside and offered him some coarse tea (*shibucha*). We spoke of many and sundry things, and he told me of the

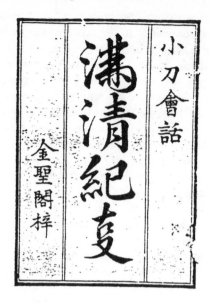

Inside Cover of the *Man-Shin kiji* (Kansai University Library)

many rumors he had picked up from Chinese when he had visited Nagasaki. I enjoyed his stories a great deal and was much entertained by him. Eventually, at the sound of the bell at sunrise, this fellow suddenly sought some rest, so I took him by the sleeve and invited him to stay with me, but he declined. When he was about to depart, he took from his package a single volume and gave it to me, saying that it was a book about the recent, strange stories from another land. When I later picked it up and began reading, I saw that it contained stories and adventures full of shocking events. Rather than enjoy reading it by myself alone, I thought I would make it available for all to read, though it is written entirely in Chinese characters, which I have put into *hiragana*.

This was, of course, a complete fabrication, and it is signed at the end: 'Mumei Sannin.' It bears no date.

Color portraits of the principal characters of the novel follow the autobiographical preface on successive pages, one to a page; an explanation is attached to each of these pictures in the following order: 'Shōtōkai sōtaishō Kō Shūsen' (Hong Xiuquan, Commander-in-Chief of the Small Sword Society), 'Shōtōkai daini no tōryō Yō Shūei' (Yang Xiurong, Second-in-Command of the Small Sword Society), 'Shōtōkai no chōhon So I' (Su Yi, a Small Sword Society Ringleader), 'Shoshū shishi, Ryohaku no chishin Shu I, nochi ni Shōtōkai no gunshi to naru' (Zhu Wei, Sagacious Official from Lübo, Magistrate in Various

Departments, Later Became a Strategist for the Small Sword Society), 'Tōetsu ken no shu Tō [Tō] Jun, nochi ni Shōtōkai no gun ni kuwawaru' (Deng Shun, Lord of Tengyue County, Later Joined the Masses of the Small Sword Society), 'Unryōsan no gōtō Chō Kaku, nochi ni Shōtōkai no gun ni kuwawaru' (Zhao Jue, Bold Bandit from Yunlong Mountain, Later Joined the Masses of the Small Sword Society). There are double-page pictures inserted at various points in each volume within the body of the text as well.

In the first section of volume one, entitled 'The Bandit Origins of the Taipings and the Small Sword Society in the Great Qing Dynasty,' and in the next section as well entitled 'The Early History of Hong Xiuquan,' the vestiges of the sort that have been tracked down about the Small Swords and the early years of Hong Xiuquan and passed down to us nowadays are completely absent. It is a work of pure fiction.

The content of the novel runs as follows. There was a chivalrous lad by the name of Hong Quanzhong in Yangzhou's Ganquan county, but he was a good-for-nothing and later became a thief. He had an infant son by the name of Hong Xiuquan, and eventually the father was captured and executed. Hong Xiuquan was disdained and humiliated by his neighbors because his father's sinful deeds had culminated in capture and death. Thinking of this bitterly, he vowed to become the leader of a nation and take revenge on those who insulted him. At that time he met an elderly man by the name of Su Yi. The old man was also a man of great will, but because he was already well along in years, he sought for Xiuquan to follow in his footsteps and so taught him the sorcery into which he claimed to have been initiated by Southern Barbarians. He (Su) informed him (Hong) that there were comrades known as the Small Sword Society and gave Xiuquan a small sword as the sign of membership in the group. Thus, when Xiuquan grasped the sorcery, he used it to punish evil men and to oppose government officials. Yang Xiurong and other mighty comrades also joined the Small Sword Society and on numerous occasions attacked the government's armed forces. Military strategist Zhu Wei generally led them in war. In the end he entrenched himself in the walled city of Shiping, Linnan county (?), Yunnan province. Military forces from Beijing attacked and overtook him there, and he is on the point of being defeated as the novel comes to a close.

Let us now take a brief look at the content of this work. The novel seems to have been written with something of a hint taken from the official reports (*fūsetsugaki*) which we cited at the start of this chapter – 'vessels from China have entered the port of Nagasaki, and they tell of a rebellious state of affairs in that country' – or from comparable items. In this official report, groups rising in rebellion within China are nowhere mentioned to be anti-Qing political groupings calling for a revival of the Ming dynasty. It noted only a simple group of thieves, like the Small Sword Society, confronting government troops in battle. Nowhere do we see any mention of fighting for some noble or just cause, but just a battle to seize the realm. It would seem as well that the novel's mention of protagonist Hong Xiuquan's making use of sorcery took a hint from the same official report which notes: 'In the final analysis, they do believe in sorcery.'

When Hong Xiuquan's teacher, Su Yi, dies in the novel, Hong 'whittled some wood himself and made a wooden image of his aged teacher.' He prayed before it, and when he came back with his followers, they worshipped the wooden icon as well. The novel here reads that 'they were bound by duty and swore an oath.' The corresponding portion of the official report reads: 'The two bandits Hong and Yang have together produced a wooden figure.... They greatly revere it, and troops in the field make their decisions about advancing or retreating on the basis of divine revelations received after praying to this wooden figure.'

From such passages, it seems clear that the novel *Man-Shin kiji* was constructed on the model of the official report cited above. Like the *Man-Shin kiji*, there is a one-stringbound-volume work about the Taiping Rebellion bearing the same title *Man-Shin kiji*. The latter, written in Kanbun, is a transcribed chronicle by a Chinese. The writer came to Japan aboard Admiral Perry's warship, arriving in the first lunar month of Kaei 7 (1854). The work circulated at first in manuscript, and later in the early years of the Ansei period was printed in a woodblock edition. In content, though, it is unconnected to the novel *Man-Shin kiji*. There is yet one further work with this same title. It covers the period of the emergence of the Taiping movement through its occupation of Nanjing in 1853 and the establishment of a capital there. It is a detailed chronological account which both follows the founding of the Taiping capital in Nanjing and continued Taiping fighting with Qing forces in various places through the seventh or eighth month of the same year. It appears to be a chronicle based on historical materials.

Chapter Eighteen

The *Man-Shin kiji* and the *Etsuhi tairyaku*

The last work (referred to at the end of the previous chapter) also called *Man-Shin kiji* is not a novel but a chronicle tracing events, based upon stories of the day. From our present perspective, it contains historical material worthy of reference. In particular, the author collected a variety of manifestos and proclamations of the Taiping forces and of rebellious groups affiliated with them, material rarely found elsewhere. As a result, this work is frequently cited by Chinese scholars as well.

The book actually begins with China's defeat in the Opium War. It records the opening of the ports at Ningbo, Shanghai, Fuzhou, Xiamen, and Hong Kong and the establishment of Christian churches at various sites by the 'barbarians,' both according to stipulations of the peace treaty. However, the Guangdong area remains in a state of unease, with bandits running rampant in the region. At this time, Hong Xiuquan (using the same character for *quan* as the *Man-Shin kiji* discussed above) learns the principles of Christianity from a British pastor in Hong Kong and reads the Bible. The barbarians then send him to Guangxi to evangelize. Feng Yunshan (later to become another leader of the Taipings) too becomes a Christian in Macao, and he returns to spread the faith in Guangxi. Some people appeal to the local authorities when Hong and Feng begin deceiving the populace with Christianity, and officials try to arrest them. Hong and Feng rally the local people, resist the government's troops, and ultimately rise in rebellion in the 28th year (?) of the Daoguang reign (1848). This anti-government group gradually grows immense, and the Qing court sends a punitive force against it, albeit unsuccessfully.

Hong Xiuquan and his followers allow their hair to grow (ceasing to wear it in a queue as demanded by the Manchu dynasty), change their style of dress (switching from Manchu to Ming styles), forbid plundering of the peasantry, and maintain strictly enforced laws as they march with reverent demeanor. They set their will on reviving the Ming dynasty, and they see the Manchus as the enemy. They move straight ahead invigorated and courageous, like Xiang Yu of Chu who destroyed his cauldrons and sank his boats (namely, determined to march ahead, even in the face of certain death, with no retreat).[a] The plan they are using follows in certain ways the restoration of the Han dynasty under Emperor Guangwu.

As can be seen in the description in the preceding two paragraphs, the book tells of the Taipings' strict military discipline and the bravery with which the Taiping troops marched forward. It also chronicles battles with Qing forces at various places as well as the patterns of strategies and attacks utilized, all with dates affixed.

For a time, the rebel army remains in Yongan in Guangxi province. Then, in Xianfeng 2 (Kaei 5 [or 1852]), they leave Yongan and surround the city of Guilin, and momentarily thereafter they raise the siege and proceed into Hunan province. Along the way, they take a number of cities and towns and set siege to Changsha (capital of Hunan). Midway, though, they lift this siege and move on to bring down Yuezhou near Lake Dongting. They next attack and take the city of Hanyang in Hubei province. They invade Hankou and occupy Wuchang. This is followed by a flotilla of over 2000 ships sailing down the Yangzi River; Jiujiang, Anqing, and Wuhu all fall to the Taipings, before they descend on Nanjing which finally falls to them. Hong Xiuquan repairs the old Ming palace there, makes it his personal residence, and posts inside and out two couplets, which read as follows:

> With our hands offered up to heaven, we shall prepare to revitalize the spirit of the great Ming.
> With our simple hearts offered up to the country, we shall eradicate the alien dress of foreign terrain.
> With 3000 courageous soldiers, we shall proceed immediately to cleanse the earth in Beijing to the north.
> Ascending to the position of Heavenly King, we shall reopen the era of Yao and Shun.

The language of these verses seems to have greatly pleased Yoshida Shōin. He cited them at the beginning of the *Shinkoku Kanpō ran ki* (Record of the Uprising in China during the Xianfeng Reign), his translation of this *Man-Shin kiji*.[1]

In the very last section of this *Man-Shin kiji*, there is mention of the uprising of the Small Sword Society in Shanghai, but this segment of text on the Small Swords has the appearance of something tacked on in the form of a postscript. The main purpose of the book was to take in the entire spectrum of actitivies of the Taiping military. Yet, it ends with a chronicling of the battles fought on a variety of fronts through the seventh or eighth lunar month of the year that the Taipings entered the city of Nanjing in March of 1853, which they made their Heavenly Capital. Even if what is recounted here does not fully accord with the detailed studies being done today in China – numerous studies have appeared, there is a Taiping Historical Museum in Nanjing, and many document collections are being assembled – it conveyed for the first time to Japan a concrete, overall picture of the evolution of the Taiping revolution and was close to being historically accurate.

At about the same time as the *Man-Shin kiji*, another work came from China (by a route that remains unclear): *Yuefei dalüe* (J. *Etsuhi tairyaku* [Outlines of the Bandits from Guangxi and Guangdong]) in one stringbound volume.[b] It records how in the year Daoguang 30 (1850):

> The rebels Hong Xiuquan, Yang Xiuqing, Xiao Chaogui, Feng Yunshan, Wei Zheng, Hu Yiguang [huang], Fan Liande, Luo Yawang, and others came together in the village of Jintian in Xunzhou, Guiping county [in Guangxi province] and formed the Society of God-Worshippers. Calling themselves the Kings of Heavenly Peace, they selected the middle of the tenth [lunar] month to rise in rebellion.

It thus notes that Hong Xiuquan, Yang Xiuqing, and the others raised an army in Jintian village in the tenth month of Daoguang 30 and called themselves the Kings of Heavenly Peace. The *Man-Shin kiji* makes no mention of the fact that the rebellion began in Jintian village, nor does it record anything of the formation of the Society of God-Worshippers. In this regard, the *Etsuhi tairyaku* is more accurate.

It records the fighting back and forth at various sites chronologically and concludes that 'in the first month of the fourth year of the Xianfeng reign [1854], Imperial Commissioner Shengbao was defeated at Linqing in Shandong province. The bandits fled on to Gaotang in Shandong, and that city eventually surrendered in the fifth lunar month.' Thus, the text chronicles events through the fifth month of 1854.

In the introduction, the punctuator and reprinter of the *Etsuhi tairyaku* notes: 'After making this investigation, I was able to learn these circumstances. I am aware that worthless volumes have already spread falsehood throughout the islands.' This would seem to point to the fabrications of the fictionalized accounts then current. We have now seen how, on the basis of the two works, *Man-Shin kiji* and *Etsuhi tairyaku*, a concrete description of the state of affairs in the Taiping Rebellion became known in Japan during the Kaei and Ansei periods.

The *Etsuhi tairyaku*, or rather *Yuefei dalüe*, was originally a Chinese work that made its way from China to Japan by ship. This is corroborated by the fact that the first half of this book is completely consistent with the chapters of a manuscript entitled *Yuexi Guilin shoucheng ji* (Record of the Defense of Guilin in Western Guangxi), held in the Nanjing Library.[2] It seems clear that it was not conveyed to Japan in the amalgamated form of a book known as *Etsuhi tairyaku*. On the basis of manuscripts printed in Japan, it was included in *Taiping tianguo shiliao* (Historical Documents on the Taiping Rebellion), compiled by the Research Institute of the Faculty of Letters of Beijing University.[3]

The *Man-Shin kiji*, or rather *Man-Qing jishi*, in one stringbound volume was transmitted to Japan in its original manuscript form by the author himself and not returned to China; later, it was in fact reimported back to China. It was the handwritten draft of a Guangdong native by the name of Luo Sen (Xiangqiao) who, when Admiral Perry arrived in Uraga Bay as envoy of the United States in Kaei 7 (1854), boarded a vessel in Perry's fleet in Hong Kong, visited Japan, and on the return voyage went ashore once again in Hong Kong. He served as a 'secretary' in matters concerning use of literary Chinese, preparing Kanbun documents to present to the Japanese government (it was claimed that they presented documents in three languages: English, Dutch, and Chinese), and carrying out brush conversations as a means of interpreting. After returning home, Luo Sen became known for his *Riben riji* (Japan Diary) (1854/11th month to 1855/1st month) which was carried in *Xiaer guanzhen* (Rarities from Near and Far), the monthly magazine published in Hong Kong. In addition, in the manuscript copy of a work entitled *Kanagawa yūki* (Kanagawa Travelogue) (bearing the old seal 'Wakagi bunko' [Wakagi Collection]), which I personally own, this same matter is laid out in the record of a discussion in brush between Luo Sen and a Japanese whose name is concealed.

Furthermore, I have in my library a manuscript copy of the *Riben riji* in one stringbound volume, and this work is included as well, based on a contemporaneous manuscript, in the first appendix of the 'Bakumatsu gaikoku kankei monjo' (Documents Concerning Foreign Relations in the Late Edo Period), in the *Dai Nihon komonjo* (Ancient Documents of Japan).[4]

I touched on the *Xiaer guanzhen* earlier and pointed out there that both Yoshida Shōin and the shogunate's Administrator for Foreign Affairs, Iwase Tadanori (Higo no kami), had both seen it. The man responsible for foreign diplomacy in the shogunate's Office of Coastal Defense, Kawaji Toshiakira, noted the following which appears in his *Shimoda nikki* (Shimoda Diary)[c] when he left for Shimoda, charged with receiving a delegation from Russia in Ansei 1 (1854): 'I have copied out the work *Xiaer guanzhen*, brought here by an American.'[5] The very fact that the man in charge of foreign diplomacy would himself have copied out a magazine in Chinese characters (edited by a British missionary) and published in Hong Kong lends evidence to the idea that *Xiaer guanzhen* was considered a valuable source of information from overseas.

Kawaji continued in the following manner:

This work is prepared by an Englishman in Hong Kong, China [Tōdo]. Each stringbound volume sells for fifteen cash, and it comes out monthly. It is like a chronicle of news of the world. The Western newspapers [namely, the Dutch *fūsetsugaki*] are not written in a Western [lit., horizontal] language and we can understand them only because they are written in Chinese characters. We have been able to see items here and there with a telescope from atop a ship's mast, following the conditions of the articles of the revised treaty of Yokohama. [Though internal details are difficult to figure out], there is much more detail to be gleaned than Japanese have done to this point.

Because the *Xiaer guanzhen* was seen as such a valuable work, it warranted the attention of the diplomatic authorities and a portion of the informed public of the day. The *Riben riji*, which was carried in the *Xiaer guanzhen* (wherein the editor noted only that it was the 'observations' [*suojian suowen*] of a 'Chinese' [Tangren], and Luo Sen's name did not appear – we know it to be his work from internal evidence), seems also to have been copied out longhand by officials and interested amateurs.

We read in the *Riben riji*: 'There is a man by the name of Hirayama Kenjirō who is sincere and erudite. He asked me about the inception of the disorder and peace in China. I showed him the entries in my daily chronicle and a plan for public order.' Hirayama Kenjirō was an official of the shogunate and one of those assigned to the welcoming party that greeted the delegation from the United States. There is also included in *Riben riji* a letter Hirayama is said to have sent Luo Sen.

It read: 'Because of the reception yesterday, I still have not had time to read it closely. I would thus like to borrow it, take it home, and read through it. I will then return it later to the Yokohama Hall [where Luo Sen was living].' So, I gave it to him. He read it through and sent it back to me, and he responded to a letter from me: 'I recently borrowed and read two stringbound volumes you lent me on the events in Nanjing and a plan for public order. I read them several times with great interest, and for the first time I understood the basis needed for public order in China. I also became aware of the honesty underpinning the learning of Luo Xiangqiao.... '

We thus learn from this citation that Hirayama borrowed and probably copied out Luo Sen's work on the disorder in China ('the events in Nanjing'). At first, the text was transcribed and passed along, only later being printed in a woodblock edition by someone. It was at this last stage that the title *Man-Shin kiji* was affixed to the work.

Earlier in this book, I mentioned that Yoshida Shōin had translated this work in Ansei 2 (1855) and titled it *Shinkoku Kanpō ran ki*, though he noted: 'I do not know the name of the author of this work, and it has no title.'[d] Shōin had learned about it from a manuscript that was circulating at the time. It was then printed in a woodblock edition, and it bore the title *Man-Shin kiji* for the first time when it appeared on page one of this edition. We learn this from the inserted note in small characters beneath the title of Shōin's work: 'This work originally bore no title. People called it *Man-Shin kiji*, and so for now we shall follow that practice.'

The brush conversation with Luo Sen which is to be found in the *Kanagawa yūki* by an anonymous author revealed the level of knowledge about the Taiping Rebellion possessed by Japanese intellectuals at the time. Luo's Japanese counterpart repeatedly queried him about 'the uprising in China.' He asked Luo: 'What is the name of the king of the Taipings and Small Sword Society?' Luo responded: 'Hong Xiuquan is the king of the Taipings, not the Small Sword Society.' He then asked Luo: 'How is their momentum? Have they already taken Nanjing?' Luo replied: 'By now they have already left Nanjing.' He asked Luo:

'Did the United States assist the Taiping king?' Luo answered: 'It neither helped nor hindered.' 'Did Great Britain assist the Qing dynasty?' he asked. 'Neither offered help. Each barbarian sought only to protect itself.' 'So, then, to whom does the way of heaven belong?' asked the Japanese. Luo replied: 'I cannot say as yet.'

Luo Sen's talent as a poet and calligrapher were remarked upon by Japanese officials and Confucian scholars at the time. Their poems written at the time of the exchange of presents appear in the *Riben riji*, and they frequently asked him to adorn their folding fans with poetry. In the space of a single month, he wrote poems on over 500 fans, and they are recorded in the *Riben riji*.

His work on the 'events in Nanjing,' namely the *Man-Shin kiji*, was reimported much later back into China; it was included, on the basis of a manuscript bearing the name 'Hong of the Tokyo Imperial Library,' in part two of *Zhongguo jinshi bishi* (Secret History of Modern China) by Menshitanhuke.[e] In the process of compiling it, a fair number of corruptions entered the language of the text, and they even affected the content, including errors in personal names.[6] Chinese scholars of the Taiping Rebellion have used this error-ridden text as a historical source and have accordingly committed errors of their own. I have done a rather detailed investigation of this matter in my study, 'Man-Shin kiji to sono hissha, waga kuni ni tsutaerareta 'Taihei tengoku' ni tsuite' (The *Man-Shin kiji* and Its Author: How [News of] the Taiping Rebellion was Transmitted to Japan).[7]

Chapter Nineteen

The *Gaihō taihei ki* and the *Shinsetsu Min Shin kassen ki*

I would like now to look at the content of two other fictional treatments of the Taiping Rebellion: *Gaihō taihei ki* (Record of Peace against the Foreigners) and *Shinsetsu Min Shin kassen ki* (New Account of the War Between the Ming and the Qing).

At the beginning of the first volume of the *Gaihō taihei ki*, there is a preface in literary Chinese by 'Hanjōken shujin' dated 'first day of autumn, Kōin [year, 1854].'[a] The Kanbun used in the preface is very odd, and it concludes: 'This work should be a warning and exhortation to women and children and an aid to the world. It will be fortuitous for all who enjoy reading it.' This is followed by doubled-paged, color-printed maps, entitled 'Tōdo kōyo no zenzu' (Complete Map of the Chinese Empire) and 'Kyōshi sōzu' (Complete Map of the Capital Area). The next displays portraits of 'Dai Shin gensui Go Jin'yū' (Marshall Wu Zhenyou of the Qing Dynasty), 'Kanpōtei kōkyū Ryū Ki' (Liu Hui of the Harem of the Xianfeng Emperor), 'Dai Shin kanshin Nei Bukyoku' (Ning Wuqu, Treacherous Minister of the Qing Dynasty), 'Minmatsu no yūshin Kan Kō' (Han Guang, Courageous Minister of the Late Ming Dynasty), and 'Dattan no yūshō Tei Kinko' (Ding Jinhu, Brave Tartar General). Then, vermillion seals with ostentatious characters are included: 'Da Qing shouming zhi bao' (Treasure of the Great Qing Dynasty's Reception of the Mandate), 'Huangdi zunqin zhi bao' (Treasure of the Emperor's Veneration of His Parents), and 'Tianzi zhi bao' (Treasure of the Son of Heaven). What meaning all of these have with respect to the text is difficult to ascertain. In addition, there are two or three double-paged illustrations in each volume.

The book begins with sections entitled 'On the Criticism of the War Councils in Beijing' and 'On the Government Forces' Setting off for Nanjing,' and there are chapters with such titles as 'Li Boyu Hides within the Enemy Position by Means of Sorcery' and 'Hong Wulong Plans for the Defeat of the Government Forces.' As I noted earlier, 'Li Boyu' and 'Hong Wulong' were both deeply involved in developing the fierce fighting with the Qing army closing in on them. In the end, the text concludes at the point at which Liu Tianchong (a general in the Nanjing army) warns Hong Wulong that a vast force from Beijing is surging in upon them. However, at the very end of this novel, the following postscript was added:

It is said the Wu Zhenyou [a Qing general] and Hong Wulong, later both brave and wise, would have both victories and defeats. At one time the Ming was on the verge of defeat at the hands of Zhenyou, and King Tiande, with a number of his commanders dead on the field, was left fighting a defensive battle with foot soldiers alone. It ultimately ended in a great defeat for him, and Yuanye, King Tiande, remained to endure by himself. With the help of brave ministers in the last days of the Ming, he wiped away his shame and moved to reunify the Ming. The story of that event shall appear in the sequel [to this book].

As this citation makes clear, the author seems ultimately to have expected a reunification of the Ming (?) dynasty. Yet, I have heard of no sequel, and if it was in fact published, successful reunification under the Ming (?) was a lost cause.

In the first chapter of this book, entitled 'On the Criticism of the War Councils in Beijing,' we read:

There was a man among the people, a descendant of the Ming house, with the surname Zhu, given name Hua, styled Yuanye. He was magnanimous and considerably dignified by nature. The institutions of the Qing dynasty at that time were unjust, and the people disobedient and bearing hatred to no small extent. Thereupon, Yuanye and Li Boyu devised a plan, forced their way into Zhejiang, and defeated Zhao Yuanzong at the battle of Lake Poyang in Jiangxi. They immediately proceeded, and the force of their onslaught at the stone walls of Nanjing made them like splintering bamboo. Many generals became fearful and fled the fortress in haste. The Ming commanders behaved with military dignity as they entered a vacant fortress surrounded by stone walls. Thus, a large number surrendered en masse, just like an assemblage of ants. [Ming] forces already were said to number some 300,000. It was the fifth [lunar] month of Xianfeng 3 [1853]. Yuanye was enthroned with the reverent title of Emperor Tiande. He then changed the reign title, and it became the first year of the Tiande reign.

Thus, this work appears to have been penned some time after receiving reports of the Taipings' occupation of Nanjing. The entrance of the Taiping armed forces into the city of Nanjing occurred in Xianfeng 3 (Kaei 6 [or 1853]). It would seem that this novel was written the following year, because the dating 'Kōin' appears in the preface. That this news from China would so rapidly come to Japan and solicit a reaction whereby it had become the stuff of fiction – and all within a year – is astounding. Perhaps this is one of the manifestations of a sensitive national consciousness amid the convulsions of that time sparked by the arrival of Admiral Perry's vessels.

In this novel, though, the leader of the anti-Qing forces is not Hong Xiuquan, but a descendent of the Ming dynasty by the name of Zhu Yuanye. We know as well that this Zhu Yuanye's enthronement as Emperor Tiande was based on a report transmitted to Japan in the previous year of 1853 (as can be seen in such sources as *Shinchō jōran fūsetsugaki*). Not only the *Gaihō taihei ki*, but the other novels mentioned earlier, were published in rapid succession, and this publication feat speaks to the shocking quality of the ripple effect set off by the reports capturing this news in Japan and the magnifying effect they had.

The *Shinsetsu Min Shin kassen ki* is also a work completely of conjecture, though 'shinsetsu' in the title would seem to suggest some distinctive meaning. Although containing elements not to be found in other works of fiction, this novel is linked to the descendents of Zheng Chenggong [Koxinga] (who had a Japanese mother), leader of an army that fought against the Qing at the end of the Ming dynasty. Furthermore, unlike any of the other novels, this one places the Ming (?) capital not in Nanjing but in Nanchang.

The same pattern to be found in other novels can be seen here as well: the insertion at the beginning of a double-paged map of China in color and four color portraits of the principal characters in the book, and within the text of each volume as well are double-paged inserts here and there. Inside the front cover to the right of the title, it reads: 'Kaei 7 [1854], Kōin, eighth lunar month, engraved for printing.'[b] To the left it reads: 'Prohibited from sale or purchase.' Beneath the title, the words 'Yamatoyo ken' is probably an assumed name of the bookshop that printed it.

On the map of Qing China that appears at the very beginning of the text, the sites captured by the Ming army (?) are colored in pink, and the following explanation is added:

China is divided into two capitals and eighteen *sheng* (provinces). A *sheng* is comparable to the five central provinces and seven districts (*goki shichidō*) of Japan. The characters for each province are drawn within boxes [on the map]. A *fu* is the site of the walled city of a feudal lord. A [descendent] of the Ming house arose and made Nanchang-fu in Hunan province his temporary capital. [In the body of this work, it is noted that Hunan used also to be called Jiangxi.] The reign title selected was Tiande. Until this point the territory taken by this Ming was divided by colors [on the map], and gradually thereafter what fell under Ming control was incorporated in later [cartographical] editions. Great attention was paid to detail.... At this time, in addition to the land held by the Ming, there are altogether 48 states (*guo*) and four islands. Distances are far vaster than in Japan.

On this map one finds the provinces of Guangdong, Guangxi, Hubei, and Hunan occupied; also, the cities of Anqing and Zhenjiang in Jiangnan province (?) are placed under occupation. However, Nanjing, which is placed in Jiangsu province, is drawn far to the north in still unconquered terrain.

There is an author's preface at the start of the body of the work. It begins:

111

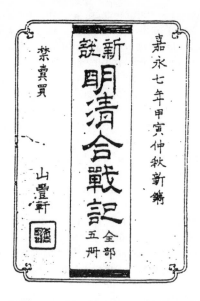

Inside Front Cover of *Shinsetsu Min Shin kassen ki* (Kansai University Library)

This book was the plan of a certain man who sought me out to compile and write it rapidly. Hence, there was no time to embellish the composition, and being very busy I completed the draft with numerous miswritten characters left uncorrected.... The change in title of the book from *Minmatsu gunki* (Records from the End of the Ming) to [*Shinsetsu Min Shin*] *kassen ki* was done at the insistence of the book buyer. The author laments that it is difficult to eke out a living freely. Be that as it may, in need of cash as I am, I had to cater to the current fashion. Yet, having heard from others of the declining state of affairs in the world, I recorded it in a rough and haphazard manner so as to call concerned people's attention to the climate of the time.

What he was effectively saying here is that he was asked to compile this work in great haste, that the idea of changing the original title from *Minmatsu gunki* to *Shinsetsu Min Shin kassen ki* was that of the bookstore, and that his readers need bear in mind the trends of the times, for in order to complete this draft he had no choice but to cater to 'current fashion.' It is known that at that time bookstores competed to put out books of this sort that 'informed' readers about trends in the world. At the very end of the passage cited above, we read: 'Recorded again by compiler Suzunari' but no details about this 'Suzunari' are forthcoming.

The text itself of this work begins with the defeat of the Chinese in the Opium War:

National prestige declined. [China] was disdained by foreign states and its own masses were disobedient.... Civil and military officials alike engaged in amusements; they were negligent in military preparedness and did not govern the people well.... The realm was in a state of disorder. Gradually governance lost its vigor, and mighty bandits arose in many places, burning down homes and slaying people. Though [the bandits] plundered wealth and violated women, local officials were far too weak to do anything about it. Though aware of these [bandits' activities], they did not pursue them. They paid no attention to the sorrows of the common folk beneath them, and in the sad situation of the ordinary people everyone – old and young, male and female, the wise and the not so wise – harbored resentment for their superiors.

The very first item discussed here is the contemporary social setting with its possibility of spawning a rebellion. Because of such a situation, a heroic female figure by the name of Dong Huaniang emerges, raises an army in Lushuang (?) county, Fujian, and becomes the leader of a Ming dynastic revival. She proceeds to travel to Hunan province to visit Zhu Wu, the last descendent (illegitimate offspring of last Ming pretender) of the Ming house who is just then engaged in a peasant uprising, and then she returns to Fujian. After numerous battles with the armies of the Qing dynasty, she succeeds in returning Zhu Wu to the Ming throne. Two men, General Gan Zhao and his brave retainer Zheng Tianlin, who came to her assistance in the cause of reviving the Ming frequently engaged Qing forces as well as ambitious British forces who were helping the Qing. She later moves her base of operations from Fujian to Nanchang in Jiangxi province, builds a walled city there, and makes it the national capital of the Ming. Inaugurating the Tiande reign, Zhu Wu accedes to the throne and enfeoffs his meritorious subjects. To this place armed forces of the Qing (with British troops as well) lay siege, and just at this point the novel comes to an end.

At the very end of the work, there is an author's postscript which reads much like the preface: 'The author notes: I have compiled in this draft stories precisely as they were conveyed to me, and thus there are no few errors of pagination and omission.... I haven't the time to enumerate the large number of mistakes. The reason is that I was in such a great hurry.'

Unlike the other novels of this sort, the *Shinsetsu Min Shin kassen ki* created a story line that is tied up with the descendents of Zheng Chenggong. It begins in its opening lines with the appearance of Dong Huaniang and is in effect a tale of the origins of 'Caozhong' (the tomb of Cao) which was erected by local people to commemorate Zheng Chenggong's mother who committed suicide. Dong Huaniang's mother, Fangshi, is violated by a 'general' (a note in the original mentions the similarity of this post to that of the ancient Japanese military commissioner) in Fujian because of her beauty. She escapes and throws herself into a mountain stream. Her body subsequently washes up on shore at the place with the 'Caozhong' stele, but 'Caozhong' was the stone monument erected by the local villagers who had earlier buried the corpse of Zheng Chenggong's mother which had come ashore, following her suicide. Fangshi floats ashore, and when the prayer is being intoned at 'Caozhong' the stone pillar falls to the ground. The story arose that Fangshi had been pregnant just at that time, and the child born to her was Dong Huaniang. We thus find first among the portraits at the beginning of the text 'Leader of the Revival of the Great Ming, Dong Huaniang,' followed by 'Brave, Meritorious Subject in the Revival of the Great Ming, the Koxinga of Today, Zheng Tianlin' and 'Commander-in-Chief of the Revival of the Great Ming, Gan Zhao, the Master of Qilong.'

Though Dong Huaniang was a completely fictitious character, in the novel Zheng Tianlin is regarded as a descendent of Zheng Chenggong, and Gan Zhao is taken to be a descendant of Gan Hui who was a general under Zheng Chenggong. Zheng Chenggong and his general Gan Hui were two men who, after the death by strangulation in Beijing (in 1644) of the last Ming emperor Zhongzhen during the rebellion of Li Zicheng, defended the legitimacy of the Ming dynastic house in south China and resisted Manchu forces to the bitter end. The author of the *Shinsetsu Min Shin kassen ki* used their descendents as figures in his work, but when they hear that Dong Huaniang has raised an army to revive the Ming, the author has Zheng and Gan hurry to Fujian from Taiwan to come to her assistance.

Zheng Chenggong opposed the invading Manchu armies and on many occasions fought against them. Although he took the city of Nanjing, he was defeated, and in the end he escaped to Taiwan. Making that island his base, he continued his resistance from there until his death. (His father, Zheng Zhilong, had switched sides midway and joined the Manchus). His mother was Japanese (née Tagawa), and he had occasion to request military support from the Tokugawa shogunate. His name seems to have become known early on in Japan as well as China. In particular, he was dramatized as Watōnai, the protagonist in *Kokusen'ya kassen* (The Battles of Koxinga) by Chikamatsu Monzaemon (1653–1724), produced on the stage in Ōsaka at the Takemoto Theater in the fifth year of the Shōtoku reign (1715). (Gan Hui too appeared in the play as the husband of Kinshōjo, Zheng's half-sister by a different mother). It was a phenomenally popular play, enjoying a long run of over three years and eliciting heartfelt applause. He became a widely known hero with whom many felt on intimate terms. Perhaps herein lies the background to his use in the *Shinsetsu Min Shin kassen ki*.

Though Gan Hui appears as a courageous general under the command of Zheng Chenggong in volume eleven of the *Mingji nanlüe* (Southern Strategy at the End of the Ming) (with an autobiographical preface dated Kangxi 10 [1671])[c] by Ji Luqi, he also appears as a strategic commander in a work by the Qing period scholar Xu Nai, *Xiaotian jinian fukao* (Chronicles of [an Era of] Small Prosperity, with Appended Annotations) (20 *juan*, preface dated Xianfeng 11 [1861]), which provides material for a study of the history of the Southern Ming – namely a history of anti-Qing resistance that continued to protect the

114

descendent of the house of Ming following the rout from Beijing and escape into southern China. In this last work, his name is written with the Chinese characters 甘輝. When Zheng Chenggong attacked Nanjing, this text describes how Gan Hui met his heroic end: 'His horse stumbled and he was captured. Gan was to be beheaded, but his martial will could not, it was said, be diverted. Sword in hand, he continued relentlessly to heap abuse [on the enemy] and he ultimately met his fate.'[1]

We know from historical materials of the period that Gan Hui lost in his battle with Qing forces, was captured, imprisoned, and died after shattering his own skull. Roughly this same story is conveyed in the *Min Shin tō ki* (Account of the War between the Ming and the Qing) (ten *juan*, with a preface dated Kanbun 10 [1670], compiled by Maezono Sōbu, a resident of Nagasaki [see Chapter 28 below]), an early text in Japan that told of the anti-Manchu struggles at the end of the Ming. Well after this work, a novel entitled *Min Shin gundan Kokusen'ya chūgi den* (Account of the Loyalty of Koxinga in the Tales of War between Ming and Qing) (ten stringbound volumes, neither author's nor [possibly] translator's name given) was published in Kyōhō 10 (1725).[d] In it, Gan Hui appears with the Chinese characters 函輝 (actually, Han Hui), and he convinces Zheng Chenggong to drive the Dutch army out of Taiwan and make that island his base of operations. Then, he himself proceeds to Taiwan, engages the Dutch in battle, and returns in compliance with Zheng's command. However, as the text continues, he is defeated as a result of the betrayal to the Qing forces of Zheng's uncle (while serving as governor-general of Simingzhou, the ancient name for Xiamen in Fujian); he comes to the aid of Zheng's wife (née Lin) and their children, and flees into the sea. The *Shinsetsu Min Shin kassen ki* seems to have a taken a hint from this work.

One further work, the *Zheng Chenggong zhuan* (J. *Tei Seikō den*) (Biography of Zheng Chenggong) by Zheng Juzhong (two *juan*, with a preface [in the Japanese edition] dated Meiwa 8 [1771]), printed and with Japanese reading punctuation by Kimura Kenkadō, may have been a source of inspiration to *Shinsetsu Min Shin kassen ki* inasmuch as both raise to center stage Zheng Tianlin, the descendent of Zheng Chenggong, and Gan Zhao, the descendant of Gan Hui, and have them leading the anti-Qing military forces. One possible reason for this connection is that the name of Gan Hui appears repeatedly – to an extent not found in other historical materials – in the Japanese reprinting of the *Zheng Chenggong zhuan*.[e]

The author of the *Shinsetsu Min Shin kassen ki* seems to have been a rather well read person. He cites such other works as *Qing su jiwen* (Account of Qing Customs) and *Jingchu suishiji* (Almanac of Chu)[f], and he inserts explanatory notes for toponyms and names of bureaucratic posts.

Chapter Twenty

Ōshio Heihachirō and Legends from the Taiping Rebellion

I have thus far offered short analyses of the various novelizations that took their material from the Taiping revolution, published in Japan during the late-Edo period. I should like at this point in the discussion to insert one major work of dramatic fiction which adopted not the style of a novel but that of historical exegesis, a work undertaken in the Taishō era, for it offers an aspect that adds considerable color to the history of Sino-Japanese relations.

I have in my collection of books a pamphlet of over 40 pages, entitled *Nankin hishi* (Secret History of Nanjing). This work bears the subtitle: 'Iwayuru Chōhatsuzoku no shinsō' (The True Facts about the 'Long-Haired Bandits'). Needless to say, 'Long-Haired Bandits' refers to the Taiping rebels themselves, and the imprint indicates that it was published in 1944 by 'Dai Ajia kensetsusha' (Greater East Asian Construction Company) (in Tokyo).

According to the pamphlet's preface, this edition is a reprint of a work by Mr. Iguchi Toraji, owner of the Shidansō, and had appeared the previous year in the journal *Dai Ajia*. In addition, it was published together with 'Ōshio Heihachirō ron' (On Ōshio Heihachirō) by Maki Tsuneharu, which also appeared in the same magazine in 1944. It is similar in content to an essay, entitled 'Ōshio Heihachirō' (*Chūō shidan*, 1921)[1] by Ishizaki Tōgoku which I had read earlier. He essentially summarized that work, changing the sentences somewhat, making it less rigid, and simplifying the cited passages analyzed in the work.

Toward the end of the Meiji period, historian Kōda Shigetomo (1873–1954), general editor of *Ōsaka shi shi* (A History of the City of Osaka),[a] published a detailed study of Ōshio Heihachirō (1793–1837) and the rebellion he led, based on important historical sources (though he does not give each and every title of the documents used): *Ōshio Heihachirō*.[b] Also, Mori Ōgai obtained a manuscript on Mino paper (handwritten, 27 pages) entitled *Ōsaka Ōshio Heihachirō bankiroku* (Accounts of Ōshio Heihachirō of Ōsaka) which is primarily a collection of stories and historical documents; and, filling in the blanks with the 'historical facts' based on Kōda's research, Mori wrote his fictional biography,

116

Ōshio Heihachirō, in the early Taishō years. He also included as an appendix a chronological biography.[c2]

A section entitled 'The Truth' in the *Nankin hishi* accepts as 'true' the material in Ishizaki's aforementioned 'Ōshio Heihachirō.' By the same token, it denies as 'falacious' the writings on this subject by Kōda and Mori. The essence of 'The Truth' is that Ōshio Heihachirō and his adopted son Kakunosuke fled Ōsaka after the uprising, escaped to Amakusa, and from there proceeded to Nagasaki where they became acquainted with one Zhou Yunshan, a leader of the 'Society of God-Worshippers,' a group opposed to the Qing dynasty, who had also taken refuge in Nagasaki. Zhou Yunshan was later to become Feng Yunshan (the Southern King), one of the leaders of the Taiping Rebellion, and with him they all traveled to Fujian, China. They then replaced Zhu Jiutao, leader of the Society of God-Worshippers, and were ceded the leadership. Heihachirō installed Kakunosuke as leader of the Society and remained himself in the background, but eventually came to take a commanding role in the revolutionary activities of the Taipings. Kakunosuke was, according to this record of the events, none other than Hong Xiuquan.

As historical materials upon which this account is based, the text cites suspicious stelae, hearsay accounts verbatim, random quotations from writings concerned with the Taipings that had come from China, and the like. The argument is advanced in an audacious manner based on wild speculation, and it concludes by noting that the material can be 'believed.'

This, however, might lead one to believe that admirers of Ōshio revered his character, supported his motives in rising in rebellion, and expressed their profound compassion and overwhelming sentiments of anguish at his frustration. The Ōshio rebellion is depicted in the following manner:

> Chūsai [Ōshio] opposed the tyranny of the shogunate [for taking no measures to help the people of Ōsaka who were suffering in a famine at that time] and raised the banner of resistance. Believing that he would martyr himself for the impoverished people, he seems much like a socialist, though his ideas were actually not like those of modern socialism. As a result of Wang [Yangming's] teachings, he did believe in equality based on the notion that all people are the same.... Thus, Chūsai's rising is not without points of resonance with socialism.

So argued Inoue Tetsujirō in an analysis of Ōshio's thought on the basis of the latter's *Senshindō sakki* (Notes from the Cavern of a Cleansed Mind).[d3]

In an appendix to his *Ōshio Heihachirō*, Mori Ōgai similarly noted that 'Heihachirō's thought was a still unawakened socialism.' Clearly such a rebellious motivation behind Ōshio's uprising shared a great deal with the causes of the Taiping Rebellion. Perhaps, argues Mori, they may have sought to revive Ōshio's thought and deeds in the Taiping revolutionary movement on the mainland. He sought to present a great drama by praising the 'heroic enterprise' of Ōshio's extremely weak rebellion which was crushingly defeated in a single day and by seeing it cross the sea to be realized in China.

117

While Ōshio did in fact rise in rebellion on behalf of the poor, starving people and oppose, plunder, and set fire to offices of the resourceless officialdom and to the homes of the merciless wealthy, his was an army of 'protest' (*kōgi*) against the officialdom and the affluent on behalf of 'helping the people' (*kyūmin*), and it was not a 'revolution' aimed at replacing the core power in the structure of political control. We know this from the placards of the movement which read: 'We are not rising out of a desire to seize the realm for ourselves.' By contrast, Hong Xiuquan did rise in rebellion out of a desire to seize the reigns of government; he planned and carried out a nationalistic political revolution to overturn the perceived enemy in the political structure of Qing control, organized a peasant army (at first made up of coal miners), fought in many places against the armies of the Qing dynasty, and established his own regime which lasted altogether for fifteen years. The main purposes of these two uprisings were thoroughly different from the time of their inceptions.

Oyabe Zen'ichirō authored a book entitled *Chingisu Han wa Minamoto no Yoshitsune nari* (Chinggis Khan was Minamoto no Yoshitsune).[e] The story that Yoshitsune's (1159–89) suicide at Kinugawa was a deception and that he actually fled to Ezo and from there to the continent has long found expression in writing, but Oyabe in one fell swoop resuscitated Yoshitsune as Chinggis Khan. Adopting a similar motif, a plot of a heroic tranformation is constructed whereby Ōshio Heihachirō too is revived on the mainland, turned into a hero who sweeps over and subdues some fifteen or sixteen provinces of China, and whose adopted son Kakunosuke attains the position of the 'Heavenly King.' Authors of such fictional treatments concocted their historical dramas with conceptions at a different dimension. I have written about this phenomenon in a short essay entitled 'Henshin no rekishi dorama' (Disguised Historical Dramas), and let me now say a few things of a more concrete nature about it.

The Ōshios, father and son, were defeated on the nineteenth day of the second lunar month of Tenpō 8 (1837), and they attempted to escape toward Yamatoji, but seeing the strict watch surrounding them, they turned and went in the direction of Kawachi, finding their way back to Ōsaka during the evening of the 24th. There they took refuge in the home of one Gorōbee of the Miyoshiya storehouse in Aburakakemachi. Gorōbee was a wholesaler of toweling (including calicos and blue-dyed objects). For many years, he had frequently visited the Ōshio family and owed them a debt for his financial circumstances. However, the Ōshios had now suddenly shown up dressed as monks and asking a great favor of him, to shelter them in a small back room at the rear of his house. They were later discovered, and on the 27th of the fourth lunar month of 1837, the local constabulary attacked the Miyoshiya storehouse. Ōshio committed suicide by setting fire to the room in which he was holed up, and Kakunosuke was also discovered as a charred corpse (there were stories as well that he was stabbed to death by his father). This is how Kōda tells the tale in his *Ōshio Heihachirō*. Inoue Tetsujirō and Mori Ōgai describe the end of the Ōshios in the same manner.

One can easily imagine that, at the time, the Ōshio incident was a great shock in the city of Ōsaka, and it would seem that a wide variety of manuscripts appeared that chronicled (and added tidbits of hearsay to) the incident.[4] Kōda cites scarcely a single document, while Ishizaki's *Ōshio Heihachirō den* (Biography of Ōshio Heihachirō)[f] is a painstaking work which cites numerous texts (and throws in some rumors) and memoranda; it is written as a meticulous 'chronological biography.' The very end of this work carries a passage entitled 'Sensei fushi jifun setsu' (The Theory That Ōshio and His Son Burned Themselves to Death):

> The deafening roar of gunfire could already be heard indoors. A fire then broke out in the room. When they saw the fire, people were terribly confused and did not know what to do. They tried to put the fire out, but in searching through it they discovered the corpses of two persons. Upon investigation they turned out to be Buddhist monks. Their bodies were scorched from head to foot, and their countenances were undetectable. The two corpses lay prostrate. There were roundtrip tickets in their pockets, which read: Monks Raimon and Kan'ei of the Tenryūji. Ōshio was using the name Raimon, and his son Shōshi [an earlier name of Kakunosuke's] was using the name Kan'ei. And, so father and son left this world together as martyrs. However, some people did not believe this story. It was said that they escaped and were living in Tsukushi [in Kyūshū]; others said they had traveled to China.

Ishizaki's theory of Ōshio as leader of the Taiping Rebellion may have developed from this point, but in his *Ōshio Heihachirō den* there is not one mention of the Taipings.

Although I have done no special study of the Ōshio uprising, manuscripts have occasionally caught my eye, and I have three in my possession at present. One such work is a small-sized volume on Mino half-pages entitled *Naniwa Ōshio sōdō ki* (Account of the Ōshio Rebellion in Ōsaka). In the afterward, the author writes: 'Composed in the first ten days of October of Tenpō 13' (1842). In content, it is essentially a collection of historical documents, including placards from the time Ōshio rose in rebellion, the battle arrays from his sorties, the names of neighborhoods afflicted in fires, various personal descriptions and personnel records given at the time, and the roadside prohibition and edict boards set up by the shogunal authorities.

Another of these manuscripts is a work in one stringbound volume on Mino paper and reads 'Naniwa ashi' (Reed of Ōsaka) on its outside cover. On its first page, though, it reads '*Ōshio gyakubō jikki* jo' (Introduction to *Account of the Rebellion of Ōshio*) by Yamada Seirin (Seizai), dated 'Tenpō 11 [1840], winter, eleventh lunar month,' and at the end it carries the title, *Ōshio sōran kikigaki* (Notes on the Ōshio Rebellion). According to the preface of this work, a man by the name of Ogura Naofusa 'collected information about the rebel Ōshio at the time and put them into a volume.' From the date of the preface, this took place roughly in the third year following the rebellion.

119

The third of these manuscripts is comprised of three stringbound volumes on Mino paper. It bears no title, but on its first page a long preface is included, 'by Hakuryū, at a temporary residence in Ōsaka, early autumn, Tenpō 8 [1837].' It says that the Ōshio rebellion took place in the second month of the year and that Ōshio and his son committed suicide on the 27th day of the third month; inasmuch as this preface was written in the seventh month, the work would have been compiled within only four or five months following the rebellion itself. It reads at one point: 'Having traveled around, I am now in Ōsaka. I took down information detailing [the rebellion] from start to finish while temporarily residing there, and compared it with [known] facts. There are ten volumes in all which I have called *Tenpō ran ki* (Account of the Uprising of the Tenpō Period).'

According to this account by Hakuryū, the text in my possession is 'comprised of various people's works and information taken down verbatim in discussions with older people.' This would indicate that he corroborated his data with other historical documents. Yet, the manuscript I have seems to be merely excerpts from an original text and not something separate from it. Furthermore, it is highly doubtful whether, as indicated in the preface, Hakuryū was actually a traveler who took up temporary residence in Ōsaka.

Kōda, whose work we cited above, noted that Ōshio and his son took refuge in the Miyoshiya, set fire to the place, thus committing suicide, and their charred remains were subsequently discovered. In his *Tenpō ran ki*, Hakuryū claims:

Heihachirō died, his body entirely consumed by the flames and his visage and abdomen by no means distinct. In his pocket there was a roundtrip ticket, and inasmuch as it was not burned up in the conflagration, it was removed. It turned out to be a ticket from Tenryūji. Heihachirō was using the name Raimon, and Kakunosuke was using the name Kan'ei. Both men had the appearance of having taken the tonsure.

In the *Ōshio gyakubō jikki* (namely, the *Ōshio sōran kikigaki*), the same account, though in rather less detail, is related:

Heihachirō had collapsed on his face, and thus a roundtrip ticket was removed from his pocket, undestroyed in the blaze. The ticket commenced from a Buddist temple named Tenryūji and was dated Tenpō 7 [1836], the previous year. He had taken the name Raimon, and Kakunosuke had the name Kan'ei. Both men appeared to have taken the tonsure.

Kōda too recounts how Heihachirō at first visited the Miyoshiya and goes on to say: 'The two men were dressed as Buddhist monks wearing a short sword in their dark gray cotton raincoats.' The accounts are also consistent on the point that Heihachirō and Kakunosuke took the tonsure once they had returned to Ōsaka. Though not written down in Kōda's *Ōshio Heihachirō*, perhaps because the author did not want to use material deemed merely hearsay, the information about the roundtrip ticket emanating from Tenryūji found in the pocket of Heihachirō's corpse and mention of the [Buddhist] pseudonyms of 'Raimon' and

'Kan'ei' were novel ideas used to dramatic effect by having the main characters transform themselves. From this data, the author of *Nankin hishi* notes that just at that time the two visiting priests, Raimon and Kan'ei, had come to rest at the home of Gorōbee: 'They decided that [the monks were] Ōshio and his son, set fire to the place, and killed the two monks. They then crucified the charred corpses whose faces were indistinguishable, thus quelling the uprising.' This is taken directly from what Ishizaki had already written.

Ōshio rose in rebellion on the nineteenth day of the second lunar month of 1837, and Gorōbee's Miyoshiya where he was hiding was attacked and he committed suicide on the 27th day of the third month (according to Mori Ōgai's chronological biography of him). For over a month after the rebellion, the whereabouts of its leader were completely unknown. In a section entitled 'Districts Hit by Arson' in the aforementioned *Naniwa Ōshio sōdō ki*, 47 *machi* (districts) and one village in Tenma are mentioned, 47 *machi* in Kamimachi, and 24 in Kitasenba, for a total of 118 *machi*. The number of homes destroyed by the fires is given as 3611, the number of ovens or hearths as 12,490, the number of vacant rental homes as 1168, the number of sheds as 223, and the number of storage facilities as 415. Because the leader of a rebellion that produced such an immense conflagration went unapprehended for over a month, his whereabouts remaining unknown, the shogunate's representative in Ōsaka Castle and the city magistrate were extremely irritated and initiated a frantic and earnest search. In the process, a wide variety of rumors and hearsay were naturally picked up.

Many and sundry inquiries and rumors that cropped up in the course of the search are recounted in *Tenpō ran ki*. These include: (a) when it was reported that he was holed up in Maya mountain, the search headed there, or he may have gone by boat to Takeshima, a deserted island in the Japan Sea between Okishima and Korea, and then continued from there to Korea; (b) he may have used Christian witchcraft, confined himself indoors deep in the remote mountains and solitary valleys, and there lived off the air; (c) he may have committed suicide and had an ally bury his corpse quietly, and then a new grave was dug for him amid the hills and fields where there were no landlords; (d) perhaps the authorities sent people to search for him in distant lands; (e) when they heard that, although there had long been some sort of evil man on Mount Kōya, those who entered the mountain never reappeared there, and they sent spies there to search for him there; and (f) ever since the days of Ōtōmiya, the 24 villages of the Totsukawa deep in the Yoshino Mountains have been a place of refuge (even now) for fleeing criminals, and thus these villages were a natural place for them to send men to apprehend him.

This sort of gossip was accepted as is in Ishizaki's *Ōshio Heihachirō den*.

The Ōshio incident became increasingly shrouded in mystery. Not only did this effectively reveal to the shogunate how completely incompetent the office of the Ōsaka Administrator was; they [stories] spread throughout the city as far as the suburban areas. Rootless and disorganized like the sound of the wind and the cry of the cranes, they attempted to regroup at Kōsan and then attacked Tenma. The people were insecure in their livelihoods; the city was surrounded and as if without any government. The longer the Ōshio rebellion continued, the more concern was cast on the authority of the Administrator's Office. Eventually they learned that suspicious persons were residing at the home of the dyer Gorōbee, who had had frequent access to Ōshio's home in Awaza. They resolutely decided that [these persons] were Ōshio and his son, and claiming quickly to be capturing them, set fire to the place in which they had been hiding and burned to death two itinerant monks from Tenryūji, Raimon and Eikan [Kan'ei?]. Ōshio and his son were by then completely burned, their bodies subsequently taken and crucified, with a placard hanging at the scene describing their crimes, and the incident came to an end. However, not one person believed this story. It was generally believed that Ōshio just had to be alive. One rumor that he was said to have boarded an American vessel and sailed to Ogasawara Island simply would not die, but in the midst of all this Ōshio fled to Amakusa in Hizen, and from there he boarded a commercial vessel bound for Nagasaki and took refuge in China.

As for the story that Ōshio went to Europe, Ishizaki cites the gravestone inscription of Akishino Teruashi (written by Akishino's son-in-law) which was erected in the tenth month of Meiji 23 (1890) at Tenryūji to the east of Ōsaka Castle. It reads in part:

> The venerable old man, known posthumously as Terusada, . . . assumed the name of Mr. Akishino. He lived in Ōsaka. In the spring of Tenpō 8 [1837], Ōshio Heihachirō rose in rebellion. Related to Ōshio through marriage, the venerable old man had long before joined in the plot. They were defeated, and Ōshio, his son, and twelve followers fled to Kawachi where they hid in a cave. Seven of them committed suicide. They then escaped by sea to Amakusa in Hizen. They remained there for over a year and then made their way by ship to China. After a long period of time, Ōshio and his son further hid their traces by making their way to Europe. The venerable old man returned to Nagasaki with three followers and there became a doctor, plying his trade between Amakusa and Shimabara.

Ishizaki also presents notes compiled by Akishino's widow (his last daughter apparently lived until about 1897) who denied the veracity of Ōshio's trip to Europe.

> In the search for Ōshio and the others, two monks were burned to death at the home of the calico-maker Gorōbee, and the matter was settled. Using this opportunity, Ōshio, his son, Akishino, and others fled for safety to Kyūshū. Father [i.e., Akishino] took refuge in the home of a relative, a

122

village headman in Amakusa by the name of Nagaoka Kōnosuke. He also became intimate with a Chinese merchant by the name of Zhou who lived in the Sūfuku Temple in Nagasaki. When he [Zhou] returned home, Ōshio and the others accompanied him to China and went to Huangpo [J. Ōbaku] Mountain. He stayed there for several years and then returned home soon, but the circumstances surrounding that are unknown. It was said that Ōshio and his son did not wish to return to Japan. Thus, the three of us returned to Nagasaki, because at that time Ōshio was said to have gone to Europe.

Ishizaki goes on from this point to note: 'For a period of time, Mr. Ōshio's trip to Europe enjoyed some currency, but in fact he never went to Europe and remained on Chinese soil.' Ishizaki argues that the Sūfuku Temple was empty and, with the destruction of the Ming dynasty, the Ōbaku monk Chōnen came there from Nagasaki, and through the good offices of the monks at the Sūfuku Temple, Ōshio and his son continued on to Huangpo Mountain in Fujian.

I would like next to examine if the rumor of Ōshio and son fleeing overseas was limited to the Ōsaka area or not. In his *Yūgei en zuihitsu* (Stray Notes in the Garden of Polite Accomplishments),[g] Kawaji Toshiakira claims that he learned of the Ōshio Rebellion on the 24th day of the second month from the head of Confucian Academy, but he was not particularly surprised by 'how extensive the matter was.' When he was in attendance at the castle on the 26th (Kawaji was then a *kanjō ginmiyaku*, financial comptroller), a courier came from Ōsaka to Edo and described the disposition of troops engaged to quell the uprising. Although the senior councilors had already withdrawn, Kawaji had heard rumors from Yabe Suruga no kami (then *kanjō bugyō* or superintendant of the finance office, former Nishimachi magistrate in Ōsaka): that Ōsaka had failed, that Hori Iga no kami (the Nishimachi magistrate) had fled to Kyoto, and that Atobe Yamashiro no kami (Higashimachi magistrate) had been hit by a cannon shell and had had his head blown to bits.

Kawaji noted: 'Heihachirō was a masterless samurai who proceeded to commit suicide in broad daylight, as it soon became clear to him that his position was untenable.' He compared it to how in times of peace people tied up their hawks and, because of a lack of military discipline at such times, people from ordinary homes would become frightened by the sounds of water fowl. A few lines later, though, he wrote: 'News arrived to the effect that Heihachirō died on the 27th and that day together with his son Kakunosuke committed suicide by being burned to death in the home of Gorōbee of the Miyoshiya in Aburakakemachi, Ōsaka. Their faces were burned beyond recognition.' He frankly admitted here his doubts, inasmuch the faces of the charred corpses were not at all clear.

In a letter to Egawa Tarōzaemon (1801–55), Watanabe Kazan (1793–1841) wrote as follows:

Item. Rumors in Bōshū have been circulating among the local people in the villages, when they go out fishing and hunting. For example, I have heard a story that Ōshio departed on an American vessel by sea. Although these are not very curious tales, a student by the name of Watanabe Kōhei [then a student in the Shōdō Academy] traveled to this area to hear these rumors; the painter Kano Sōtoku reported the same stories; and the doctor Satō Motokura passed them on as well. Thus, although I believe there are such stories and although I find it difficult to overlook or quickly detect them, we do not yet understand them fully. Have you heard any such [stories]? I would like to ascertain if there is any truth to them.[5]

Although the date of 'tenth month, 29th day' is entered on this letter, no year is recorded for it. If the American ship mentioned in the body of the letter was the Morrison, that would make it an event of the sixth month of Tenpō 8 (1837).[h] Ōshio's suicide took place in the third month of the year, and rumors of this sort were still current in and around the sixth month. Furthermore, while Kazan referred to the fact that 'these are not very curious tales,' one can still see that the idea of Ōshio's boarding the American vessel seemed incredulous to him. The mysteries surrounding Ōshio spread throughout Japan.

Perhaps Kazan may have had a particular interest in Ōshio. In 1834, the Tahara domain of Mikawa [in present-day eastern Aichi prefecture] hired Ōkura Nagatsune (1768–1856) as the director of industry to reform domainal finances. It was Kazan who had recommended Nagatsune in recognition of his scholarship. Nagatsune had lived in Ōsaka for a considerable period of time and seemed to have gotten to know Ōshio well. In his biography of Ōshio, Ishizaki notes: 'Ōkura Nagatsune was an old friend of [Ōshio] sensei.' In his biography of Nagatsune, Hayakawa Kōtarō includes a long letter from Ōshio addressed to Nagatsune, describing in great detail his state of affairs and mental attitudes following retirement; he also cites another letter, dated the seventh month probably of Tenpō 8 (1837), from Nagatsune in Tahara to a Mr. Ishii of Tanaka domain in Suruga [in present-day central Shizuoka prefecture], which states in part: 'I've received a letter from Ōshio ...' and 'my wife has gone to Ōshio's home, for she knows him well.'[6] From this evidence, Hayakawa argues that Nagatsune's wife (who was from Ōsaka) was probably related to Ōshio. This relationship between Nagatsune and Ōshio seems to have enabled Kazan to learn a considerable amount of information about Ōshio through Nagatsune.

In his *Naniwa sōjō kiji* (Account of the Riot in Ōsaka), Fujita Tōko paints a lively picture of the Ōshio rebellion.[7] According to it, Fujita wrote down precisely what he heard from Saitō Yakurō, in secret a fencer in Egawa Tarōzaemon's school and a shop employee: Possibly because Nirayama Intendant Egawa was responsible for coastal defense, he 'wanted above all else to embark on a maritime voyage, to go to Ōshima and Hachijōjima, and it was not at all easy to keep him confined indoors'; so, he sent Saitō to Ōsaka to check on Heihachirō's movements and investigate the Kinai area, in an effort either to arrest or kill Ōshio.[8]

Honda Tamesuke, who had long been on close personal terms with Ōshio, at the time of the uprising participated with the advance police force from Tamatsukuriguchi in quelling it and frankly recounted events from the fighting: 'At this time, while the castle warden and city magistrate pleaded openly to Edo, they temporized and in fact were in conflict.' He spoke with Yakurō, who had a letter of recommendation from Egawa, and recounted the cowardice of the administrator and the shrinking hesitation of the vanguard troops. These admissions would lead one to accept the account as highly reliable.

Yakurō, though, claims that he returned without having met Heihachirō, and when he came to Edo, news of the deaths of Ōshio and his son had already arrived via the shōgun's Ōsaka Castle representative. Tōko concludes: 'Although there was no doubt that in appearance the burnt body was that of Heihachirō, the townsmen who hid him were not so sure and we cannot say for certain that it was Heihachirō. Yakurō seems to have had his doubts, too.'

Maki Tsuneharu's 'Ōshio Heihachirō ron' (which is appended to the *Nankin hishi*) takes a extremely witty view of the notion that Ōshio and son escaped from Ōsaka:

> As the means most suitable to his escape from Ōsaka, Ōshio set a huge fire within the city. Naturally, as soon as the fire erupted, everyone in Ōsaka scrambled to escape with their property and goods in the vessels large and small that floated on the waterways accessible from all directions in the city.... Ōshio observed the situation, boarded a boat previously outfitted, and passed through the Inland Sea from the mouth of the Yasuharu River.... The local officials, as was their practice, imagined by virtue of their office that they would rapidly search in earnest through the hilly areas primarily of Yamato and Kishū. While smiling self-satisfiedly, they apparently discovered that he had made good his escape to Nagasaki.

Maki imagined that, if Ōshio did escape from Ōsaka and did make his way to China, this manner and route of escape were conceivable.

Chapter Twenty-One

Various and Sundry Images of Hong Xiuquan

On the matter of Ōshio's alleged meeting with Zhou Yunshan (later, Feng Yunshan) in Nagasaki and their trip together to China, Ishizaki Tōgoku notes: 'The problem here is the identity of Mr. Zhou, said to be a Chinese merchant, with whom Ōshio and his son embarked on their journey. In the various works we have examined, I recall a work by Ōkura Nagatsune, entitled *Kiyō ki* [Account of Nagasaki], which mentions this.' It is not clear what work this *Kiyō ki* refers to. I, for one, have never heard of such a work by Ōkura, and after a brief examination of his writings, no work by this title comes to the fore. Nonetheless, Ishizaki quotes from it as follows:

> Recently, a talented young Cantonese by the name of Zhou Yunshan came to Nagasaki. He is well-versed in both Dutch medical science and studies of the *Yi jing* (Classic of Changes). I gained considerably through a meeting with him, and if he were to wish to remain permanently on Japanese soil, I would make such a recommendation to the feudal lords. Last year Yunshan formed something called the Triads. He was arrested while spreading his [religious] message locally [in China] and by dressing up as a merchant escaped certain death. He now says that he has collected his books to take long-term refuge in Japan.

Ishizaki next turns to the frequent religious rebellions and riots in south China at that time, and he mentions the uprisings of the White Lotus and Tianli sects before looking at the uprising of the Triad rebels. He notes that the Triads, on suspicion of having plundered and pillaged while carrying on their evangelical work, met with repression by officials. Their leaders were executed, and others dispersed in every direction. One of those leader, Zhou Yunshan, beat a hasty retreat to Japan, he claims. And, with the dismemberment of the Triads, its remnant followers came together in the Society of God-Worshippers, which had already existed for some time, and gave it renewed strength. The Triads regarded heaven as father, the earth as mother, and the four seas as brothers; Ishizaki argues that they now moved another step forward by reverencing 'God.' This

Society of God-Worshippers was an organization founded, he notes, by a Cantonese named Zhu Jiutao in the early years of the Daoguang reign period, about the same time as the Triads formed.

Ishizaki then goes on to relate a fascinating story he learned from a man named Wang Wentai (allegedly a Japanese), an 'expert on Guangdong,' when he visited China. He prefaces the story by noting that 'it is based on points that are legendary.'

> One day three soothsayers visited the 'Society of God-Worshippers.' One was Hong Xiuquan, another was Feng Yunshan, and the third was known only as the 'great man from the Eastern Sea.' In other words, he was the teacher of Hong and Feng. Since Feng was a refugee from the 'Triads,' he was of course acquainted with Mr. Zhu [Jiutao], and he introduced the two men. I long lived in the enchanted land on the Eastern Sea, and having mastered the religion of the Triads, I returned home, and this man was none other than our teacher, the 'great man from the Eastern Sea.' In questions and answers with the 'great man from the Eastern Sea,' the latter won acclaim and thus came to gain control over the 'Society of God-Worshippers' as its religious leader.

At this point, Zhu Jiutao queries the 'great man from the Eastern Sea' over a period of three days, first about Daoism, then concerning Chan Buddhism, on to practices aimed at achieving immortality, and finally from matters of kings and usurpers to the realm to God (the original text marks this as Christianity).

> As a result, the 'great man from the Eastern Sea' refuted the arguments about practical affairs one by one, and Mr. Zhu surrendered. The 'Society of God-Worshippers' was ceded to the 'great man from the Eastern Sea.' Mr. Zhu ultimately went back and disappeared in Langshan [namely, the original base of the Society of God-Worshippers].

Ishizaki noted at the time that, if the 'great man from the Eastern Sea' was, at the time of this story, a Japanese, he was certainly an interesting fellow, whoever he was. He then goes on to explain the story in his own distinctive manner as follows. When he first heard the story from a friend ten years earlier, he had thought that it was some sort of fictional account (though he claimed never to have seen such a novelistic treatment), but the basis of the story of this now deceased friend 'was unfortunately much debated.' Whether based on fact or fiction,

> We only have conversational fragments from which we can reconstruct the gist of the story.... Be that as it may, without being too bold, *I believe* that the 'great man from the Eastern Sea' was our own 'Ōshio sensei' and that Feng Taoshan was the name adopted by Zhou Yunshan with whom he traveled from Nagasaki. As a result of this, *some now say* that Hong Xiuquan was Ōshio Kakunosuke [emphasis Masuda's].

127

By 'bold' he seems to have had in mind wild speculation.

The 'Society of God-Worshippers' has legendary aspects to it. Chinese historians have inquired into the background of this Hong Xiuquan, who it is said to have trained there. Hong was from Huaxian in Guangdong province, born in the seventeenth year of the Jiaqing reign [1812]. Early in his life, though, both of his parents died and he was left an orphan, traveling here and there to carry on his studies. He was a highly gifted young man, imposing physically, and talented, and he made a living through divination. Feng Yunshan, who hailed from the same area as Hong, launched the 'Society of God-Worshippers' and used his native talents to become a religious leader. When he was a child, he was separated from his parents and studied here and there. Thus, it was said that he was born deep in the mountains of Huaxian, but no one really knew if this was so.

This line of argument is that since scarcely anyone, it would seem, knew Hong Xiuquan or anything of his background, it may be justifiable to assume that Ōshio Kakunosuke furtively assumed his identity.

The portion of the text above that describes Hong Xiuquan is taken over almost entirely from 'Zei ming ji' (Record of Bandit Names) in the 'Fuji' (Supplementary Records) of the *Pingding Yuefei jilüe* (Brief Record of the Quelling of the Rebels of Guangdong and Guangxi) by Du Wenlan.[a1] In this work, we read as follows:

The leader of the rebels, Hong Xiuquan, came originally from Huaxian, Guangdong, and was born in Jiaqing 17 [1812]. His body[2] was chubby and he was somewhat literate. His father's name was Guoyou; and both he [Guoyou] and [Hong's] mother died when Hong was young. Xiuquan was a drinker and gambler [Ishizaki called him 'highly gifted and imposing physically']. He made a living by telling fortunes. Earlier, a devious man from Guangdong by the name of Zhu Jiutao had been preaching on behalf of the 'Society of God-Worshippers.' Xiuquan and his fellow local Feng Yunshan followed him [Zhu] as their teacher.[3] Later, Xiuquan became a religious leader.

The *Yuefei jilüe* was a Qing dynastic account and thus, of course, treated the 'rebel' Hong Xiuquan and his clique as 'rebellious bandits.' At the time, though, Hong Xiuquan was an unknown rebel leader with no rank who had suddenly emerged from a mountain village of Guangdong (Hong had failed the first stage of the civil service examinations several times). Other than those close to him, it would seem, his background was not at all widely known. The Qing military had certainly sent out spies and tried to gain information from captives, but only got rumors and stories which were many and conflicting.

The *Yuefei jilüe* was compiled by Du Wenlan from Xiushui, Zhejiang, when he was the Hubei salt distribution commissioner, on the orders of Huguang Governor-General Guanwen (1798–1871, a bannerman, style Xiufeng). He used as source material the reports based on memorials to the throne from a punitive force of the Qing army. This force, however, suffered many defeats; not only did it find it extremely difficult to garner information on the various groups of the rebel army, but it often embellished and fabricated material to its advantage.

Ishizaki's ideas are based on the accounts given in the *Yuefei jilüe*, as he simply conveyed the data from it and regarded Hong Xiuquan's background as unknown. Research in recent years has significantly clarified much about the family line, relations, youth, young adulthood, and other aspects of Hong's life.

Before Hong Ren'gan, Xiuquan's paternal cousin (nine years his junior), who from youth had been particularly close to Xiuquan and would later become the most powerful leader in the Taiping movement, joined the rebels at Nanjing, he was taken under the wing of a Swedish missionary by the name of Theodore Hamberg (Han Shanwen, 1819–54) who was preaching in the Guangdong region. Hamberg later wrote a work in English on the basis of what Hong Ren'gan told him in conversations and the notes Hong passed to him: *The Visions of Hung-Siu-tshuen and Origin of the Kwang-si Insurrection*. This was later translated into Chinese by Jian Youwen (Jen Yu-wen) as 'Taiping tianguo qiyi ji' (Record of the Taiping Uprising).[4] Thereafter, Hong Xiuquan's family relations and the character of the man himself as well as the early activities of the movement (with Feng Yunshan) became much better understood. The 'Taiping tianguo qiyi ji' was published in 1935, and it appeared together that year with a reprint of the 1854 English original.[b] Furthermore, Aoki Tomitarō translated it into Japanese under the title *Kō Shūzen no gensō* (The Visions of Hong Xiuquan)[c]; he used both the original published in Hong Kong and Jian's Chinese translation as a basis for his own edition.

The term Aoki used was 'visions' which appeared in the Chinese edition as 'strange visions.' Let me now say a few words about the nature of Hong's divine possession. When in 1837 Hong Xiuquan failed the local civil service examinations for the third time, he suddenly became ill (some say over the shock of failing the examinations). He rented a sedan chair, returned to his home town, and lay sick in bed, unconscious for 40 days. During this period he fell into an extraordinary delirium. In it he ascended to heaven and received a revelation from an old man with golden hair and a black coat; he fought with devils and exterminated evil demons; and he received the mandate of heaven and became king. He blurted out all manner of things to his father and elder brothers, so it was assumed that he was in the possession of devils. They summoned a faith healer to rid him of the devils, and they also called a doctor to try and heal him, but with no effect.

After about 40 days, his delirium abruptly cleared up, and he returned to his normal self. Later, he had occasion to read *Quanshi liangyan* (Good Words to Admonish the Age), which he had long owned, a work distributed by a man by the name of Liang Fa, who had worked among the missionaries on the streets of Guangzhou. He discovered in it many things that fit well with his experiences in the extraordinary spiritual world of his great illness some years earlier. Finally, he converted to Christianity and began to spread the gospel among the people. His many 'visions' from his experiences while under the influence of intense delirium are described in Hamberg's work.

Toward the end of 1935, Jian Youwen visited Hong Xiuquan's home village of Guanlubu in Huaxian, was shown the clan geneology of the Hongs (one of the branch families thereof), and subsequently published a report on the many historical materials he examined there: 'You Hong Xiuquan guxiang suo dedao de Taiping tianguo xin shiliao' (New Historical Sources on the Taipings Discovered on a Visit to Hong Xiuquan's Native Place),[d] replete with the numerous photographs he had taken at the time. Luo Xianglin too made an investigative trip to Hong Xiuquan's native village in the spring of 1936 and wrote up a report primarily concerning Hong's family line: 'Taiping tianguo Hong Tianwang jiashi kaozheng' (A Textual Study of the Lineage of the Taiping Heavenly King Hong).[e]

From these reports, there is no evidence of his having taken another surname as one would expect from the rumors (and Qing military information) mentioned above. As for the origins of Hong's family, their ancestors (details can be found in Jian's study) were Hakkas who moved from Jiaying department (now, Meixian), Guangdong province, to reclaim remote terrain in a village in the mountains, living off agriculture and rearing cattle.

Much has been written on the basis of these historical materials about Hong Xiuquan's origins in a variety of books by specialists on the Taiping Rebellion: Guo Tingyi, *Taiping tianguo shishi rizhi* (Daily Historical Record of the Taiping Rebellion)[f]; Luo Ergang, *Taiping tianguo shigao* (Draft History of the Taiping Rebellion)[g]; and Jian Youwen, *Qing shi Hong Xiuquan zaiji* (Historical Record of Hong Xiuquan in the Qing),[h] among others. In particular, the first chapter, entitled 'Tianwang Hong Xiuquan zhi chushen' (The Origins of Heavenly King Hong Xiuquan) (running a total of 43 pages) of volume one of Jian Youwen's magnum opus, *Taiping tianguo quanshi* (Complete History of the Taiping Rebellion),[i] a work in three volumes and 2318 pages, comprises a detailed examination on the basis of a broad range of sources; Jian again went to Hong's native place and adds notes gleaned from his descendents and local old-timers. It is the most detailed study.

Let me now turn to several features of Hong's life. He was born in 1814; his father was named Jingyang, his grandfather Guoyou, his elder brother Renfa, and his next elder brother Renda. At age seventeen he worked as a village school teacher, and on three successive occasions he traveled to the provincial capital to sit for the *xiucai* examinations; each time he failed. Around this time he received a religious tract, entitled *Quanshi liangyan* from a Christian missionary in the streets of Guangzhou. This work is now no longer extant in China, but an edition of the Guangzhou printing held in the Harvard University Library was reissued by the Taiwan publisher Xuesheng shuju in 1965; the new edition includes as well a long explanatory text by Deng Siyu with the title 'Quanshi liangyan yu Taiping tianguo geming zhi guanxi' (The Relationship between

Good Words to Admonish the Age and the Taiping Revolution). Later, under the influence of this work, Hong became a Christian. Together with his friend and fellow native Feng Yunshan (who apparently did not undergo baptism), he founded the Society of God-Worshippers and began their proselytizing activities. This work was one sort of missionary tract written by a Cantonese by the name of Liang Fa (or Liang Afa) who received baptism at a branch of the London Missionary Society set up in Guangzhou by the British missionary Robert Morrison, and there Liang had helped Morrison in his work spreading the gospel.

A number of Japanese works on Chinese and Qing history, written in the early and mid-Meiji era on the basis of Qing court documents, frequently use the *Yuefei jilüe* as a principal source. For example, in volume 8 of the *Shinchō shiryaku* (Brief History of the Qing Dynasty),[j] by Satō Sozai (Bokuzan, 1801–91), we find the following:

Xiuquan's native place was Huaxian, Guangping [*sic*. Guangdong]. When he was forty or more years of age, he had long hair, wasp-like eyes [sic.], a broad visage, and a chubby body, and he was somewhat literate. His father's name was Guoyou; and both he [Guoyou] and [Hong's] mother died when Xiuquan was young. Xiuquan was a drinker and a gambler. He traveled along [China's] waterways, telling fortunes to support himself....[5] Earlier, a devious man by the name of Zhu Jiutao had been preaching the Christianity of the 'Society of God-Worshippers,' which was also known as the Three Dots Society.[6] Xiuquan and his fellow local Feng Yunshan followed him [Zhu] as their teacher. Soon thereafter, Xiuquan became the religious leader.

This information is taken directly from the *Yuefei jilüe*.

In volume 2b of a work entitled *Saikin Shina shi* (Recent Chinese History),[k] co-authored by Ishimura Teiichi and Kōno Michiyuki, we read:

Xiuquan was from Huaxian, Guangdong. He was somewhat literate and made a living by telling fortunes. Earlier, a devious man by the name of Zhu Jiutao had been preaching on behalf of the 'Society of God-Worshippers.' Xiuquan and his fellow local Feng Yunshan went there and took him [Zhu] as their teacher. Using their skills, they traveled to Guangxi and lived in Penghua Mountain.

This material also comes directly from the *Yuefei jilüe*.

It would be accurate to call Sone Toshitora's *Shinkoku kinsei ran shi* (Account of the Uprising of Recent Times in China)[l] the first history of the Taiping Rebellion written by a Japanese (later revised by Soejima Taneomi). In his introductory remarks, we read:

This book has a few small points that differ from works published at the time in our country, such as *Shinshi ran'yō* (A Overview of the History of the Qing) and *Gen Min Shin shiryaku* (Brief History of the Yuan, Ming, and Qing). As recorded in the preface to this work, I have written this on the basis not solely of Chinese books, but have read widely in foreign accounts and traveled to see the actual places.

However, when it comes to the question of Hong Xiuquan's origins, Sone largely follows the *Yuefei jilüe* account:

This man [Hong Xiuquan] was large in stature, cutting a gallant figure, imposing physically and broadly learned. He was born in Jiaqing 17 [1812] in Huaxian, Guangdong, and early in life lost his parents. Being poor and finding it difficult to acquire an education, he drifted from place to place, and over the course of time made contact with like-minded men. From time to time, he traveled along [China's] waterways, telling fortunes to support himself. Earlier, there was a devious man by the name of Zhu Jiutao had been preaching a religion that worshipped God. Xiuquan and his fellow local Feng Yunshan followed him [Zhu] as their teacher. After Jiutao's death, his followers all called upon Xiuquan to become their religious leader.

I am not entirely sure whether Ishizaki used these early- and mid-Meiji period Japanese writings on Chinese and Qing history or whether he directly took his material from Du Wenlan's *Yuefei jilüe*, but as we noted in a quotation above, following his discussion of Hong Xiuquan, he added:

As noted above, Hong Xiuquan, the founder of the Taiping Heavenly Kingdom, was born in Huaxian, Guangdong. As no one knew anything of his background, he and Feng Yunshan wandered aimlessly, reading fortunes, wearing their hair in an oddly long fashion. The year of his birth, Jiaqing 17, corresponds to Bunka 9 [1812] in Japan, making him just 26 [East Asian style – JAF] at the time of Ōshio's uprising. That makes him the same age as Kakunosuke. Just because they were the same age does not, of course, make them the same person, but there certainly were not many men wandering about Guangdong with long hair, reading fortunes. When you put together the stories to the effect that a refugee from the 'Triads' [Zhou Yunshan] came from an enchanted land in the Eastern Sea with his teacher, then the time and personages *certainly do fit* Ōshio and his son [emphasis Masuda's].

This is really a piece of wild speculation.

While Hong Xiuquan was said to have been a man from Huaxian, Guangdong in Chinese works, Ishizaki denies this by asserting that Hong was none other than Ōshio Kakunosuke. He goes on to say: 'In fact, to avoid the Opium War, the three men [Ōshio, father and son, and Zhou Yunshan] made their way by reading fortunes from the Fujian region and drifted ashore at Guangdong. Perhaps it is a fact that they took control over the "Society of God-Worshippers."' Furthermore, on the subject of the Society of God-Worshippers, he adds the following, idosyncratic explanation:

> The Society of God-Worshippers is based in Daoism to which it adds Christianity. It is extremely superficial. With this foundation, Zhou Yunshan admired Ōshio *sensei*. Although Ōshio *sensei* reverenced the teachings of Wang Yangming, he was a man of great self-discipline, well-versed in Daoism, Zen, and particularly Christianity. Thus, in questions concerning religious principles, he clearly surpassed Zhu Jiutao, but because of this he had no desire to be the religious leader of the Society of God-Worshippers. His approach to religious instruction in such a case as this in which the times and human feelings were so thoroughly different could have been Daoism or perhaps classicism or perhaps religion. When *sensei* saw this, *doubtless* he then allowed Hong Xiuquan [or Kakunosuke] and the talented Zhou [or Feng Yunshan] to proselytize in the Society of God-Worshippers entirely with Christianity and so pass on his religious beliefs [emphasis Masuda's].

We know from a memorial sent from the Qing military in the field at the time that Zhu Jiutao was a Triad leader. However, since the natures of the Triads and the Society of God-Worshippers which was Christian were different, it would have been extremely strange for Zhu Jiutao who allegedly founded the Triads (?) to have reorganized the Society of God-Worshippers. This is thus probably just a story of the time. After the fall of the Ming dynasty, the Triad organization was a secret anti-Qing (anti-government) society in south China that came together on the basis of a nationalistic (pro-Han) ideology to 'revive the Ming.' Although Zheng Chenggong (Koxinga) was said to have been a proponent of it,[7] it was originally a secret society with branch organizations in various locales (each with its own leader and often with different names). One can find a wide assortment of theories about it in the historical sources, but I cannot fathom on which basis Ishizaki put forward the idea that the Triads were formed in the early Daoguang reign of the Qing period by Zhu Jiutao. We know much of the inner workings of the Triads, because Tao Chengzhang, a friend and fellow local of Lu Xun as well as an activist who led the Guangfuhui, or Restoration Society, a late-Qing revolutionary organization, was connected to the Triads at that time. Just after the 1911 Revolution, though, he was assassinated in a power struggle with a member of the group.

There are a number of theories about the origins of the Triads (after Zheng Chenggong's death, perhaps beginning in the Kangxi reign, perhaps during the Yongzheng reign), but one of the most thoroughly researched works based in the sources (including Chinese documents held in the British Museum in London) is Xiao Yishan, 'Tiandihui qiyuan kao' (A Study of the Origins of the Triads).[8] Although no firm time period has been established for its formation, most scholars generally agree on the Kangxi or Yongzheng era. While it emerged as an anti-Qing group, it had many local leaders of various branch organizations, and some seem to have become bandit groups. At the time that the Taipings rose in rebellion, many were allied with the Triads on the point of opposition to the Qing dynasty, but the latter were frequently weak organizationally and were thus bought off by the Qing military. Luo Ergang's study, 'Taiping tianguo yu Tiandihui guanxi de wenti' (The Problem of the Relationship between the Taipings and the Triads),[9] gives numerous examples, on the basis of considerable research, of relations between the two groups at various sites.

As concerns Zhu Jiutao, I know of two studies: Xie Xingyao, 'Lao Wanshan yu Zhu Jiutao kao' (A Study of Lao Wanshan and Zhu Jiutao)[10]; and Luo Ergang, 'Zhu Jiutao kao' (A Study of Zhu Jiutao).[m] The latter relies on the account given in the *Yuefei jilüe*, arguing that Hong Xiuquan and Zhu Jiutao were, respectively, leaders of the Society of God-Worshippers and the Triads and had no mutual ties; and it explains in concrete terms the basis of why the *Yuefei jilüe* erroneously records that Hong took Zhu as his teacher. The main point here concerns a report to the Qing court from a military force on the scene about a deposition from a Taiping prisoner of war to the effect that Zhu was called the 'Taiping King.' In his study, Luo examines a number of such reports on the basis of a meticulous methodology. He convincingly shows that Zhu Jiutao was a pseudonym used by Qiu Changdao. Furthermore, in the first year of the Xianfeng reign (1851), the core of Zhu Jiutao's organization was wiped out in Hunan, and the Qing court sent an army to take him prisoner. Various reports confirm that in Xianfeng 5 (1855) Zhu Jiutao was captured at Chenzhou in Hunan.

In Japanese studies of Chinese history written in the early Meiji period, we find works that identify Hong Xiuquan, quite apart from the *Yuefei jilüe*, as the follower of one Hong Deyuan (not Zhu Jiutao) who became a religious leader. In volume four of his *Shinshi ran'yō*,[n] Masuda Mitsugu (Gakuyō, fl. 1877) notes:

> Hong Xiuquan was a man of Huaxian, Guangdong. When he was forty or more years of age, he could copy out writing and he was somewhat literate. His surname is unknown. He had earlier joined a religious association [earlier referred to as the Tiandinghui; its leader named as Hong Deyuan]. When Deyuan passed away, he [Xiuquan] assumed the surname Hong and replaced [Deyuan] as religious leader. In addition, he added Christianity and called himself the younger brother of Jesus and the younger, second son of the Heavenly Father Jehovah.

In his *Man-Shin shiryaku* (Brief History of the Manchu Qing dynasty)[o] as well, Masuda recounted basically the same facts about Hong Xiuquan.

In volume five of the *Gen Min Shin shiryaku*,[p] compiled by Ishimura Teiichi, we read:

> Hong Xiuquan was a man of Huaxian, Guangdong. When he was forty or more years of age, he had long hair, wasp-like eyes [*sic*.], a broad visage, and a fat body, and he was somewhat literate. His surname is unknown. He had earlier joined a religious association [the Tiandinghui]. When [Hong]

Deyuan [earlier mentioned as the head of this association] passed away, he assumed the surname Hong and replaced [Deyuan] as leader of the group. In addition, he added Christianity and called himself the younger brother of Jesus and the younger, second son of the Heavenly Father Jehovah.

These two works have essentially the same text here. They differ from the aforementioned *Shinchō shiryaku* and *Saikin Shina shi* which are thought to have been based on the *Yuefei jilüe* in that Hong Xiuquan, taking over from Hong Deyuan and not from Zhu Jiutao, inherits even the surname Hong and becomes leader of the religious group. Moreover, in these texts we find mention of neither the Triads nor the Society of God-Worshippers, but the Tiandinghui, although 'Tiandinghui' is thought to be a local provincialism for the Triads. As for the succession of leadership from Hong Deyuan to Hong Xiuquan, described in both of these texts, as well as the descriptive passages before and after, this is touched on only briefly as a rumor in an appendix to the *Yuefei jilüe*, although it appears to derive from a different source.

It seems as though the base text upon which these works were composed was the *Dunbi suiwen lu* (Random Notes of a Defended Nose) by Chuyuan Tuisou. 'Chuyuan Tuisou' was the pseudonym of Wang Kun who worked as a scribe in the Qing military camp engaged in battle with the Taipings.[q] His introductory remarks begin: 'Following the encampment, I assisted in drafting documents, as we swiftly rode through five provinces....' This text, the *Dunbi suiwen lu*, was among those transcribed in manuscript and brought back to Japan by Takasugi Shinsaku, Nakamuda Kuranosuke, and the others aboard the *Senzaimaru* which visited Shanghai in Bunkyū 2 (1862). It was about this time that the text first began circulating in Japan. There is an 1864 manuscript edition in two stringbound volumes of this work listed in the *Iwase bunko tosho mokuroku* (List of Books in the Iwase Collection) – the Iwase Collection can be found in Nishio city, Aichi prefecture. It initially became known in the manuscript edition, and it seems to have been printed with Japanese reading puctuation around the time of the Meiji Restoration (no date of publication is given) in three stringbound volumes. We turn next to a discussion of this work.

Chapter Twenty-Two

The *Dunbi suiwen lu* and Various Other Writings about the Taiping Rebellion

In 'Yuekou jilüe' (Brief Record of the Rebels of Guangdong and Guangxi), in *juan* 1 of the *Dunbi suiwen lu* (Random Notes of a Defended Nose), we read as follows:

> Hong Xiuquan was a man of Huaxian, Guangdong. When he was forty or more years of age, he had long hair, wasp-like eyes [sic.], a broad visage, and a fat body, and he was somewhat literate. His surname is unknown, though some say it was Zheng. In Daoguang 25 [1855] he went to Guangxi and joined a religious association. It so happened that when Hong Deyuan [mentioned earlier in the text as the leader of an association known as the Tiandinghui] passed away as a result of illness, he came to assume the surname Hong and replaced [Deyuan] as leader of the group.... In addition, he added Christianity and called himself the younger brother of Jesus and the younger, second son of the Heavenly Father Jehovah.

Comparing this account from the *Dunbi suiwen lu* with those of two texts cited earlier, the *Shinshi ran'yō* and the *Gen Min Shin shiryaku*, one can see that they are virtually identical. Inasmuch as both the *Shinshi ran'yō* and the *Gen Min Shin shiryaku* were written in Kanbun, they effectively lifted the sentences directly from the *Dunbi suiwen lu* as is. This parallels precisely the case of the *Yuefei jilüe* as compared to both the *Shinchō shiryaku* and the *Saikin Shina shi*.[a]

The *Dunbi suiwen lu* was printed with punctuation for Japanese readers and, it seems, enjoyed a rather wide readership in Japan. As noted earlier, apparently this work was originally brought to Japan by Takasugi Shinsaku (1839–67), Nakamuda Kuranosuke (1837–1916), Hibino Teruhiro (1838–1912), and the others who traveled to Shanghai aboard the *Senzaimaru*, the shogunate's trading vessel, between the fourth and seventh lunar months of Bunkyū 2 (1862).

In his *Yū-Shin goroku* (Five Records of a Trip to China),[b] Takasugi Shinsaku lists the 'books copied by Nakamuda,' and among them we find the *Dunbi suiwen lu*. There is a note in the text at this point which reads: 'Relied on a copyist in Nagasaki.' Because this was a 'book [that had been] copied,' we know that it was copied out in Shanghai and brought home to Japan, but we do not know if the original from which it was copied was a printed text or if it was a manuscript itself (the latter is more likely the case). However, in his *Nakamuda Kuranosuke den* (Biography of Nakamuda Kuranosuke),[c] Nakamura Kōya (1885–1970) mentions the maps and book titles of the volumes purchased by Nakamuda in Shanghai; we find there 'thirteen stringbound volumes of books and manuscripts concerning the Long-Haired Bandits.' Probably, the *Dunbi suiwen lu* was included among these.

In his *Zeiyūroku* (A Record of Warts and Lumps)[d] as well, Hibino Teruhiro first describes the Taiping Rebellion which he witnessed with his own eyes in Shanghai at the time and the population dislocations it caused. He then notes: 'I have written down over the past few days all matters concerning the bandits, having ascertained them particularly through the *Dunbi suiwen lu* which I myself copied out.' Thus, just like Nakamuda, Hibino too made a copy of this work and returned with it to Japan.

These men were the first Japanese to travel to Shanghai and see on the spot the 'Long-Haired Bandits' about whom firm knowledge was so difficult to come by in Japan till then. To that end, they appear to have made copies of such works describing circumstances at the time in considerable detail, before returning home with these materials. In addition to the *Dunbi suiwen lu*, we find among the list of 'books copied by Nakamuda' such texts concerning the Taiping Rebellion as: *Tianli yaolun* (Important Observations Regarding Heavenly Principles), *Taiping zhaoshu* (The Taiping Imperial Declaration), *Taiping lizhi* (Taiping Ceremonial Regulations), *Tianming zhaozhi shu* (The Book of Heavenly Decrees and Proclamations), *Zizheng xinpian* (A New Treatise of Aids to Administration).[e]

For the entry corresponding to the seventh day of the fifth lunar month [1862] in his 'Shanhai enryū nichiroku' (Daily Record of a Stay in Shanghai) (in his *Yū-Shin goroku*), Takasugi Shinsaku notes: 'The reverberations of gunfire were heard by all on land at dawn, and this had to have been fighting between the Long-Haired Bandits and the Chinese. I thought that if only I could go verify this [report] and see the fighting firsthand, I would be so happy.' In his entry for the tenth day of that same month, we find: 'At dusk a Dutchman came and told us that the Long-Haired Bandits were three *li* [about one mile] outside Shanghai. The next morning we would certainly be able to hear artillery fire. The [Edo shogunal] officials expressed great surprise, but I on the contrary was ecstatic.' And, several days later on the sixteenth: 'We again heard artillery fire all morning long.'

Under his entry for the seventh day of the sixth lunar month, we learn that the shogunal officials in the Japanese party made an inspection of the suburbs of Shanghai, and Takasugi accompanied them. 'Many small [Buddhist] temples were destroyed, the work of the hands of the bandits.' When they went to examine a Confucian temple, 'the English have lived here since the bandit rebellion began, and it has been changed into a barracks for troops. Inside the temple the troops sleep on their guns. What I saw was inexplicably deplorable.'

Although the foreign concession area was secure during the period when these Japanese visited Shanghai, in the outskirts of the city Taiping forces were just waiting for an opportunity. Just at that time, Loyal King Li Xiucheng had made his camp at Suzhou and was contemplating an attack on Shanghai. Thus, the men who traveled to Shanghai aboard the *Senzaimaru* wrote reports of this sort and brought back to Japan a variety of source materials on the Taipings.

No date is recorded for when the Japanese edition of the *Dunbi suiwen lu* was printed. At the end of the main text, we find: 'Prepared by Itō Yukimiki, Naniwa' (i.e., Ōsaka). This would clearly indicate who had punctuated the text, but the publisher remains unclear. A work in two stringbound volumes, entitled *Jinling guijia zhitan* (Account of the Plunder in Nanjing in 1853–1854 [publ. 1856]), by Xie Jiehe, which appears on the list of books brought back to Japan at the same time (as well as in Takasugi Shinsaku's account), was also printed with Japanese punctuation. On the inside of its front cover, it reads: 'Printed by the Nishodō, Naniwa, winter late in Meiji 2 [1868].' It also bears an inscription: 'Prepared by Takami Inosuke of Iga.'[f] This might mean that at about the same time the *Dunbi suiwen lu* was also printed in Japan.

I have in my possession two Japanese editions of the *Dunbi suiwen lu*. Both have the title on the inside front cover, and both carry the 'introductory remarks ... personally recounted by Chuyuan Tuisou' at the beginning of the text. They then carry a preface by Yao Jiyun, dated the eighth lunar month of Xianfeng *jiayin* or 1854, followed by the titles of each of the eight *juan* of the work. As cited above, we find in the first *juan*, 'Yuekou jilüe,' a brief biography of Hong Xiuquan who succeeds to the leadership of the Tiandinghui after the death of Hong Deyuan. The last page of the text (inside the back cover) where an inscription might be written is blank in one of my texts and carries just the following note in another: 'Japanese, Chinese, and Western Bookstore, Ogawa Gihei of Masuya-chō, Ōtsu, Ōmi domain.' Judging from the two facts that the Japanese punctuator given at the end of the text proper was 'Itō Yukimiki of Naniwa' and that the bookseller was 'Ogawa Gihei of Ōtsu,' it would seem that this work was published in the Kansai area. Furthermore, because dates of the 'application' and 'permission' (for printing) of the aforementioned *Jinling guijia zhitan* are recorded in the *Kyōhō igo Ōsaka shuppan shoseki mokuroku* (List of Books Published in Ōsaka from the Kyōhō Reign Forward),[g] while such information for the *Dunbi suiwen lu* cannot be found in such book lists, perhaps the initial Japanese punctuator of the text printed the work himself without permission.

Bibliographically speaking, it seems that the first printed edition of the *Dunbi suiwen lu* has not been passed down to the present, for it was apparently banned both by the Qing government and by the Taipings. In the opening statement of Xie Xingyao's 'Dunbi suiwen lu ba' (Postface to the *Dunbi suiwen lu*) (in his *Taiping tianguo congshu shisan zhong* [Thirteen Works in a Collection on the Taipings]),[h] he notes: 'This book is a work of the Xianfeng period, though its circulation was highly limited. Woodblock printed editions of it are exceedingly hard to come by now. Printed editions of it are extremely rare. Editions one may see today are either manuscripts or those printed in Japan.'

The *Taiping tianguo ziliao mulu* (Bibliography of Source Materials on the Taiping Rebellion)[i] mentions the *Dunbi suiwen lu* in eight *juan* and gives both a manuscript edition of Xianfeng 9 (1859) in one stringbound volume held in the Beijing Library as well as a privately printed edition by Wang Kun in two stringbound volumes, dated Guangxu 1 (1875), 'held by Xie Xingyao.'[j] Perhaps Xie obtained this latter private reprinting by Wang Kun after having written that 'editions one may see today are either manuscripts or those printed in Japan.' This 1875 edition of the *Dunbi suiwen lu* was the one used in volume four of *Taiping tianguo*, the documentary collection compiled by the Zhongguo shixuehui (China Historical Association) and published in 1952. (A comparison with the Xianfeng edition in the Beijing Library reveals a small number of discrepancies).

The manuscript editions of this text brought to Japan, as noted above, were from Bunkyū 2 or 1862, and the manuscript held in the Iwase Bunko dates to early in Bunkyū 4 or 1864 (in the second lunar month of that year, the reign title was changed to Genji). Both are thus manuscripts dating prior to the reprinting of Guangxu 1 (1875, which corresponds to Meiji 8). Hence, the text obtained in Shanghai by Takasugi and the others was either the Xianfeng edition or a copy made from it and brought back to Japan. As for the reprinting of Guangxu 1, I have seen three copies of it in the collection of Fujita Toyohachi (1869–1929), which is now in the Tōyō Bunko. They are all identical. However, the Tōyō Bunko's *Fujita bunko mokuroku* (List of Books in the Fujita Collection)[k] errs in giving the author of this work as Yu Qinsheng, apparently the result of some sort of misunderstanding.

In the 'introductory remarks' to the *Dunbi suiwen lu*, we read as follows: 'I was an expectant official in Guilin. Obeying my charge, I went to the encampment and wrote down correspondence. We covered five provinces. Along the way, I compiled a volume of recorded personal observations. After the bandits fled to the eastern provinces, I left my post on a plea of illness. I copied down reports and regularly recorded the discrepancies in the stories reported.' To elaborate a bit, he was at his bureaucratic post in Guilin, and then entered the military camp as assigned. There he became a scribe and rode about on campaigns with the Qing armed forces in their battles with the Taiping Army in five provinces: Hunan, Hubei, Jiangxi, Anhui, and Jiangsu. After the Taipings entered Shandong, he used the pretext of illness to quit his appointment. He then compiled a volume of reports, and unsubstantiated rumors were not, as a rule, included in it.

When Wang Kun was serving as the circuit intendant of Yongning in Sichuan, he was censured by Instructor (*xuezheng*) He Shaoji and was dismissed from office by Governor-General Huang Zonghan (He's relative by marriage), both of which angered him greatly. A man of perverse nature, Wang Kun included in his work that it was impossible that all of the women in He's family had been the objects of Taiping obscenities. He went on to add extraordinary contempt with countless words of calumny for the high official for whom he bore such hatred. When He Guiqing became governor-general of the Liang-Jiang provinces, he ordered the woodblocks for this book burned, according to Xue Fucheng (in his *Yongan biji* [Notes from an Ordinary Hut]).[1] Yet, argues Xie Xingyao, while the personal attacks are immoral, there are places in the text worthy of consultation in which Wang directly describes invaluable historical materials that he saw firsthand.

Luo Ergang, however, has written an article entitled 'Yibu Taiping tianguo de jinshu' (One Work Banned by the Taipings).[m] In it he quotes from a manuscript entitled the *Jieyu hui lu* (Account of Burning to Ashes), which was banned as a Taiping work. He then discusses the 'introductory remarks' of the work in which the author claims to have recorded things he personally witnessed. Through a detailed analysis of the content of this work, Luo concludes that it was a forgery, and thus one cannot consider it a Taiping work. His textual research is extremely detailed and cannot be gone into here. However, inasmuch as the *Dunbi suiwen lu* was banned both by the Qing government and by the Taipings, one probably did not see it much in general circulation. (It is said that an edition was printed in Tongzhi 2 [1863] under the changed title *Chaobao suiwen lu* [Random Notes from Documents] and is held in the Nanjing Library). The fact that this book was reprinted in Japan roughly at the time of the Meiji Restoration under such circumstances is worthy of particular note from the perspective of Taiping bibliography.

If I may be permitted a bibliographic digression, let us return to the subject of the relationship between Ōshio Heihachirō and the Taipings. One thing about which we raised serious doubts was the question of how it was that Ōshio, in the words of Ishizaki Tōgoku, was 'a man thoroughly conversant in . . . Christianity.' How are the Wang Yangming School [of which Ōshio was a professed adherent] and Christianity linked? Ishizaki argues that 'Ōshio's thorough knowledge of Christianity [*Kirishitan*] was well known from studies done already at the time of the incident involving Mizuno Isanori and Toyoda Mitsugi.' Then, Ishizaki cites a work of unclear authorship, entitled *Ōshio den* (Biography of Ōshio [Heihachirō]), as follows:

> After the incident involving Mizuno Isanori [an incident following Mizuno's own death – Masuda] settled down, I was looking into mysterious texts that had been confiscated and learned that they were records entirely in a secret language. Thus, not one person from the shogunal administrators on down could understand a word of it. It seemed as though only Heihachirō had completely mastered it so that he could comprehend its meaning in great depth after just one reading. People of the time all sighed in respect and declared him divine.

After the uprising, all traces of Ōshio and his son soon disappeared. 'Many stories tell that Mitsugi studied the magical methods of Christianity from his books which she received from him directly, then hid herself in a ravine deep in the mountains, and attempted all manner of magical tricks.' Ishizaki then comes to a far-fetched conjecture: 'Thus, the fact that Mr. Ōshio was thoroughly conversant with Christianity and, of course, that he acquired this tradition from Hong Xiuquan and Feng Yunshan further demonstrate this,' presumably referring to the theory of Ōshio's Christianity.

The 'incident of the Christian heretic,' which arose in the Kyoto-Ōsaka area during the Bunsei years [1818–30] and in which Toyoda Mitsugi (a woman), who allegedly received her training in Christian witchcraft from Mizuno Isanori, was the 'principal offender,' was judged to be one of Ōshio's three achievements while in office (according to Kōda Shigetomo). Ōshio was said to have rushed to use it to enhance his reputation. Kōda, however, raises doubts about whether Toyoda Mitsugi, Ōshio's follower, was really a Christian. While one can see in the records (depositions and affidavits) the facts that they uttered incantations to 'Zensumaruharaiso' (Jesus, Mary, and Paradise), prepared for the baptism, and secretly kept pictures of 'Tentei Nyorai,' still from their depositions we see a kind of dualist or heterogeneous nature in which they had stolen money entrusted to them to perform incantations and prayers, such as offerings to the fox god.

That Ōshio acquired much knowledge of Christianity or training in it as a result of this scrutiny is extremely doubtful, if not altogether laughable. Under the circumstances at the time, his was an investigation and an effective judgment of what was deemed a thoroughly 'heterodox religion.' Thus, it is unimaginable that he would have found any need to study the fundamental religious principles or doctrines of Christianity at all. It was a judgment based solely on an investigation into their conduct and behavior from the biased perspective against this 'heterodoxy.'

Ōshio's written judgment on this case seems to have circulated rather widely and was included in 'Shiryō sōsho (6)' (Series of Historical Materials), in *Shiseki shūran* (Collection of Historical Documents).[n] It appears as well in an appendix to the aforementioned three-stringbound-volume manuscript in my collection, and I also have a thin manuscript of the written judgment itself, entitled *Kirishitan kyō jahōsha keizaisei sho* (Report on the Adjudication of the Guilt for Heterodox Practices of the Christians). After examining these materials, we find not so much as a particle of evidence to substantiate the idea that the investigation covered the religious principles or doctrines of Christianity. Thus, from our present perspective, reasoning to the contrary borders on nonsense. At least, as seen in the judgment in the case involving his follower Toyoda Mitsugi, Ōshio was not 'a man extremely learned in the Christian religion,' and fragments such as Ishizaki's assertion that he studied 'mysterious [Christian] texts that had been confiscated' cannot be accepted.

Westerners refer to the Christianity practiced by the Taiping rebels as 'Taiping Christianity,' thus stressing its distinctiveness. The American missionary, Issachar J. Roberts, with whom Hong Xiuquan studied Christianity

141

in Guangzhou early on, later visited the Taipings' Heavenly Capital (Nanjing) and spent some time there, observing conditions under the Taiping Heavenly Kingdom. When he left Nanjing, though, he reported on the Christianity of the Taipings: 'They are carrying out their political objectives with their ridiculous religious pretensions.'[1] However, Luo Ergang argues that the Society of God Worshippers 'used a certain kind of training in Christianity as the foundation and forged it into an intellectual weapon in the Chinese peasant revolution of that time. It also used certain Christian religious ceremonies and made them a means of organizing the revolutionary multitudes.' He goes on to say that:

> The Society of God-Worshippers first and foremost synthesized a simple anti-feudal egalitarianism – peace for all peasants throughout the realm, equality of all people, equal land distribution, and the like – with a certain egalitarian idea within Christian doctrine, and they created a 'revolutionary God.' This meant that all people throughout the realm, regardless of who they were, were the sons and daughters of the Lord, and before God commoners were the equal of the emperor. By using their God in Heaven, they attacked the emperor on earth, the highest ruler in feudal society. It was thus an attack on the spirit of heirarchy of the feudal system that had been in China for several thousand years. The religion of the Society of God-Worshippers also made use of the God of Christianity to attack all of the feudal superstitions and the authority – from Confucius to King of Hell – that the landlord class used to oppress the peasants, and it liberated the Chinese peasantry from the shackles of ancient myths.... The religion of the God-Worshippers advanced yet another step and merged both with a certain egalitarianism in Christianity and with ancient Chinese ideas of Great Harmony (*datong*). In so doing, they hauled down to earth a visionary Heavenly Kingdom (*tianguo*) and created the Taiping 'Heavenly Kingdom' of freedom and equality, in which 'the entire realm was a single family, all enjoying great peace,' without exploitation or oppression.[2]

Luo Ergang also argues that although the religion of the Society of God-Worshippers included two sides, religious superstitions and revolutionary thought, in their early years the superstitious element played an extremely important organizational role. In subsequent years when the 'Heavenly Capital' was erected at Nanjing, though, it occasioned the opposite effect on the internal structure of the Taiping movement. Yang Xiuqing, using the pretext of the 'Heavenly Father's Descent to Earth' (whereby the Heavenly Father or God descended to Earth and took possession of Yang's body), sought to usurp Hong Xiuquan's position of authority, and Hong Xiuquan had Yang killed, for his 'treason was divulged by Heaven.' 'As a result of the conflict between Hong and Yang,' claims Luo, 'the superstitious disguises of the Heavenly Father and Heavenly Elder Brother were completely stripped off, and this made the masses indifferent to religion.' So saying, Luo sees the religious aspect of the Taiping movement as a disguise – a means of forging political cohesion – basically for the purposes of revolution.

In the third volume of Jian Yuwen's three-volume work, *Taiping tianguo dianzhi tongkao* (Comprehensive Analysis of the Institutions of the Taipings),° there is a section entitled 'Zongjiao kao' (Analysis of Religion) which is subdivided into three parts: 'The Personal Religion of Hong Xiuquan,' 'Taiping Christianity,' and 'Foreigners' Views of Taiping Christianity.' The analysis runs to 488 pages and goes into great depth and detail. Jian shows that, seen historically, Christianity went threw many different changes depending on time and circumstances. 'We cannot deny the capacity of Christianity to undergo change and to develop naturally, nor can we deny the providential power of Chinese believers to transform it themselves. No one would deny that that was a genuine time of great tumult, and we all must recognize accordingly that [the Taipings] had a distinctive form of Christianity.' On the basis of these premises, Jian concludes that '"Taiping Christianity" was one strain in the history of Christianity which evolved and took shape in China.'

In exposing the superstitious nature of their religious beliefs, Luo touches on how Eastern King Yang Xiuqing – originally a peasant from a mountain village who worked in the local hills and made charcoal, he was a ruthless creature with a natural gift for strategic leadership – tried to unseat and replace Heavenly King Hong Xiuquan and how he was killed by Hong in retaliation. When Hong discovered Yang's plan for a coup d'état, he immediately sent secret messengers to his kings, who were in the midst of battle at various sites in the country, calling them to return to the 'Heavenly Capital.' Northern King Wei Changhui was the first to return to Nanjing, and he attacked and killed Yang Xiuqing without delay. Not only was Yang himself cut down, but allegedly his entire family and all the officers and troops under his command as well, some 20,000 men and women in all meeting their deaths. This occurred in late August and early September of Xianfeng 6 (1856), though historical records give differing exact dates.

Wei then replaced Yang, took effective control over the Heavenly Capital, and brought his own pressure to bear on the Heavenly King. Returning to Nanjing after Wei was Assistant King Shi Dakai, who like Wei had reason to despise Yang's tyranny, and he reprimanded Wei for carrying out the massive slaughter of Yang's whole family and all his military forces. When Wei Changhui then tried to kill Shi Dakai, Shi escaped alone by clinging to a rope furtively let down the ramparts of the city and fled to Anhui. Wei proceeded to murder all of Shi's family members remaining within the city (roughly occurring on September 20, 1856). Having left the Heavenly Capital, Shi assembled an army in the Anhui region and attempted to break into the Heavenly Capital to punish Wei Changhui. When he learned that Shi's huge army was approaching, Hong Xiuquan in response rallied an anti-Wei group within the city and had them attack and execute Wei. The latter's decapitated head was then sent to Shi Dakai in Ningguo (Anhui) for inspection (in November).

143

Eventually, Shi Dakai reentered the Heavenly Capital at the head of his large armed force and was given power over state affairs for the 'Heavenly Kingdom.' In just over eight months' time, he departed the Heavenly Capital with an armed force under his command, attacking on the Anhui front, and he never returned to Nanjing. Hong Xiuquan's two elder brothers (by a different mother) and confidantes – the Tranquillity King Hong Renfa and the Blessing King Hong Renda – fell out with Shi, and even Hong Xiuquan was said to have feared that Shi, like Yang Xiuqing and Wei Changhui before him, would come to outshine the Heavenly King and assume his position. When he learned of the atmosphere in the capital, he severed all personal contacts himself.

In this manner, internal dissension continued unabated with the power struggles among the various kings, the power-holders among the Taipings, and one by one from the very beginning of the uprising they lost their leading generals (the Southern King Feng Yunshan and the Western King Xiao Chaogui having already died in battle). Gradually, the signs of a thorough internal breakdown became more and more apparent. After Shi Dakai's departure, the principal military powers supporting the Taiping movement were the young Chen Yucheng and Li Xiucheng, fellow provincials from poor peasant families in Guangxi who had both worked as hired laborers. Both had also received Taiping kingships. Li Xiucheng was captured after the fall of the Heavenly Capital, and in the deposition he was compelled to write (whether it is entirely the work of Li Xiucheng or not remains in doubt), he noted: 'The dispute between the Assistant King [Shi Dakai] and the Tranquillity King and the Blessing King having caused the Assistant King to march far away from the capital, the morale of the soldiers and the people was broken and troubled.... No one was seeing to affairs at the [Taiping] court, and there was not a single capable general in the field.'[P] These statements also indicate that the Taipings were clearly on the verge of collapse.

Ishizaki explains this internal dissension in extremely simple terms, by stating that it was due to the fact that Hong Xiuquan was a Japanese. 'The Eastern King Yang [Xiu]qing intended to usurp the throne for himself, and [Hong Xiuquan] ultimately had Wei Changhui murder him. Wei Changhui too was later killed [by Hong]. In short, these events occurred at the time of the founding [?], although in fact *they rebelled when they ultimately learned that Hong was a Japanese.*'[3]

Furthermore, Ishizaki says nothing about the fact that these gruesome power struggles among the leaders of the Taipings weakened the Taiping movement, but on the contrary notes the following:

> The elimination of these rebel officers was by no means a cause for the weakening of the Taiping Rebellion. The Taipings retained their strategic position at Jinling [Nanjing], drew back to Jing-Chu in the West, joined it with Qing-Qi[q] in the north, terrain covering several thousand *li*, with armed forces numbering a million, and many strong leaders and valiant officers scattered about like the stars in the sky. They continued to defeat

the armies of Zeng Guofan, Zuo Zongtang, and Liu Mingchuan at various sites, and the government's forces showed not the least fight in them.

Even after the dissension among the central Taiping power-holders, fighting with the Qing armies continued, but Ishizaki does not recognize the gradual movement toward destruction – 'no one was seeing to affairs at the [Taiping] court, and there was not a single valiant officer in the field' – but writes with an empty optimism.

Chapter Twenty-Three

The *Kan'ei shōsetsu* and the *Riben qishi ji*

The Taiping movement was, of course, an anti-Qing revolution which arose toward the end of the dynasty, a struggle which rocked the foundations of Manchu rule and nearly succeeded in toppling it. If we return 210 years prior to the rebellion, we find, in the very last years of the Ming dynasty, a war of resistance fought by Han Chinese against the Manchu armies which had invaded Chinese soil from Manchuria to the northeast. The Ming state was on the verge of collapse, and the war sent shock waves as far away as Japan. News of the great tumult of this dynastic transition in China and the ethnic clash it engendered were conveyed to Japan at the time. I would like now to examine how the news was received and what response was made in Japan at the time.

Earlier in this work, we noted that the descendents of the anti-Manchu heroes of the late Ming, Zheng Chenggong and his General Gan Hui, appear as extraordinary, fictional heroes in popular Japanese novelistic treatments of the Taipings, such as *Shinsetsu Min Shin kassen ki* (1854). The complex events that transpired on the mainland during the collapse of the Ming dynasty were not only treated as popular topics, for they also created all manner of sensations among the authorities of the Edo shogunate.

Zheng Zhilong, although originally the head of a band of pirates, was the leader in the Fujian region of the anti-Manchu popular movement of the time. He and his son, Zheng Chenggong (or Koxinga [Coxinga], as he later became known), both had ties to Japan. In particular, Zheng Chenggong (Prince of Yanping) was the son of Zhilong and a Japanese woman, and the fact that he was 'half-Japanese' makes it effectively impossible to deny that (some) Japanese have felt an emotional intimacy with him.

Because of the close ties the two Zhengs had with Japan, they sent a number of emissaries to the Edo shogunate, seeking weapons and requesting military assistance. The shogunate deliberated about many policy responses, investigated the matter keenly, and was deeply pained about whether or not to plunge in and dispatch troops overseas. This is the subject matter of the oft-cited work, *Kan'ei shōsetsu* (Account of the Kan'ei Era).[a] The word 'shōsetsu' in the title does not carry its current meaning of 'novel' or 'fiction,' but was a chronicle of the affairs of the Kan'ei period (1624–30) under the third Tokugawa Shōgun Iemitsu, written shortly after the events themselves in a conversational, historical style. Other works of this sort exist as well, such as the *Keichō shōsetsu* (Account of the Keichō Era [1596–1611]) and the *Genna shōsetsu* (Account of the Genna Era [1615–24]).

In one section of the *Kan'ei shōsetsu*, we find the following:

Koxinga massed his men and set off to besiege a place known as Takasago [Taiwan]. At that time, he respectfully sought [military] assistance from Japan and humbly offered all manner of rare gifts. The Nagasaki Administrator sent word [of these gifts to his superiors]. If assistance was not forthcoming, worried [Iemitsu], what would be his reputation. The 'Three Houses' [major collateral lines of Kii, Owari, and Mito], the Senior Councillor [Ii Naotaka], and others were summoned for consultation.

At this time, the Three Houses (*shinpan* daimyōs) proposed to Iemitsu that he name them each Commanders-in-Chief and send them on a military expedition, but Ii Naotaka rejected the idea, saying: 'As for the sending of military assistance, I humbly believe that there is no merit in it whatsoever and that it will be utterly useless.' Although Iemitsu 'was much concerned thereafter, the Senior Councilor's objection was a plausible conclusion, and there were no instructions for assistance [to be sent]. The gifts were returned by the Nagasaki Administrator.'

There was a postface (in Kanbun) to the *Kan'ei shōsetsu* (in this edition of the *Zoku shiseki shūran* text) by Hayashi Nobuatsu (or Hōkō), dated 'Kyōhō 3' (1718). In it, he notes:

This work has been passed down from the Kan'ei period and is said to convey the narrative of [Iemitu's] trusted vassals, Nagai Hyūga no kami, Matsudaira Iga no kami, Yagiumi Tajima no kami, Captain Sakuma, and others. My ancestor, Hayashi Dōshun [Razan], was privy to discussions among the officialdom, and I note some differences in the details, but it would be difficult to prove.... I have copied this out anew and presented it to the shogunal authorities. It may be useful for further reference.

However, in the present edition of *Kan'ei shōsetsu* in the *Zoku shiseki shūran*, this postface is cut midway (perhaps corresponding to the tail end of the first half of the work), and the aforementioned section containing Koxinga's request for military assistance appears in the latter half or after the postface. Thus, it seems as though this section of the text differs from that in which Hayashi claimed to correct discrepancies of detail between what 'Hayashi Dōshun was privy to' and what was discussed by the trusted vassals of the shōgun. Perhaps someone later added this portion to the text. In any event, the 'facts' of this story in general were clearly handed down at the time. Because these stories were only later transcribed, inconsistencies may unavoidably have cropped up in the telling. For example, the Koxinga (Zheng Chenggong) in the text cited above was in this instance a reference to his father, Zheng Zhilong. This error was soon pointed out in a work known as *Taiwan Teishi kiji* (Chronicle of the Zheng Family of Taiwan) (published in Bunsei 11 [1828]) by Kawaguchi Chōju, who was in charge of the Mito domainal historical records.[b] We know this because the document requesting military assistance was presented to the shogunate by Zheng Zhilong's emissary, via the Nagasaki Administrator, and was subsequently included in *Ka-i hentai* (The Transformation from Civilized [China] to Barbarian [Manchu]), a text we shall discuss in the next chapter.

Although we do find in the *Kan'ei shōsetsu* the 'Three Houses' vying with one another to request a military expedition, there is another chronicle as well. An item entitled *Teishi enpeigan ra fuku fūsetsu* (Zheng's Request for Military Reinforcements, with Appended Report) in the *Tsūkō ichiran* by Hayashi Fukusai reads:

> As the Great Ming fell ever more into chaos, Zheng Zhilong of Fujian, promoting a descendent of the emperor, the Prince of Tang, fought against the Tartars. Although there was no clear victor, because they were such a great enemy, Zheng Zhilong planned with a subordinate of his by the name of Cui Zhi to send a merchant by the name of Lin Gao as emissary to Nagasaki. ([Note in original:] Upon investigation, Lin Gao arrived in Nagasaki in the twelfth lunar month of Shōhō 2 [1645]). Although they were requesting military assistance from Japan, Shōgun Iemitsu had doubts about their presentations and did not give permission [for the request].

This passage, quoting from the *Nanryū kun iji* (Memories of Master Nanryū [Tokugawa Yorinobu, Lord of Kishū]), indicates that Iemitsu harbored doubts and refused permission.

In another text, volume 65 of the *Daiyūin tono ojikki* (Chronicle of Shōgun Iemitsu)[c] by Narushima Motonao (1778–1862, the shōgun's private Confucian teacher and head of the shogunate's library), there is an entry for the tenth lunar month of Shōhō 3:

> It has become known that when Zhilong humbly requested military reinforcements, a proposal was forthcoming from the Three Houses. The lords of Kii, Owari, and Mito called together a number of men and requested the dispatching of a military expedition. However, according to the *Nanryū kō furyaku* (Outline Geneology of Lord Nanryū), Lord Yorinobu said that sending an expedition from Japan would not be successful and not only would be humiliating for the Japanese but would insure a long-term enemy of a foreign land, and it would cause eternal harm. Even if Japanese troops were to win victories and gain terrain, it would be like rocky soil, of no advantage to the country, in fact inviting disasters in years to come. He did not know if it would be good for their reputation to grant this request.

Furthermore, the text notes: 'If the *Nanryū kō furyaku* mentions the Houses, there is no doubt about it.' This would indicate a recognition of the value of the historical materials recorded in the *Nanryū kō furyaku* and a confidence in its accounts. It effectively refutes criticism of ideas about the *Kan'ei shōsetsu* as a work of gossip.

One document still remains, however, that substantiates the fact that deep within private shogunal circles preparations seem to have been underway for a military expedition. In the first volume of his *Shinchō zenshi* (Complete History of the Qing Dynasty), Inaba Kunzan (Iwakichi, 1876–1940) has a chapter entitled 'Minmatsu Shinsho ni okeru Nihon no ichi' (The Place of Japan in Late Ming and Early Qing).[d] On the one hand, citing records from the *Kan'ei shōsetsu* in this section, he argues that the shogunate was not positively inclined toward a military expedition; yet, citing 'Tomita monjo' (Tomita Documents) (privately held by Tomita Takahiro in Fukushima City), a collection of letters of the time from Itakura Shigemune (the shogunate's representative in Kyoto) to his nephew Shigenori, he notes that 'the shogunate had clearly already issued some sort of expeditionary order to Itakura Shigemune, a collateral relative of the shōgun, and Shigemune had confided his personal views about it to his nephew, Mondo no suke Shigenori.'

In a February 1891 article entitled 'Tokugawa Iemitsu no Shina shinryaku no kito' (Tokugawa Iemitsu's Plan for the Invasion of China) published some time ago in the journal *Shigakkai zasshi*,[e] by Ogura Hidenuki, these Tomita Documents are cited. And, in a chapter of his book *Zōtei kaigai kyōtsū shiwa* (History of Overseas Contacts, Revised Edition),[f] Tsuji Zennosuke affirmed this 'plan' and made it a subject of his book.

Let us look at this section from these Tomita Documents themselves. (There seem to be some small errors of transcription or misprints in the portion cited in the *Shinchō zenshi*, so I shall follow the photographic reprints from those documents that appear in *Zōtei kaigai kyōtsū shiwa*).

- We plan to sail aboard ships to China [lit., the Great Ming], construct a military camp, and then wait.
- It would not be a lost cause.
- If we press forward, we can then build a moat around our encampment.
- In all there is one Japanese general and ten assistants.
- There are ten feudal vassals with annual stipends totaling one million *koku* of rice.
- [Item omitted]
- The feudal vassals in all gave 10,000 *koku* of rice to one cavalryman and either three or five foot soldiers. [Tsuji estimates that there were in excess of 20,000 troops].
- [Item omitted]
- If we do take China, we very much hope that you [i.e., the Japanese government] would offer military reinforcements.

- If we sail to China without incident, the vessels carrying the men would all need be destroyed. We pray that you will peruse the above document and then burn it. Concluded.

The instructions to burn and dispose of this document after perusing its contents indicate that the plan was moving ahead under top secret conditions. The document bears no signature, and in spite of the directions to destroy it, it [obviously] survives. These facts might lead us to conclude that this is not the original item but a copy of it. Even if it were a copy, though, the very fact that such a document exists would seem to indicate that this story is not a wholly baseless piece of fiction.

While the shogunate was secretly making preparations to dispatch troops as per the request of Zheng Zhilong, doubts were raised in deliberations within the government over Zheng's statement of request. When an emissary was about to be sent to Nagasaki, reports were received there to the effect that Fuzhou had already fallen to the Manchus and that the Prince of Tang who had made Fuzhou his base was, together with Zheng Zhilong, in retreat. These matters were reported to the shogunate, and the expedition was called off. Also, a document informing the various feudal lords of these events is included in the present edition of *Tsūkō ichiran* (volume 212).

News that Fuzhou, where the Prince of Tang (Emperor Longwu) had set up his base with assistance from Zheng Zhilong and his son Zheng Chenggong, had come under attack by Qing armies and fallen proved apparently to be a major shock in Japan. We know this from items such as the following (dated the tenth lunar month of Shōhō 3) which appears in the aforementioned *Daiyūin tono ojikki* (volume 65).

It was learned in recent intelligence coming from Nagasaki that the armies of the Ming had been defeated at Fuzhou and the Ming ruler had been killed. Retainers [in Edo] of [daimyōs] Matsudaira Nagato no kami Hidenori, Matsudaira Shintarō Mitsumasa, Matsudaira Ukyōdaifu Yorishige, Matsudaira Awa no kami Tadahide, Matsudaira Aki no kami Mitsuage, Date Tōtōmi no kami Hidemune, Matsudaira Dewa no kami Naomasa, Hosokawa Higo no kami Mitsunao, Nabeshima Shinano no kami Katsushige, Tachibana Sakon no shōgen [Captain of the Left Guards] Tadashige, and Arima Chūmu no shōsuke Tadayori were ordered to be attentive to the eventuality of foreign vessels arriving. Minister of State Komatsu Chūnagon Toshitsune, Matsudaira Echigo no kami Mitsunaga, Matsudaira Satsuma no kami Mitsuhisa, Mori Naiki Nagatsugu, and Kyōgoku Tango no kami Takahiro acted similarly.[g]

This would indicate that warning directives went out to the domains along the coast. In the past the Tartar pirates of the 'Yuan' had made raids on Japan and greatly frightened the Kamakura shogunate. Thus, on this occasion, when the Tartar 'Qing' attacked the 'Great Ming' and took Fuzhou on China's southeastern coast, the base held by the Ming's last descendents, we can see that the shogunate's rapid commencement of preparations 'to be attentive to the eventuality of foreign vessels arriving' indicates how greatly the collapse of the Ming exerted a ripple effect on Japan.

At first, the capital of the 'Great Ming' at Beijing was attacked and taken by the Qing armies. After the Chongzhen Emperor committed suicide, descendents of the Ming imperial house bearing the surname Zhu gained followings around the country. The base established by the Prince of Fu at Nanjing fell, then the base of the Prince of Lu at Shaoxing also fell; they escaped to Zhoushan Island. The Prince of Tang set up a base at Fuzhou and was there barely able to remain in existence. Both Zhoushan and Fuzhou were points from which trading vessels came to Nagasaki, and both were thus nodes linking Japan and China. Zhoushan was an isolated island which merely had a resistance capacity because of its mountain fortresses. Fuzhou, though, was situated in a corner of the mainland, and there the Prince of Tang was enthroned as emperor bearing the reign title Longwu. News that the Longwu Emperor's castle had fallen and that he had fled (he was later caught and executed by the Manchus), thus, in one manner or another caused considerable shock in Japan.

Aside from the request for military reinforcements by Zheng Zhilong and others supporting the Prince of Tang at his Fuzhou base, there are records in China that indicate an application for military assistance from a group supporting the Prince of Lu in Eastern Zhejiang (Shaoxing and Zhoushan). In this instance, I am referring to the *Riben qishi ji* (Record of Requesting Help from Japan) by Huang Zongxi (Lizhou). It chronicles the unsuccessful efforts by Huang Xiaoqing (younger brother of Huang Binqing, the real power at Zhoushan) and Feng Jingdi, attendant censor to the Prince of Lu, who came to Nagasaki to request assistance. On this question, though, we can find no documents, such as might be found in the *Ka-i hentai*, to substantiate such a story. It would be best if the two accounts were in general consistent, thus corroborating one another's story; were this not the case, it would be precarious to try to establish the facts of the case. Not to follow such a careful procedure would, effectively, exceed the reach of reasoned conjecture and scrutiny. However, all manner of conjecture and scrutiny have been attempted for this case of 'requesting Japanese help,' and the source of proof always returns to Huang Zongxi's *Riben qishi ji.*

The date of Huang Xiaoqing and Feng Jingdi's request for Japanese assistance varies widely according to the historical sources (of which there are many in China), but *Riben qishi ji* gives the date as the third year of the reign of the Prince of Lu (in Japan it was the first year in the Keian reign period [1648]). Although this dating remains unclear in Japanese records, it seems that the account given in the *Riben qishi ji* has generally been accepted in China as fact. (This work is included in: *Xingchao lu* [Records of the Itinerant Court]; and later in *Jingtuo yishi* [The Forgotten History of Jingtuo], compiled by Chenhu Yishi; and *Lizhou yizhu huikan* [Collected Posthumous Writings of Huang Zongxi]).[h]

This is supported, among the historical materials for the [itinerant] Southern Ming, by two sources compiled and published at the end of the Qing by Xu Zi – an account in *juan* sixteen of *Xiaotian jinian fukao* (Chronicles of [an Era of] Small Prosperity, with Appended Annotations) (20 *juan*, preface dated Xianfeng 11 [1861]) and in the biographies section of *Xiaotian jizhuan* (Biographies of [an Era of] Small Propserity). In the biographies of Feng Jingdi that appear in works of the Kangxi reign of the early Qing as well – such as in the *Nanjiang yishi* (Forgotten History of the Southern Reaches) by Wen Ruilin, the *Haidong yishi* (Forgotten History East of the Sea [Taiwan]) by Wengzhou Laomin, and the *Dongnan jishi* (Accounts of the Southeast) by Shao Tingcai (most of which were passed down in manuscript form and only published in the late Qing period) – all seem to have been taken over without change from the *Riben qishi ji*. Although they lack 'biography' sections, the 'Jianguo ji' (Records of the Administrator of the Realm) in the *Lu chunqiu* (Rise and Fall of Lu) and the main body of the *Dongnan jishi* (Records of the Southeast) by Zuoyin Feiren [pseudonym of Zha Jizuo] both follow accordingly.[i] Rather than all taking their information directly from Huang Zongxi's work, perhaps they all drew upon stories (?) from the same source. In any event, they all effectively repeat the same thing, and the content of their accounts is somewhat odd from our perspective.

The request for assistance from Japan from Feng Jingdi, who appears in the various 'biography' sections of the works cited above (with the exception of *Dongnan jishi* [Accounts of the Southeast] where his biography is missing; he is mentioned in the biography of Wang Yi), for all intents and purposes seems to have been based upon Huang Zongxi's work (or both on a common ancestor). According to this account of the story, both Feng Jingdi and Huang Xiaoqing were promised an expeditionary force by the 'King of Satsuma,' with whom Cui Zhi had become intimate after a number of trips to Japan; thus, they went as emissaries in search of help to the 'island of Nagasaki.' Just at that time, the story goes, Japan had concluded a war with Westerners (Portuguese?), and permission for their delegation to come on land was not forthcoming. The King of Satsuma heard that Feng Jingdi and his associates had been refused permission to land at Nagasaki; taking this as an 'embarrassment to Japan,' he decided, in consultation with the Tokugawa shōgun, to send criminals from various islands, and he sent 300,000 Hongwu cash (some sources give a figure of 100,000). There was, however, a brothel in Nagasaki, and Huang Xiaoqing had shut himself up tightly inside, apparently forgetting that he had sailed to Japan to request assistance; he was thus ridiculed by the Japanese and lost all interest in a military expedition. This is the general story, with slight differences depending on the text consulted.

Despite the fact that some of what is recorded in this account – in its more specific details – appears to be rather factually strange material, Feng Jingdi and Huang Xiaoqing probably did come to Japan regardless of the absence of any mention of such in Japanese records. Zhang Huangyan (Cangshui) has a poem entitled 'Song Huang Jinwu [Xiaoqing] Feng Shiyu [Jingdi] qishi Riben' (Sending Off Lord of the Imperial Insignia Huang [Xiaoqing] and Attendant

Censor Feng [Jingdi] to Seek Assistance from Japan' in his poetry collection, *Qiling ji* (Collection of Curious Fragments). It would seem highly bizarre to have composed a poem of this sort for an entirely fictional incident. Zhang Huangyan was a soldier-scholar who, together with Zheng Chenggong, led troops in an attack on Nanjing where Qing forces had camped. When later apprehended, he refused to surrender in allegiance to his captors and was put to death. His epitaph (included in *Zhang Cangshui ji* [The Writings of Zhang Huangyan])[j] was written by Huang Zongxi, not someone later, and perhaps Huang patterned his *Riben qishi ji* after Zhang's life.

Zhang Huangyan's writings, *Zhang Cangshui ji* (the *Qiling ji* can be found in this collection as well), were proscribed by the Qing government, and were scarcely known. Late in the Qing period, the anti-Manchu nationalist Zhang Taiyan printed them to propagandize the anti-Qing revolutionary cause. There is now as well a 1959 edition published by Zhonghua shuju.

Something evident in the *Riben qishi ji*, and its traces can be found in the *Ka-i hentai*, is the recording of the fact that they came to Japan for help, carrying Buddhist texts as gifts, but they failed. A monk by the name of Zhanwei who had returned home from Japan told them that, because the Japanese treasured such Buddhist texts, if they brought them to Japan, they would succeed in their request for assistance. The monk encouraged Ruan Jin, an 'admiral' under the Prince of Lu, and Ruan sent Zhanwei together with his own younger brother, Ruan Mei, also in the navy, as an emissary carrying [Buddhist] texts 'in the winter of 1649.' However, earlier Zhanwei had referred to himself as the 'saint of the golden lion,' and thus incurred the suspicion of being connected to Catholicism and ended up under arrest and exiled from Japan. The second time he arrived with the emissary and was banished, his request for assistance having failed, and so he returned to China with the Buddhist texts he had brought along. Thus the story is recounted in the sources.

A document somewhat in correspondence with this account can be found in the *Ka-i hentai* (volume 1), but it is unrelated to the matter of seeking assistance from Japan. This is a document which reads at its very end: 'Japanese translation of a document sent to the Nagasaki Administrator from the Prince of Lu of the Great Ming ... [dated] X day of the tenth lunar month of the fourth year [1649] of the reign of the Prince of Lu, the administrator of the realm.' We have no original for the 'Japanese translation.' The main contents of the document are first laid out – the 'saint of the golden lion came from Japan, and explaining his aspirations on behalf of Buddhism and [Buddhist] texts, said he wished to travel to Japan with another as emissaries, carrying a statue of the Guanyin Bodhisattva and a complete set of the Buddhist scriptures, and thus to spread the Buddhist law.' Then, an explanation is attached to the document which indicates that this was hearsay added at a later date.

The golden lion was a Chinese monk [Tōsō] who traveled back and forth to Nagasaki. He lived and worked within the domain of [the lord of]

Nabeshima. Returning to China, he feigned to speak in the name of the authorities. Receiving a complete set of the Buddhist scriptures from Senguan [a reference to Zheng Chenggong, but for Zheng to come up in this context is extremely strange and thus may be an error based on rumor – Masuda], he returned to Japan and won great fame for himself. When the false claim became known, he was banished from the territory of [the lord of] Nabeshima and sent home. Rumor has it that he was imprisoned.

It is not entirely clear if this matter concerning the 'saint of the golden lion' (as he appears in Japanese accounts) was conveyed in connection with the request for assistance in China or if it was conveyed in Japan unrelated to matters concerned with such requests. The *Xiaotian jinian fukao* and other texts merely say that he sought military assistance.

Within the second section of the *Siming congshu* (Collection of the Siming Mountains),[k] there is one *juan* entitled 'Feng Wang liang shilang mulu' (Epitaphs of the Two Attendant Censors, Feng [Jingdi]) and Wang [Yi]); there it is included as the work of Quan Zuwang (Sheshan). It is doubtful that these are actually writings of Quan Zuwang, as they are probably the work of a later author using his name. (They are not included in the 'Sibu congkan' edition [volume 95] of the *Jieqi ting ji* [Collection from the Jieqi Pavillion], the collection of Quan Zuwang's poetry and prose essays).[l] On the issue of requesting assistance from Japan, it is consistent with the accounts and essentially the same in content as the *Riben qishi ji*; frequently sections are identical word-for-word.

On the other hand, Quan Zuwang's 'Lizhou xiansheng shendao beiwen' (Epitaph for the Late Master Lizhou [Huang Zongxi]) (included in *juan* 1 of *Jichi ting ji*) which recounts the career of Huang Zongxi is without a doubt the work of Quan himself, and it is often cited as such. Although Huang Zongxi never stated it himself, the text of the 'Lizhou xiansheng shendao beiwen' claims that he in fact went to Nagasaki as co-emissary with Feng Jingdi to seek assistance from Japan; a note in the text adds at this point: 'This was Lord Feng's second trip seeking help.' This matter is altogether absent from the epitaph for Feng Jingdi, cited above, and if this were also the work of Quan Zuwang, the texts should be consistent on this point. Furthermore, Quan seems to have been boasting about this point [in his epitaph for Huang]: 'No scholars have yet mentioned the eastern travels of the Lord [Huang]'; and 'After the passage of a hundred years [following Huang's death], men will then be able to consider it.' Such digressions cannot be found in the epitaph for Feng Jingdi, and from the perspective of this point, Feng's epitaph appears to be the work of a hand other than Quan Zuwang's.

In any event, Quan's thesis that Huang traveled to Japan to seek assistance was first articulated by him, though the evidence to support it is weak, and it is not widely accepted. (Neither the *Xiaotian jinian* nor the *Xiaotian jizhuan* accept it). More recently, Liang Qichao and others, though, have believed it to be true and, thus, in the next chapter of this work, I would like to examine it in more concrete terms.

On the Japanese side, documents indicating that in addition to Zheng Zhilong, his son Zheng Chenggong and his son Zheng Jing (Jinshe), among others, came to Japan seeking help have been collected in the *Ka-i hentai*. In the next chapter, I would like to examine both this work and another work which used it to a considerable extent when compiled: *Tsūkō ichiran* ('Tōkoku bu' [Section on China]).

Chapter Twenty-Four

Details Concerning the
Riben qishi ji

As we noted in the previous chapter of this work, the very beginning of the *Riben qishi ji* recounts how Zhou Cuizhi made contact with the King of Satsuma and requested assistance and how the Tokugawa shōgun promised to send troops to help. This name, Zhou Cuizhi, appears in other texts as Zhou Hezhi, such as the *Nan tian hen* (Traces of Heaven in the South) by Lingxue zuanxiu (Compiler Ling-xue)[a] and the *Nanjiang yishi* (Forgotten History of the Southern Reaches) by Wen Ruilin.[b] Inasmuch as the latter appears to be an expanded and revised version of the former, it should not be surprising that they contain the same material. The *Xiaotian jinian fukao* and *Xiaotian jizhuan*, both by Xu Zi, also have 'Zhou Hezhi,' but an 'annotation' in the latter carries the following note: 'Upon investigation, it was learned that the character *cui* is an error for the character *he*, which is popularly abbreviated as *cui*. Despite this, the *Riben qishi ji* still has Cuizhi.

Let us look at a passage in the *Riben qishi ji* that concerns Cuizhi and the request for Japanese assistance:

> Zhou Cuizhi, style Jiujing, came from Ronghua, Fujian. When he was young, he was unable to read. He left home and became a pirate on the seas. He was very able in speech and followed the orders of his fellows. He had been to Japan and was known for being an excellent shot. He forged a father-son bond with the King of Satsuma.... In the spring of the *yiyou* year [1645], Emperor Siwen [Longwu] made him Naval Commissioner-in-Chief [he had previously become the company commander of Huanghua-guan], and as the assistant to Huang Binqing set sail for Zhoushan [Island].

The text then goes on to describe the matter of military assistance:

> That winter Cuizhi sent another man to Satsuma to appeal about the sad chaos in China and to request the sending of a brigade of troops.... Indignant, the shōgun promised to dispatch in the fourth month of the next year 30,000 troops; they would provide their own compliment of warships,

military supplies, and weaponry; and would thus offer to the Chinese for several year's use this large fighting force.

Whether or not this last passage is accurate, when we ponder generally when this man Cuizhi lived and when he went to Japan to request military assistance, we must first look to the mention of either fall or winter of the *yiyou* year, as recorded in the *Riben qishi ji*. According to the compiler and annotator of the *Xiaotian jinian fukao* (see the 1957 edition from Zhonghua shuju), *yiyou* is 1645, the second year of the Shōhō reign in Japan.

Two letters requesting military assistance which Cuizhi allegedly brought to Japan are now included in the *Ka-i hentai*.[c] As pointed out long ago by Kondō Shigezō, one of them can also be found in the *Zoku zenrin kokuhō ki* (Valuable National Records of Our Good Neighbor, Continued) and the *Zoku zenrin kokuhō gaiki* (Valuable National Records of Our Good Neighbor, Further Accounts, Continued); it is also in the *Shiseki shūran* and *Zoku gunsho ruiju* (Collection of Writings Classified, Continued).[d] For neither of these letters do we know the name of the addressee, but the date is written at the very end: 'twelfth day, twelfth [lunar] month, Longwu 1.' This corresponds to Shōhō 2 [1645] in Japan, the *yiyou* year, and thus is consistent with the date given in both the *Riben qishi ji* and the *Nanjiang yishi*. Furthermore, the letter that appears in the *Ka-i hentai* and these other texts carries the phrases: 'The reign name was changed to Longwu.... [Cui] Zhi was ordered to serve under the Barbarian-Pacifying General, and Zhi was given the post of advance naval commander.' This information also matches precisely with the *Riben qishi ji* and the *Nanjiang yishi*. The Barbarian-Pacifying General refers to Huang Binqing; Huang had been given investiture by the Longwu Emperor as the Barbarian-Pacifying Count.

According to the *Ka-i hentai*, at the very end of the letter, it states that the person who brought Cuizhi's letter was 'specially delegated Assistant Commander Lin Gao' (the *Zoku zenrin kokuhō ki* and *Zoku zenrin kokuhō gaiki* both state: 'specially delegated Assistant Commander Gao Qi'). In the Chinese texts, *Riben qishi ji* and *Nanjiang yishi*, however, the name of the bearer of the letter is not given. They do state: 'In the fourth month of the next year, [the shōgun] promised to send 30,000 troops, ... and he awaited the arrival of an envoy from China. Cuizhi was elated.... Councilor Lin Yuewu was appointed as emissary to go east [i.e., to Japan] on the eleventh day of the fourth month. As Yuewu was about to set sail, [Huang] Binqing called it off.' It remains unclear if Assistant Commander Lin Gao (or Gao Qi), who had allegedly carried the letter requesting help as Cuizhi's envoy in the second year of the Shōhō reign, was the same person as Lin Yuewu, who had tried to go to Japan to request military help in the fourth month of the following year, or another person. The names are different, and it would seem they were different men.

Although the name 'Lin Gao' cannot be found in the Chinese sources, the name 'Lin Yuewu' can and in other works as well. In the biographies section of the *Nanjiang yishi* (*zhuan* 53), he is given as a military commander in the biography of Zhou Hezhi. However, it also says that he was a friend of Cuizhi and assistant commander, and that when Zheng Zhilong tried to surrender to the government's armed forces, Lin Yuewu gave eight reasons why it was unacceptable to do so. The *Xiaotian jinian* notes that when Zhou Cuizhi recaptured a harbor entrance in the first lunar month of the *dinghai* year (1674), he had staff officer Lin Yuewu and Regional Commander Zhao Mu guard it.

Let us look now at the contents of the letters from Cuizhi. Although full of florid language and phrasing, their essence was a 'request for assistance.' One letter 'asks to borrow 3000 troops,' while the other 'requests 3000 soldiers.' Both sought an expedition of 3000 men. The letter that 'requests 3000 soldiers' goes on as follows: 'The enemy [i.e., the Qing military] has superior capability in the use of bows and arrows. Because [Cui] Zhi's forces are so poorly outfitted for armor, they are unable to sustain a battle and [thus] incur many injuries. I believe that Japanese armor is the envy of the entire world and that they defend against bows and arrows like gold or stone.... I earnestly desire that [Cui] Zhi be allowed to trade for 200 suits [of such armor] at a fair exchange.' In short, what Cuizhi sought from Japan was 3000 soldiers and 200 suits of armor. However, in neither the *Riben qishi ji* nor the *Nanjiang yishi* do we find such precise figures for military personnel and weaponry.

The letters that Cuizhi's mission carried seeking assistance were brought to Nagasaki. After they are mentioned in the *Ka-i hentai*, the text goes on to comment: 'The two letters from the aforementioned Cuizhi were brought to Nagasaki by Lin Gao. They were then forwarded to Edo, so that the senior councilors would be able to examine them. Shunsai [Hayashi Shunshō, 1618–80] read it before the shōgun [Iemitsu].' Perhaps, as stated in both the *Riben qishi ji* and the *Nanjiang yishi*, only after they first went to Satsuma, did they then present their letters to the Nagasaki Administrator, which was the official route to the Edo shogunate, but this does not accord with Japanese records, and perhaps the *Riben qishi ji* and the *Nanjiang yishi* based their accounts simply on hearsay.

According to the *Ka-i hentai*, the envoy Lin Gao stayed in Nagasaki, while the letters were transmitted to the shogunate. Matsudaira Izu no kami Nobutsuna and Ii Kamonnosuke Naotaka examined their contents, and through the Nagasaki Administrator, informed Lin Gao that 'this was not a matter to be promptly brought to the attention' of the shōgun and they 'were to convey to Lin Gao that he was to return home with alacrity.' The document informing Lin Gao of this at the time bears the name of Hayashi Shunsai written in his own hand, and it is now included in the *Ka-i hentai*.

The following year [1646] Cuizhi was about to send Lin Yuewu to Japan as an emissary to invite the Japanese army, but, as noted in the *Riben qishi ji*, he was stopped by Huang Binqing just at the moment of departure. Once again the next year, the *Riben qishi ji* records: 'In the third month of 1647, Cuizhi recaptured the two walled towns of Haikou and Zhendong [both in Fuqing county, Fujian]. His adopted son, Lin Gao, was sent to accompany the Prince of Peace and

Prosperity (Anchang wang) on a mission to request assistance from Japan.[1] He returned without success.' The next year again, 1648, Feng Jingdi persuaded Huang Binqing to send his young brother, Huang Xiaoqing, and Feng to Nagasaki, but the 'king' (in fact, it was the Nagasaki Administrator) did not permit him to come ashore and proceed.

If we are then to reorganize the above accounts of requests for military assistance from Japan, as recorded in the *Riben qishi ji*, we find the following situation:

1. In the winter of 1645, Zhou Cuizhi sent someone to Satsuma, who appealed on behalf of the 'sad chaos' in China, and requested the sending of 'a brigade' of troops.
2. The following year, 1646, Lin Yuewu was about to be sent off as emissary to Japan to invite a Japanese army to China, but at the last moment he was stopped by Huang Binqing.
3. In the third month of the next year, 1647, Cuizhi had his adopted son, Lin Gao, accompany the Prince of Peace and Prosperity to Japan to request military assistance, but they returned empty-handed.
4. The following year, 1648, Feng Jingdi and Huang Xiaoqing traveled to Nagasaki to seek help, but were not allowed to come on shore. Xiaoqing spent a goodly amount of time at local brothels; he thus lost all credibility, and his reinforcements were not forthcoming. He did, though, received 100,000 Hongwu cash for military provisions.
5. In the winter of 1649, a Buddhist monk by the name of Zhanwei returned from Japan. He told Ruan Jin that if he made presents of Buddhist scriptures from Putuo Shan monastery and sought Japanese assistance, he would be successful. Ruan Jin, accordingly, sent his own younger brother, Ruan Mei, a naval officer, as emissary to Nagasaki.[2] However, since Zhanwei, who accompanied them on the trip, had referred to himself in Japan as the 'saint of the golden lion,' he had been seen as a Catholic infiltrator and had been arrested. In fact, though, he was just a Buddhist priest and was exiled from Japan. When Ruan Mei learned that he had been misled, he loaded the texts back on his ship and returned home.

These are the five instances of Chinese requests for military assistance from Japan that are recorded in the *Riben qishi ji*. It is doubtful that they can be factually verified, for much of the evidence is unconfirmed hearsay collected after the fact. For example, the following, cited earlier, is of dubious quality: 'Indignant, the shōgun promised to dispatch in the fourth month of the next year 30,000 troops; they would provide their own compliment of warships, military supplies, and weaponry; and would thus offer to the Chinese for several year's use this large fighting force.' Similarly, what follows seems simply to be an exaggerated manner of expression: 'He had the roads, bridges, post stations, and inns over the route from Nagasaki to Edo – some 3000 or more *ri* long – repaired, and thus awaited the arrival of the emissary from China.'

When we look at the evidence from the Japanese side, the *Ka-i hentai*, we learn that on the basis of reports from Nagasaki, orders were issued from the shogunate to the Nagasaki Administrator to conduct negotiations in Nagasaki and resolve the matter there. In other words, it is virtually impossible that they would have so courteously welcomed an envoy from the losers requesting assistance, by repairing the roads and bridges and reoutfitting the post stations and inns. In fact, we find in the *Ka-i hentai* a severe indictment of the language used in the letters from Cuizhi, which both displays the Japanese sense of dignity and censures the rudeness of the language used. Thus, in the final analysis, it is highly doubtful that what we have seen recorded in the *Riben qishi ji* actually transpired.

The *Riben qishi ji* has traditionally been attributed to Huang Zongxi who served the Prince of Lu in eastern Zhejiang, and thus the assistance sought concerned matters primarily under the control of the Prince of Lu. The author of the text could not help, one would assume, but be ignorant of the help sought by the Longwu court in Fujian to the south. Although such data is not to be found in the *Riben qishi ji*, a letter requesting help was sent to Japan by Zheng Zhilong, a follower of Longwu, and it is included in the *Ka-i hentai*. For the thirteenth day of the eighth lunar month of Longwu 2 (1646), we find the following entry in that text: 'The Longwu Emperor's emissary, Huang Zhengming, crossed the sea and sought assistance from Japan. There were several letters from Zheng Zhilong. Two letters were for the Shōhō Emperor of Japan, and three more were for the shōgun, with three to the King of Nagasaki. All were accompanied by gifts.' The contents of these letters are not recorded, but the *Ka-i hentai* carries an explanation. It says of Huang Zhengming:

> He was captured at sea by the Tatars [the Manchus] and was unable to come to Japan. Thus, on a small vessel, as his own emissary, [Zheng] Zhilong arrived in Nagasaki with his letters and gifts as well as the letters of [Huang] Zhengming. In the tenth month of that year, a report was issued from Nagasaki to Edo, and a senior councilor informed [the shōgun] of its content. My late father [Hayashi Shunshō] read it before the shōgun.

The shogunal authorities deliberated over these letters, as the text notes:

> Deliberations ensued for several days. The two *dainagon* from Owari and Kii came to Edo, and Shunsai read the aforementioned letters out loud. Abe Tsushima no kami, who was on monthly duty, took possession of the letters. With all of his daily paperwork, he held onto them closely and had no cause to show them to anyone. He was ultimately unable to copy them, but because he attended daily meetings, he relayed their content to my father who recorded it himself, as follows.

What follows is the general contents of these letters. The main points therein are:

- In the tenth month of the third year of the Shōhō reign, two letters were sent to the Shōkyō Emperor from the great general and pacifier of barbarians,

160

Marquis Zheng Zhilong. One letter had appended an imperial edict from the Longwu Emperor.... It sought the loan of a powerful military force. Although mention of 5000 troops had already been made,[3] inasmuch as the enemy was formidable, they needed more. A gift was included together with the edict.

- In an enclosure to the Shōkyō Emperor from the same person, an imperial edict commanded Huang Zhengming to offer up the letter and request the loan of a powerful military force....

- In the three letters to the shōgun from the same person, two letters concerned primarily the matter of borrowing troops and the rough seas encountered by the emissary's vessel. The third letter concerned Zheng Zhilong's wife and children; they requested ten girls and ten slaves from Japan. It mentioned that one young son [perhaps indicating Zheng Chenggong's younger brother, Shichizaemon] missed his mother and wanted to summon her to China.... [Zhi]long's son [Chenggong, Koxinga] had served the Great Ming for sixteen years; he had married a woman who had given birth to [Zhilong's] grandchild. Accordingly, the King of China [Longwu] kindly honored him by naming him an imperial son-in-law and enfeoffing him as the Earl of Loyalty and Filiality. He led over 100,000 people. The mother honored the son and was thus enfeoffed along with her husband....

- [Of the] three letters passed to the King of Nagasaki from this same person, two concerned the request for military aid. The third concerned his wife and children, effectively the same manner of expression as treated in the letters, mentioned above, to the shōgun....

- In the letter from Huang Zhengming, emissary of the King of China (Tōō), to the Shōkyō Emperor, only the request for military assistance is mentioned....

As for the terms of address used in Zheng Zhilong's letter, conveyed by emissary Huang Zhengming – 'Zhengjing huangdi' (Shōkyō Emperor), 'Shang jiangjun' (shōgun), and 'Changqi wang' (King of Nagasaki) – an investigation was carried out in Japan to determine whom they referred to. Also, each and every term employed in the letters for the 'Shōkyō Emperor' and the 'shōgun' was meticulously scrutinized, and the detailed items that underwent scrutiny are included in a section entitled 'Difficult Questions' in the *Ka-i hentai*. The texts reports that with this list of scrutinized items in hand, 'the shōgun ordered the lord of the Funai Castle in Bungo, Hine Oribemasa, together with Naitō Shōhei to go to Nagasaki as the shōgun's representatives. They met with emissary Huang Zhengming and conveyed the shōgun's decision on this matter. The emissary was ordered to return home. However, if he [the Chinese envoy] had more to say on the issue, then the Japanese representatives were to take it down and report the matter to Edo.' Just before this in the text we read: 'Perhaps military assistance would be sent on this occasion. After several days of deliberations, it was generally decided that it would not.' Thus, it had already been generally decided that military assistance would not be dispatched, and this they seem to have tried to pass on to the emissary by 'convey[ing] the shōgun's wishes on this matter.' In fact, however, we know that it had not been so decided; 'if he [the Chinese envoy] had more to say on the issue,' then they were to take it down and report to the authorities in Edo. In other words, we can see the readiness, depending on circumstances, to respond positively to a request for military assistance. This point is substantiated by the *Kan'ei shōsetsu* and the 'Tomita monjo,' cited above.

Although the sending of Huang Zhengming to Japan does not appear in the *Riben qishi ji*, we do find it in other Chinese historical materials. In volume eight of the *Siwen daji* (Great Record of the Siwen Emperor),[e] an account of the events surrounding the Longwu court based in Fujian, there is the following note: 'Bandit-Pacifying Marquis Zheng Zhilong put forward a plan to revive [China] by acquiring Japanese military assistance. The emperor [Longwu] permitted him to proceed. Huang Zhengming was made the primary emissary, and carrying on the color of [Ming] garments he ascended to the rank of *shū* ? [the text is missing a character here] and set off on his mission in great splendor.'

Can we say, then, that Zheng Zhilong's proposal, accepted by Longwu, to send Huang Zhengming to Japan does not appear in the *Riben qishi ji*? While Huang's mission remained in Nagasaki, awaiting a definitive response from the *bakufu*, reports were conveyed to Nagasaki that Fuzhou had fallen and the Longwu Emperor had sought refuge elsewhere; at this, the request for military assistance was abandoned. The *Ka-i hentai* has the following to say on this matter:

> On the seventeenth day of the tenth month, a letter, dated the fourth day of the tenth month, arrived from Nagasaki. It said that, in the latter part of the eighth month, the Tatars had invaded Fujian and destroyed Shanheguan [perhaps the text meant Xianxiaguan]. The men of the Great Ming were inadequate to the task, and they surrendered.... Because the letter on this matter had arrived, there was no need to send Oribemasa and Shōzaemon [Shōhei? – JAF] to Nagasaki. Yamazaki Gonhachirō [the Nagasaki Administrator] learned through an interpreter that Fuzhou had already fallen and that the reinforcements were no longer necessary. Emissary Zhengming was informed that his gifts would not be accepted [under the circumstances] and that he was to return home.

We noted earlier with respect to Feng Jingdi that, although there were numerous documents about the case surrounding him in China, nothing is to be found in Japan. Chinese materials indicate that, in the final analysis, it was the permission of the influential Huang Binqing of Zhoushan that enabled Feng and Huang Xiaoqing to sail for Japan. Let me note here, though, that Huang Binqing's name does appear in the *Ka-i hentai* by chance.

The content of his letter is not given, but the writing on its cover alone was copied into the text. The very first line reads: 'An auspicious morning in late summer, *jichou* year, in the reign of Longwu, restorer of the Great Ming.' Next, on what must have been the middle of the cover, is the place for a seal and below it written horizontally: 'The great benefactor of the world.' The next two lines read as follows: 'A letter of Huang Binqing, imperially ordered master of suppression of the barbarians, presented by Shi Qi, his assistant regional commander.' A note is appended by way of explanation: 'One character was forgotten.' It would seem that an assistant regional commander by the name of Shi Qi [the third character of his name has been lost – JAF] delivered a letter from his superior, Huang Binqing. However, no mention is made of the letter's content nor is an explanation given of its general intent, unlike other letters that appear in the *Ka-i hentai*. Perhaps, it was not passed along to the *bakufu* as an official letter.

What is indicated as the *jichou* year of the Longwu reign (1649) was already after Longwu's base in Fuzhou had fallen and he had fled. The *Ka-i hentai* adds the note: 'The *jichou* year of the Longwu reign is dubious,' and then continues: 'In the *dinghai* year [1647], the Ming emperor changed reign titles from Longwu to Yongli. Therefore, Huang Binqing failed to use the Yongli reign title but continued to use the Longwu title.'

The *jichou* year of the Longwu reign corresponds to the second year of the Keian reign in Japan. According to the *Riben qishi ji*, Feng Jingdi and Huang Xiaoqing, with the permission of Huang Binqing, arrived in Nagasaki to seek military assistance in the previous year, the *wuzi* year [1648], which corresponds to the first year of the Keian reign. If this appeared on the face of the letter carried by Feng and Huang, it was off by a year. Perhaps Huang Binqing sent another emissary by the name of Shi in the year following the arrival of Feng Jingdi and Huang Xiaoqing, or perhaps Mr. Shi sought help entirely on his own and simply used Huang Binqing's name. We just do not know for sure. In any event, we should make note of the fact that, although Feng Jingdi's name fails to appear in any Japanese historical records, the name of Huang Binqing, who it is thought ordered him to make the trip to Japan, does appear in the Japanese historical record, albeit faintly.

The *Riben qishi ji* notes of Feng Jingdi that he went to Japan as an envoy seeking military assistance, failed to achieve his goal, and returned home. Feng himself, however, left an account of his search for help from Japan in the *Fuhai ji* (Record of a Trip across the Sea). Mention is made of 'Feng Jingdi's *Fuhai ji*' together with the *Riben qishi ji* and similar works as historical records that 'detailed events concerning [the Prince of] Lu, Administrator of the Realm' in the 'prefatory remarks' to the *Nanjiang yishi*. Among the materials listed in the 'prefatory remarks' to the *Nan tian hen*, too, that 'detailed events concerning [the Prince of] Lu, Administrator of the Realm,' we again find, together with the *Riben qishi ji*, mention of 'Feng Jingdi's *Fuhai ji*.'

In his *Wan Ming shiji kao* (An Examination of the Historical Records of the Late Ming),[f] Xie Guozhen looked at over 1000 historical works concerning the late-Ming period, and for the principal ones among them he transcribed the prefaces and postfaces from the originals, adding his own exhaustive investigation and explanations. As a guide to historical material necessary for research in this area, there is much in it to aide our work. In *juan* 12, Xie mentioned the *Fuhai ji*, noting only: 'It is a work by Feng Jingdi (Jizhong) from Ciyu of the Ming era. At the time of the Prince of Lu, Administrator of the Realm, Jizhong was right attendant censor for military affairs. He had once sought military assistance from Japan. His writings include *Fuhai ji*. He died with the fall of Zhoushan.' There is no introduction to the contents of the *Fuhai ji* and no examination of it. Possibly Professor Xie did not see the text himself.

There is included in volumes 98–100 of the *Siming congshu* (Collection of the Siming Mountains) a work entitled *Feng shilang yishu* (Posthumous Writings of Attendant Censor Feng) (8 *juan* with 3 *juan* of appendices), but the *Fuhai ji* is not in it. Just the title of this work remains now, and it seems to be a phantom work at that. If, indeed, a work entitled *Fuhai ji* penned by Feng himself has been passed down to our time intact, then we might learn more about the truth of his mission requesting aid, but at present that would be mere speculation.

I have seen a work with the title *Fuhai ji*[g] which is a photolithographic edition of an old manuscript (supposedly in the former collection of Wang Lipei of Hunan). It is also appended to the photolithographic edition of an old manuscript by Qian Bingdeng, *Suozhi lu* (A Record of What Is Known). The original manuscript of this *Fuhai ji* bears as its author's name Zhang Linbai, while Feng Jingdi's name appears nowhere. The copier of this manuscript added an appendix to the work, which notes: 'This work was written and given its title by Zhang Linbai. Zhang Linbai did not investigate the various ministers of Lu, but he examined the case of the request for help from Japan and learned what Xu Fuyuan had done. He has disguised his name to pass in the world.' An explanatory note by Li Zongtong from Gaoyang in the first *juan* continues in this vein: 'Zhang used an alias, and in fact it was Xu Fuyuan who went to Japan to request assistance,' but no analysis or corroboration is provided. As for Xu Fuyuan, there is a brief mention of him in the *Ming shi* (History of the Ming Dynasty),[h] but in *Xiaotian jizhuan* (*juan* 41, 'liezhuan' no. 34) there is a rather detailed biography of him. The trip to Japan in search of military assistance, though, is absent from it. Perhaps it was some sort of misunderstanding on the part of the manuscript copier, perhaps simply confusion.

The work looks at men like Huang Binqing, Zhou Cuizhi, and Wu Zhongluan who were based on Zhoushan Island, and gives brief biographies of such figures as Zheng Zhilong, Zheng Hongkui, and Zheng Chenggong, and examines their mutual relations. At the end, the Prince of Lu employs Zhanwei to convey an oral message and sends Ruan Mei off to Japan as assistant emissary loaded down with Buddhist texts to seek help. The story is the same as that recorded in the latter half of the *Riben qishi ji*.

Although Feng Jingdi's name appears nowhere in this text, there may be reason to believe it was his work. In it, the Prince of Lu initially does not give his permission, but then wishes that Ruan Jin's plan be put into action:

With one powerful minister as principal emissary [Feng Jingdi?], he made his [i.e., Ruan Jin's] younger brother, the naval commander Ruan Mei, assistant [emissary]. The multitudes pressed for the Great Earl Wu Zhongluan to go, [too]. Master Wu was old, and [the emissaries] were selected from the lesser lords. Were I not to go, it was decided to have been impossible. I put on the garb of a rank 2 official, was given the official long gown and sash, feted at a banquet by the Prince, and then sent off. . . .

After this point in the text, the ship sails toward Nagasaki and when it docks there, the author notes: 'Ruan Mei's ship arrived. In gauging the strength of the wind and waves, he said that they had not been particularly bad. Thus, I knew why the Buddhist texts had been loaded onto my ship.' Later, again, the first person singular as author of the *Fuhai ji* appears in the texts several times: 'On this day, I called for an interpreter to board the ship,' and 'he wanted me to come ashore to greet me.'

In the section on 'Zhou Hezhi' in the *Nanjiang yishi*, we find the corresponding reference to Ruan Mei as the assistant emissary and Feng Jingdi as the principal emissary on this mission. However, in the *Fuhai ji*, Ruan Mei and Zhanwei travel together, and when Zhanwei is discovered as having called himself the 'saint of the golden lion,' he is thought to be a Christian from the West and exiled; the story follows just what appears in the *Riben qishi ji*. However, the account of Feng Jingdi traveling to Nagasaki with Huang Xiaoqing, as is found in the *Riben qishi ji*, is nowhere to be found in *Fuhai ji*.

The *Siwen daji*, cited above, is a chronicle from the era of Longwu (the Siwen emperor) who was based in Fujian province. There is also the *Lu chunqiu*,[i] which chronicles the political history surrounding the Prince of Lu (who was not an 'emperor' but 'Administrator of the Realm'), the last Ming descendent, based in eastern Zhejiang and a rival of Longwu. In an entry for Yongli 5 (1651, corresponding to Keian 4), the *Lu chunqiu* carries the following: 'In the seventh lunar month that fall, they requested provisions from Japan. The king [to whom this refers is uncertain] permitted the rapid transport by sea of several thousand *shi* of food provisions.' This is then followed by the an explanation:

Earlier, in the *dinghai* year [1647], the Prince of Peace and Prosperity received orders from the Administrator of the Realm to seek help from Japan. . . . He had reached the island of Nagasaki,[j] and an island interpreter reported [this matter] to shōgun Minamoto [Tokugawa]. . . . First-degree graduate Ling Shihong and first-degree graduate Feng Jingdi traveled on with a letter from State Minister Zhang Kentang and a letter in blood [indicating a desperate request] from Huang Binqing, master of suppression of the barbarians. By chance, four Christian vessels lost their wind, were shipwrecked, and came on shore. Thereupon, shōgun Minamoto raised an army and fought them off. He comforted them [the Chinese] in the request for military provisions. The request for foodstuffs was the third trip of the Administrator of the Realm.

This citation makes it clear that no troops were forthcoming, but in their place military provisions were sent, and that this request for supplies of autumn 1651 was the third of the Administrator of the Realm (the Prince of Lu). Although unable to obtain the requested military assistance, they were aided with military supplies, and this would seem to indicate that in fact their primary aim was troops, which this voyage was the third attempt to secure.

In the *Riben qishi ji* it states that Cuizhi sent his adopted son, Lin Gao, to Japan to accompany the Prince of Peace and Prosperity in the *dinghai* year, and Huang Binqing dispatched Feng Jingdi and Huang Xiaoqing in the *wuzi* year. The *Lu chunqiu* records these events occurring one year later. This may be an example of conflicting records or discrepancies in accounts among those items taken to be fundamental in the historical materials. Perhaps it was due to a report transcribed well after the fact. Thus, relying solely on a certain quantity of historical narratives is, in fact, no more than groping speculation. We have no alternative, though, save lining up what appear to be the vestiges of historical facts.

I should like next to consider what appears in the entry for Yongli 3, the *yichou* year (Keian 2 [1649]), in the *Lu chunqiu*: 'In winter, the eleventh month, Chamberlain Yu Tunan was sent to Japan to establish friendly relations.' The fact that Yu Tunan came to Japan for this reason cannot be found in any of the Japanese historical records I have perused. But perhaps this was one example of increasingly frequent numbers of vessels coming to Japan on friendly terms (and possibly seeking aid).

Chapter Twenty-Five

Satsuma, Japanese Pirates, and Ming China

Zhou Cuizhi (perhaps Zhou Hezhi) arrived in Japan, and, as described in the *Riben qishi ji* and other Chinese texts, 'forged a father-son bond with the King of Satsuma.' This may have been no more than Cuizhi's own self-promotion or perhaps a narrative of interesting exaggerations by rumor-mongers. We should not overlook the fact that the relationship between Satsuma and Cuizhi or someone like Cuizhi, namely a Chinese pirate-trader of that time, may be based on wildly inaccurate or baseless stories. Let me dig a bit further into this question now.

According to the biography in Wen Ruilin's *Nanjiang yishi*, when Cuizhi was 'nearly 40 years of age,' he 'saw that the realm was on the verge of chaos and became indignant.' Seeking to make himself 'useful to the imperial court' by bringing an end to all 'illicit acts' of the sort carried out till then by pirates, 'he was given the post of company commander of Huanghuaguan, and he kept an eye on merchant vessels.'

As for the extent of the influence that Cuizhi, a pirate himself at the time, had, we find the following account in *juan* 7 of the *Siwen daji*: 'Zhang Kentang reported to the Longwu Emperor that Cuizhi was an able seaman and had over 50 vessels and over 2000 troops at his disposal. To expiate his crimes and achieve victory, he [Cuizhi] asked to be brought under the banner of the minister [Zhang].' This citation would indicate that Cuizhi controlled a large number of ships and was a pirate leader with a large number of troops, but that he had surrendered and joined forces with Zhang Kentang.

If, as the *Nanjiang yishi* states, when Cuizhi was only 40 years of age, he quit his life as a pirate to become an official, he probably came to Satsuma before then. If, however, as the *Riben qishi ji* and the *Nanjiang yishi* note, he sent an emissary to the lord of Satsuma domain and 'appealed on behalf of the sad chaos in China, and requested the sending of a brigade of troops' in the winter of the *yiyou* year (1645), then counting backward from that year he would have been coming to Satsuma in his thirties or twenties, during the Genna or Kan'ei periods. In China, since Longwu ascended the throne in Fuzhou in the *yiyou* year, this would correspond to the late Wanli or Chongzhen reign periods.

At this time *wakō* (C., *wokou*) [lit., Japanese pirates] activity was on the decline, but they had left a trail, it would seem, in their aftermath. According to Chen Mouheng's *Mingdai wokou kaolüe* (A Summary of Japanese Pirates in the Ming Period),[a] in Genna 2 (1616) pirates attacked Fujian (citing the *Fujian tongzhi* [Comprehensive Gazetteer of Fujian]), and again in Genna 4 (1618) they attacked Jieyang in Guangdong (citing the *Guangdong tongzhi* [Comprehensive Gazetteer of Guangdong]). Needless to say, the *wakō* were a mixed group of Japanese pirate bands and Chinese coastal pirate groups. The Chinese pirates – principal among them being such men as Wang Zhi, Xu Hai, and Chen Dong – continually plundered sites along the coast and played havoc with the local people's lives. The government worked diligently to bring them under control, but the pirate bands fought the government armies and had sufficient power not to be outdone. Zheng Zhilong, who supported the Longwu Emperor of the Southern Ming and held effective power to control the Longwu court, had originally been a pirate, and Cuizhi was his mighty general with whom they had supported Longwu.

From this perspective, it becomes perfectly plausible that Cuizhi came to Japan at the time effectively in the role of one of these aftermaths. As for his relationship with Satsuma, we learn from a work by Zheng Shungong, *Riben yijian* (A Mirror of Japan),[b] that Satsuma was a base of operations for the *wakō*.

The *Riben yijian* in four stringbound volumes was the work of Zheng Shungong who came to Japan as an envoy of the Ming over the period generally of Jiajing 34–36 (1555–57); his objective was to propose to the Japanese authorities a way of controling the *wakō*. He then wrote this work on the basis of a large number of historical documents and personal investigations. It is a guide to Japan in many areas, and there are a variety of maps inserted in the text. Noteworthy in particular is the narrative concerning his own views about the *wakō* based on personal observations. In a sub-section entitled 'Fengtu' (Topography) in *juan* four in the section 'Qionghe huahai' (Investigating the Rivers and Discussing the Seas), he notes:

> Many of the ordinary people of Satsuma are merchants, and a large number are bandits [namely, *wakō*]. In the *bingchen* year of the Jiajing reign [1556], a local bandit by the name of Kamon threatened and attacked Xu Hai [a pirate who acted as a guide for *wakō*; see below]. For the past twenty years, the area of Takasu [in another section, 'Beilu' (Captives) in *juan* 6, there is a note indicating that the two characters 高州 are to be read 'Takasu' in Japanese] has been a place for drifters and vagrants to lay low. Over this period of time, some 100 local families there have taken as many as 200 to 300 of our [Chinese] people prisoners, and they have become Japanese slaves. They are coastal people from Fuzhou, Xinghua, Quanzhou, and Zhangzhou.

Dubious as the accuracy of these numbers may be, inasmuch as they are recorded here it would seem that already from the late Ashikaga period (1392–

1573) many people from the Fujian area had been taken captive by *wakō* and were living in Satsuma. Even if they had no contact at all with *wakō*, it would appear that there were Fujianese who came and went at Satsuma, either in connection with the many fellow provincials already resident or with their descendents. Both the *Riben qishi ji* and the *Nanjiang yishi* record that Cuizhi was a man from Fujian. Perhaps the fact that the pirate Cuizhi 'came and went' at Satsuma was related in some way to the tail end of *wakō* activity.

In addition, they generally followed a pattern of behavior in which they were engaged at the time in trade (largely secret trade), while using that as cover for the piratical plunder and theft committed against the cargo on others' ships. Thus, at times they assumed the guise of traders, remaining pirates nonetheless.

About Zheng Shungong, the author of the *Riben yijian*, we find the following mention in the *Jiajing dongnan pingwo tonglu* (Comprehensive Account of the Suppression of the Japanese Bandits in the Southeast during the Jiajing Period): 'At first, the Japanese monk Seiju arrived in Ningbo to accompany Zheng Shunchen who was to be sent [to Japan] by Minister Yang Yi.' This text, the *Jiajing dongnan pingwo tonglu*, was printed in 1932 [in one *juan*] from a manuscript held in the 'Guoxue tushuguan' (Library of National Learning) in Nanjing. In fact, as Liu Yizheng points out in his postface to the photolithographic edition, it is the same as the entry, 'Riben' (Japan), under 'Bingbu' (Board of War) 33, in *juan* 169 of the *Guochao dianhui* (Institutes of the Dynasty) [preface dated Tianqi 4 (1624)] by Xu Xueju.[c]

While the *Guochao dianhui* follows chronologically from 'Hongwu 2' (1369) through the Yongle, Xuande, Zhengtong, Chenghua, Hongzhi, and Jiajing reigns, however, the *Jiajing dongnan pingwo tonglu* begins abruptly with 'Jiajing 31 [1552]' after a brief prefatory note about the initial Jiajing years. In others words, the latter was a chronicle of an era in which the harm caused by *wakō* had become particularly severe, and it ends with 'Longqing 2 [1568]' (as does the *Guochao dianhui*). A Ming-era edition of the *Guochao dianhui* is held in the Naikaku Bunko (I was able to copy the section entitled 'Japan' therein), but it has recently been reprinted in Taiwan by Xuesheng shuju in four stringbound volumes.

Emissary Zheng Shunchen, who was sent to Japan by Minister Yang Yi, appears in both the *Jiajing dongnan pingwo tonglu* and the *Guochao dianhui*. He is probably the same person as Zheng Shungong, author of the *Riben yijian*. The following entry on Zheng Shungong can be found in the *Ming shi* (under 'Waiguo' [Foreign States] 3, *juan* 322):

Zheng Shungong, who had been sent on a mission [to Japan] by Yang Yi, went overseas to spy on [the foreigners]. He departed and reached Bungo island. The king of the island again sent the monk Seiju as emissary who came by boat; he acknowledged their guilt, saying: 'As for the recent infringements, in every case dishonest Chinese merchants have secretively taken locals from the islands. [Ōtomo] Yoshishige [1530–87] knows nothing of this.'

Additionally, the *Riben guo zhi* (Treatises on Japan) (preface dated Guangxu 23 [1897]) of Huang Zunxian (a Qing diplomat stationed in Japan in the early-Meiji period) has the following to say about Zheng Shungong in *juan* 5, 'Lin jiao zhi' (Treatise on Contacts with Neighbors) (part 2):

> In the first year of the Kōji reign period [1555, corresponding to Jiajing 34], Governor-general Yang Yi of the Ming dispatched Zheng Shungong who proceeded to Hirado in Hizen (?). He was able to meet with Ōtomo Yoshishige, and reprovingly said: 'We have had friendly ties for many years. Why are [your people now] causing havoc to our shores and taking our people prisoner? Stop behaving in this manner at once.' Yoshishige passed along this information to Shōgun [Ashikaga] Yoshiteru. [The shōgun] ordered his lords to a meeting.

Huang Zunxian does not precisely indicate what source he based this information on, but materials on the Japanese side that I have seen generally agree. I would like to discuss one text, 'Yoshū Nojima shi shin tai Minkoku ki' (Chronicle of the Invasion of the Great Ming by Mr. Nojima of Yoshū), in volume 5 of Kasai Shigesuke's *Nankai chiran ki* (Chronicle of War and Peace in the Southern Seas),[d] where there is an entry, 'Tei Shun kō' (Marquis Zheng Shun[gong]), which reads as follows:

> After the collapse of Ōuchi Yoshitaka's rebellion, Ōtomo Yoshishige pacified the domains of Buzen and Chikuzen. Just at that time, there was sent to the state of Japan from the Great Ming an imperial letter, which read: 'China and Japan have carried on licensed trade for many years now. Recently, these good ties have declined, and all invitations have been severed. Furthermore, with every passing year Japanese pirate ships increasingly have come and assaulted the coast of the Great Ming. It is my hope that you will be able to bring a stop to these acts of piracy and restore peace and security to the people. For that reason I have written this letter, and it will certainly be beneficial when our old friendship is restored to harmony.'
>
> The emissary from the Great Ming, a man by the name of Marquis Zheng Shun, arrived at the port of Hakata. Because Ōtomo Yoshishige of Bungo controlled the western provinces at that time, he was seen as the King of Japan, and the imperial letter was delivered to him. He described his feelings, saying: 'The so-called King of Japan is, in fact, the master of the royal domains [namely, the emperor]. I hold control over the western provinces and only protect them as a pillar, for I am not the king. In Japan at present the eminent lords of various states are in a state of war, and they do not uphold the morality of a king's rule. There is thus no need to report this to the court. In addition, every day we ceaselessly make war preparations to protect our holdings, continue our internecine strife, and have no time to dispatch troops to other domains. [The piracy] is only the

work of bandits on islands. An order from the court will make no difference.' The emissary heard this and returned.[1]

How the coming of emissary Zheng Shungong was dealt with by Japan seems to have been conveyed accurately or nearly so in the aforementioned *Nankai chiran ki*. Seen as a whole, the *Riben yijian* appears to confirm what was pointed out earlier in the *Ming shi*, that Zheng 'went overseas to spy on foreigners.' What it chronicles in this connection contains points in great detail not to be found elsewhere, but the conflict over the suppression of the *wakō* was not concretely recorded.

What the *Riben yijian* has to say in connection with Satsuma is based on the conclusion that Zheng Shungong came to Japan at the time, and investigated and 'spied' on the *wakō* issue from many angles. Although we cannot now affirm this completely, I do think it possible to say that there are a fair number of facts to that effect.

At the time, Satsuma and China (in the southeast) retained contacts, and Satsuma's 'Bōnotsu' in the southwest corner of Kyūshū was flourishing as a strategic harbor in the Ming-Japanese trade. In *juan* 231 of his work, *Wubei zhi* (Treatise on Military Preparedness) (preface dated Tianqi 1 [1621]), Mao Yuanyi included a subsection entitled 'Jinyao' (Harbor Strategies), under 'Riben kao' (Study of Japan), part 2 of 'Si yi' (Four Foreign Peoples). Mao has the following to say about Japan's 'Strategic Ports':

> The country has three harbors, and each is a place where merchant vessels congregate, ports[2] opening out onto the high seas for traffic. They are along the western coast: Bōnotsu [belonging to Satsuma], Hakatanotsu [belonging to Chikuzen], and Anotsu [belonging to Ise]. Bōnotsu is considered the main route, as foreign vessels must come and go through there. Hakatanotsu is the central port, ... and Anotsu is the last port.

From the foregoing, it appears that at the time Bōnotsu in Satsuma was seen as the 'main route' for those traveling from southeast China to Japan. Ships came first there and then continued on to Hakatanotsu or Anotsu. Since there was as well the route from Ningbo (in Zhejiang) or Zhoushan through the Gotō Islands and then on toward Hakatanotsu, to call Bōnotsu the 'main route' would seem to indicate that he was speaking of cases involving travel to Japan primarily from Zhejiang and Fujian in the southeast or the Guangxi-Guangdong region. At that time, many traveled via the Ryūkyū Islands to Satsuma, and thus the Ryūkyūs served generally as a relay or intermediary between Satsuma and the Ming dynasty.

Earlier than the *Wubei zhi*, however, there is a text known as the 'Riben rukou tu' (Diagram of the Japanese Invaders) in Zheng Ruoceng's *Riben tuzuan* (Maps of Japan) (with a preface dated Jiajing 40 [1561]).[e] In a section in this work entitled 'Satsuma,' the following explanation is given: 'The *wakō* came along the main route to Fujian and Guangdong.' Under 'Gotō,' it says: 'The *wakō* came

津要

問有三津皆商舶所聚通海之江也、西海道有坊
津薩摩州　　州花旭塔津所筑前州伊勢州三津惟
坊津為総路客船往返必由花旭塔津為中津地
方廣闊人煙湊集中間海商無不泊此地有松林
方長十里有名中里松士名洗齊煞橫乃前先也有
一術名大唐街與人留彼相俟今畫為倭也洞津
為木津地方又遠與山城相近貨物或偹或缺惟
中津無不有貿易川銀金銅錢悉経祀名曰乃隔

From the *Wubei zhi* section entitled 'Jinyao' (Kansai University Library)

along the main route to Zhili, Zhejiang, and Shandong.' In the section entitled 'Tsushima,' we read: 'The *wakō* came along the main route to Korea and Liaodong.' From these and other various 'main routes' – 'from there they entered Quanzhou and Zhangzhou,' 'from there they entered Fuzhou and Xinghua,' 'from there they entered Ningbo,' 'from there they entered the Qiantang River area,' 'from there they entered the Yangzi River area,' and the like – the points along the Chinese coast that were invaded are indicated. The three strategic harbors just given in the *Wubei zhi* are removed from *wakō* activity and seem more closely connected to general trade and intercourse.

Until Kan'ei 12 (1635) when the Tokugawa shogunate, wanting to maintain control in foreign intercourse, limited Chinese vessels entering ports to that of Nagasaki, Bōnotsu flourished for a time as a center of Ming trade. The curious products from overseas that were gathered here are the subject of Kawashima Genjirō's chapter, 'Tōsen ni karamaru Bōnotsu no seisui' (The Rise and Fall of Bōnotsu, Entangled among Chinese Vessels) in his work, *Nankoku shiwa* (Historical Tales from the Southern Lands).[f] He visited Bōnotsu, investigated it, and added his own study.

Kawashima recorded that he visited Shimabara Eiji, a descendant of Shimabara Kamonnosuke, a trading family from Bōnotsu in the distant past, and examined an old document in his collection. It was an official shogunal license to trade with the Ryūkyū Islands given to 'Shimabara Kamonnosuke, captain of the *Tenjinmaru*,' signed by Shimazu Yoshihisa, dated ninth day, eleventh month, Tenshō 12 (1584). A scholar of such matters – he was the author of such works as *Tokugawa shoki no kaigai bōekika* (Overseas Traders in the Early Tokugawa Period) and *Shuinsen bōeki shi* (A History of Trade by Licensed Vessels)[g] – he wrote that the 'Tokugawa shogunate pioneered in the licensing of merchant vessels from overseas.' In particular, it was essential that these shogunal licenses have clearly written on them the name of the vessel and of the captain.

This ship's captain, Shimabara Kamonnosuke, was widely known as Kiuemon, and he successfully operated a shipping enterprise; from this we know that he sent vessels in the direction of the Ryūkyūs. He apparently did well in his actual shipping trade, but in Keichō 5 (1600), he sailed to China and proceeded to Beijing. He had been ordered by the Shimazu family to repatriate to China the Ming General Mao Guoke, who had been brought back to Japan as a hostage by Shimazu Yoshihiro during the invasion of Korea [under Hideyoshi a few years earlier]. He departed from Bōnotsu with a hundred or more men under his command, placed Mao Guoke on board, and proceeded first to Fuzhou, and from there they were escorted as far as Beijing. The Ming emperor Shenzong [r. 1573–1620] granted Kiuemon an audience and threw a sumptuous banquet for him. The foregoing is based on Kawashima's research; in fact, it can be found in Shimazu Hisatoshi's *Sei-Kan roku* (Account of the Expedition against Korea) (Kanbun 11 [1671])[h] and Tokunō Michiaki's *Seihan yashi* (Unofficial History of the Western Domains) (Hōreki 10 [1760]?).

The matter of repatriating prisoner Mao Guoke can also be found in the *Nanpo bunshū* (Literary Collection of Nanpo) (printed in Keian 2 [1649]).[3] 'Nanpo' was the literary style of a monk by the name of Bunshi who was respectfully treated by Satsuma domainal lords – Shimazu Yoshihisa, Yoshihiro, and Iehisa – in the Keichō and Genna reigns. He held a post in which he was responsible for diplomatic correspondence.

Among works that contain records about Nanpo, although it cannot be considered a study of him, is the *Nanpo Bunshi ōshō* (Nanpo, Monk Bunshi)[i] by Mori Keizō (Taikyō). Among the pieces collected in the *Nanpo bunshū* are all manner of official documents written on behalf of the Satsuma lord. These include: 'Letter Presented to the Emissary of the Great Ming,' 'To Merchants of the Great Ming,' 'To Yi Wuzi of the Great Ming,' 'Letter to the Provincial Military Commander of Fujian in the Great Ming,' 'Letter to a Barbarian Chief,' 'Reply to a Barbarian Chief,' 'Reply to a Ship's Captain of the Southern Barbarians,' 'Letter to a Ship's Captain from the State of Luzon,' 'Reply to the State of Annam,' 'Reply to the King of the Ryūkyūs,' 'Reply to the Official of the Ryūkyūs,' and 'Reply to the King of Zhongshan.' A look at these documents reveals the state of commercial interactions and trade between Satsuma at the time and China, the Ryūkyūs, and the states to the south. We also learn that they earnestly hoped for continued flourishing trade with these lands.

The Ming General Mao Guoke (Weibin), who (according to Kawashima) was taken prisoner by the Satsuma army during the invasion of Korea, also appears in

173

the *Nanpo bunshū*. Using the subsequent return of Mao to Ming China as a pretext, a document was drawn up that planned for the revival of trade relations between the Ming and Satsuma.

In a document, 'Pedigree of the Line of Yoshihiro,' included in the first volume of *Nanpo bunshū*, there is mention of Yoshihiro's and his son's description of the fighting that had transpired with the Ming armies in Korea:

> The military commanders of the Great Ming sent an army of several million troops to attack [the Satsuma army's base] in Sach'ŏn.[j] Yoshihiro and his son fielded several tens of thousands who did not fight but surrendered. For this reason, he lifted up his belt and charged forward into the millions of troops. In a brief period of time, the [Ming] army crushed them.... Then, Counselor-in-Chief Long Ya sought peace talks with our military forces.... Finally, responding to his request, the Great Ming General Mao Weibin was made a hostage, and he was placed on board ship and returned with them to Japan.

In another section of this volume, entitled 'Funeral Eulogy for Those Lost in the War,' there is the following note: 'The Great Ming general, his arrows spent and his bowstring broken, ultimately surrendered to us. We took this General Mao Guoke as hostage, together boarded ships, and returned home.' As for the later repatriation of Mao Guoke, we find the following in the 'Letter Presented to the Emissary of the Great Ming' (this text opens with: 'Respectfully submitted by Fujiwara Iehisa, lord of Satsuma domain in the land of Japan, to the emissary of the Great Ming....'):

> Earlier, the Chinese named Mao Guoke was resident in Korea and Japan for three or four years. We demonstrated extreme respect for the [Ming] imperial court. We dispatched a vessel and sent along official Kiuemon to repatriate [Mao] to the land of China. We have yet to investigate whether or not [Mao] Guoke is in good health, but to this day someone has been assigned to watch out in this matter.

Among the documents which speak of Chinese vessels coming to Satsuma and the flourishing trade they brought, these describe the depth of the relationship between the Ming and Satsuma. Kawashima informs us that the person referred to herein as the 'official Kiuemon' was Shimabara Kamonnosuke. Kawashima does not clearly indicate what the historical sources are for his assertion that Mao Guoke, prisoner of war from the Korean campaign, was repatriated to China, but he was probably basing himself in *Nanpo bunshū*, *Sei-Kan roku*, and *Seihan yashi*.

Might not the 'Kamon,' who appears in the entry on Satsuma in the aforementioned 'Qionghe huahai' from the *Riben yijian* – 'In the *bingchen* year of the Jiajing reign [1556], a local bandit by the name of Kamon threatened and attacked Xu Hai' – point to 'Shimabara Kamonnosuke' (Kiuemon) or perhaps the author linked the two names. Although I cannot point precisely to historical documentation, this does in any event provide corroborative evidence that such a powerful overseas trader from Satsuma existed at the time. It also seems to bear some relationship to my own excavations, mentioned earlier, about Cuizhi's coming to Japan and 'forging a father-son bond with the King of Satsuma.'

One further work about the ties between Satsuma and the *wakō* should not be overlooked. There is a section entitled 'Kouzong fenhe shimo tupu' (Complete Illustrated Treatise Analyzing the Vestiges of the Pirates) in *juan* 8 of the *Chouhai tubian* (Illustrated Text on Coast Defenses) (preface dated Jiajing 41 [1562]) by Hu Zongxian.[k] In it we find an explanation of Chen Dong, who is known as a leader of *wakō*, along with Wang Zhi and Xu Hai: 'He was the head of the personal scribes of the younger brother of the lord of Satsuma domain and had many men of Satsuma under his command.' Whether this is true or false, this entry in the *Chouhai tubian*, a Chinese text, does also describe an extremely close bond between Satsuma and the *wakō*.

Chapter Twenty-Six

Satsuma, Ming China, and
the Invasion of Korea

From the extant historical materials, we can at best generally trace the relationship between Satsuma and Ming China. On Hideyoshi's military expeditions to Korea, and particularly the movements of the Satsuma army at that time, these traces can be found in Shimazu Hisatoshi's *Sei-Kan roku*. I first examined the copy of this text held in the Naikaku Bunko (originally held in the Asakusa Bunko). I later learned that it was included in the *Shimazu shiryō shū* (Collection of Historical Documents on Shimazu)[a] and printed with annotations based on the manuscripts held in the collection of Shimazu Hisamitsu.

In an introduction to the *Sei-Kan roku* provided by Hayashi Shunsai, we learn that Shimazu Hisamitsu, grandfather of Shimazu Hisatoshi, the compiler of this work, joined in the Korean Expedition in the army of Shimazu Yoshihiro: 'How could the veracity of this work, the truth of this chronicle, ever be compared to common street chatter!' In other words, *Sei-Kan roku* should be regarded as historical material with a high degree of reliability, and it contains much information concerning the relationship between Satsuma and Ming China.

Does this then mean that the events recorded in the *Sei-Kan roku* (and, for that matter, Tokunō Michiaki's *Seihan yashi*), such as Shimabara Kiuemon's escorting of two large vessels, the repatriation of Mao Guoke who had been taken as a hostage during the the Korean Expedition and brought back to Japan, and Shimabara's audience with Ming Emperor Shenzong and the extravagant banquet held in his honor in Beijing, are all true? I have attempted to find confirmation in the *Ming shilu* (Veritable Records of the Ming Dynasty), but was unable to locate any record of Shenzong's holding an audience for Shimabara. Yet, in the *Liangchao pingrang lu* (The Record of Level Land over Two Eras) by Zhuge Yuansheng (preface dated Wanli 34 [1606]),[b] we read:

> On [Wanli] 28/4/18 a Japanese vessel carrying Mao Guoke arrived from Changguo in Ningbo. By imperial command it was soon sent home. It bore aloft a large banner on which was written: 'Pacify the barbarians and sing

triumphantly.' The king of Japan sent one letter to Xing Jinglüe and another to the Fujian Governor Jin Xueceng. With each he included a present of [Japanese] weaponry, horses' armor, and a golden helmet. They were placed in a box together. On board ship was one Japanese commander, 50 to 60 Japanese soldiers, and an additional twenty to 30 persons outside the imperial command from Zhangzhou and elsewhere who were repatriated. On that day a wind from Jiushan blew and burst into Dinghaiguan that night. The area was terrified and doors were shut. Brigade Commander Lu was sent to investigate and went to see the Zhejiang provincial military commander. A military officer wanted to kill the Japanese to acquire [military] merit, but he was not allowed to do so. Ultimately, a banquet was held with entertainment. The provincial military commander ordered that they be rewarded with silver medals, woven caps, and oxen and lambs.... The provincial military commander dispatched people to go to the Meihuasuo in Fujian. Together with Jin Shengwu, they set sail from their home village. In the eighth lunar month they were able to set off and departed for home.

As we see here, the escart party for Mao Guoke passed through Dinghai from Ningbo en route to Meihuasuo in Fujian. From there they retraced their steps to Japan. Thus, they were received not by Emperor Shenzong but by the Zhejiang provincial military commander. Perhaps the report of their traveling as far as Beijing and being received by the emperor was embellishment passed along by Shimabara Kiuemon.

When the army of Shimazu Yoshihiro and that of Ming General Mao Guoqi confronted one another, a woman from Yoshihiro's camp appeared with a letter. She was captured by a patrol and brought before General Mao. The letter was from Guo Guoan. Mao then had it sent on to Counselor Shi Shiyong. The *Sei-Kan roku* records:

> [Shi] Shiyong was overjoyed and said: 'Guo Guoan is a Chinese. *When I once sailed to Japan, I met with Guoan at a place called Bōnotsu in Satsuma domain* and had an intimate conversation. Now, he is happily in Yoshihiro's camp. Our troops think that Guoan is a spy, and they are more than willing to destroy the Japanese camp.' However, because of the details of what Guoan had said, Shiyong wrote up a letter and relied on a Korean merchant to deliver it to Guoan. Soon thereafter, Guoan himself replied in writing. His general point was that he was now in Korea, in the camp of Shimazu Yoshihiro [emphasis Masuda's].

Shi Shiyong reported that he had conspired with Guo Guoan in the Satsuma army and had wanted to destroy that army, but in the *Sei-Kan roku* Guo ultimately helped Satsuma with military strategy and won great victory.

The point that a woman had arrived at the military camp of General Mao Guoqi with Guo Guoan's letter from the Shimazu camp is recorded as well in the

Wubei zhi and the *Liangchao pingrang lu*. The *Sei-Kan roku* (and the *Seihan yashi* which is thought to have been based upon it) cite passages from the *Wubei zhi* and the *Liangchao pingrang lu*, and it appears to have been written on the basis of these two works. For example, in a section entitled 'Chaoxian kao' (A Study of Korea) in *juan* 239 of the *Wubei zhi*, we find: 'A mounted patrol caught a woman coming from the Japanese camp. She produced a letter from her pocket.... [Mao] Guoqi helped as Zhuge Xiu explained: "It's from Guo Guoan." He spoke with Counselor Shi Shiyong. Shiyong was overjoyed and said: "Guo Guoan is a Chinese. We were in Japan together once, and together pledged meritorious deeds on behalf of the [Ming] dynasty. Now he is here and they say he is a spy."' The *Liangchao pingrang lu* is more abbreviated than this, but contains a similar report. The *Sei-Kan roku* took this over in its entirety.

As concerns Guo Guoan (Lixin), in volume 13 of the *Seihan yashi* (preface dated to the Hōreki era [1751–64]) we find the following:

> Lixin was a man of Fenyang during the Ming era. He used the styles Guoan and Guangyu. He went to the capital to sit for the civil service examinations. He arrived late and returned home. There was a boat set to sail for Japan, and Guangyu, wanting to see Japan, boarded it. It arrived and docked in the Satsuma capital in Bunroku 2 [1593].[c] He was at that time 23 years of age [by East Asian count]. Lord Yoshihisa detained him and compelled him to remain in Satsuma. He then took Fenyang as his family name and was given Lixin as his given name. To handle correspondence, he and a priest from the Daiji Temple accompanied the troops. Lixin's descendent was named Funyō [Ch. Fenyang] Shigeuemon.

After the Korean Expedition, Guo Guoan and his descendents seem to have become naturalized men of Satsuma. Guo and one Xu Yihou who (from Tenshō 19 [1591]) had also been in the employ of Yoshihisa in Satsuma – he was said to have been seized together with his ships in Guangdong – became liaisons who jointly submitted a document (effected in Wanli 20 [1592]) which secretly reported to China on Hideyoshi's sending of troops to Korea. This matter can be seen in an appendix, entitled 'Jinbao Wo jing' (Recently Reported Japanese [Bandit] Alarms), in the Ming work, *Quan Zhe bingzhi kao* (A Study of the Military Institutions for Protecting Zhejiang Province) (see below).

As noted above, the *Sei-Kan roku* points out that Counselor Shi Shiyong of the Ming armed forces said: 'When we once sailed to Japan, I met with Guoan at a place called Bōnotsu in Satsuma domain.' The *Liangchao pingrang lu* (under 'Riben' [Japan], part 2, in *juan* 5) adds a note: 'He hailed from Wujin. With an introduction from the Fujian provincial military commander, in [Jiajing] 26 [1547] he went to the home of Xing Jinglüe [in the *Sei-Kan roku*, this read: 'Commander Xing Jie']. During the third month, he left and returned to the camp of Mao' Guoqi. He does indeed appear to have been a man originally active in the Fujian area, and he thus seems in this period to have made a trip to Satsuma.

We have already noted something of relations between Satsuma and the Fujian region when we looked at the case of Zhou Cuizhi, and we find in the *Seihan yashi* (volume 13) the following record:

In the spring of Bunroku 3 [1594],[d] the Taikō [i.e., Hideyoshi] ordered Lord Ryūhaku [i.e., Yoshihiro's father, Yoshihisa, who had not left for the front because of his advanced age] to send a letter to Fujian, conveying wishes for peace. Earlier, Konishi [Yukinaga]'s emissary, Naitō Hida no kami, had gone to China and had not yet returned. They did not know if peace was a reality. Thus, they tried to convey from Satsuma to Fujian a token of gratitude. You Ming of the Fujian local censorate and Xu Yu, censor-in-chief, replied in a letter relating that they would give relief to troops and the people. They then sent another letter with the same intent. Lord Ryūhaku presented the two letters [to Hideyoshi].

Another note was inserted at this point: 'Note: The two letters to Lord Ryūhaku remain extant today.' At the time of the first military expedition to Korea, when Hideyoshi tested the Ming side concerning peace talks so as to save the situation, he ordered Shimazu Yoshihisa to convey a document to the Fujian officialdom. He may have done this because of the relationship that Shimazu had established with Fujian.

Another person who had established a link between Satsuma and Ming China over the Korean Expedition was Son Jirō; he served in the war effort as an interpreter for the Ming forces. In the *Sei-Kan roku*, it is reported that Son was born Zhang Mao in Nanjing: 'However, at age fifteen he lost his mother, and he feared poisoning by his stepmother. He ran away to Japan and was cared for by the local people in a place called Tamimoto in Ei county, Satsuma domain. And so he passed the years. In Tenshō 16 [1588] he heard a report of his stepmother's death and returned to Nanjing. Yet, inasmuch as he had spent so much time in Japan, he was called upon to act as an interpreter.'

According to the *Sei-Kan roku*, Terasawa Shima no kami of the Satsuma army heard from Son Jirō criticism from the Ming commanders of the great defeat visited by the Ming forces on Yoshihiro at Sach'ŏn. At that time, Son Jirō conveyed an evaluation of Mao Guoqi's battle defeat in five areas. The means by which Zhang Mao – Son Jirō – who was said to have hailed from Nanjing, came to Satsuma and was cared for by local people is not recorded, but the fact that he joined the Ming military forces as an interpreter in situations involving negotiations between the two armies appears to be much like Guo Guoan's joining the Satsuma armed forces to help in document communication. We cannot overlook the roles they played behind the scenes in negotiations between the two side at the time of the Korean Expedition.

We have already noted that in the *Chouhai tubian*, Chen Dong, a *wakō* leader, is referred to as 'a personal scribe of the younger brother of the lord of Satsuma domain.' This seems to have been considered a false report in Japan.

In volume eight of his *Ishō Nihon den* (Treatises on Japan under Different Titles) (author's preface dated Genroku 1 [1688]),[e] Matsushita Kenrin (Seihō) transcribed the *Hu gong Zongxian jiao Xu Hai benmo* (The Full Account of Hu Zongxian's Destruction of Xu Hai) by Mao Kun, which is included in *juan* 57 of Jiao Hong's [1541–1620] *Guochao xianzheng lu* (Dynastic Biographies [ca. 1616]).[f] In it we find the sentence: 'Chen Dong was a former military scribe for the younger brother of the king (*wang*) of Satsuma.' To this is added the note: 'There was no king of Satsuma, but rather a lord [*shou*; J. *kami*]. . . . The name of the younger brother of the lord of Satsuma remains unclear.'

In volume 282 of his *Ya shi* (Unofficial History) (author's introduction dated Kaei 4 [1851]),[g] entitled 'Gaikoku den (Min jō)' (Chronicles of Foreign Lands, the Ming, Part 1), Iida Tadahiko [1799–1860] quotes from precisely the same spot in the *Guochao xianzheng lu* to say that Chen 'Dong was a former military scribe for the younger brother of the king of Satsuma.' The text then notes: 'Investigation reveals no such person yet to be described in any Japanese work.'

The expression, 'king of Satsuma,' is unclear and probably was the result of a false report, but depending on how we approach the question, it may not have been completely without basis. Perhaps it refers to Shimazu Yoshihiro, younger brother of Shimazu Yoshihisa. Perhaps it was someone like Yoshihiro. In a section entitled 'On the Invasion of Chen [Dong] and the Japanese Bandits' of the 'Jinbao Wo jing' – namely, warnings about the *wakō* (in this instance, a reference to Hideyoshi's expedition to Korea) – which is included in Hou Jigao's *Quan-Zhe bingzhi kao* (printed in the Wanli reign of the Ming dynasty), we again find: 'The *kanpaku* [Hideyoshi] knew his intentions somewhat [the text earlier noted that the lord of Satsuma revered the Ming dynasty], and ordered the younger brother of the lord of Satsuma, Takekura [Yoshihiro], to take troops under his command.'

The 'Jinbao Wo jing' reports for Wanli 19 (1591, Tenshō 19 in Japan) that Xu Yihou and Guo Guoan, both then resident in Satsuma, together asked Zhu Junwang who was returning home aboard a Chinese vessel to convey a report to China (no specific address is given; it just says Qingtai). It reached China in the second month of Wanli 20 (Bunroku 1). The timing is a bit off here, for it was from the Jiajing 30s and 40s (1551–71) that the 'Japanese pirates' were at their strongest and most threatening, namely twenty or more years prior to this event. According to Shimazu Narioki's *Shimazu shi keifu ryaku* (A Brief Geneology of the Shimazu Family), Yoshihiro was born in Tenmon 4 (1535), and thus he was already in his twenties in Jiajing 34–35 (1555–56) when, according to the *Chouhai tubian*, Chen Dong invaded at the head of troops from Hizen, Chikuzen, Bungo, Izumi, Hakata, and Kii. Thus, equating 'the younger brother of the lord of Satsuma' with Yoshihiro falls within the scope of possibilities. However, it does not fall within the realm of reasonable inference to my satisfaction.

Claiming to be 'the younger brother of the king of Satsuma' probably carried distinctive authority among the pirates who maintained ties with the *wakō*. Thus Xu Hai asked Chen Dong to take his place and work as a scribe. It says of Xu

Hai in Mao Kun's *Hu gong Zongxian jiao Xu Hai benmo*: 'He took large amounts of Chinese goods and gold that he had plundered, bribed the younger brother of the king, and deceivingly asked that [Chen] Dong be employed as a scribe.'[h] The text mentions 'deceivingly,' and thus it accepts the point that it was a scheme by Xu Hai to deceive Chen Dong, but in any event he was trying to gain favor with 'the younger brother of the king of Satsuma.'

When the *Ishō Nihon den* cited the above reference to 'deceivingly asked that [Chen] Dong be employed as a scribe,' it changed the text to: 詐請東付罪書記. In the Ming edition of the *Guochao xianzheng lu*, however, we read: 詐請東代署書記. The *Ishō Nihon den* took the expression 代署 as 付罪. Inasmuch as the characters are similar in appearance, perhaps they were incorrectly transcribed in the initial drafting stage of the text, for Matsushita Kenrin's explanation of the latter phrase, which he took to be an error, makes no sense.

The *Ishō Nihon den* is a broad collection of accounts concerning Japan found in Chinese and Korean documents (in 127 sections) from antiquity forward. It took over 30 years to compile (according to the *Sentetsu sōdan zokuhen* [Collection of Biographical Notes on Wise Men of the Past, Continuation] of Tōjō Kindai [Nobuyasu, 1795–1878], vol. 3)[i] and is an extraordinarily useful work, but there are errors of this sort in it. In the area of punctuation, too, there are unreliable points. In the entry under 'Jinyao' in the *Wubei zhi*, we find the sentence: 'Trade using silver, gold, and copper coins relied on the *jingji* by the name of Nakayori.' He misplaced Japanese reading punctuation in the latter half of this phrase, because he misunderstood the meaning of the term *jingji* (broker, agent). Kita Shingen (Seiro) noted this point in his *Baien nikki* (Plum Orchard Diary) (Kōka 2 [1845]).[j] At present I do not have the original edition of the *Ishō Nihon den* (I have seen it), and I am basing what I write on the misreadings of this passage that appear in both the *Shiseki shūran* and the *Kōgaku sōsho* (Collection of Imperial Learning) of Mozume Takami.[k]

I should note in passing that there is a note beside the characters 'Xu Hai' in the margin of *Hu gong Zongxian jiao Xu Hai benmo*, which appears in the *Kōgaku sōsho*. It reads: 'The two prefectures of Cangzhou and Xuzhou in Zhejiang province.' Not to know who the famous Xu Hai, a leader of *wakō* on a par with Wang Zhi, and to mistake his name for a toponym is a major error.

Mao Kun's *Hu gong Zongxian jiao Xu Hai benmo*, cited in the *Ishō Nihon den*, is an important document for *wakō* studies. It describes in detail how Governor-General Hu Zongxian plotted, maneuvered, and eventually crushed the powerful pirate chiefs led by such men as Wang Zhi, Xu Hai, Chen Dong, and Ye Ma who were intimately tied to the *wakō*. As we find in the *Ming shi* ('Wenyuan zhuan' [Biographies of Literary Men], *juan* 287), Mao Kun (Lumen) 'enjoyed speaking of military matters.... When the *wakō* issue was pressing, he was invited to Hu Zongxian's staff, and together they made military preparations.' He thus helped Hu Zongxian devise strategies to deal with the *wakō*. Although his essay describing the circumstances surrounding the defeat of these pirates does indeed contain portions particularly lauding Hu Zongxian, it never deviates far from the actual circumstances. His work is mentioned under part 6 of the 'biographical materials' heading of the 'History Section' of the *Siku chuanshu zongmu tiyao* (Outline of the Catalog of the Complete Libraries of the Four Treasuries).

The aforementioned 'Jinbao Wo jing,' included as an appendix in the *Quan-Zhe bingzhi kao*, is a report on Hideyoshi's military expedition to Korea. Before the main text begins there is a section on Satsuma and the Chinese residents there at the time, including material seen scarcely anywhere else. As Xu Yihou states:

In the *xinwei* year [Longqing 5, Genki 2, 1571], my ship was passing through Guangdong and was captured. Fortunately, the lord of Satsuma in Japan liked to use unorthodox methods and thus saved our lives. Every time it was [Chinese] villainous sorts who drew the *wakō* into wreaking havoc with our great [Ming] state. They took prisoners of merchants and fishermen and turned around and sold their wares. It is all very sad. In the *yiyou* year [Tenshō 13 (1585)], I [Xu Yihou] and the others fearfully reported to the lord of Satsuma on the murders of Chen Hewu, Qian Shaofeng, and some ten or more others, that their wives and children were dead, and that the remaining bandits had gone off to Cambodia, Siam, Luzon, and elsewhere. A small number of pirate vessels awaited them there. In the *dinghai* year [Tenshō 15 (1587)], Hideyoshi brought down Satsuma, Hizen, and Higo, and the pirate ships stealthily set out to sea. I accompanied the lord of Satsuma to an audience [with Hideyoshi]. He risked death in an appeal to Hideyoshi, and as a result the order to have [the pirates] executed was rescinded. There were still two pirate leaders who had not been captured. From that time forward till the present day, there has been peace on the high seas.

...Those Chinese who lived for a long period of time in Japan all belonged to bands of pirates. Not one of them, I believe, ever dared speak the truth [about Hideyoshi's expedition]. Furthermore, all villagers who operated shops were not well versed in national affairs, and not one of them either ever spoke the truth about this.

This citation reveals that even in the Hideyoshi era there seem to have been, in addition to Xu Yihou and Guo Guoan, a fair number of Chinese residents in Satsuma. Furthermore, these Chinese apparently served as guides for the *wakō* and frequented the Chinese coast. Inasmuch as Xu Yihou claimed that he was taken prisoner from his ship in 1571, the year of Wanli 19 (1591) when the secret report was written and sent corresponds to twenty years later. He lived in Satsuma for these twenty years and observed a wide variety of circumstances in Japan during this period; also reports on conditions in Japan, relying on information from Chinese ship captains who had been there, were sent back from time to time to China. This report by Xu Yihou on the military expedition of Hideyoshi appears to have reached the central government, for we find a memorial dated Wanli 22 from He Qiaoyuan, director in the Ministry of Personnel, in the *Ming shi* (*juan* 320, 'biographies,' no. 208, 'Gaikoku' [Foreign Lands] 1) which reads: 'In Wanli 19 a Chinese taken prisoner by the name of Xu Yi[hou] wrote [a report] which reached home.'

Chapter Twenty-Seven

Zheng Chenggong and Guoxingye (Kokusen'ya, Koxinga)

The facts described in both the *Sei-Kan roku* and the *Seihan yashi* concerning Shimabara Kiuemon's repatriating Mao Guoke to China, traveling through Fujian province as far as Beijing, and then being received in an audience by Emperor Shenzong are certainly open to doubt; nothing of the sort is reported in Chinese documents. As noted above, he did travel as far as Meihuasuo in Fujian, as pointed out in the *Liangchao pingrang lu*, and the rest would appear to be an exaggeration developed as the story circulated. An investigation of the *Ming shilu* reveals no evidence of his traveling to Beijing and having an audience with Shenzong. All of which is to say that I have yet to hear any stories such as those reported in the *Sei-Kan roku* and the *Seihan yashi*. If we are to corroborate this material with Chinese documents, we need to examine such works as the *Ming shi*, the *Ming shi jishi benmo* (Records of the Ming in Full [80 *juan*]) by Gu Yingtai (d. 1689), the *Ming shi gao* (Draft History of the Ming Dynasty [310 [*juan*] by Wang Hongxu (1645–1723), the *Ming tongjian* (Comprehensive Mirror of the Ming Dynasty) by Xia Xie, and the *Ming ji* (Records of the Ming Dynasty [60 *juan*]) by Chen Hao and Chen Kejia.[a] I was, however, unable to locate any references to these events and finally I examined the *Ming Shenzong shilu* (Veritable Records of the Reign of Shenzong of the Ming Dynasty), published in Taiwan by the Institute of Historical Linguistics, Academia Sinica, but it, too, revealed nothing of this sort.

I would like to look now at something which may help explain all this. In *juan* 348 of the *Ming Shenzong shilu* (dated the sixth month of Wanli 28 [1600]), there is a report from Zhejiang Governor Liu Yuanlin, given as a memorial from the 'Ministry of War,' which contains the following:

A lookout caught sight of a foreign vessel. There were several official Chinese and foreigners aboard. Upon investigation it was learned that Company Commander Mao Guoke[b] had been sent to the Japanese military camp by Brigade Commander Mao Guoqi to operate as a spy. The present ruler [Tokugawa] Ieyasu [has ordered] Japanese to send this man back by

184

ship. Also, last year they bound and sent home men taken prisoner and a bandit leader [probably the leader of a group supporting the *wakō* named] Ji [Li] Zhou, altogether eleven men. Thus, [Mao Guo]ke was handed over and punished [together with the other eleven?].

The text then goes on as follows:

> It was decided that the Fujian governor would also carry out an investigation, and finally the civilians and soldiers taken prisoner were to be taken back under protection to the respective original places from whence they had come, and they would be guaranteed by the local village leaders.

This memorial from the Ministry of War was composed in the bureaucratic language of the time, and there are passages within quite difficult to decipher, but the general thrust can be gleaned from the above citations. The phrase 'sent to the Japanese military camp ... to operate as a spy,' according to the *Liangchao pingrang lu* and the *Wubei zhi*, meant that Mao Guoke among others carried a warning proclamation into the Japanese military camp to encourage peace talks. Just then the Ming army had suddenly attacked the Japanese, and Mao Guoke and his associates evacuated with the Japanese forces and were taken back to Japan.

In the account given in the aforementioned *Ming Shenzong shilu*, there is nothing mentioned about the treatment accorded the Japanese who escorted Mao Guoke back home. We have only that the Ministry of War memorialized a report from the governor of Zhejiang and that the Ministry of War memorialized concerning instructions to the governor of Fujian. Perhaps on the basis of these, the accounts in the *Liangchao pingrang lu* and the *Wubei zhi* – namely, that he was escorted as far as Meihuasuo in Fujian – should now be regarded as fact.

I would like now to add something to a point raised earlier. In Chinese historical texts that discuss the Korean Expedition – the *Ming shilu*, the *Ming shi*, the *Ming shi jishi benmo*, the *Ming shi gao*, the *Ming tongjian*, and the *Ming ji* (it is discussed as well in the *Liangchao pingrang lu*) – they write the name 'Shimazu' [lords] of Satsuma as it would have been pronounced phonetically in Chinese with three characters [lit. 'Shimanzi'].

The Japanese army was divided along three routes or fronts. The eastern route force was based in Ulsan and was dubbed 'Kiyomasa,' and the western route force was based in Songnim and was dubbed 'Yukinaga.' [The surnames] Katō and Konishi [of the generals after whom these armed forces were named] were not used. However, the middle route force was based in Sach'ŏn and was dubbed Shimazu [Shimanzi]. This method of naming [by using the surname Shimazu] was not in conformity with [using the given names] Kiyomasa and Yukinaga.

The *Ming shi* (*juan* 320), for example, notes the following under 'Waiguo zhuan 1 (Chaoxian)' (Treatises on Foreign Lands 1 [Korea]): 'At that time the Japanese were divided into three. The eastern route force was called Kiyomasa and was based in Ulsan. The western route force was called Yukinaga and based in Songnim and Yekyo; it built ramparts over a distance of several *li*. The middle route force was called Shimazu and based in Sach'ŏn.' The *Liangchao pingrang lu* also gives 'Shimazu' and 'Shimazu Yoshihiro.'

It would seem, then, that from prior to the Korean Expedition the Shimazu family was generally known in China at the time as 'Shimazu' [namely, by the pronunciation of the name, rather than the correct characters], while at the time of the Korean Expedition the name of Kiyomasa and Yukinaga first became known. In any event, it is odd to read [the given names] 'Kiyomasa' and 'Yukinaga' next to [the surname] 'Shimazu.'

Among the works I have examined, only Mao Yuanyi's *Wubei zhi* (*juan* 239)[c] follows the consistent pattern of 'Kiyomasa,' 'Yukinaga,' and 'Yoshihiro.' The *Liangchao pingrang lu* has both the Japanese and the Chinese renderings for Shimazu, probably because it is an edited collection of historical documents. Particularly sharp is the following entry in the *Ming Shenzong shilu* (*juan* 329, entry for the twelfth month of Wanli 26 [1598]): 'The Japanese commanders exhausted their strength in coming to the aid of Yukinaga in the west. Regional Commander Chen Lin went to the head of his officers and men, rallied the rank-and-file troops, and fought vigorously. He shot to death the great Japanese general Shimazu and took a number of his commanders alive.' Inasmuch as he placed 'the great Japanese general Shimazu' next to 'Kiyomasa' and 'Yukinaga,' as commanders, respectively, of the eastern, western, and central route forces, 'Shimazu' would point to Shimazu Yoshihiro. The portion of text cited here is the record of a report from Xing Jie, the Chinese commander of the expeditionary force. The *Ming shilu* similarly copies the reports from various bureaus and the expeditionary forces; it is not particularly discerning as a source (for example, it gives different characters at different times for Mao Guoqi's name). Although it is called the *shilu* or 'veritable records,' its accounts are just an accumulation of raw material, and it certainly would be dangerous to accept it uncritically as fact.

The *Ming shilu* in circulation is based entirely on immense manuscript works, and thus it did not undergo a thorough and detailed examination of all the material recorded in it so as to present a unified work. Furthermore, in the process of transcribing material, mistakes and omissions cropped up. There is now being published in Taiwan a *Ming Shenzong shilu jiaokan ji* (The Veritable Records of the Shenzong Reign of Ming Dynasty, Checked for Errors)[d] which examines the manuscripts used in the 596 *juan* of the text for errors, and it turns out that there were quite a few differences in characters in the manuscript editions.

Zheng Zhilong was based in Fujian at the end of the Ming dynasty, supported the Longwu Emperor as the descendent of the Ming imperial house, resisted the invasion of the powerful Qing military, and sought military support from the Japanese. I have already devoted a fair number of pages to him, to investigations of the account given in the *Riben qishi ji* in which Zheng and his general, Zhou

Cuizhi, requested military assistance from the king of Satsuma, to the relationship between Zhou Cuizhi and Satsuma, and to the relationship between the Ming and Satsuma going back to the time of Hideyoshi's Korean Expedition. If we might return to this for a moment, I would like to add a bit on Zheng Chenggong.

While Zheng Zhilong was in Hirado, he sired a child of mixed ethnicity, Zheng Chenggong, with a Japanese woman, and thus the child was half Japanese. Chenggong continued to support the Ming pretender even after Zhilong surrendered to the Manchu armies. Supporting the Ming to the bitter end, he took refuge in Taiwan and refused to submit, a man brimming with a sense of loyalty, the basis of the Japanese martial ethos. This was a quality much praised by Japanese scholars and literary men later in the Tokugawa era. Chikamatsu Monzaemon's (1653–1724) play, *Kokusen'ya kassen* (The Battles of Koxinga), attracted extraordinary popularity, and Watōnai, Zheng Chenggong's childhood name in the play, was widely extolled by townsmen of that time.

In the Bunsei reign period (1818–30), a three-volume work, *Taiwan Teishi kiji* (Chronicle of the Zheng Family of Taiwan) (1828), was compiled by historian Kawaguchi Chōju on the orders of the daimyō of Mito domain. Conscientiously citing numerous historical texts, he examined in concrete detail the anti-Manchu movement of the Zheng family and wrote his work in the annalistic format in literary Chinese. Also, on the order of the daimyo of Hirado, the Confucian official Asakawa Zen'an (Kanae [1781–1849]) wrote *Tei shōgun seikō den* (Biography of General Zheng Chenggong) (Kaei 3 [1850]) in literary Chinese. This work was originally written as an inscription; at its very end, we read: 'It was ordered that the biography Zheng had composed be engraved on stone at Senrihama so as to preserve it as an ancient relic.' As it turned out, the text became too long for the stone being carved, and later the Confucian official Hayama Takayuki (Gaiken) was instructed to compose a text (1852), inscribe it in on stone, and fix the stele at Senri (near Kawachiura where Zheng Chenggong had been born). The inscription in included in the *Dai Nihon shōgyō shi* (History of Commerce in the Great Japan)[e] by Suganuma Teifū, a native of Hirado, and in the *Hirado bōeki shi* (History of Trade in Hirado), appended to the former. In his work, *Kaigai iden* (Strange Stories from Overseas),[f] Saitō Setsudō (Masanori) dealt with three men active in overseas affairs: Yamada Nagamasa [d. 1633], Hamada Yahee, and Zheng Chenggong. As Saitō noted:

> Zheng Damu [Chenggong] indignantly took the lead in performing heroic deeds. He summoned the declining sun from the place where it sets, and isolated without any support he faced the rising enemy. He would not submit despite countless frustrations for he had the ways of our General Kusunoki Masashige [1294–1336]. For several decades his descendents continued to serve the proper ruler in a corner [of the realm], again just like Mr. Kusunoki. Perhaps he was impregnated with our eastern essence.

We see here the reason that men of that time praised Zheng Chenggong.

According to Kitani Hōgin,[g] Chikamatsu's play *Kokusen'ya kassen* was 'based on rare accounts of which we find no comparable examples in the history of drama. The play opened in the eleventh month of Shōtoku 5 (1715) and lasted through its final show in the second month of Kyōhō 2 [1717]. Over a three-year period [1715–17], it lasted a lengthy seventeen months [Kyōhō 1 had an intercalary first month] and played every day to packed houses. Similar cases are extremely rare indeed.'

Zheng Chenggong acquired the name 'Guoxingye' (Kokusen'ya, Koxinga), because the Longwu emperor of the itinerant Ming gave him the Ming imperial name or 'national name' (*guoxing*) of Zhu; he was also known as Zhu Chenggong. In Chikamatsu's usage the character *xing* in *guoxing* was miswritten 性, but historical evidence indicates that 姓 is correct. The last character '*ye*' (*ya*) carries an honorific meaning in China, and it is attached to given names.

A *kyōgen* production, *Kokusen'ya*, was staged a second time in the first month of Kyōhō 5 (1720) (three years after the initial performance closed), a third time in the fifth month of Kyōhō 16 (1731), a fourth time in the seventh month of Kan'en 3 (1750), and then repeatedly after that and always with great success, according to Kitani. It thus exerted a wide influence in many areas, for '*jōruri* [ballad dramas] and *kabuki* were, needless to say, adapted in novelizations, storybooks, novels, *nō* chants, and paintings, as well as various kinds of toys, dolls, candies, and clothing.' Zheng Chenggong as 'Koxinga' gained over-whelming popularity among the urban dwellers of Japan.

With the extraordinary popularity of *Kokusen'ya kassen*, Chikamatsu wrote *Kokusen'ya gonichi no kassen* (The Later Battles of Koxinga) in 1717 and *Tōsen banashi ima Kokusen'ya* (Koxinga and the Story of the Chinese Vessels) in 1722. Also, Kitani notes that Ki no Kaion (1663–1742) wrote *Keisei Kokusen'ya* (Koxinga, the Demi-Monde Version),[h] and Nishiki Bunryū wrote *Kokusen'ya tegara nikki* (Diary of the Exploits of Koxinga), a playbook in the *bunyabushi* (a style of chanting *jōruri* music).

These are all texts of plays, but many novelizations and storybooks concerned with Koxinga also were published. Kitani mentions, among others, Kiseki's (1667–1736) *Kokusen'ya Minchō taiheiki* (Koxinga's Chronicle of Peace in the Ming) and [Ki no Kaion's] *Kokusen'ya gozen gundan* (Koxinga's Military Tales), Hachimojiya Jishō's *Fūryū Keiseiya gundan*,[i] Ishida Gyokusan's *Kokusen'ya chūgi den* (Koxinga's Biography of Loyalty and Righteousness), and Bokutei Yukimaro's *Kokusen'ya kassen*.

Furthermore, quoting from the *Nansui man'yū shūi* (Gleanings from Travels in the Southern Waterways), Kitani argues that the 'Rōmon' (Tower Gate) scene [in Act III] of *Kokusen'ya kassen* was translated into Chinese by a Nakasaki interpreter by the name of Shū Bunjizaemon. He cites one passage at the very beginning: 'The story goes that an official came several times to Tangshan. He wanted to attack the Manchu ruler and revive the greatness of the Ming dynasty. So, he summoned righteous men of valor. One night Watōnai, accompanying an elderly woman, went to the lion's castle in which resided Gan Hui of the Wuchang Army.'

The text of *Kokusen'ya kassen* in 90 folio leaves, seven lines to a page, of Takemoto Chikugo no jō [another name for the important puppet play chanter Takemoto Gidayū I], held in the Tōyō Bunko Library, was published in photocopy form by Nihon koten bungaku kankōkai in 1972 with an explanatory pamphlet by Tsutsumi Seiji appended. He notes, in addition to those works mentioned by Kitani, a large number of works with plots involving Koxinga: the novel *Ima Watōnai Tōdo bune* (The Chinese Vessels of Watōnai) by Kan Rakushi and the popular picture book edition of *Kokusen'ya kassen* (The Battles of Koxinga) published with the artwork of Shimai Kiyomitsu; the *kibyōshi* text, *Kokusen'ya hanjō* (The Prosperity of Koxinga) (Tenmei 2 [1782]), written by Iba Kashō, and the popular illustrated edition *Kokusen'ya yamato banashi* (The Japanese Story of Koxinga) (Bunka 12 [1815]) by Tōzaian Nanboku, among others.

On Zheng Zhilong we have a detailed account right up to his surrender in 'Zheng Zhilong shoufu' (Zheng Zhilong Pacified), in *juan* 76 of *Ming shi jishi benmo* (preface dated 1658) by Gu Yingtai of the early Qing. There is as well a rather detailed record in Huacun kanxing shizhe's *Tan wang* (Tales of Travels) (1 *juan*), under a section entitled 'Feihuang shimo' (A Full Report on Feihuang). The *Tan wang* is a work of the late Ming to early Qing, for at the very end of its description of Zheng Zhilong, it recounts: 'After a short time, he submitted to the dynasty and repaired to Shengjing [the Manchu capital].' The *Tan wang* discusses 27 anecdotes generally from the Chongzhen period (1628–44) of events in the lives of descendents of the Ming house. It is listed in the table of contents of the history section of the *Siku quanshu zongmu tiyao* with an explanatory note and is now included in the reference work, *Shuo ling*.[j] In the *Tan wang* Zhilong is called 'Huangfei,' and in the *Zheng Chenggong zhuan* (Biography of Zheng Chenggong) (to be discussed below) his style is given as 'Huangfei,' but in the *Wujing kaizong* (Origins of the Military Classics) and the *Ka-i hentai*, it is given as 'Feihong.' The *Taiwan waiji* (see below) and the *Xiaotian jizhuan* both give 'Feihuang.'

The *Wujing kaizong* is a work of the late Ming, claiming to be 'compiled by Huang Xianchen of Futian' and with a preface dated the fourth month of Chongzhen 9 [1636].[k] It was reprinted in Japan in seven stringbound volumes with Japanese reading punctuation in Kanbun 1 (1661). It would seem that this work was published before Zheng Zhilong surrendered to the Qing forces, when he was still fighting for military glory in the Nanhai area. The book is a 'military classic' explaining tactics and strategies as well as giving illustrations of weaponry and battle arrays. In it we find a work entitled 'Gujin mingjiang' (Famous Commanders Past and Present) which offers capsule biographies of celebrated military leaders from the Zhou, Spring and Autumn, and Warring States periods through the late Ming. At the end of the Ming section, Zheng Zhilong is mentioned. There it states that his style was Feihong and that during the Chongzhen era 'he repeatedly called on the generals-in-chief and regional commanders of three provinces, carried out the affairs of the area commander, and was appointed commander of the Nan-Ao region.' It goes on to state: 'He trained troops for ten years and did not use up a single grain of public rice.' This refers to the era in which he was most active militarily in Nanhai. However, later Zheng Zhilong surrendered to the Manchus when they invaded Fujian, and this is recounted in the section 'Erchen zhuan' (Biographies of Those Who Served Two Authorities) in *juan* 63 of the *Xiaotian jizhuan* and in the section 'Nichen zhuan' (Biographies of Rebellious Officials) in *juan* 80 of the *Qing shi liezhuan*.

One three-volume work on the life of Zheng Chenggong is *Taiwan Teishi kiji* (Bunsei 11 [1828]) by Kawaguchi Chōju of Mito domain. It is an annalistic account in Kanbun for which Kawaguchi widely investigated related Chinese documents from the Ming and Qing dynasties as well as documents left in Japan, checked them for accuracy, and then compiled the work. It begins in Keichō 17 (Wanli 40 [1612]) as Zheng Zhilong and someone by the name of Zuguan came for an audience with the *bakufu* at Sunbu [present-day Shizuoka city], and it ends in Genroku 13 (Kangxi 39 [1700]) when on the edict of the Qing ruler Zheng Chenggong and his son Jing (who died in Taiwan) are returned for their funerals at their ancestral home in Nan'an, Fujian province.

At the end of his work, Chōju notes:

> The affairs [discussed herein] are based on an assortment of writings and have been checked for their veracity. Literary texts add complexities and literary adornments, and I have imposed order on this. Although I deal primarily with the Zheng family, I also touch on matters concerning the late Ming dynasty. Over the course of some 80 years of time, there was order and chaos, flourishing and decline, rise and fall, and thus when the mandate of heaven and the minds of men set on a course of action, this may be seen in general terms.

This statement enables us to see the main principles of compilation of the work. Kawaguchi's book is discussed in *juan* 13 of Xie Guozhen's book, *Wan Ming shiji kao*, and I think it should be cited as a document worthy of special attention in the study of the Zhengs, compiled in Edo-period Japan.

At the beginning of the *Taiwan Teishi kiji*, the author gives an explanation of Taiwan, citing several works, and then at the very start of the annals section of the work, he cites from such Japanese writings as *Butoku taisei ki* (Compilation on the Martial Arts), *Koku shi* (National History), and *Butoku hennen shūsei* (Annalistic Compendium on the Martial Arts). He then notes: 'In Keichō 17 [1612], Zheng Zhilong and Zuguan of the Ming had an audience with the *bakufu* at Sunbu. The shogunate politely asked him questions about the affairs in foreign lands. Zhilong presented a gift of medicines.' This account is not to be found in any Chinese source on the subject.

Kawaguchi then goes on to cite the *Zheng Chenggong zhuan* to say 'Zhilong had the style of Feihuang' and to cite the *Wujing kaizong* and the *Ka-i hentai* to say that 'later he was called General Feihong.' His father's name was Shaozu, and he served as storehouse commissioner for Cai Shanji (Ye Shanji, according

From the Japanese edition of the *Taiwan Teishi kiji* (Kansai University Library)

to the *Zheng Chenggong zhuan*), the prefect of Quanzhou (Fujian), and Zhilong was his eldest son. 'At birth he was very good-looking,' states the text, citing the *Zheng Chenggong zhuan* and the *Tan wang*, 'and after he had matured a bit, his bravery and skill far surpassed others of his generation, modeling himself on men of the time, perhaps Qi Jiguang. He had extraordinary literary skills and knew everything there was about music and dance.' After a falling out with his father, Shaozu forgave and went after him, while Zhilong departed to find an ocean-going vessel. At the appointed time of its departure, the ship raised its sail, and he pleaded with a wealthy merchant who permitted him on board, and so he eventually made his way to Japan. At the time he was eighteen years of age, he was in Hirado (Bizen) [in present-day Nagasaki prefecture] using the name Hirado Rōikkan. Later he made frequent trips to Japan aboard merchant vessels. So, the text relates, citing the *Tan wang*, the *Zheng Chenggong zhuan*, the *Nanjuku shū* (Collection of the Southern Academy), the *Ka-i hentai*, the *Ryūkyū shiryaku* (Short Gazetteer of the Ryūkyū Islands), the *Nagasaki yawa sō* (Nagasaki Evening Chats), and other texts.

In an entry under Keichō 7 (1602), we read that 'before this occurred bandits arose in the Nanhai,' and their leader was one Yan Zhenquan (the *Zheng Chenggong zhuan* gives his name as Yan Siqi). Zhenxiang was known as the 'Japanese leader' (*Nihon kōra*; *kōra* was apparently a corruption of *kashira* meaning 'leader'), and had occupied some terrain on Taiwan at the head of a group of rural Japanese. They split up the area with a gang of thieves into ten strongholds to hold onto the land. Zhilong together with his younger brother Zhihu joined Zhenxiang's party. They plundered four cargo vessels from Thailand, and Zhilong's wealth was the greatest of the ten. Eventually, Zhenxiang died, and at the persuasion of the other bandits Zhilong became chief and traveled the seas. The text draws this information from the *Tan wang*, the *Zheng Chenggong zhuan*, the *Ming shi jishi benmo*, and other works. Booty from looting and pillaging gradually led to great wealth, and the Ming forces could not fight them off. A pacification order was issued. Because Zhilong had once been in Cai Shanji's debt, Cai encouraged him to surrender, which ultimately Zhilong agreed to do, according to the *Zheng Chenggong zhuan* and the *Ming shi jishi benmo*.

In another entry under Keichō 7, we read: 'While Zhilong was initially in Hirado, he married a woman, née Tagawa of a samurai family. She gave birth to Chenggong and a younger brother Shichizaemon'; this material is drawn from the *Zheng Chenggong zhuan* and the *Tagawa Shichizaemon sojō* (The Petition of Tagawa Shichiuemon). The *Taiwan Teishi kiji* goes on to discuss the activities of Zheng Zhilong, but the birth of Zheng Chenggong digresses from the accounts of the text. I would like now to look at the *Zheng Chenggong zhuan*, so frequently cited by the *Taiwan Teishi kiji*, because this work has been one of the most influential historical sources on Zheng Chenggong in both China and Japan.

Fujiwara Ietaka's collection of random pieces, *Ochiguri monogatari* (The Story of Fallen Chestnuts), originally circulated in manuscript form (Bunsei 6 [1823], published by Asō Tomotoshi). It was later included in the first volume of the *Hyakka zuihitsu* (The Random Pieces of 100 Authors).[1] Although it is unclear just when it was written, it contains material on Tokugawa Iemitsu's going to the capital in the Kan'ei period (1624–44) and on the chanting of Buddhist sutras at Ninnaji in the spring of An'ei 9 (1780). Because it is a collection of transcribed observations from this period, it probably was written in the late An'ei period or the early Tenmei or Kansei periods. It largely records material within aristocratic circles, but therein one finds a section covering comparative historical facts concerning Zheng Chenggong. It is doubtful that what it says in this context was based on anything substantive, but a close look at the content of what is relates leads us to the conclusion that it essentially took material from the *Zheng Chenggong zhuan* and translated it into Japanese.

In addition to scattered reports transmitted from Nagasaki, knowledge among Japanese about Zheng Chenggong at the time – what sort of man he was, as well as changes in the times or circumstances – was, as can be seen in the *Ochiguri monogatari*, principally drawn from the *Zheng Chenggong zhuan*. In the second month of An'ei 3 (1774), the *Zheng Chenggong zhuan* was reprinted with Japanese reading punctuation in Ōsaka, Japan and the author of the *Ochiguri monogatari* probably saw the reprinted text.

One text known to recount the vestiges of Zheng Chenggong was the *Cixing shimo* (Full Account of the Imperial Gift of a Surname) in one *juan* by Huang

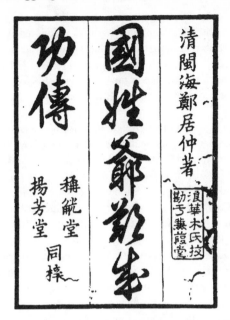

Japanese reprint edition of the *Zheng Chenggong zhuan* (Kansai University Library)

Zongxi. Also, the *Taiwan waiji* (Account of Taiwan) (preface dated Kangxi 43 [1704], 30 *juan*) by Jiang Risheng (Dongxu),[m] written in the style of a serialized novel, describes the rise and fall of the Zheng family over a 63-year period from the birth of Zheng Zhilong through the surrender of Zheng Keshuang: 'People from Fujian recounted in great detail what transpired in Fujian, sufficient to pick and choose from for the history of the country' (from the preface by Chen Zheyong).[n]

In Japan, however, people became familiar with this information primarily from the Japanese reprint edition of *Zheng Chenggong zhuan*. The text in two stringbound volumes was punctuated and introduced into Japan by Kimura Kenkadō (Kōkyō) of Ōsaka, and he published it based on the original edition which came into his possession.[o] Even now this reprinted edition can be found occasionally on the book lists of used book stores, and I have a copy of it myself. After it was reprinted, all subsequent Japanese biographies of Zheng Chenggong seem to have been based upon it. The *Taiwan Teishi kiji* also has much that derives from it.

Before it appeared, one work published in Japan that discussed Zheng Chenggong in some detail was the *Min Shin tō ki* (Chronicle of the Battles between Ming and Qing) (with a preface dated Kanbun 1 [1661] by Ukai Nobuyuki). Based on reports conveyed to Nagasaki, it appears to be largely rooted in fact, but is written in novel form full of hyperbole. It was, though, published while Zheng Chenggong was alive, in the very year that he first occupied Taiwan. (The *Min Shin tō ki* will be discussed in the next chapter). Also, a general outline of Zheng Chenggong is conveyed in the *Nakasaki yawa sō* (Kyōhō 5 [1720]) by Nishikawa Joken (1648–1724),[p] who was from Nagasaki, under the title, 'Takasago no koto narabete Kokusen'ya monogatari' (On Taiwan and the Story of Koxinga). It recounts much that is in the *Min Shin tō ki*.

The original text that Kimura Kenkadō used for his reprint edition is now held in the Naikaku Bunko. After his death the text became part of his former library which the shogunate acquired from his descendents. In the book, in addition to the library seal of his collection ('Kenkadō zōsho in'), we now find the following library seals: 'Asakusa bunko,' 'Shōheizaka gakumonjo,' and 'Nihon seifu tosho.' The reprint edition omitted the original preface (dated the second month of Kangxi 41 [1702]) by the author Zheng Juzhong (Yizou [*jinshi* of 1706]) and included only a preface by a Japanese (Kinryū Dōjin) and postface (by Akutagawa Kan). Thus, the background of this particular text is unclear in the reprinted edition. In his *Wan Ming shiji kao*, Xie Guozhen mentioned this work, but, having not seen the original, he based himself on the Japanese reprint edition and just transcribed the preface to that edition by Kinryū Dōjin.

According to author Zheng Yizou's own preface, the *Zheng Chenggong zhuan* was originally appended to the *Mingji suizhi lu* (Record of a Fulfilled Will in the Late Ming). The folds in the pages of the book carry the title 'Mingji suizhi lu' and in rather small characters below it we find 'Daoshang fuzhuan' (Appended Account of the Island). 'Daoshang' undoubtedly referred to the island of Taiwan. According to the preface, the *Mingji suizhi lu* was put together from the following works: *Mingji bianwu* (Distinguishing Errors about the Late Ming) (4 *juan*), *Jiang Min shilüe* (Brief Account of Jiangsu and Fujian) (6 *juan*), *Ming yu xingguo lu* (Account of the Itinerant Ming) (16 *juan*), and *Ming yimin lu* (Account of Ming Remnants) (1 *juan*). To these the *Zheng Chenggong zhuan* was added, it would appear, as an appendix.

Inasmuch as the *Mingji suizhi lu* appears on the Qing Council of State's 'list of books banned and to be destroyed,' it probably did not circulate extensively. Thus, in Xie Guozhen's *Wan Ming shiji kao*, the original is not even registered. In his *Qingdai jinshu zhijian lu* (Record of Works Known to Have Been Banned in the Qing Period),[q] Sun Yaoqing lists the *Mingji suizhi lu* in 2 *juan* (part of the full text); and because he claims it to be an 'old manuscript,' we know that he must not have seen the original.

Xie Guozhen mentions the *Mingji suizhi lu* in his *Wan Ming shiji kao* and notes: 'It is a short introduction appended to the *Daoshang fuzhuan*, held in the Naikaku Bunko in Japan.' Apparently, the *Mingji suizhi lu* is scarcely available even in China. In an explanatory note, Mr. Xie writes of the author Zheng Yizou: 'Detailed facts about him are not known.' Yet, an explanatory note in *juan* 13 of the *Zheng Chenggong zhuan* draws on the *Dongyue rulin houzhuan* (Later Confucian Biographies from Fujian) (1 *juan*) by Chen Shouqi (1771–1834) to point out that 'Zheng Yizou was from Haicheng, Zhangzhou and was a *juren* of Shunzhi 13 [1656]. Indifferent to bureaucratic advancement, he returned home to find rest. He acquired a thatched hut in the foothills of the white clouds and created the Nanbing Wenshe (Literary Society of Retirement in the South).' There is some sort of contradiction here between Xie's and Zheng's accounts. The text goes on further to note: 'Those who studied there came from as far away as Japan. Ki[mura] Kōkyō of Naniwa [Ōsaka], Japan, proofread the text for errors.' This seems to indicate that those who studied at Zheng's Nanbing Wenshe brought the text to Japan, and thus Kimura Kenkadō obtained it. But what really happened? Having not seen the *Dongyue rulin houzhuan*, I cannot judge whether the phrase, 'those who studied there came from as far away as Japan,' was part of the entry in the *Dongyue rulin houzhuan* or a portion added by Mr. Xie himself.ʳ

The author refers to his introduction as a 'Corroborative Introduction' (*Zhengxin xu*). In it he notes: 'It has been nearly 60 years from the fall of the Ming dynasty till today. People have departed and the wind has died down. Even with conscientious men of wisdom and attentive men of talent, we cannot be completely free of errors.' However, while 'I could not walk the length and breadth of Kyūshū and see the whole terrain, ... I looked where the traces led and did not forget to investigate in detail. Men of great moral character and wisdom from far away who are concerned with the same matters as I have kindly written me letters. My knowledge remains incomplete.' For corroborative purposes – in other words, to establish the veracity of events from the time of the fall of the Ming dynasty – he gathered historical materials with painstaking care: 'I shall later return to this and order it all by categories.' It would seem that the accounts given in this work have a high degree of credibility.

Chapter Twenty-Eight

The *Min Shin tō ki*

I have already touched on one Japanese work, written in a mixture of Chinese characters and Japanese *kana*, detailing the activities of Zheng Chenggong; it is the *Min Shin tō ki* (preface dated 1661)[a] which appeared early on. It was written some 113 years before Kimura Kenkadō's reprint of the *Zheng Chenggong zhuan* appeared. Because it was written in a dramatic style, in the form of a novel of military affairs, it necessarily contains colorful adornments to its descriptions. However, many texts cite its accounts as historically accurate. This can be seen even in studies of more recent vintage, from the *Taiwan Teishi kiji* on. In that year of 1661, Zheng Chenggong seized Taiwan from the occupying Dutch forces and made it his consummate base of operations. However, at the very end of volume ten of the *Min Shin tō ki*, we read that Zheng Chenggong attacked the outpost held by the Dutch (Anpingcheng) and brought about their surrender soon thereafter. Thus, we can see that this book was written on the basis of the most recent reports and information available at the time.

More concretely, at the end of the preface by Ukai Nobuyuki (Sekisai, 1615–64) at the beginning of the text, we find that it was written in 'the first ten days of the eleventh month of Kanbun 1 [1661].' That Zheng Chenggong died in Taiwan at age 39, namely in the fifth month of the next year, Kangxi 1 (1662), is consistent with accounts from the *Zheng Chenggong zhuan*, the *Taiwan Teishi kiji*, the *Taiwan waiji*, and the *Xiaotian jinian fukao* (as well as the *Xiaotian jizhuan*). Among these works, the *Taiwan waiji* and the *Xiaotian jinian* both supply the date as the eighth day of the fifth month. In this instance, it would appear that the *Xiaotian jinian* was based on the *Taiwan waiji*; at other points in the *Xiaotian jinian*, the compiler notes that accounts from the *Taiwan waiji* are more reliable than those of the *Mingji nanlüe* (Southern Strategies of the Late Ming).[b]

It was said that Zheng Chenggong died of illness, but there are many hypotheses about the cause of his death. In many books we then find that he caught cold on the first day of the fifth month, sat cross-legged on the floor to suppress it, argued with his subordinates, and mounted a platform to observe vessels coming from the Pescadores Islands; he then suddenly died on the eighth day of the month. Any number of theories seem to have been circulating as to its cause. Perhaps, while reading the *Taizu zuxun* (Ancestral Admonitions from [Ming] Taizu) (the Longwu Emperor was said to have contributed a preface to this work), he said 'with what dignity may we look upon our former emperor [Longwu] who is beneath the earth,' tore at his head (or covered his face) with both hands, and died in a fit of anger (as told in such texts as the *Taiwan waiji* and the *Xiaotian jinian*). Perhaps, he became insane, bit off his fingers, and died (as told in such texts as Lin Shidui's *Hezha congtan* [Collected Stories of Hezha][c] and the *Qing shi gao* [Draft History of the Qing Dynasty]). Perhaps, he contracted malaria and died (as told in such works as Irisawa Tatsukichi's *Unsō zuihitsu* [Random Notes from a Villa in the Clouds] and Inagaki Magohee's [Kigai] *Tei Seikō* [Zheng Chenggong]).[d]

In his work, 'Zheng Chenggong de siyin kao' (A Study of the Cause of Zheng Chenggong's Death),[e] Li Tengyue, a medical doctor (perhaps his degree was from a Japanese institution inasmuch as he cites numerous Japanese writings) of the 'Taiwan Documents Committee,' introduced these various theories, widely referred to many types of historical works (58 in all), and added a study of his own. He concluded that 'the onset of his [i.e., Zheng's] illness came from a cold he had caught, which appears to have been a kind of sickness accompanied by a sudden rise in temperature' related, Li argues, to the poor climate of Taiwan.

In additional remarks, Dr. Li Tengyue cites many historical writings to analyze in medical terms Zheng Chenggong's nature and disposition. He claims that Zheng was of bilious temperament in terms of the Greek theories of humors and of type-O blood; according to the views on mental illness of [the German psychiatrist] Ernst Kretschmer (1888–1964), he was a cruel ruler and egotist; in body type and temperament of a similarly mentally ill person, he was close to depressive insanity. This perspective should probably be taken into account when considering Zheng Chenggong the man, who was reputed to be strict in military discipline and morals and executed transgressors without mercy.

From the date of Ukai Sekisai's preface to the text, Kanbun 1 (1661), we know that the *Min Shin tō ki* was written about one-half year before the sudden death of Zheng Chenggong. The year that it was printed, perhaps 1661 or perhaps the next year, however, is not given at the end of the text where it only reads: 'Printed by Tanaka Shōhee.' This was the case for the edition of the text which I have seen in the Naikaku Bunko, a first printing or near first printing (the form of the Chinese characters in the book's title are different from later editions; the Naikaku Bunko has a text of a later printing as well). I have a copy of a later printing in my library; except for the fact that it lacks the phrase 'Printed by Tanaka Shōhee,' it is entirely the same as the first printing with no date given. We do, though, know that the printer of the *Min Shin tō ki*, 'Tanaka Shōhee,' was a Kyoto bookstore, because on the final page of the *Tsūzoku Kokusen'ya chūgi den* (Popular Biography of the Loyal and Righteous Koxinga) (nineteen *kan*, in *katakana*, with illustrations), we find: 'Tanaka Shōhee

197

Bookstore, woodblocks prepared by Nakamura Shinshichi,' and next to 'Tanaka Shōhee' are the characters for 'at the edge of the Gojō Bridge in Rakuyō [Kyoto].'

The actual body of the *Min Shin tō ki* begins as follows. In the first year of the dynasty (1368), the meritorious official Liu Ji (Bowen) who had helped the first emperor of the Ming, Zhu Yuanzhang, to found the great Ming dynasty observed the heavens and predicted the rise of the great Ming, and after the passage of 280 years, he predicted the rise of the Qing dynasty with a reign title of Shunzhi. The story then unfolds, generally following historical facts, as Li Zicheng brings down the Ming and the Qing invades. The texts describes the battles fought at a number of points within the country between the invading Qing armies and the forces supporting descendents of the Ming dynastic house. The story then proceeds primarily to depict the sudden rise of Zheng Zhilong and Zheng Chenggong and the battles in which they engaged. Finally, as touched upon earlier, Chenggong, finding his position in China proper untenable, plans to seize Taiwan and he attacks the Dutch military there.

The principle reason the author of this work wrote his book was to try to convey an image of Zheng Chenggong as a hero who supported the Ming to the bitter end and resisted the invading Qing. He even referred to the forces of Zheng Chenggong as the 'official army' (*kangun*). As a work that closely followed the historical facts of Zheng Chenggong's career, it seems to have been based on detailed historical reports of the day.

Let us now take a look at Ukai Sekisai's preface to get at how this book was composed.

Through an introduction, Maezono Sōbu of Nagasaki in Hishū, came to visit my humble cottage. He said to me: 'Recently, the Great Ming has lost its virtue, the integrity of the national terrain has been severely harmed, and the gods of the soil and grain are ?[1] The northern barbarians have taken advantage of these troubles to assume control over the country. Their state is called Da Qing, and they have changed to the reign title Shunzhi.... Zheng Zhilong from Quanzhou once took refuge for several years in Matsuura, Hishū, Japan. People called him Hirado Ikkan. He then returned home but could not bear to sit and watch his homeland be overthrown.... Sounding the tocsin of righteousness, he raised a force of men and repeatedly reported his military victories. Unfortunately, he fell into the hands of the barbarians' court and did not fulfill his heart's desire. How terribly sad! Hirado's son was Chenggong.... He deeply resented his father's unhappy fate.... He thereupon personally led a band of men to attack cities and plunder terrain, ... and tried to bring down Yingtianfu [Nanjing], but he failed and retreated.... His heart's desire, though, had not yet been broken. He retreated an inch to advance a foot in an effort to attain his long-cherished wish. He was truly a heroic man. My [i.e., Maezono's] father was surnamed Xu and came from Quanzhou in the

Ming. He came to our country [Japan], and I was born in Nagasaki. My father died when I was seven years of age. My relatives now live in our old village, and every year a merchant vessel comes to Nagasaki. Among the family papers [they brought] were reports of the bandits' upheavals in China. According to merchants' stories, furthermore, they took down copious notes which filled several volumes. Others then edited them into a complete account. They spoke with Mr. Kurogawa and Mr. Tsumagi, the local pacification officials [i.e., the Nagasaki Administrators]. They went as far away as the capital [Kyoto] to speak with Lord Makino of Sado domain. I would like this volume to spread throughout the realm.

However, the writing in this volume is vulgar and unsophisticated. The language is abstruse, and the meaning will not be conveyed. Thus, I request your [Ukai's] editorial comments to make this a straightforward piece of work. Please do not turn me down without looking at it.

Having received this request from Maezono, Ukai Sekisai replied:

Books that recount the disorders in Ming China include *Jingguo xionglüe* (Grand Plan for Managing the State [by Zheng Dayu, nine *juan*, 1645]), *Huang Ming jishi benmo* (Full Account of the August Ming Dynasty), and *Mingchao xiao shi* (Short History of the Ming Dynasty [by Lü Bi, eighteen *juan*]). I have heard that they have even come to Japan. However, these works have been taken into government offices and are not available to be read. I happily await their importation soon by [Chinese] merchants. Once we can refer to them and select material from them, then we shall not err on matters of date, person, or place, nor shall we get words and events out of order.

He seemed to be speaking in a rather hesitating manner at the time. Maezono fully understood, but since he had come from far away, he could not wait for these documents indefinitely. He noted:

I forcefully requested them over and over, and after several days my request was granted. I have made a selection of about half of the draft; and corroborated it with the *Zhongxing weilüe* (Great Plan for Revival)[2] to pick out the reading material and use examples as items for explanation.

Sekisai then went on to say:

He also added the 'Yudi beikao' (Geographical Reference), the 'Huang Ming dixi' (Imperial Lineage of the August Ming Dynasty), the 'Zhuge Kongming bazhen tu' (Zhuge Liang's Eight Tactical Dispositions of Troops), the 'Zheng Chenggong zhen tu' (Zheng Chenggong's Troop Dispositions), the 'Nanbei Zhi[li] tu' (Diagrams of Northern and Southern Zhi[li]), and the 'Duojiashagu dao tu' (Map of Takasago Island [Taiwan]). Altogether there were eleven *juan* which he named the *Min Shin tō ki*.

As this citation indicates, the *Min Shin tōki* came together in the following manner. Maezono, son of a man from Quanzhou (Fujian province) – within the Zheng family's range of activities – and born in Nagasaki, received certain historical documents concerning Zheng Chenggong from relatives who lived in his family's hometown in China and from Chinese ships that sailed to the port of Nagasaki. He then compiled them and brought them to Ukai Sekisai's home in Kyoto to have them selected and edited with the aim of publication. This explanation, of course, holds only if Sekisai's preface is trustworthy.

In the edition of this work that I have seen, held in the Naikaku Bunko, the 'Zheng Chenggong zhen tu', the 'Nanbei zhi tu', and the 'Duojiashagu dao tu' are missing, while a work entitled 'Fujian sheng Zheng Zhilong xitu' (Chart of the Lineage of Zheng Zhilong of Fujian Province) is included. Thus, this edition is not a complete first edition of the text. Although the text that I own is a later edition, it is the same as the original edition. However, the diagrams and charts section is quite different and seems to have been added at a subsequent date. It begins with the 'Yudi beikao' and this is followed by a 'Tianwen chandu tu' (Astronomical Chart) which contain two two-sided global maps. The North and South Poles are indicated on it, and the equator and meridian lines have been added; also, latitude and longitude lines have been drawn in, so that it is arranged as a world map. This map is followed by a 'Tianxia zongtu' (Map of the Entire Realm) which forms a complete map of China. This in turn is followed by separate maps of the various provinces of China: 'Bei Zhili tu' (Map of Northern Zhili), 'Nan Zhili tu' (Map of Southern Zhili), 'Shanxi sheng tu' (Map of Shanxi Province), 'Shandong sheng tu' (Map of Shandong Province), 'Henan sheng tu' (Map of Henan Province), 'Shaanxi sheng tu' (Map of Shaanxi Province), 'Zhejiang sheng tu' (Map of Zhejiang Province), 'Jiangxi sheng tu' (Map of Jiangxi Province), 'Huguang sheng tu' (Map of the Huguang Provinces), 'Sichuan sheng tu' (Map of Sichuan Province), 'Fujian sheng tu' (Map of Fujian Province), 'Guangdong sheng tu' (Map of Guangdong Province), 'Guangxi sheng tu' (Map of Guangxi Province), 'Yunnan sheng tu' (Map of Yunnan Province), and 'Guizhou tu' (Map of Guizhou). There is also a 'Jiu bian tu' (Map of the Nine Peripheral Areas), namely a map of the regions surrounding China. Next is a 'Xuanji yuheng tu' (Chart of *xuangji* and *yuheng*), a chart of the 'armillary sphere,' said to have been used for astronomical observation in antiquity. This is followed by a 'Xia Yu zhishui tu' (Chart of [King] Yu of the Xia Bringing the Waterways under Control); next is a 'Shengchao diwang kao' (Study of the Rulers of the August Dynasty [Ming]) which briefly traces the emperors of the Ming dynasty; this is followed by the 'Zhuge Liang bazhen tu' (Zhuge Liang's Eight Tactical Dispositions of Troops), a chart of Zhuge's battlefield preparations. Then we find two topographical maps, 'Beijing cheng' (The City of Beijing) and 'Nanjing cheng' (The City of Nanjing), a map of the Fujian coastline, and a 'Dayuan cheng tu' (Map of Taiwan).

These were all at the time designed to clarify material concerning China for the general reading public and to provide preparatory knowledge. The maps were placed in the first *juan* before the main text of the work.

I am unaware of any detailed study of Maezono Sōbu himself. He does not appear in *Nagasaki senmin den* (Biographies of Former Men of Nagasaki).[f] Whether this was his real name remains in doubt. The characters for his given name Sōbu are strange. Yet, in Nishimura Joken's *Nagasaki yawa sō*, we read: 'The fact that Koxinga was an military commander of incomparable ingenuity is amply demonstrated in the *Min Shin tō ki* by a Nagasaki man.' This would seem to indicate that he was not a fictional personage.

According to a brief biography of Ukai Nobuyuki (Sekisai) found in the *Sentetsu sōdan zokuhen* by Tōjō Nobuyasu (Kindai), he was born in the Kanda district of Edo in Genna 1 (1615), and after reaching age twenty he traveled to study in Kyoto. He received training at the Naba Academy, and he boarded there for several years. He later opened his own private academy in Aburanokōji where he taught, and he became known for his historical studies. At age 32 [Japanese style], he served Aoyama Daizennosuke, the lord of Amagasaki. Fifteen years after moving there, in Manji 3 (1660) when he was 46 years of age, he gave up his stipend and returned to Kyoto. There he acquired a reputation the equal of Yamazaki Ansai and Mōri Jōsai. In Kanbun 4 (1664), he passed away at age 50 at his thatched cottage in Horikawa.

After rejecting a stipend and settling in Kyoto, Sekisai, in response to a request from a bookstore, revised and punctuated old Chinese volumes for Japanese reprinting. These were greatly welcomed by the public, and, as noted in the *Sentetsu sōdan zokuhen*, he was able to live off the fees he charged for these services. The text mentions Sekisai's punctuation of Kanbun works, but does not reveal how many such volumes he worked on. Many of these works, though, were multi-volume. The *Kindai meika chojutsu mokuroku* (List of Writings by Well-Known Modern Authors)[g] by Tsutsumi Asakaze gives the following works among those he supplied with Japanese reading punctuation (supplemented by information from *Kinsei Kangakusha denki chosaku daijiten* [Great Encyclopedia of Biography and Writings of Kangakusha of the Early Modern Era][h] by Seki Giichirō and Seki Yoshinao): *Zhuzi yulei daquan* (Complete Text of the Recorded Conversations of Master Zhu) (140 *juan*), *Wubei zhi* (100 *juan*), *Han wen* (Writings of Han Yu) (40 *juan*), *Liu wen* (Writings of Liu Zongyuan) (36 *juan*), *Du shi jizhu* (The Poems of Du Fu with Collected Commentaries) (24 *juan*), *Huainan honglie jie* (Explanation of the *Huainanzi*) (21 *juan*) (by Gao You of the Later Han), *Sishu daquan* (The Four Books in Their Completeness [i.e., with commentaries]) (23 *juan*) [compiled in the Yongle reign of the Ming], *Wanxing tongpu* (Collected Geneologies of Manifold People) (140 *juan*) [by Ling Dizhi], *Lishi gangjian bu* (Commentary to the Ordered Mirror in History) (40 *juan*), *Bohu tong* (Comprehensive Meanings from the White Tiger Hall) (four *juan*) [by Ban Gu of the Later Han], and *Fengsu tongyi* (Comprehensive Understanding of [Ancient] Institutions) (four *juan*) [by Ying Shao]. From this list it would appear that Sekisai introduced numerous Chinese works to Japan with Japanese reading punctuation. His accomplishment in making them available in Japan was truly immense.

Sekisai got to know well Chen Yuanyun (or Yuanbin, 1595–1671), who made his way to Japan at the end of the Ming dynasty. As Imazeki Tenpō has noted, we 'can see connections to Chen Yuanyun' in the works punctuated by Sekisai.[3] What exactly this 'connection' was – the books selected for punctuation or the method of fixing punctuation – is not made clear. After Sekisai's death, at the request of his son, Chen Yuanyun wrote Sekisai's inscriptional epitaph. Today, it is said, this stele still exists on the hillside behind the Enkōji Temple in Kyoto.[4]

We have already noted that the story of Zheng Zhilong's efforts to obtain Japanese military assistance to resist the attacks of the Manchu armies can be found in the *Ka-i hentai*. In that same text, we find letters from Zheng Chenggong, son of Zheng Zhilong, to the shōgun, and from Chenggong's son, Zheng Jing (Jinshe), to the Nagasaki Administrator. However, letters from members of the Zheng family seeking military assistance from Japan as well as collected reports on the movements of the Zhengs are organized and recorded in *Teishi enpeigan ra fuku fūsetsu* (Requests of the Zhengs for Military Assistance with Appended Reports) which fill three volumes (212–14) of the *Tsūkō ichiran*. These reports draw on such works as the *Taiwan Teishi kiji* and the *Zheng Chenggong zhuan*, and use the insertion of 'reference' notes here and there to correct errors or point up uncertain points in these works.

From the Meiji period forward, there have been a large number of biographies and studies of Zheng Chenggong in Japan as well. These would include from the Meiji period: Higashi Seijun [Takusha] *Tei Enpei jiryaku* (Account of Zheng, [Prince of] Yanping)[i] (in Kanbun); Maruyama Masahiko, *Tei Seikō* (Zheng Chenggong); and Miyazaki Raijō, *Tei Seikō*[j]; also, Tatemori Kō (Shūkai), *Tei Seikō den* (Biography of Zheng Chenggong) from the Taishō period; and Inagaki Magohee, *Tei Seikō* (mentioned above). Furthermore, after Japan seized control over Taiwan from China as a consequence of the Sino-Japanese War of 1894–95, many times the name of Zheng Chenggong came up in the books and journals that examined or introduced the land regulations concerning Taiwan and its history.

Although unlike works of this sort, I would like to take special note of the *Tei Seikō den* by Hiseki. Hiseki [lit., 'firm of character' – JAF] was the penname of a Chinese who lived in Japan during the Meiji era. However, Zhang Taigu's *Biming yinde* (Index of Pennames)[k] gives two names, Wang Shuming and Chen Shiyi, for those who used the penname Hiseki [or Feishi, in Chinese]. We cannot be sure which of them it was, but the book itself was published in 1904 by the 'Shinkoku ryūgakusei kaikan' (Chinese Overseas Hall) in Tokyo, and Feng Ziyou mentions it in the 'references' to his 'Kaiguo qian haineiwai geming shubao yilan' (A Survey of Revolutionary Writings at Home and Abroad Prior to the Founding of the Republic).[l]

This was a work that reflected the support of the overseas students who called for an anti-Manchu revolution at the end of the Qing dynasty, were sympathetic to Zheng Chenggong's unyielding spirit of resistance, and advocated nationalism. They were saying that Zheng Chenggong was not an international hero, but a Chinese hero: 'Rather than glorify world heroes, it is best to praise Chinese heroes!' We find here the fervent anti-Manchu nationalism of that time.

I would like to take special note of one further point with respect to this book. The work itself claims: 'The author's reference materials were taken largely from Japanese writings.' Perhaps this was a result of the author's not having been able to consult many Chinese historical writings while he was a student in Japan, and because the historical sources with respect to Zheng Chenggong by Japanese, which had been sufficient to stimulate and arouse them at the time of Zheng's activities, stimulated the Chinese when they read them later. The author lists seventeen items of 'reference materials,' and among them are Maruyama Masahiko's *Tei Seikō*, Miyazaki Raijō's *Tei Seikō*, Kawaguchi Chōju's *Taiwan Teishi kiji*, and Inō Yoshinori, *Taiwan shi* (Chronicle of Taiwan),[m] altogether fourteen of them by Japanese. Only three works listed were Chinese: Yu Yonghe, *Wei Zheng jishi* (Accounts of the False Zheng); Jiang Risheng, *Taiwan waiji*; and Huang Cheng, *Qi Min lu* (Fujian Chronicle of Tears).

These volumes were emotionally charged biographies of Zheng Chenggong written by overseas Chinese students amid the winds of anti-Manchu revolution. Although research on these writings remains incomplete, they were biographical accounts of Zheng Chenggong who was chosen with the aim of furthering the revolutionary cause, and they praised his spirit. They formed a distinctive genre of writings. In particular, we should note from the perspective of the history of Sino-Japanese cultural interactions the fact that they were composed principally on the basis of Japanese historical work.

Recent Japanese studies of Zheng Chenggong that I have seen include: Inagaki Magohee, *Tei Seikō*; and Ishihara Michihiro, *Tei Seikō*.[n] These are detailed works that treat Zheng Chenggong from a variety of angles and make use of numerous historical materials. The former, possibly because it was written in Taiwan, contains many illustrations, and concerning the battles over Taiwan, it makes use both of Chinese historical sources as well as foreign materials, in particular Ludwig Riess's *Geschichte der Insel Formosa*.[o] The latter also brings together numerous historical works and provides a list of references numbering more that 50 which is divided into Japanese, Korean, Chinese, and Western works. For Chinese publications on this topic, there is: Yu Zongxin, ed., *Ming Yanping wang Taiwan haiguo ji* (Record of Maritime Taiwan under the Prince of Yanping of the Ming).[p] This last work is written in the form of a detailed chronology.

Taiwan was Zheng Chenggong's final base of operations, and it appears that the number of people studying him increased dramatically after the Guomindang moved its government there. In 1950 the journal *Wenxian zhuankan* (1.3) ran a 'special issue commemorating the birth of Zheng Chenggong,' which carried a number of articles on him. The first among was the introductory piece mentioned above by Li Tengyue, 'Zheng Chenggong de siyin kao.' In addition, 'Cixing Chenggong shiji ji Ming Zheng yidai youguan shishi nianbiao' (Evidence of the Imperial Gift of a Surname to Chenggong and a Chronology of Historical Facts Relating to the Zhengs in the Ming Dynasty), edited by Lin Xiongxiang and Chen Shiqing, offers a detailed chronology that puts together events surrounding the Zheng family and related historical facts. Among the studies are 'Zheng Chenggong zheng-Tai shulüe' (Short Account of Zheng Chenggong's Attack on Taiwan) by Mao Yibo and 'Zheng shi shixi ji renwu kao' (A Geneology of the Zhengs and a Study of Their Character) by Liao Hanchen. There is also a 'Zheng Chenggong yanjiu cankaoshu mulu' (Bibliography of Studies and Reference Works on Zheng Chenggong) by Lai Xiangyun, which divides such work into Chinese, Japanese, and Western languages and gives the names of works as well as their authors or editors. However, for dates of publication it uses the Western calendar for Western books, and for Chinese and Japanese books, it lists 'Qing publication,' 'Republican-period publication,' 'Meiji publication,' 'Taishō publication,' and 'Shōwa publication.' Roughly 200 book titles are given, but they seem arranged in a somewhat haphazard manner.

Huang Dianquan's *Zheng Chenggong shishi yanjiu* (A Study of the Historical Facts about Zheng Chenggong)[q] is a pamphlet, but it contains a considerable number of related photographic plates with notes at the beginning of the text. Ding Lüjin's *Yanping shijia* (Family Geneology of [the Prince of] Yanping)[r] is best described as a historical novel, divided into 26 chapters. It covers four generations of the rise and fall of the Zheng family, and keeps fairly close to the historical record.

Wu Fa's *Taiwan lishi zhaji* (Detailed Account of Taiwan's History)[s] cites works concerning Zheng Zhilong and Zheng Chenggong, when they were in Taiwan, and frequently offers observations from its own perspective. Particularly worthy of note here is a reference to a Dutch account of 1675, *Het Verwaardloosd' Formosa* (Neglected Formosa),[t] by Frederick Coyett, the Dutch governor of Taiwan. He notes that Zheng Chenggong had under his command two companies of 'black soldiers,' many of whom had been brought along to Taiwan as former Dutch slaves. Many Chinese texts reveal that Zheng Chenggong had units under his command of 'steel men,' namely troops outfitted with iron armor, but the fact that he had 'black units' is scarcely to be seen elsewhere – perhaps there were Malays among them.

Among works on Taiwan and Zheng Chenggong presently being compiled, one detailed account that cites numerous historical sources on the Dutch and Spanish attacks on Taiwan and on Zheng Chenggong's recovery of the island is the *Taiwan sheng tongzhi* (Comprehensive Gazetteer of Taiwan), *juan* 9, 'Geming zhi' (Treatise on the Change of Regimes) and 'Quhe pian' (On Being Rid of a Burden).[u] Detailed discussion of the history of the anti-Qing resistance by Zheng Chenggong and his descendents can be found in the same work, *Taiwan sheng tongzhi, juan* 9, 'Geming zhi' and 'Ju-Qing pian' (On Resisting the Qing).

The *Zheng shi shiliao* (Historical Materials on the Zheng Family)[v] is made up of three volumes [in thirteen *juan*], but it is comprised of selections from materials concerning the Zhengs taken from the *Ming Qing shiliao* (Historical Materials on the Ming and Qing).[w] It is effectively a base work on the Zheng family.

Appendix:
Yamamoto Ken (Baigai)

Kansai University and Yamamoto Baigai

In the 'Chronology' included in the *Kansai daigaku shichijū nen shi* (A Seventy-Year History of Kansai University),[a] there is the following note under Meiji 28 (1895): 'A special course of study was instituted in September. It enabled there to be short training courses in reading texts, composition, mathematics, and foreign languages.' In the main body of this work we also find: 'We must take particular note of the creation of the special course of study.... It would correspond in today's parlance to a general liberal arts curriculum. Yamamoto Ken was hired as a lecturer to teach textual reading and composition as the basis for legal studies.' There is also a note, entitled 'Bekka setchi no jijō' (Facts about the Establishment of the Special Course of Study), following this which reads in part:

> At that time, Yamamoto Ken, who used the style Baigai, was hired as a lecturer. He lectured here on *Sanyō ikō* (The Literary Remains of Rai Sanyō)[b] and *Kinsei meika bunshō* (Selections from the Writings of Famous Modern Authors). He had participated in the planning the Ōsaka Incident and was the patriotic man of will who drafted the famous 'Declaration of Korean Independence' at the request of his leader Ōi Kentarō. At the time he lectured here he was 44 years of age [Japanese style].

Thus, Yamamoto Baigai was teaching there during the formative period of 'Kansai Law School,' the forerunner of Kansai University, but he was as well a man who must, of course, be mentioned in any discussion of the history of modern Sino-Japanese relations. Indeed, the *Tō-A senkaku shishi kiden* (Biographies of East Asian Pioneer Men of Will)[c] has a rather extensive entry on him. He has a detailed, four-volume chronological autobiography, which he signed *Ken shuroku* (Personal Record of [Yamamoto] Ken). It was typeset and printed (though not put on sale) by his students in 1931, after his death. Entitled

Baigai sensei nenpu (Chronological [Auto-]Biography of Master Baigai), it carries at the beginning a reminiscence and description by his student, the artist Suga Tatehiko, of the 'pursuit of knowledge' at Yamamoto's private academy. Yamamoto had opened a Kangaku or Chinese studies academy in Ōsaka, and he had many students there.

An entry for 1896 in this chronological autobiography reads as follows: 'In the middle of August, I developed eye trouble and had to abandon reading and writing. From the previous year, I had been going to Kansai Law School to lecture on *Wenzhang guifan* (Models of Literary Prose; ed. Xie Fangde [1226–89]).[d] At this point I had to stop.' This evidence leads us to the conclusion that Yamamoto taught in the special course at Kansai Law School from September 1895 until August 1896.

An Early Love of History

According to his chronological autobiography, Yamamoto was born in Takaoka, Kōchi prefecture in 1852 (Kaei 5), and he died at Ushimado, Okayama prefecture in 1928 at the age of 76. He was reading Chinese texts from his youth: 'My young mind loved history [books] but did not enjoy the classics,' reads the entry for his twelfth [Japanese style] year, 'and I particularly liked reading the *Zizhi tongjian* (Comprehensive Mirror for Aid in Government).'[e] Already at age ten, 'I had read through the *Shi ji* (Records of the Grand Historian) and the *Zuozhuan* (Commentary of Mr. Zuo), and I was reading the *Twenty-One Dynastic Histories*.'[f] The chronological autobiography goes on to explain: 'I could read unpunctuated Chinese texts well.' At age thirteen, 'I enjoyed discussing current events.... I also derived special joy from gathering together and writing down material concerning the trends of the time from books.' We see here an early proclivity toward history and the problems involving issues of the day. This youthful predilection for reading may have contained the sprouts of Yamamoto's later opposition to the government and struggles on behalf of freedom and popular rights.

At age fourteen, he was summoned to appear before the daimyō of Tosa domain, and he composed the following poem in Chinese:

The golden candle burns resplendently before your beautiful seat,
How can a mere child bow down before your countenance?

The next year his devotion to historical texts continued – 'I reread the *Zizhi tongjian* for the sixth time this year' – and he completed his reading of the *Twenty-Two Dynastic Histories*.[g]

By the same token, 'Western Learning' was being taught in many of the domains, and according to his chronological autobiography Yamamoto, at age seventeen in the inaugural year of the Meiji period, studied English at the Kaiseikan in Kōchi. 'Studying English,' though, 'did not strike my fancy and I quit after about two weeks.' At age nineteen in 1870, he became a student at the

Shidōkan in Kōchi; it was a school specializing in Kangaku and his father was a teacher there. He worked there as assistant to a teacher of punctuating Chinese texts. The following year, when the Shidōkan was closed as part of the policy to abolish the feudal domains and institute a nationwide system of prefectures, a call went out from the capital for the study of English, and it was requested that the teachers at the 'Translation Bureaus' (perhaps under prefectural control) set up English departments. Some were even hired by Keiō University. He first studied the English grammar from the *Kakken bosu*, but 'in less than ten days, I was studying by myself and reading geography and history.' He was in fact confident enough to note: 'I surpassed by fellow students.'

A look at his *Zōsho mokuroku* (Book Listing)[h] reveals a large percentage of Chinese texts. At the very end, however, is a 'Section of Western Books,' which lists a total of eleven works including *First Book in English Grammar*, *Longman's New Reader No. 4*, *New National Readers (1–5)*, *Elementary History of the United States*, *New Physical Geography*, and *World We Live (Manry's Geographical Series)*, among others. The grammar, *Kakken bosu*, was this *First Book in English Grammar*.

When he was twenty in 1871, he departed for Tokyo where he entered the Ikuei Academy which stressed Western Studies and additionally offered instruction in Chinese Studies. While serving as an assistant in Kangaku, he studied Western Learning under the Dutchman T. H. Reich.[i] The chronological autobiography mentions that he studied about England and Germany there, going on to note that 'Reich particularly enjoyed geography and I did as well. He used geography in his classes every day. That I later knew the geography of the world and set my will on overseas affairs was surely a gift I received from him.' In the aforementioned *Zōsho mokuroku* is a listing of the geography texts in English which, it would appear, he read at this time.

No details are given concerning the extent to which he pursued his 'studies of England,' but 'while I was in the academy, at Reich's request I translated into English a biography of Tokugawa Ieyasu, which he then touched up.' Later, 'when I was working in the Ministry of Public Works, at the request of Professor Malcolm, I translated an English novel into Japanese.'

From Telegraph Operator to Newspaperman

In 1874 Yamamoto became a telegraph operator [a level of technical official below that of engineer – JAF][j] as a means of support. The following year he was sent on business to Ōsaka, and from that time forward his ties with the city of Ōsaka developed. There he went to work for the Kōraikyō Telegraph Office. 'Ever since I was young,' he wrote of this time, 'I had always revered Toyotomi Hideyoshi. I thus set my heart on settling in Ōsaka, and at this time I came to Ōsaka. I heard that the grave of Kimura Nagato no kami [the early Edo-period warrior, Kimura Shigenari] was in Wakae, and I went there immediately to pay my respects.' The next year he brought his parents from Tosa to Ōsaka. They all took up residence in Ōsaka in a rented home in Minami-atsuto-chō where they lived together.

In 1877 the Seinan War [namely, the rebellion of Saigō Takamori] erupted, and Yamamoto was sent on business into the area of the fighting. After entering a site of particularly severe fighting near Taharazaka, he noted: 'Bullets were whizzing by and the place was strewn with corpses.' After his return from the war, Yamamoto worked for both the Kawaguchi and the Kōraikyō Telegraph Offices, but the following year, 1878, he quit his job as a telegraph operator for the Ministry of Public Works. As he wrote, 'futilely I held this great goal in my heart, and I was waisting my efforts on spotty, poor workmanship. I thus quit my job.' His 'great goal' was to further the cause of the Popular Rights Movement, and to that end he became a newspaper reporter, for it seemed that he would thus be able to have recourse to public opinion through speech and action. After quitting his telegraphy position, he wrote: 'I wanted to set up a newspaper office in Kyoto.' Although he went to Kyoto many times, 'it never got off the ground.'

In 1879 Yamamoto joined the staff of the *Ōsaka shinpō*. The following year he married a woman from Tosa. That year (1880) he wrote his *Kōgai yūkoku ron* (On Indignant Patriotism), and he serialized a novel, *Yaezakura matsunomidori* (Florid Cherry Blossoms, the Glory of Pine Green), in the *Ōsaka shinpō*. In his chronological autobiography, he noted: 'It won great esteem, with a professional teller of military tales recounting it.'

Although the latter text is now nowhere to be found, the *Kōgai yūkoku ron* is held in the National Diet Library in Tokyo. It was published in 1880 by Nakao Shinsuke of Ōsaka and is a small volume of some 150 pages. It is virtually overflowing with Yamamoto's passion and indignation on behalf of freedom and popular rights. His fellow provincial Ueki Emori (1857–92) contributed a preface and helped in the revisions. In his own 'prefatory remarks,' Yamamoto wrote: 'I talked it over with my friend Emori, and I revised it several times in places where it was unsatisfactory.' In Ueki's preface, he noted: 'Although we had slight differences of opinion about this or that in the text, it was an excellent work for propogating popular rights. I thus rejoice on behalf of the country and celebrate on behalf of freedom.' As for its contents, Chapter One is an 'Overview.' Chapter Two is entitled 'The Origins of Popular Rights,' and Chapter Three is 'Limiting the Powers of the Government.' The final chapter, fourteen, is entitled 'Avoiding Violence.' In his 'prefatory remarks,' Yamamoto noted that 'this book is principally aimed at persuading villagers and woodcutters.... I thus did not employ refined, elegant language, but worked to use ordinary prose. Anyone should be able to read it.'

Yamamoto Baigai on People's Rights

In the first chapter, 'Overview,' Yamamoto argued that in the Asian countries of China, Turkey, and Persia, 'people's rights were being taken away with each passing day, leaving them in a tragic state scarcely able to enjoy life.' By contrast, 'there were the petty barbarians, the Normans, the Saxons, and the Gauls of France and England.' They 'long ago sought popular rights and often fought against their government and armies over the past few centuries.... Ultimately, legal institutions were established leading to their present wealth and strength.' He also noted: 'Although the United States of America, for example, was in fact populated by immigrants from the extremely poor people of Europe, it has now acquired wealth and strength surpassing the rest of the world. This is the major reason for it.' Furthermore, 'the ebb and flow of national rights is based on the ebb and flow of people's rights. If the people's rights do not grow, they will lack that by which to grow strong.' This viewpoint appears to be drawn from the knowledge of world history which Yamamoto had acquired as a young man.

'The nation is not the sovereign's nation,' he noted at one point in his second chapter. 'It is the people's nation. The people are not the sovereign's people. They are the people of the realm. The government is not the sovereign's government. It is the government of the people.' Thus, in connection with the acquisition of popular rights, he argued that 'popular rights are not something conferred by a sovereign. They should be restored to the people by the government which must quickly find a way to restore them to all people without distinction' (Chapter Two). Because popular rights are innate to the people, Yamamoto argued that they should with all alacrity be taken back from the sovereign and the government. He also vitriolically denounced the autocratic sovereign who oppressed the people:

> Originally, autocratic government treated the people with oppression, a practice which became ordinary, and the people themselves fell into a state of servility and cowardice. Ultimately, they looked up to their sovereign as one deserving unlimited honor, and governments, taking advantage of this weakness, increasingly nurtured their own authority, degrading the people to the same level as oxen or horses.... With supreme authority, the sovereign oppressed the people to the point of privatizing the realm.

And, at another point, he noted:

> The prerogative to make laws and run an administration all reverted to the sovereign alone. In matters of the realm, the sovereign thus saw everything as a function of what was in his personal interest. This gradually bred a mood of lethargy.... He entrusted his authority to a prime minister to administer the most important affairs of state.... Without paying it any mind, he [the prime minister] increasingly entrenched his own position. As an exhibition of his power, he stood preeminent over all private individuals. With the most important matters of state within his ken, ... his authority surpassed even that of the sovereign several fold, and the evil done by him was also much worse than the sovereign's.

Thus, he argued that if limitations were not placed on the power of a government that combined such a sovereign and sovereign power, there would be no

210

happiness for the people. 'Because of this, if we do not limit the power of government, we cannot hope to see people's rights prosper. The people will be deprived of happiness and will decline to a state in which they will be unable to enjoy their lives' (Chapter Three). He thus stressed the fact that people's rights were not something conferred upon them but were to be obtained when the people resisted their government and took back their rights. As he pointed out:

> People's rights originally protected the people's freedom, and to that end brought them happiness and enabled them to live with security. Originally they were the mechanism by which the tyranny of government was destroyed and thereby the people's freedom could not be obliterated. In order to make use of this mechanism, the people must be outfitted with the tools sufficient to resist government. Without such tools, they will continue as always to yield all rights and be unable to extend their rights. [Chapter Four]

Here we find the basic principles underlying the work of Yamamoto Baigai and contemporary activists in the Popular Rights Movement.

Off to Okayama

The *Chigo shinbun* (Children's News) was inaugurated in Okayama in 1881. Yamamoto was invited to serve as editor-in-chief, and he moved to Okayama in March of that year. That winter, however, *Chigo shinbun* incurred the displeasure of the government and was temporarily shut down. It was closed down once again in the spring of the following year and was finally banned outright. That year Yamamoto met Kobayashi Kuzuo for the first time, and, as he notes in his chronological autobiography, 'we vowed to devote our energies to the Jiyūtō (Liberal Party) and discussed the idea of establishing another newspaper.' Kobayashi later became a close friend of Yamamoto's, and when the former died in 1920 Yamamoto wrote his funerary inscription. Kobayashi came from Okayama and for many years had studied French with a Frenchman; he had also researched French law. He used his learning to protest the shackling of freedom and the repression of speech by Japan's clan-dominated government of that time. He called for the pressing need to open a parliament, and he presented to the authorities a written memorial on the establishment of a parliament and a petition on behalf of his fellow provincials. He was actively involved in the Popular Rights Movement.

After the closing of *Chigo shinbun*, the *Chūgoku nichinichi shinbun* (Daily News of Western Honshū) was founded with Yamamoto as editor. As he noted, however, 'at that time, the government's oppression was becoming worse with each passing day, and many lecture societies and social gatherings were being broken up. In March several of us received punishments. I had to pay a fine of 10 yen.' He also pointed out: 'At an invitation, I went to Kasaoka in Bichū [in the southwest corner of present-day Okayama prefecture] to attend a gathering which was disbanded and fined 12 yen.' We can thus see that the government's intervention and repression of speech and meetings were particularly severe. The *Chūgoku nichinichi shinbun* was banned less than a month after its first issue appeared. Yamamoto 'planned its revival with Kobayashi and others but it never materialized.'

In financial dire straits during this period, Yamamoto frequently had to move from one friend's home to another. As he noted: 'My financial situation was becoming increasingly worse, as my opposition to the government grew increasingly more sharp. My hatred for the government's tyranny burned within me, but the privations I was suffering made it impossible for me to do anything about it.' In his chronological autobiography, Yamamoto had the following to say:

After the Satsuma Rebellion came to an end, the government's despotism grew extreme. First, the Risshisha (Set the Will Society) in Tosa domain arose, later becoming the Aikokusha (Patriotic Society). They memorialized and petitioned for the creation and opening of a diet. At one point they formed a 'Kokkai kisei dōmeikai' (Association for the Establishment of a Diet), and it became the Jiyūtō. At this time, the Kaishintō (Progressive Party) was formed, the Kyūshū kaishintō (Kyūshū Progressive Party) was formed, and the Kinki jiyūtō (Kinki Liberal Party) changed its name to the Rikken seitō (Constitutionalist Party). All opposed the government on the basis of their respective points of view. The government then proclaimed 1890 as the year in which a diet would convene, while restricting men of will with legal conditions placed on their assemblages. Its cruelty and despotism were felt everywhere. The obstructions to men of will were followed by fines. Such was the situation at that time.

In November of that year Yamamoto left Okayama and returned to Ōsaka. While he 'still had no livelihood after returning to Ōsaka,' Sugita Teiichi (1851–1920) and others of the Echizen jiyūtō (Echizen Liberal Party) started up the *Hokuriku jiyū shinbun* (Liberal Newspaper of Northern Honshū), and Yamamoto was invited to serve as assistant editor. He thus repaired to the city of Fukui. The next year the newspaper stopped publication due to exhaustion of funds, and Yamamoto once again returned to Ōsaka.

The Opening of a Kangaku Academy in Ōsaka

When Yamamoto was 31 in 1883, his chronological autobiography notes, he 'divorced his wife on certain grounds,' but the reasons are not indicated. At that time he went with his wife to her family home in Kōchi 'to explain the situation and to obtain permission.' He then returned from Kōchi to Ōsaka by himself, and 'thereafter, I remained at home where I opened a private academy to teach students. I had but to support one household.' From that time forward,

Yamamoto began work as the instructor of a Kangaku academy to support himself. He also 'shut myself up to read and write, for half a year never stepping outside the door.' It seems, though, that he had not fully relinquished his desires for political reform, and 'when Prime Minister Itagaki [Taisuke, 1837–1919, the Jiyūtō prime minister] returned from Europe, he gave a speech at the Jiyū Pavilion in Nakanoshima. I went there to listen, but that's all.' By 'but that's all' he seemed to be implying activity on behalf of the Popular Rights Movement.

The following year, there was a fire and he moved to Morimura in the east of the city. For all his efforts, Yamamoto's proclivity to speak on behalf of the political movement could not be forestalled. Invited to join the staff of the *Rikken seitō shinbun* (Constitutionalist Party News), half the day he would work at the newspaper office, and half the day he taught students in his academy. When the cooperation between the Jiyūtō and the Rikken seitō fell apart, Yamamoto, as a member of the former, resigned from the newspaper staff. The Jiyūtō thereupon established in Ōsaka the Sōkikan, and 'I once again became involved [in the movement].' As before, 'I was entrusted with party work,' and he traveled to Tsuruga in Echizen. Subsequent travels took him to Bizen, Mimasaka, Hōki, Izumo, Iwami, Aki, and Bingo.

On the Eve of the Ōsaka Incident

At the tail end of his entry for Meiji 17 (1884) in his chronological autobiography, Yamamoto described the situation on the eve of the 'Ōsaka Incident.'

Kobayashi Kuzuo was in Tokyo, and there he frequently met with the French Minister from late summer and early autumn on. He was eventually introduced to Itagaki Taisuke, and they reached an accord: a plan for the independence of Korea. They sought out Gotō Shōjirō to shoulder the movement in Korea. To this end, they requested from the French government a loan of one million francs and a battleship. At this time, the French had their own designs on Annam [to China's south] and were only too happy to stir up an incident between Japan and China to the north. News of Prime Minister Ferry's approval of the request arrived. Kobayashi then reported on circumstances to that point in detail. It seemed as though his principal aim was to use the uprising for independence in Korea to provoke violence between Japan and China, take advantage of the government's press of business, call for a rebellion, and overthrow the government.

Thus, in order to construct in Japan a society with popular rights quickly, the radicals within the Jiyūtō had the following plan. By supporting a rebellion of the Korean independence movement of Kim Ok-kyun (1851–94), they would induce a conflict with China, which saw Korea as a vassal state, and throw the Japanese government into turmoil, bringing it down. The French government together with Kobayashi established contact to facilitate the execution of this plan of action. 'At this time,' notes his chronological autobiography, 'the whole affair was kept completely in secret, its details conveyed to no one. Letters to and from the French were all held by Kobayashi himself.'

At the beginning of his entry for 1885 in his chronological autobiography, we read: 'On January 5, I made a rare trip into the city. On behalf of the Korean movement, I did not return home, but boarded a vessel directly for Tosa and there consulted with party friends.' That year [actually, 1884 – JAF] the Sino-French War erupted over Annam. 'Troops from China and France engaged in battle over Vietnam. Kobayashi Kuzuo was in Tokyo, involved in plans with the French minister and exchanging letters with Admiral Courbet. Kobayashi often wrote me and told me what was transpiring,' but Yamamoto does not offer any concrete details at this point. After Kobayashi urged him to come to Tokyo and there revealed to him a detailed plan for the rebellion in Korea, Yamamoto promptly offered support.

> A letter from Kobayashi Kuzuo arrived summoning me to Tokyo post-haste.... At dusk on [July] 7, I arrived in Yokohama and then proceeded immediately to Tokyo where I met Kobayashi. Kobayashi reported that several stalwart men had been sent to Korea to kill high-level officials and thus spark conflict with China. We would then take advantage of this opportunity and rise up in rebellion.... I supported the rebellion. I further asked about the co-conspirators and was told they were Ōi Kentarō and Isoyama Seibee. I also asked about the order of events in which the plan would be carried out. Kobayashi said: 'Money has already been provided. We're waiting for the opportunity to present itself, and Isoyama [who was director of the Yūichikan, a boarding house in Tokyo where young Jiyūtō men of will gathered] will lead these brave men directly to Nagasaki where they will rent a ship and sail to Korea.' I said: 'That's great! Since there are only a few conspirators, there will be no leaks. When the opportunity presents itself and the brave men are ready to depart, they will need vessels to take them from Yokohama to Nagasaki.' ... I drafted a manifesto for distribution to announce when the rebellion in Korea would commence and also discussed matters concerning funds. On the 18th I boarded the *Shin-Tōkyōmaru*, returning home on the 19th.

Yamamoto had mentioned to Kobayashi about sailing from Yokohama to Nagasaki, but in fact the leaders, having gathered in Ōsaka to head for Nagasaki, were arrested in Ōsaka. This became known as the 'Ōsaka Incident.' The manifesto composed by Yamamoto was entitled 'Declaration of Korean Independence,' and it is included in his chronological autobiography. It reads in part as follows [in literary Chinese – JAF]:

> Righteous Japanese troops declare to all men of the world. The independent nation of Korea was a state founded and developed by the

Yi family. It never sought intervention by other states. The Qing used force to subjugate it and rendered it a vassal state, compelled it to pay tribute, destroyed its national authority, and divested it of freedom.

Funding Problems and Arrests

The circumstances surrounding the Ōsaka Incident are described in great detail in the following works: *Ōsaka no goku* (Jail in Ōsaka)[k]; Itagaki Taisuke, gen. ed., *Jiyūtō shi* (History of the Liberal Party)[l]; and the aforementioned *Tō-A senkaku shishi kiden*.[m] I would like to cite here from the last of these works:

> When they were at long last ready to begin the uprising in Korea, they first needed to prepare an elegant manifesto to win over the people's hearts. They had to rely on someone who was especially talented at composition in literary Chinese, and they thus called upon the Ōsaka scholar of Chinese studies, Yamamoto Ken, styled Baigai, revealing their plans to him and asking him to write it.... He was extremely encouraged and readily consented. Content in his simple life of celibacy and vegetarianism, he always rejected eating meat. In spite of this, he said, 'I need strength to write this manifesto. First, it'll be wine; next, I'll order a meal of octopus and crab. Sure, I'm a vegetarian, but you can tell from the Chinese characters as we write them that 'octopus' and 'crab' are insects [because they each contain the radical for insect – JAF]. Eating insects should be no problem for a vegetarian.' While drinking wine from a large cup with octopus and crab, he pondered what he would write, and then he composed the profoundly vigorous piece below.

The text then quotes the declaration Yamomoto wrote, adding: 'This declaration was then translated into English and French by Kobayashi who had made arrangements to send it to various foreign newspapers.' The *Tō-A senkaku shishi kiden* then continues:

> The declaration came about in this manner. The death-defying men rallied together under Isoyama and others. They were able to produce explosives, and gradually their weaponry was prepared.... Energetic political figures helped out in the plans both publicly and privately. The number of participants soon exceeded 80.
>
> When their plans were on the verge of being put into action, essential funding did not materialize as desired. Both Ōi and Kobayashi were busily and excitedly involved in every manner of affair, but the activities of the Jiyūtō politicians were constantly under government scrutiny, and every little move they made was closely observed by the watchdogs of the authorities. That meant, of course, that they had to be extremely careful in carrying out their aims, and they were unsuccesssful in explaining the

content of their plans in order to appeal to the anger and chivalrous spirit of the nation. Thus, they fell into worse financial staits, and it became clearer with each passing day that their expectations of ever succeeding were seriously in doubt.

The procurement of funds proved disappointing, and decisive action could only be undertaken when it would already be too late. As the final means at their disposal, 'they had no choice but to adopt emergency measures, for they were performing a great task on behalf of the state': they began plundering, as in Kanagawa prefecture and elsewhere. 'The funds obtained through this means of seizure were collected by Ōi.' Carrying the money in their hands, the first, second, and third group of conspirators massed in Ōsaka with their explosives, the cans in which they were placed, and their swords. The explosives brought by Kageyama [Eiko] of the second Ōsaka brigade were placed in Yamamoto's care. Thus, 'Ōi still remained in Tokyo to collect funds, but Kobayashi, Isoyama, and other leaders made their way to Ōsaka one after the next. Ōsaka became the base of operations for those who would carry out the job.'

Unable to secure sufficient funds – Yamamoto's chronological autobiography notes that he approached his friends in Akō in Harima [present-day southwestern Hyōgo prefecture] for contributions – they attacked and robbed the Senjuin Temple, which was well known for its wealth in Shigisan, Yamato [present-day Nara], a wealthy farmer in Takaichi, Yamato, and Okahashi Kiyoshi. Isoyama concealed his whereabouts, and Arai Shōgo took over his leadership position. One by one they traveled from Ōsaka to Nagasaki in preparation for the voyage overseas. According to his chronological autobiography, Yamamoto, Ōi, and Kobayashi sent off a group with Arai and Kageyama from Umeda train station [in Ōsaka].

While one group was preparing for the trip in Nagasaki, the entire plot was disclosed and arrests commenced. There are two possible sources of the disclosure: one group of conspirators involved in robbery as a means of securing funds throughout Ibaraki and Chiba was caught and confessed; or someone in the Jiyūtō office was in fact a spy, and his reports made it possible to know of the plot and make the wholesale arrests. First, Ōi and Kobayashi were picked up in Ōsaka, while Arai and Kageyama were taken in Nagasaki; in all 58 persons were incarcerated at one of two jails in Ōsaka, Nakanoshima, and Horikawa. According to his chronological autobiography, when Yamamoto learned of the arrests of Ōi and Kobayashi, he surmised that 'the police were certain to pay a visit' on him as well; he did not leave his home, but waited and continued teaching his students at his academy until the police did, in fact, arrive.

After a preliminary investigation lasting some eighteen months, a judicial judgment was reached on this incident in the fall of 1887. The three leaders, Ōi Kentarō, Kobayashi Kuzuo, and Isoyama Seibee, received the heaviest sentences, 'six years of minor imprisonment.' Arai received a term of 'five years of minor imprisonment,' while Yamamoto received a sentence of 'one year minor imprisonment and ten months of supervision.' As his autobiography notes, 'I was interrogated on the charge of causing foreign troubles and for violating the criminal regulations concerning control over explosive substances.'

Getting to Know Judge Inoue Misao

Yamamoto discussed his life in prison in his chronological autobiography, and details of the court's decision can be found in *Tō-A senkaku shishi kiden*, though the defendents seem to have been treated rather magnanimously in view of the fact that they had committed acts of treason. Not only was public opinion sympathetic to them, but, as is made clear in Yamamoto's chronological autobiography, both Appellate Court Judge Kojima Korekata (Iken, 1837–1908) and the presiding Judge Inoue Misao (d. 1905) opposed the government's intentions and wanted to hand down lenient sentences.

> Originally, Kojima and Inoue both intended to judge on the charge of stirring up troubles overseas. I happened to hear that the government considered the violation of the criminal regulations concerning control over explosive substances to be a particularly severe offense and sought to have it dealt with severely. Public opinion, however, was completely on the side of the men of valor [i.e., the defendants], seeking either a light term or a magnanimous sentence. On the evening of the 23rd, the judges met and prepared a written judgment before orders from the government had arrived. We waited all through the night, but they still had not finished.... The judges probably were not in agreement with the government and thus wanted to offer a lenient judgment. They thus had to act before the government's orders arrived.

The presiding judge at the time was Inoue Misao. After he completed his term in prison and was parolled, Yamamoto seems to have become on intimate terms with Inoue and other penal officials. We know this from his chronological autobiography which notes: 'I remained in contact with Judge Inoue Misao, the Horikawa Prison's head doctor Tamiya Yukiharu, and the head of general affairs at the prison, Kakuyama Rikichirō, after leaving prison. Tamiya and Kakuyama later sent their sons to study with me.' Judge Inoue with whom Yamamoto became friendly following his prison term is well known as one of the founders of Kansai Law School. It would appear that Yamamoto's invitation to teach at Kansai Law School was the result of Inoue's recommendation, but there is no mention whatsoever of this in his chronological autobiography.

The defense in the Ōsaka Incident was led by Hoshi Tōru (1850–1901) and included as many as sixteen other attorneys. Among them several had subsequent ties with Kansai University: Shibukawa Chūjirō (an administrator), Sunagawa Yūshun (a director), and Mori Sakutarō (a trustee).

When he was released from prison, Yamamoto returned to running his academy. He also kept up a relationship with the press, as a writer for the *Aikoku shinbun* (Patriots' Newspaper) which commenced publication in Kōbe in 1890 and as editor for the *Shinonome shinbun* (Dawn News). As he noted, though, 'more often than not I didn't go into the office, but would draft an article and send it in.'

That year, 1890, the Imperial Diet convened for the first time. Yamamoto lamented: 'Everyone is congratulating each other, because they've attained this without spilling any blood.... The throng dreads the sight of blood. How can they even speak of politics! The tyranny of clique government is still with us, with mediocre people dominating politics and current affairs worsening on a dayly basis.' With the amalgamation the following year of the Jiyūtō and the Kaishintō, Yamamoto noted: 'I was strongly opposed to this.... The comrades who had struggled' ten years earlier 'to bring down clique government were nowhere to be found' in the (new) party now. 'They had fallen over the course of time.... I thus resolved to sever my connection to the party.'

In 1894 Japan finally did commence hostilities with China over Korea. 'Several times I sent the authorities position papers,' he noted in his autobiography, but details of their contents are not mentioned. The following year he lectured on the *Wenzhang guifan* at Kansai Law School. In 1896 he had to cease reading and writing due to eye problems and discontinued his lectures.

Travel to China and Contacts with the Reformers

In the spring of 1897, his eye troubles healed, and that fall he set off for China. He boarded the *Genkaimaru* at Kōbe and arrived in Tianjin via Pusan and Inchon. From there he proceeded to Beijing. He then turned and proceeded from Shanghai up the Yangzi River, visiting Hankou via Suzhou. The return voyage downriver stopped at Nanjing before returning to Shanghai. In December he headed back for Japan. Yamamoto entitled his narrative of this voyage *Enzan sosui kiyū* (Travelogue of the Mountains of North China and the Rivers of South China) (two stringbound volumes, in literary Chinese); it was published in 1898 [in Ōsaka] though not put up for sale. He took a camera with him during his travels and took photos of the scenery at the places he visited. After he returned to Japan, he asked a friend to use these photos as the basis for real-life paintings, and these he inserted here and there in the text of *Enzan sosui kiyū* with lithography.

Throughout his trip, Yamamoto persisted in wearing Japanese dress. As he viewed the famous ancient sites in China, he was filled with historical impressions, and he described their present state. In Shanghai he had particularly close contact with Chinese reformers active in journalism, and they spoke at length of current events.

Kojō Teikichi (1866–1949) and Fujita Toyohachi (Kenpō, 1869–1929) were living in Shanghai at that time, translating into Chinese articles and editorials from the Japanese press for, respectively, *Shiwu bao* (Contemporary Affairs) and *Nongxue bao* (Agronomy). Through these two men he was able to meet Luo Zhenyu (1866–1940) at *Nongxue bao* and Wang Kangnian (Rangqing, 1860–1911) and Liang Qichao (Rengong, 1873–1929) at *Shiwu bao*. Zhang Taiyan

(Binglin, 1869–1936) also paid a visit on him at this time, and Yamamoto went with Wang on one occasion to meet Zhang Jian (1853–1926). Yamamoto exchanged an assortment of views with these men and indicated general agreement with many of their positions.

For December of 1897, he noted in his chronological autobiography, 'the Chinese Ji Kan, Wang Youling, and Kang Tongwen paid me a visit. From that time forward many Chinese did so.' From contacts made during his travels in China, Yamamoto became active on behalf of the reformers who fled to Japan the next year following the 'Hundred Days Reform Movement.' In an entry for 1898 in his chronological autobiography, he noted: 'Last year I traveled in China, and my contacts with Chinese have become rather broad since'; 'I have exchanged many letters with Wang Rangqing'; 'I have translated a number of works for the Chinese Luo Zhenyu and sent them to Shanghai.'

Furthermore, he wrote: 'Kang Mengqing came to visit. Mengqing, *ming* Youyi, is from Guangdong, an elder cousin of Kang Changsu. Changsu, *ming* Youwei, is styled Nanhai. He has served at the Qing court and worked for reform.' He then went on to write:

> On September 23, there was a report of a political change in China. The Empress Dowager was unhappy with the earnest reform efforts of the Qing emperor, and she finally placed the emperor under house arrest. She banished Minister of Works Zhang Yinhuan to Xinjiang and ordered beheaded six men, including Lin Xu, Tan Sitong, and Kang Guangren [Kang Youwei's younger brother]. Changsu, Liang Rengong, and Wang Shaoyun took refuge here in Japan. Rengong, *ming* Qichao, had the childhood name of Zhuoru. I got to know him in Shanghai. Shaoyun bears the *ming* of Zhao.

Although Yamamoto said nothing here of whatever plans or schemes he may have had with respect to the 1898 Reform Movement, his chronological autobiography notes:

> On September 27, I went to Tokyo because of the incident in China. . . . On October 5, I returned to Ōsaka and formed a group which was called the Nis-Shin kyōwakai (Sino-Japanese Cooperative Society). . . . At the end of October, I heard that Kang Changsu, Wang Shaoyun, and Liang Rengong had gone to Tokyo. On the 29th, I went to Tokyo together with Kang Mengqing and met with all three men.

To help these men in their work, 'on the 7th, I held a party at the Biichi Pavilion with Yamada Shunkei, Izumida Jirō, and Kajima Nobushige, among others. I proposed the matter of the Nis-Shin kyōwakai. Many people were in attendance.'

Qingyi bao and the Datong School

It was not long thereafter that Liang Qichao and others began publication in 1898 of the thrice-monthly *Qingyi bao* (Journal of Pure Discussion), and when overseas Chinese living in Japan in 1899 established the Datong School, they contacted Yamamoto and sought his cooperation. In an entry for 1899 in his chronological autobiography, he noted: 'In the winter of last year, Kang Mengqing went to Yokohama and began to publish *Qingyi bao* [nominally owned by Feng Jingru and edited by Liang Qichao – Masuda]. I was asked to write for it.' A look at the full run of *Qingyi bao* now reveals that from the second number there was a column under the title 'Lun Dong-Ya shiyi' (On Conditions in East Asia), and these serial editorials were signed 'Baigai Yamamoto Ken.' Also from the second number, there was a space at the end of each issue for 'places serving as agencies for the journal,' and there one may find 'Mr. Yamamoto, head of the Baiseisho Academy, No. 1 Tanimachi, Higashi-ku, Ōsaka.' From the third number, though, the words 'Mr. Yamamoto' were no longer printed. In other words, Yamamoto's academy served as an agency for the sale of *Qingyi bao* in Ōsaka.

Once again, his chronological autobiography went on to say: 'People from Guangdong contributed funds and created the Datong School in Yokohama to teach Chinese students.[n] Through Mengqing's introduction I was asked to serve as headmaster. I could not abandon my own academy and move, so I had to turn down the offer.' The fact that Yamamoto would be invited to serve as headmaster for the Datong School, built by determined overseas Chinese for the purpose of educating their children, is an indication of the trust he had inspired in them.

In the tenth issue of *Qingyi bao*, there was an article entitled 'Datong xuexiao kaixiao ji' (Record of the Opening of the Datong School). Similarly there is a detailed account of the school in the *Geming yishi* (Unofficial History of the Revolution)[o] by Feng Ziyou who was a student in its first class. Kang Youwei's disciple, Xu Qin (Junmian), took up the post as the school's principal, though former Minister of Education Inukai Ki (1855–1932) was asked and accepted a place as honorary principal. According to the article in *Qingyi bao*, in addition to Inukai, the following Japanese attended the opening ceremonies of the school: Ōkuma Shigenobu (former prime minister, 1838–1922), Takata Sanae (1860–1933), Mochizuki Kotarō (1865–1927), Nakanishi Masaki, Kashiwabara Buntarō, Hirayama Shū, and Miyazaki Torazō (1870–1922), fifteen invited guests in all.

On March 14, 1899, Yamamoto received a telegram from Tokyo and left for the capital. Narahara Nobumasa (1863–1900), a secretary in the foreign ministry, acting on the position held by Foreign Minister Aoki Shūzō (1844–1914), asked Yamamoto to get Kang Youwei, Liang Qichao, and Wang Zhao (1859–1935) to leave Japan for the United States. The Foreign Minister considered it harmful for diplomatic relations with China to have these three men in Japan [the Qing government had made this request of the Japanese Foreign Ministry – Masuda], and in view of his close ties with Kang Mengqing, they sought to use Yamamoto to effect this plan. However, as he wrote, 'a hunter cannot bare to enter the lair of a trapped bird and kill it,' and Yamamoto refused the request of the Foreign Ministry. Through Kang Mengqing, Yamamoto

220

revealed to the three men that the Japanese government intended to expel them. Glad to obtain this information from him, the three men then promised to proceed to the United States. Kang Youwei received 15,000 yen from the Foreign Ministry and set off first (to Canada), but Liang and Wang refused to leave because they felt that the amount of travel funds provided by the Japanese government was too small. This story is recounted in Yamamoto's chronological autobiography.

In 1900 the Boxer Uprising erupted in China, and troops sent from eight nations, including Japan, Great Britain, Russia, France, Germany, and Italy, entered Beijing from Tianjin. At the time Yamamoto wrote in his autobiography: 'I wrote to Prime Minister Yamagata [Aritomo, 1838–1922] and Foreign Minister Aoki, forcefully arguing for an overall plan to help the Chinese government,' but concrete details of his 'forceful argument' are not given.

In November 1901, he noted that 'Liang Qichao has asked that I translate *Seiji hanron* (Outline of Government).' It is unclear if this request ever materialized or, if so, whether he ever sent it to Liang. In February of the following year, Liang inaugurated his semi-monthly journal *Xinmin congbao* (New People's Miscellany) in Yokohama, and published serially his famous essay 'Xinmin shuo' (On the Renovation of the People). Perhaps Liang needed a translation of *Seiji hanron* as a reference work for his writing. An investigation of the early issues of *Xinmin congbao* does not turn up the name of this work in Yamamoto's translation.

Furthermore, the *Yamamoto bunko tosho mokuroku* (Book List of the Holdings in the Yamamoto Collection) does indicate two works entitled *Seiji hanron*. The first is in one stringbound volume, published in 1895, 'by Woodrow Wilson of the United States, translated by Takata Sanae.' The second is in two stringbound volumes, published in 1883, 'by George H. Eaman [?], translated by Kobayashi Eichi.'

A Quiet Life in Okayama

In 1904 Yamamoto moved to Ushimado in Okayama prefecture. 'Ever since I bathed in waters off Ushimado again,' he noted, 'I wanted for three years to move there,' and 'Ushimado was in a remote area by the sea, an area good for nurturing mind and body.' Thus, he selected this place and moved there largely for health reasons. One further reason may have been that, since the start of the Russo-Japanese War that year, 'people's minds are unsettled. I unexpectedly sensed this among my new students.'

As an 'Afterward' to this year in his chronological autobiography, Yamamoto added: 'My written and published work over the past few years include *Enzan sosui kiyū*, 'Dong-Ya shiyi,' and *Riben wendian* (Grammar of Japanese).... 'Dong-Ya shiyi' was published in the Yokohama journal *Qingyi bao*, and *Riben wendian* was published by a Chinese in Shanghai.' He then went on to list the 'foreigners who have visited me over the past few years.... Among the Chinese were Jiang Shixing, Song Shu, Wang Kangnian, Luo Zhenyu, Li Jun, Wang Zhao, and Liang Qichao. Among the Koreans were Yi Tuho and Cho Ŭiyŏn.' This is an indication that Yamamoto's acquaintances of this period were linked with questions concerning East Asia.

According to his chronological autobiography, when Yamamoto was 66 in 1918, he visited Harbin via Korea, before settling back down in Ushimado. In the Hiroshima area, Shikoku, and the Kyoto area, he gave invited lectures at a host of places, attended meetings of poetry and tea ceremony groups, enjoyed fishing, and generally spent his last years in leisurely pursuits. His chronological autobiography ends in August 1927, probably because he became weak due to illness and 'while sick my fingers trembled, I couldn't write.' He died in Ushimado in September 1928 at the age of 76. According to his will, Yamamoto's books were donated to the Okayama Prefectural Library. Although we do now have the *Yamamoto bunko tosho mokuroku*, his entire collection is said to have been destroyed during the war.

Travelogue and Historical Poems

Today, two works by Yamamoto, a one-volume work entitled *Enka manroku* (Travels amid Smoke and Mist) and *Baiseisho eishi* (Historical Poems from the Baiseisho),[P] are held in the Hakuen Collection of Kansai University Library. The two printers were former students and friends of Yamamoto's, and while the former work appeared while he was living, the latter appeared a full year after his death.

Enka manroku is a short narrative (in literary Chinese), only fourteen leaves in length, of Yamamoto's travels in the cold, misty valleys of Sanuki and Shōdojima. In the margins of each page are short Chinese poems contributed by various literary men, such as Kubō Rakoku (the printer?). Also, at the end the impressions and comments of several men are added, and among them are such complimentary passages as that of [the Confucian scholar] Fujiwara Nangaku (1842–1920): 'This piece of writing is meticulous in structure, vigorous in its language. It is worthy competition for San'gan and Senshū. It deserves our praise and appreciation.' Perhaps Nangaku's last sentence was a consequence of his own origins in Sanuki. This connection, it would seem, was the means by which this thin volume ended up in the Hakuen Collection.

The *Baiseisho eishi* is a collection of poems by Yamamoto written in the seven-character line quatrain style, dealing with historical personages from Japan and China. Although titled 'historical poems,' they are more historical evaluations for which Yamamoto borrowed a poetic form. Many also have added to them impressions and comments in an apparent effort to explain the poems' contents. Chinese and Japanese historical figures, well over 100 in all, are taken up, from Sugawara no Michizane, Kusunoki Masashige, Zhuge Liang, Wen Tianxiang, Fang Xiaoru, Lin Zexu, Toyotomi Hideyoshi, Tokugawa Ieyasu, Nawa Nagatoshi, Ishida Mitsunari, Katō Kiyomasa, and Yui Shōsetsu to Saigō Takamori, Ōkubo

Toshimichi, Etō Shinpei, and Soejima Taneomi. He also has pieces in it not confined to a single individual, such as 'Wakō' (Japanese Pirates), 'Toku Hōjō kyūsei shi' (Reading the History of Nine Generations of the Hōjō Family), 'Toku Fushimi sen ki' (Reading the Chronicle of the Fushimi War), 'Toku Saden' (Reading the *Zuozhuan*), 'Toku Sanyō gaishi' (Reading [Rai] Sanyō's *Unofficial History of Japan*), 'Hyō Tōbu hōchū' (Comment on the Murders Carried out by Tang and Wu), 'Toku kagaku jigen' (Reading the Elementary Learning and Simple Language), 'Hyō tōsō' (Comment on Clique Fighting), 'Hyō sei-Kan eki' (Comment on the War against Korea), and 'Hyō Yasokyō' (Comment on Christianity). He also included poems on historical texts and historical facts. As a whole they amount to short pieces of intrepid historical criticism.

If we were to derive from this work characteristics of Yamamoto's view of history, we find his sense of values most plainly apparent in his own likes and dislikes which were rather different from general views of history at the time. We can see here a kind of rebellious spirit at work. For example, in his poem about Tokugawa Ieyasu, he wrote: 'Old friendships were ephemeral to him. How could one prolong them alone? In one's lifework one had only oneself. The most injurious approach one could take was to engrave slander on a bell. After first establishing a government, he wanted to keep it in his family forever.' Similarly, another poem about Ieyasu is stinging: 'His craft and deceit were like that of an old fox. He sought help and endured suffering, but always used deception. He planned his whole life only for his own family. Old friendships and new favors were not part of his vision.'

Diametrically opposite is a poem he wrote for Ishida Mitsunari: 'He summoned the men with whom he had established ties of obligation, and their might was a force to behold. The tide of fortune was against him, and he was soon killed. From times past, historians have frequently written falsely about him, saying he was deceitfully servile and slandered loyal officials.' In his poem for Ōno Harunaga, he wrote: 'He sacrificed his own life in loyalty to his lord to repay a debt of gratitude. Who might grace his doorway now? There have been few such heroic figures ever. For whatever reason, historians have spread false tales about him.' And, by way of explanation, he added: 'Past historians have said that men of great fairness emerged in the Tokugawa era, but this is false.'

In his poem about Katō Kiyomasa, he wrote: 'To the old bandit's [Ieyasu] many schemes, he [Katō] added treachery. He willing accepted restraint with hands tied. Sadly, good and bad were based on his partiality, and vainly he obtained a large fiefdom.' To this Yamamoto added: 'Kiyomasa and Masanori were both related by marriage to Hokuchō [i.e., the Asano family, Hideyoshi's wife], and throughout their lives submitted absolutely to the control of Ieyasu. They received large fiefdoms, which gave no advantage whatsoever to their lord [the Toyotomi house]. When their lord's family perished, his fiefs were seized as well. It was as if they were unaware of this dishonor.'

Yamamoto noted in his chronological autobiography something that can be seen in these historical poems as well: 'Ever since I was young, I had always revered Toyotomi Hideyoshi. I thus set my heart on settling in Ōsaka.' However, the hatred he felt for Tokugawa Ieyasu (in Yamamoto's words, he was as crafty as an 'old fox') who had seized Hideyoshi's position and replaced him appears repeatedly, and he expressed it with particular maliciousness. Whether or not this point of view is justified, it is a clear indication of Yamamoto's basic sense of human nature.

Commentary on the *Nihon gaishi* (Unofficial History of Japan) and on the Chinese Revolution

In his poem on the *Nihon gaishi* of Rai Sanyō (1780–1832), Yamamoto offered a stinging evaluation: 'When he [i.e., Rai] described affairs, he generally wrote impressionistically, based on unfounded talk. His powerful pen in this piece was frequently deceptive, threatening the common run of men by indiscriminately showing off his talent.' After this poem, he added a long note: 'Ever since the Meiji Restoration, Sanyō's *Nihon gaishi* has become thought of as the best work of history. Shisei [Sanyō's style] used his wide knowledge and great talent, there not being a single standard history or popular account that had escaped his perusal. Still, Mr. Rai's *Nihon gaishi* is no more than a piece of fiction. It should not be regarded as a work of history.'

Thus, Yamamoto argued, it was not a work of history, but historical fiction. The reason he offered is as follows:

The Kawagoe battle took place in broad daylight. One Honma, with a lantern as his standard, fought with Daidōji and died. Shisei argued that since a work by one Hiratsuka claimed that the lantern standard was extraordinary, the battle must have been fought at night. One cannot lose sight of the facts when depicting the events of history. Shisei thus, according to his own idea of things, changed daytime to night.

Similarly, at the battle of Tennōzan, Horio Mosuke ascended first from the west, laid an ambush, and waited, and when the army of Matsuda Tarōzaemon arrived from the east, his men fired at them all at once and wiped them out. Sanyō argued that both armies came along the same route. He claimed that because the enemy's archers and riflemen were lying in wait, it was an uninteresting battle, but his version of the story twisted the facts. At the battle of Shizugatake, Lake Yoko was about 2.5 miles in circumference, and Sakuma Morimasa arrived in the evening by the northern edge of the lake. Nakagawa Kiyohide's fort was located close by, to the east of the lake. 'If he [Sakuma] followed the lake around to the south, he would come to the foothills of the mountains by dawn.' Even if they were to have gone slowly from north of the lake to the foothills, it would have taken no more than the time necessary to eat a meal. And if they set out at twilight to the south, who knows how far they might have gotten by dawn? After leveling this sort of cross-examination, Yamamoto took Sanyō to task: 'His neglect of topography was like this as well.'

Finally, the *Nihon gaishi* in its opening volume lamented the fact that the court's authority had fallen into the hands of the warrior class, and in his chronicles of the Tokugawa house, he forcefully extolled the shogunal government. This was a clear contradiction in the points being made: 'Which of these is his judgment?' Yamamoto concluded: 'People today all sing the praises of the *Nihon gaishi*. Ever since the Meiji Restoration, people have used this work to understand government. How strange!'

As noted earlier, Yamamoto was sympathetic to and worked on behalf of the late-Qing reform group of Kang Youwei and Liang Qichao. Inasmuch as Kang and Liang were struggling to protect the Qing emperor and institute reforms, they were no revolutionaries but just reformers. Irrespective of whether it was linked to this, Yamamoto was in agreement with those Chinese who wanted to overthrow the Manchu dynasty, and still he was opposed to republicanism after the revolution in favor of a monarchical form of government. Among his historical poems is one entitled 'Hyō Shinkoku kakumei' (Comment on the Chinese Revolution), and in it we find the following: 'Heaven will help the Chinese people and overturn the Manchu Qing. A military encounter is brewing for some future day. Sadly they are recklessly intoxicated with republicanism, but they need a wise sovereign to secure the four borders.' To this he added the following note:

> That the Manchus run the government is the shame of the Chinese. This certainly makes sense. It would be best to select and install a wise ruler, for failing that, the present fighting will continue unabated. The present situation resembles the regional dominance of commanderies in the Tang dynasty. Nothing restrained them. This is much like the vain intoxication with republicanism: The sovereign lacks the virtue and influence to pacify them.

Although it appears as though this was a work of 1921, from our present perspective Yamamoto, nurtured by the old culture and with his 'fervent belief in the way of Confucius,' demonstrated certain temporal limitations about which there is nothing we can do.

Rongo shiken (My Views on the Analects)

Yamamoto noted that in his early years he enjoyed the histories more than the classics, but in his later years he devoted his heart and soul to his *Rongo shiken* (unpublished). According to an entry for October 1911 in his chronological autobiography, Yamamoto 'began a second draft of *Rongo shiken*' at that time, and the following year he noted: 'I worked on a second draft of *Rongo shiken* from the spring on, and even the blistering hot days did not halt my brush.' Under 1913, he wrote: 'I completed a third draft of *Rongo shikō* [probably a misprint from *Rongo shiken*] this year.' For November 1914, he wrote: 'I began a fourth draft of *Rongo shiken* in the fall and I reorganized its structure.' For 1915, 'I completed a fifth draft of *Rongo shiken* on December 28'; for 1922, 'I completed a seventh draft of *Rongo shiken* in the spring'; and for January 1923, 'I have been at work editing and punctuating *Rongo shiken*, completed on the 26th.' In a postface to his *Baiseisho eishi* of December 1923, we find: 'I have not returned to my study to work on *Rongo shiken*.' At that time serious stomach trouble prevented him from writing. These references indicate that after retiring to Ushimado, Yamamoto devoted a number of his last years to writing *Rongo shiken*, although he passed away before seeing it completed.

Although Yamamoto claimed to have enjoyed the histories more than the classics when he was young, it would seem that he came to devote himself to the task of writing an explanation of the *Analects* of Confucius because it was with this work that he ran his academy and instructed his students. In an entry for 1889, the year after his prison sentence was completed and he was released and returned home, his chronological autobiography noted: 'I published some of my writing, and I noted the dates on them counting from the birth of the Sage [Confucius].' Also, for 1905, the year he moved to Ushimado: 'Ever since I first gathered the academy students together in 1889 and carried out the ceremony of prayer to Confucius, I have always done so every year on the *shangding* day in spring and autumn. I still do it here in Ushimado.' These references indicate that since he opened his academy and began teaching students, particularly as the years passed following his release from prison, Yamamoto seemed to be becoming a Confucianist.

Poetry as the Avocation of the Confucian Scholar

The *Baiseisho eishi* has 'Introductory Remarks' by Watanabe Tokujirō, one of Yamamoto's disciples, in which he offers an explanation of the dictinctive character of Yamamoto's historical poetry. He argues that it is better to see them as the expression of a particular historical perspective than as poems stressing such and such a meter or rhyme scheme. This may have been a general point of view shared by these men at the time. Yamamoto himself seems to have considered his poetry the work of a young hand, worthy of no praise at all. In an entry for 1895 in his chronological autobiography, he wrote as well:

> I was unskillful in poetry and thus did not ordinarily write many [poems]. . . . After being released from prison in 1888, I frequently went with my late father on journeys to the outskirts of the city or to a poetry club. Although I worked hard at composing poetry, few of them are worth reading. By the time my father passed away, I was still poor in the composition of poetry. For this reason I have written scarcely any poems over the past year.

Watanabe Tokujirō had the following to say in his 'Introductory Remarks':

> The master was born into a hereditary Confucian household in Sagawa domain of Tosa, continuing his grandfather's work. Although he lived by

the classics and prose writing, early on he dedicated himself to a patriotic concern for the public welfare, and he traveled about the land to make contact with many men of will. The master was very much one of those men who used Confucianism to vehemently argue the issues of the day. His prose was thus particularly strong in historical analyses. Furthermore, the spiritual acuity of his insight and the preeminence of his argumentative skills gave rise to the idea that he surpassed his predecessors. Nevertheless, he himself called his poetry, which dared not even adhere to the rules of meter and style, the avocation of a Confucian scholar. Thus, while seen from the perspective of his poetry alone, there is much that might be suggested, one must never assess the master's poetry in comparison to that of poets. This collection should be read more with his historical analyses in mind. I for one cannot agree with aimlessly discussing it on the basis of the rules of meter and style.

His Self-Composed Epitaph and Inscription

On the back side of the page with Yamamoto's photo at the beginning of the *Baiseisho eishi*, he included an epitaph and inscription that he wrote for himself. Carving his own epitaph, it was an autobiography which he wanted to leave for posterity. It is simple, and I would like to conclude this piece by introducing it in full.

The master's posthumous name was Ken, his *azana* was Eihitsu, his childhood name was Hantarō, and his style was Baigai. He was from Tosa domain. His late father's posthumous name was Ren, and his mother's maiden name was Myōjin. As a young man he devoted himself to concerns of the nation, and he was incarcerated for several years before being pardoned. He opened an academy in Ōsaka and in his later years moved to Ushimado. He was born on the twelfth day of the second month of Kaei 5 [1852]. He died on XXXXXXXX. His funeral was held at XXXXXX. The master believed fervently in the way of Confucius, and his worry on behalf of conditions of the day never flagged until his death. He despised Christianity. He behaved with honesty and integrity, and he did not go along with the mainstream. Inscription signed:

How insignificant this miniscule body
Buried beneath stone.
One thousand years from now,
Nay, will anyone appreciate me?

Inscription composed and executed by Yamamoto Ken himself.

For the former set of eight blank spaces (XXXXXXXX), it should read: September 6, 1928. For the latter six blank spaces: 'Ushimado, Okayama prefecture.'

Three phrases in the text belie a certain conceit and self-praise on Yamamoto's part: 'As a young man he devoted himself to concerns of the nation'; 'his worry on behalf of conditions of the day never flagged until his death'; and 'He acted with honestly and integrity, and he did not go along with the mainstream.' Still, when the lines, 'One thousand years from now,/ Nay, will anyone appreciate me?' reveal a tinge of loneliness contrary to his vanity. They strike one as the voice of an old political activist who has been disappointed.

Postface. There is a text entitled *Tsuitōji* (Memorial Address) by Kokubo Kishichi which is owned by one of Yamamoto's descendents. In it one finds the following lines: 'When the late Count Itagaki founded the Jiyūtō in 1881, Yamamoto joined together with other fellow locals. He was on particularly friendly terms with two of them, Kataoka Kenkichi and Nakae Chōmin.' This would lead us to believe that Yamamoto joined the Jiyūtō from the very beginning.

Notes

Note: All numerical notes are those of the author; alphabetical ones are those of the translator.

INTRODUCTION

a. Helpful in the preparation of this brief introduction to the life and work of Masuda Wataru were the following two articles: Matsueda Shigeo, 'Masuda Wataru san no omoide arekore' (Various memories of Mr. Masuda Wataru), *Bungaku* 45 (May 1977), 548–52; and Katayama Tomoyuki, 'Hensha atogaki' (Editor's postface), in *Seigaku tōzen to Chūgoku jijō, 'zassho' sakki* (The Eastern Movement of Western Learning and Conditions in China: Notes on 'Various Books') (Tokyo: Iwanami shoten, 1979), pp. 351–61.

b. (Tokyo: Sairensha, 1935). Published after the war as *Chūgoku shōsetsu shi* (Tokyo: Iwanami shoten, 1962).

c. (Tokyo: Iwanami shoten, 1935). A fuller edition was published after the war in thirteen volumes: (Tokyo: Iwanami shoten, 1956, reprinted 1964).

d. Initially published in *Chūgoku koten bungaku zenshū* (Complete Works of Classical Chinese Literature) (Tokyo: Heibonsha, 1959), volume 22; published separately by Heibonsha in 1963; and reprinted in *Chūgoku koten bungaku taikei* (Series on Classical Chinese Literature) (Tokyo: Heibonsha, 1979), volumes 40–41.

e. (Tokyo: Kōdansha, 1948, reprinted 1956); Chinese translation, *Lu Xun de yinxiang*, by Zhong Jingwen (Changsha: Hunan renmin chubanshe, 1980). Other works by Masuda concerning Lu Xun include: *Ro Jin no kotoba* (Lu Xun's Words) (Tokyo: Sōgensha, 1955); and *Ro Jin annai* (A Guide to Lu Xun) (Tokyo: Iwanami shoten, 1956). He also wrote *Chūgoku bungaku shi kenkyū, bungaku kakumei to zen'ya no hitobito* (Studies in the History of Chinese Literature: The Literary Revolution and People on Its Eve) (Tokyo: Iwanami shoten, 1967).

CHAPTER ONE

a. (Tokyo: Iwanami shoten, 1966).

b. In *Meiji ishin shi kenkyū* (Studies on the History of the Meiji Restoration), ed. Shigakkai (Tokyo: Fuzanbō, 1929, 1930), pp. 432–58.

c. The Kaiseijo, earlier known as Kaisei gakkō, was the shogunate's school for teachers of Western learning and Western-style mathematics. In 1863, its name was changed to

229

Bansho shirabesho; in 1868, the Meiji government restored its original name as Kaisei gakkō; it was renamed the next year Daigaku nankō; and, after several more name-changes, it became Tokyo University in 1877. The edition of the *Wanguo gongfa* cited here is held in the collections of Harvard-Yenching Library and the library of the University of California, Berkeley.

1. The person who entered the Japanese reading punctuation in the text is not made explicit, but it was Nishi Amane (1828–97) according to Ōtsuki Nyoden, *Nihon Yōgaku hennen shi* (Chronological History of Western Learning in Japan), with additional annotations by Satō Eishichi (Tokyo: Kinseisha, 1965).

d. Also held in the collection of the Hoover Institution, Stanford University.

e. The text of the Shigeno translation with extraordinarily helpful annotations can be found in *Honyaku no shisō* (Ideas of Translation), volume 15 in the series, *Nihon kindai shisō taikei* (Compendium on Modern Japanese Thought), ed. Katō Shūichi and Maruyama Masao (Tokyo: Iwanami shoten, 1991), pp. 43–90. There is an appended essay by Zhang Jianing on the textual history of the *Wanguo gongfa* as well (pp. 381–405). One other volume in this line, held in the collections of Harvard-Yenching Library and the Starr Library (Columbia University), is Theodore Dwight Woolsey (Wuerxi, 1801–89, translated by W. A. P. Martin), *Gongfa bianlan* (Guide to International Law) (Beijing: Tongwenguan, 1877).

f. In his *Kinsei Nihon no kokusai kannen no hattatsu* (The Development of Modern Japan's International Conception) (Tokyo: Kyōritsusha, 1932), pp. 26–50.

g. Respectively in his *Ishin shi sōsetsu* (Essays on Restoration History) (Tokyo: Gakuji shoin, 1935), pp. 25–58; and *Meiji ishin* (The Meiji Restoration) (Tokyo: Hakuyōsha, 1943), vol. 1, pp. 107–46.

2. In his 'Kaigai chishiki' (Knowledge from Overseas), in *Kinsei sōdan* (Modern Stories) (Tokyo: Hokkai shuppansha, 1944 [pp. 174–230]), Watanabe Shūjirō writes: 'In a letter dated fourth month, 1868, Saigō Takamori [1827–77], considered the man who had contributed the greatest military exploits to the political cause of the Restoration, included the words: "I responded to the English minister that Tokugawa Yoshinobu would be treated according to international law (*bankoku kōhō*) and would not be subject to attack." Can we see here how the understanding of international law at that time offers a glimpse into the political situation?'

h. An 1880 edition (Beijing: Tongwenguan) of this translation can be found in the Harvard-Yenching Library and the Starr Library, Columbia University.

3. In *Meiji bunken mokuroku* (Bibliography of Meiji Documents), ed. Takaichi Yoshio (Tokyo: Nihon hyōronsha, 1932), the reading 'Gatchin' is written in Japanese syllabaries beside the Chinese characters for Hobson's name. This is incorrect.

i. A copy can be found in the collection of Harvard-Yenching Library, published by the Hui'ai yiguan.

j. No copies of *Xiyi lüelun*, *Fuying xinshuo*, and *Neike xinshuo* are apparently to be found in library collections in the United States, according to the printed catalogues available. I recently found the first and third of these, dated Ansei 5 (1858) and Ansei 6 (1859), respectively, as well as an 1857 edition of *Quanti xinlun* for sale in a printed catalogue of the Tokyo bookstore, Tōjō shoten.

k. (Tokyo: Kokusho kankōkai, 1914), three volumes.

4. At the time, Japanese intellectuals were able to read Kanbun (classical Chinese). Precisely because the population of Kanbun-readers was so overwhelmingly large, these medical texts could be diffused in Japan and made use of.

5. I would like to add the following note. Western medical science, it is usually argued, was introduced to China by foreign missionaries at the end of the Ming dynasty. Jean Terrenz (Deng Yuhan, 1576–1630) – Swiss missionary to China, friend of Galileo, and a man knowledgeable in medicine – worked, together with Matteo Ricci, to

implement calendrical reforms. He also prepared – working with Li Zhizao (1565–1629) in Hangzhou in the waning years of the Chongzhen reign (1628–44) at the end of the Ming – an abridged translation of the work of Andreas Vesalius (1514–64), a Belgian considered the father of modern anatomy, under the title *Renshen gaishuo* (Outlines of the Human Body) in two *juan*. It seems that this text on human anatomy was not at all widely disseminated in China, nor was it conveyed to Japan. Had it been introduced to Japan, it probably would have helped Sugita Genpaku in his painstaking work of translating *Kaitai shinsho* (New Work on Dissection, 1774) in his *Rangaku kotohajime* (The Beginnings to Dutch Learning).

CHAPTER TWO

a. A copy may also be found in the collections of the Hoover Institution, Stanford University, and the Starr Library, Columbia University.

b. The Masuda Bunko, held at Kansai University in Suita, holds another edition of this work: Kikusui Kyozō, 1868, in two stringbound volumes. See *Kansai daigaku shozō Masuda Wataru Bunko mokuroku* (Listings of the Books in the Masuda Wataru Archive Held at Kansai University) (Kyoto: Dōbōsha, 1983), p. 62.

c. In *Bakumatsu Meiji Yasokyō shi kenkyū* (Studies in the History of Christianity in the *Bakumatsu* and Meiji periods) (Tokyo: Ajia shobō, 1944); (Tokyo reprint: Nihon Kirisutokyōdan shuppankyoku, 1973), pp. 177–204. In this later edition, 'Shina' has been changed to 'Chūgoku' throughout.

d. A copy may also be found in the collections of Harvard-Yenching Library and the Starr Library, Columbia University.

e. A copy may also be found in the collections of Harvard-Yenching Library and the Starr Library, Columbia University.

1. Theories concerning 'dynamics' (Ch. *lixue*, J. *rikigaku*) can already be seen in the 1854 (Kaei 7) work, *Rigaku teiyō* (Summary of the Physical Sciences), compiled and edited on the basis of Dutch books by the physician and Dutch Learning scholar Hirose Motoyasu. My copy of this work has a first part with four stringbound volumes and a second part with one [Kyoto: Tennōjiya Ichirōhee].

f. Copies of the original can be found in the Starr Library, Columbia University and Harvard-Yenching Library. There are also two reprints held in the collection of the latter: Changsha: Shangwu paiyinben, 1939; and Taibei: Xuesheng shuju, 1965, six volumes.

2. The word used for 'geometry' is pronounced *jihe* in Chinese, much like the first part of the term in Latin, *Geometria*, and some have considered it a loan into Chinese; there was also a certain sense of free translation introduced in the characters chosen to convey the sound, for they ordinarily mean 'some' (as in some money or some time). On this subject, Watanabe Shūjirō writes in his *Kinsei sōsetsu*: 'An *English-Japanese Dictionary* published as early as 1862 translated geometry as *sokuryōgaku*. Nonetheless, from the Meiji period forward the term *kikagaku* (Ch. *jihexue*) became the conventional term for geometry. The fact that some people criticized as inappropriate the use of the Chinese characters now read *kikagaku* (but potentially misread, reflecting the ordinary meaning of the term) and not using the term for geodesy reflects a desire to translate the actual meaning of "geometry" into Japanese.'

I also have a text by Wylie entitled *Shuxue qimeng* (Rudiments of Mathematics) ([in two *juan*] with a postface dated 1853 by his disciple Jin Chengfu). The place of publication is not indicated, as only the year is given on the cover. Since my copy carries the designation '*kanban*' (official publication), we know it to be a Japanese reprint. It contains such technical terms as reducing fractions to common denominators (*tsūbun*), reducing fractions to lowest terms (*yakubun*), repeating decimals (*junkan shōsū*), extraction of square roots (*kaihei*), and logarithms (*taisū*), and it has a table of logarithms as an appendix. A one-volume Japanese reprint is listed as well in the *Naikaku Bunko Kanseki bunrui mokuroku* (Catalogue of Chinese Books in the Naikaku Bunko [Tokyo: Naikaku Bunko, 1956]). In this same catalogue, a Japanese reprint of a book entitled *Daishuxue* (Elements of Algebra, by Augustus de Morgan) (J. *Daisūgaku*) is listed as well, 'orally translated by Wylie, transcribed by Li Shanlan,' dated 'Meiji 5 [1872], proofread by Tsukamoto Ki.'

g. (Tokyo: published by Kariganeya Seikichi, printed by Kikuma gakkō meishinkan).

h. There is also a Meiji 36 (1903) edition of this work in the Masuda Bunko.

3. He later served as one of three assistants to the Bible Translation Committee (comprised of three foreign missionaries) founded in 1874, and he was of particular help to James Curtis Hepburn (1815–1911). We can now see that he used as a reference the Chinese translation of the Bible and that he adopted unchanged from that translation the Gospels, the Acts of the Apostles, Revelations, and the like. I have made a preliminary comparison of the Chinese and Japanese translations of the Bible and found an enormous amount simply carried over from the former into the latter. The translation of the Bible began in Japan in 1874 and was completed in 1880. See Yamamoto Hidetaru, *Nihon Kurisuto kyōkai shi* (History of the Christian Church in Japan) (Tokyo: Kirisuto kyōkai jimusho, 1929). The great efforts to which Okuno went in punctuating and translating this and other Chinese texts are manifest. I also own a three-volume *Kunten Kyūyaku seisho* (Old Testament with Reading Punctuation) (1883) and *Kunten Shin'yaku seisho* (New Testament with Reading Punctuation) (1884) – both published in Yokohama by the 'American Bible Company' – which are the Chinese translation of the Bible with reading punctuation and Japanese syllabaries added to indicate inflection in Japanese. These seem to have circulated rather widely, for some appeared with different bindings from the same publishers. I also have another work translated by Okuno, *Jidu shilu* (The True Story of Christ, J. *Kirisuto jitsugaku*), 'written by Alexander Williamson, transcribed by Dong Shutang of the Qing' (published by Iijima Seiken, 1882 [in Tokyo]).

CHAPTER THREE

a. No such work appears in the Masuda Bunko. Masuda apparently meant the *Chikan keimō jukka shobu* (Elementary School Lessons of the Circle of Knowledge), and incorrectly wrote as the title what this work actually is, a Japanese reprint of the Chinese text.

b. (Hong Kong: Ying-Hua shuyuan [London Missionary Society Press], 1856). A copy of the 1864 second edition is held in the collection of California State Library, Sacramento.

c. (Kamakura: Mikuni sha, 1940); (Tokyo: Nagasaki shoten, 1941); (Tokyo reprint: Heibonsha, 1963).

d. (Tokyo: Takayama shoin, 1940).

e. (Tokyo reprint of 1882 original: Gengendō, 1940). Also in volume 17 of *Meiji bunka zenshū* (Collected Writings of Meiji Culture), ed. Yoshino Sakuzō (Tokyo: Nihon hyōron sha, 1927–30).

f. The expression *honjo* is here translated as 'main office,' although Honjo might as well refer to a district in Edo. Thanks to Professor Zhou Qiqian for pointing out this possibility to me.

1. These can be found in Yamaguchi Muneyuki, *Zenshū mishū Hashimoto Sanai kankei shiryō kenkyū* (Studies of Historical Materials Concerning Hashimoto Sanai Not Found in His Collected Works) (Kurume, 1940, not for sale).

2. Narushima Ryūhoku has also written: 'Yanagawa sensei ryakujō' (Brief biography of Professor Yanagawa) and 'Yanagawa sensei itsuji' (Unknown facts about Professor

Yanagawa), both included in *Ryūhoku ikō* (Ryūhoku's Posthumous Manuscripts) (Tokyo: Hakubunkan, 1892–93) in two volumes. Narushima notes that he enjoyed a 'particularly close friendship with' Yanagawa, and he lauds the latter's genius to the stars.

3. Ōtsuki Fumihiko, *Fukken zassan* (Miscellaneous Collection of Fukken) (Tokyo: Kōbundō shoten, 1902).

g. In his *Bakumatsu Meiji Yasokyō shi kenkyū*, pp. 123–39.

CHAPTER FOUR

1. I have seen only a copy of this work, not the original.

2. Morrison was the author of a history of the countries of the world, entitled *Gujin wanguo gangjian lu* (Narrative Record of the Countries of the World, Past and Present), which was reprinted in Japan in the Meiji period [with reading punctuation by Ōtsuki Masayuki in three stringbound volumes, Tokyo: Higashinari Kamejirō, 1874]). As for Lin Zexu, many are the sections in Wei Yuan's *Haiguo tuzhi* which bear the mark of Lin's 'explanation.' More will follow on this theme.

a. The bibliographic information that follows comes from examination of these works in the Masuda Bunko at Kansai University: *Shuxue qimeng*, two *juan*, by Alexander Wylie (postface dated Xianfeng 3 [1853]) and an Edo reprint of the same text; *Yinghuan zhi lüe*, ten *juan*, by Xu Jiyu (Zongli yamen, Tongzhi 5 [1866]) and a Japanese reprint of the same edition with reading punction added by Inoue Shun'yō and Moriogi Sonosa no kami Ryūho (published by Miyajima Yaisaemon et al., printed by Taibikaku, Bunkyū 1 [1861]); *Diqiu shuolüe*, by Richard Quarterman Way (1819–95) (Ningbo: Huahua shengjing shufang, Xiangfeng 6 [1856]) and a Japanese edition with reading punction by Mitsukuri Genpo (Edo: Yorozuya Hyōshirō, Man'en 1 [1861], printed by Rōsōkan); there is a Japanese edition of the *Wanguo gangjian lu*, entitled *Bankoku kōkan roku wage*, four stringbound volumes, translated by Ōtsuki Kiyoyuki and Watanabe Yakurō (Tokyo: Toriya Gisaburō, 1874, printed by Kafuseisha); *Da Yingguo shi*, eight *juan*, translated by William Muirhead (Shanghai: Mohai shuyuan, Xianfeng 6 [1856]);

b. Copies of this text can be found in the collections of the Starr Library, Columbia University, and the Harvard-Yenching Library.

3. See *Kondō Seisai zenshū* (Collected Works of Kondō Seisai) (Tokyo: Kokusho kankōkai, 1906), vol. 3.

4. See Ayusawa Shintarō and Ōkubo Toshiaki, *Sakoku jidai Nihonjin no kaigai chishiki* (Tokyo: Kangensha, 1953).

c. A copy of the original can be found at the Harvard-Yenching Library.

d. (Tokyo: Min'yūsha, 1900).

5. Fukuchi also notes that Iwase had a bit of training in Dutch Learning. Kurimoto Joun (1822–97), administrator in the foreign office who was resident in France in the *bakumatsu* period and who rushed home when news of the Meiji Restoration reached him (and later became head of *Hōchi shinbun*), has noted that Iwase worked hard to turn general Dutch Learning toward more knowledge of English studies. In his letters to Hashimoto Sanai, Iwase addressed them in English and horizontally to: 'Sanai (sama) Higo' (see *Hashimoto Keigaku zenshū*, vol. 6, letters).

e. In *Hashimoto Keigaku zenshū* (Collected Works of Hashimoto Keigaku) (Tokyo: Unebi shobō, 1943).

6. Iwase and Hashimoto were agreed (as was Shungaku for that matter) in their desire to see Hitotsubashi Yoshinobu succeed to the position of shōgun.

f. Published posthumously in two volumes by the Yao shoten (in Tokyo) in 1896, with a preface by Katsu Kaishū (1823–99).

g. (Shanghai: Commercial Press, 1927); (Hong Kong reprint: Taiping shuju, 1964).

7. In Yoshida Shōin, 'Shotoku zasshū' (Collected Letters), section two of *Shōin sensei icho* (Posthumous Works of [Yoshida] Shōin), ed. Yoshida Kurazō (Tokyo: Min'yūsha, 1909), volume 2.

8. In Yoshida Shōin, 'Yūshitsu bunkō' (Manuscripts in a Darkened Room), in *Shōin sensei icho* (Tokyo: Min'yūsha, 1908), volume 1.

9. On Iwase Higo no kami, Kurimoto Joun has written 'Iwase Higo no kami to jireki' (Account of Iwase, Lord of Higo), in *Hōan jūshu* (Ten Pieces from the Gourd Hut) (Tokyo: Hōchisha, 1892). Kurimoto and Iwase studied together at the Shōheikō, the official *bakufu* college. This essay describes Iwase's personality and career in a little more detail. For even greater detail on Iwase, see Ōta Kumatarō, 'Iwase Tadanori,' in a special issue (autumn 1926) of *Chūō shidan* (published by the Kokushi kōshūkai) on the subject of 'individuals in the late Tokugawa and Meiji eras.'

h. In *Tōkō sensei ibun* (The Literary Remains of Takasugi Shinsaku) (Tokyo: Min'yūsha, 1916).

i. Not for sale (printed by Nakamuda Takenobu in 1919).

10. Included in *Bunkyū ninen Shanhai nikki* (Diaries of Shanghai in 1862) (Tokyo: Zenkoku shobō, 1946).

CHAPTER FIVE

1. With Russians already beginning to appear from time to time in Hokkaidō to the north, in Kansei 9 (1797), Ōhara Sakingo (Donkyō, d. 1810) wrote *Hokuchi kigen* (Alarming Words about the Northern Lands) in 1797. The edition of this work in my possession, dated 1888, was published as a supplement to the *Tōkyō nichinichi shinbun*, with an introduction by Fukuchi Gen'ichirō (1841–1906). Furthermore, in the tense atmosphere with Russian and British ships off Japanese and Chinese coastal waters, Koga Dōan (1788–1847) in 1838 (Tenpō 9) wrote *Kaibō okusoku* (Speculations about Coastal Defenses). My woodblock-printed edition of this work, dated 1880, carries prefaces by Yamagata Aritomo (1838–1922) and others [Tokyo: Hidaka Seijitsu, one stringbound volume]. Both works attracted considerable attention.

   During the Kaei reign period (1848–54), as British and American ships arrived at Japanese shores and imperial instructions on strictly enforcing coastal defenses were isssued several times, Shionoya Tōin wrote the *Chūkai shigi* (Personal Views on the 'Chouhai' Chapter [Wei Yuan's first chapter in the *Haiguo tuzhi*]); my edition of this work [dated 1851] carries the tag 'Tōin's unpublished manuscripts' and is a copy of that owned by Tamura Hisatsune, daimyo of Kashiwahara. In 1853, with the arrival of Perry's ships at Uraga and Putiatin's at Nagasaki, the *Kaibōbi ron* (On Coastal Defense Preparedness) by Fujimori Tenzan (Kōan, 1799–1862) appeared; my edition of this work is a copy with a postface dated Kaei 6 or 1853. These works too created a major sensation. When Townsend Harris arrived to demand a commercial treaty with Japan, views on coastal defenses were already an established phenomenon.

   Translator's note. Ōhara's work is also to be found in *Chihoku gūdan* (Stories about the North), ed. Ōtomo Kisaku (Tokyo: Hokkō shobō, 1944).

a. (Suita: Kansai daigaku Tōzai gakujutsu kenkyūjo, 1967).

b. (Shanghai: Taidong tushuju, 1925), two volumes.

2. (Beijing: Renmin chubanshe, 1958), pp. 633–40. This work comprises volume 5 of his *Zhongguo sixiang tongshi* (Comprehensive History of Chinese Thought). [It appeared separately in 1956 with the subtitle: *Shiqi shiji zhi shijiu shiji sishi niandai* (From the Seventeenth Century Until the 1840s)].

3. In *Zhongguo jindai sixiang shilun wenji* (Historical Essays in Modern Chinese Thought) (Shanghai: Renmin chubanshe, 1958), pp. 11–25.

c. It is hard, so far removed in time and space and with Masuda no longer alive, to know if he really found these absurd arguments the least bit convincing or interesting. Like the opening quotation to this book from Mao's *On the People's Democratic Dictatorship*, such use of contemporary Chinese references were probably being used largely to add some sort of authority to the topic under discussion. In other words, Wei Yuan's thought certainly is important in and of itself and influential in nineteenth-century Japan, precisely as Masuda has shown and will show further. To drop citations about the 'progressiveness' (in Marxist-Leninist terms) of his thought not only has no place in this discussion; it is virtually meaningless, unless the author is merely trying to demonstrate that contemporary Chinese scholars (and hence the Chinese government) accept Wei Yuan as 'important.' This phenomenon is not unique to Japanese scholars.

d. (Beijing: Sanlian shudian, 1957).

4. Also, the *Yapian zhanzheng shiqi sixiang shi ziliao xuanji* (Selected Materials on the Intellectual History of the Period of the Opium War), ed. Editorial Selection Group on Modern History of the Modern History Institute of the Chinese Academy of Sciences (Beijing: Zhonghua shuju, 1963) first transcribes Wei Yuan's introduction to the *Huangchao jingshi wenbian* (pp. 1–2) and then proceeds to his introductions to the *Shengwu ji* (pp. 73–74) and the *Haiguo tuzhi* (pp. 74–75), followed by the first four sections of 'Chouhai pian' from the main text of the *Haiguo tuzhi* (pp. 75–86).

e. (Beijing: Zhonghua shuju, 1959).

f. In *Yinbingshi wenji* (Collected Essays from an Ice-Drinker's Studio) (Taibei: Taiwan Zhonghua shuju, 1960), vol. 3 (originally published in 1902).

5. I have searched through the three volumes of the *Dai Saigō zenshū* (Collected Works of the Great Saigō Takamori) (Tokyo: Heibonsha, 1926–27), but I have been unable to find any reference to the relationship between Saigō and the *Haiguo tuzhi*. Perhaps, Liang Qichao was mistaken.

g. Japanese woodblock edition (preface dated 1871 by Katsu Kaishū), 1 volume. The *Seiken roku* was written originally in Kanbun. Masuda's edition is in one stringbound volume, printed in Tokyo by Morita Tetsugorō. This translation follows Masuda's modern Japanese rendition with help from Charles Terry's somewhat outdated English version, as it appears excerpted in *Sources of Japanese Tradition*, ed. Ryusaku Tsunoda, Wm. Theodore de Bary, and Donald Keene (New York: Columbia University Press, 1964), vol. 2, pp. 105–07. I take responsibility for all errors.

6. I have a one-volume copy of this work in which Shōzan discusses policies for coastal defense. It is included in Fujita Mokichi, *Bunmei tōzen shi* (A History of the Eastward Movement of Civilization) (Tokyo: Hōchisha, 1886).

h. Edited by Yoshida Kurazō (Tokyo: Min'yūsha, 1908–09), two volumes.

CHAPTER SIX

1. Yoshimoto Noboru, *Kaishū sensei: Hikawa seiwa* (Katsu Kaishū: Pure Conversations from the Icy Stream) (Tokyo: Kyōkan bunbō, 1902); revised edition (Tokyo: Kōno Seikōkan, 1909).

a. *Saiyū nikki*, in *Yoshida Shōin zenshū* (hereafter, *YSZ*), ed. Yamaguchi ken kyōikukai (Tokyo: Daiwa shobō, 1976), volume 9, pp. 23–107.

2. Furthermore, according to the *Tōin sensei nenpu* (Chronological Biography of Shionoya Tōin), edited by Tōin's grandson, Shionoya Tokitoshi (Seizan) (n.p.: Shionoya On, 1923), *Ahen ibun* (in seven volumes) was compiled by Tōin in Kōka 4 (1847) when he was 39 years of age [East Asian style]; 'prior to that time the Opium War had occurred in China, and with the growing sense of crisis felt [in Japan], *sensei* said that we had to make preparations. Thus, he compiled the *Ahen ibun* in seven

volumes. Such domains of Chōshū, Satsuma, Saijō, and Sakura dispatched men to copy this text which hence served as a warning.' From this we learn that various domains vied to chronicle the Opium War in China as an 'exhortative lesson' (*imashime no kagami*) which might bear upon the destiny of Japan itself.

b. The original in nine stringbound volumes by Hara Nensai (1774–1820) is in Kanbun: (Ōsaka: Kawachiya Shigebee, et al., 1816; Gungyoku shodō, eight *kan*), held in the collection of the Harvard-Yenching Library. Other editions in the Masuda Bunko include: (Tokyo: Shōeidō shoten, 1899) and (Yūhōdō shoten, 1920). It was translated into Japanese and edited by Oyanagi Shigeta (1870–1940) (Tokyo: Shun'yōdō shoten, 1936).

c. The two works by Takano Chōei can be found in the collection of the Harvard-Yenching Library. *Yume monogatari* has been reprinted in *Watanabe Kazan, Takano Chōei, Kudō Heisuke, Honda Toshiaki*, ed. Satō Shōsuke (Tokyo: Chūō kōron sha, 1972). *In'yūroku* can be found in the Naikaku Bunko. Chen's work has been printed in many editions, such as: (Taibei: Taiwan yinhang, 1958).

d. Yamaga was a lineal descendent of the great philosopher Yamaga Sokō (1622–85). See *YSZ*, 7:27, n. 1. Masuda mistranscribes the date here, as it should be eighth month, 23rd day, the same date as the letter itself; see *YSZ*, 7:80–81.

e. In *Noyama goku bunkō* (Manuscripts from Noyama Prison), in *YSZ*, 2:333–35. The original Kanbun texts of the *Noyama goku bunkō* have been annotated by Andō Kiichi, *Kunchū Yoshida Shōin sensei Noyama bunkō* (The Noyama Prison Manuscripts of Yoshida Shōin with Annotations) (Yamaguchi: Yamaguchi-ken kyōikukai, 1932).

3. From this point on, Shōin is refering to 'Yi zhan' (On war), the third part of 'Chouhai pian' in *juan* 1 of the *Haiguo tuzhi*.

f. In *Noyama goku bunkō*, in *YSZ*, 2:322–23.

g. In *YSZ*, 2:93–131. The Chinese author was Luo Sen.

4. See my '*Man-Shin kiji* to sono hissha, waga kuni ni tsutaerareta "Taihei tengoku" ni tsuite' (The *Man-Shin kiji* and its author, how the 'Taiping Heavenly Kingdom' was transmitted to Japan), in *Torii Hisayasu kyōju kakō kinen ronshū* (Essays in Honor of Professor Torii Hisayasu on the Occasion of His 61st Birthday) (Tenri: Torii Hisayasu kyōju kakō kinen, 1972).

5. The 100–*juan* edition which I own is a reprint edition of the Guangxu 1 (1875) text; it carries a postface by Zuo Zongtang (1812–85) and was published by Shanghai shuju in 1895. In the 60–*juan* edition [Taibei reprint of the 1847 edition: Chengwen chubanshe, 1966] from *juan* 53 on and in the 100–*juan* edition from *juan* 84 on, both texts are concerned with issues of manufacturing cannons, ships, explosives, and telescopes; also, it covers the earth and astronomy, and in various sections there is material on coastal defenses and military preparedness.

h. The *Xiaofang huzhai yudi congchao* is a work in 84 stringbound volumes (*ce*), comp. Wang Xiqi (1855–1913), originally published in Shanghai (Zhuyitang, 1877–97). Lin Zexu's *Sizhou zhi* appears in the 82nd *ce*. It has been reprinted several times: (Taibei: Guangwen shuju, 1964; Taibei: Taiwan xuesheng shuju, 1975).

CHAPTER SEVEN

1. In the prewar period, 'Sibei buyao' was a series of reprints of fine works published by Zhonghua shuju.

2. Also it might be argued that, because those responsible for the Opium War, with the cruel consequences it brought, were still alive and held power as high officials of the court, there was reason to fear it.

a. See Chapter Ten below for more on this work.

b. Kimura Kaishū's work (Tokyo: Kōjunsha, 1892) has been reprinted: edited by Nihon shiseki kyōkai (Tokyo: Tokyo University Press, 1978), 2 volumes; Katsu Kaishū's work (Tokyo: Kunaishō, 1891) has been reprinted: (Tokyo: Hara shobō, 1968), 2 volumes; Naitō Chisō's work (Tokyo: Tōgaidō, 1888 or 1889); Ōkuma Shigenobu's work (Tokyo: Waseda University Press, 1913) has been reprinted: (Tokyo: Jitsugyō no Nihonsha, 1913); and Yoshino Maho's work (Tokyo: self-published, 1883), seventeen *kan*, has been reprinted: (Tokyo: Gannandō shoten, 1968).

c. (Tokyo: Min'yūsha, 1892); reprinted several times, such as: (Tokyo: Min'yūsha, 1926); (Tokyo: Heibonsha, 1967); (Tokyo: Tokyo University Press, 1978).

3. In the 'Zhongguo jindai shi ziliao congkan' (Publication Series of Materials on Modern Chinese History) series, there are six volumes of documents entitled *Yapian zhanzheng* (The Opium War) (Shanghai: Shenzhou guoguangshe, 1954); the sixth volume includes 'Yapian zhanzheng shumu jieti' (Explanation of Writings on the Opium War).

d. Rev. ed. Rong Mengyuan (Beijing: Sanlian shudian, 1954), pp. 3–33.

e. Liang's work has been reprinted several times: (Beijing: Zhonghua shuju, 1959); and (Taibei: Wenhai chubanshe, 1970). Yao's work (Shanghai: Xin zhishi chubanshe, 1955) was reissued more recently: (Beijing: Renmin chubansha, 1984).

4. Shi Daogang has put forth the thesis that 'Daoguang yangsao zhengfu ji' was not the work of Wei Yuan at all, but actually fourteen years prior to the revised edition from the Shenbaoguan, its ancestor text, 'Yingjili yichuan rukou ji' (Account of the plunder by the barbarian ships of England) (later retitled 'Yangwu quanyu' [The origin of Western affairs]) by Li De'an was published in Tongzhi 4 (1865); and borrowing Wei Yuan's name, he made a series of revisions to the text, thereby changing its original appearance. Shi's view has given rise to a debate with Yao Weiyuan who thoroughly denies this entire position. The May 3, 1959 issue of *Guangming ribao* carried an essay by Shi entitled 'Guangyu "Yangwu quanyu" yishu' (On the essay 'Yangwu quanyu'); and in the December issue of *Lishi yanjiu* that year, Yao published a rebuttal entitled 'Guanyu 'Daoguang yangsao zhengfu ji' de zuozhe wenti' (Questions concerning the author of the 'Daoguang yangsao zhengfu ji'). The debate was not over, for in the April 1960 issue of *Lishi yanjiu* Yao responded with '"Daoguang yangsao zhengfu ji" zuozhe wenti de zaishangquan' (Renewed discussion of the questions of authorship of the 'Daoguang yangsao zhengfu ji'), and it spawned a variety of rebuttals. The reason this text was later included in the *Shengwu ji* has given rise to a number of different points of view. I do have sufficient space to give a detailed explanation for the position I have taken, and while each point can convincingly be made, it cannot be made decisively.

CHAPTER EIGHT

a. The factory director, or *opperhoofd* as he was known in Dutch, was referred to by the Japanese as *Kapitan* or 'Captain.' See Grant K. Goodman, *Japan: The Dutch Experience* (London: The Athlone Press, 1986), p. 13.

1. Preface dated 1870, contained in *Tōin sonkō* (Extant Writings of [Shionoya] Tōin), [Tokyo: Yamashiroya Kiyoyoshi], *kan* 4.

b. (Tokyo: Minyūsha, 1894); (Tokyo reprint: Tokyo University Press, 1979).

c. The name of the 'Captain' is given here in Japanese syllabaries; I have been unable to identify him.

d. (Tokyo: Kokusho kankōkai, 1913).

e. (Tokyo reprint: Tōyō bunko, 1958–60), four volumes.

f. In his *Nichi-Ran bunka kōshō shi no kenkyū* (Studies in the History of Japanese-Dutch Cultural Interaction) (Tokyo: Yoshikawa kōbunkan, 1959), pp. 178–200. This work was reprinted in 1986.

g. Published as the third issue of *Nihon kobunka kenkyūjo hōkoku* (Tokyo, 1937).

CHAPTER NINE

a. See Dona Torr, ed., *Marx on China, 1853–1860: Articles from the 'New York Daily Tribune'* (London: Lawrence & Wishart, 1968).

b. Adapted from W. G. Beasley, trans. and ed., *Select Documents on Japanese Foreign Policy: 1853–1868* (London: Oxford University Press, 1955), p. 131.

c. Covering the period from Kōka 2 (1845) to Ansei 6 (1859).

d. Respectively: appended to the *Dai Nihon komonjo* (Ancient Documents of Japan) (Tokyo: Shiryō hensanjo, Tokyo Imperial University, 1922); and in Ishin shi gakkai and Maruyama Kunio, eds. (Tokyo: Zaisei keizai gakkai, 1942–44), six volumes.

e. Ed. Ishin shiryō hensan jimukyoku (Tokyo: Meguro shoten, 1937–40), five volumes.

f. The *Masuda Wataru bunko mokuroku* lists two unsigned manuscript copies of this text, one formerly belonging to Imazeki Tenpō. The *Yifei fanjing lu* can be found in the Chinese collections of both the Harvard-Yenching Library and the Hoover Institution (Stanford University). The former is a two-volume Japanese manuscript edition, and the latter is dated Kaei 4 (1851) and contains Japanese reading punctuation; hence, both should really be listed as *Ihi hankyō roku* and placed in their respective Japanese collections.

g. Included in volume six of the documentary series *Yapian zhanzheng* (The Opium War), ed. Zhongguo shixuehui (Shanghai: Xin zhishi chubanshe, 1955), six volumes.

1. I may be getting ahead of myself, but let me mention the [unsigned] *Renyin Zhapu xunnan lu* (Record of Those Who Gave Their Lives at Zhapu in 1842), cited as a 'book still being sought' in section nine of the aforementioned 'Yapian zhanzheng shumu jieti'. It, too, is an extremely rare work in China, but I have a copy of it in my own collection. Published in the 24th year of the Daoguang reign (1844), compiled by Shen Yunshi.

h. (Tokyo: Meiji shoin, 1905).

i. A copy of this work (dated Ansei 4), printed by the Meirindō, can be found in the Harvard-Yenching Library, listed as a Chinese work, *Yifei fanjing wenjian lu* in six *juan*; inasmuch as this title circulated solely in Japan, it should be in the Japanese collection and titled *Ihi hankyō bunken roku*.

j. (Tokyo: Yoshikawa kōbunkan, 1962).

k. Edited by Hattori Unokichi (1867–1939), and, according to the introduction, compiled by Kanda Kiichirō and Nagasawa Kikuya (Tokyo: Bunkyūdō shoten, Shōundō shoten, 1933).

l. (Tokyo: Teikoku chihō gyōsei gakkai, 1914).

2. In the revised edition of the *Seikadō bunko Kanseki bunrui mokuroku*, there is the addition of an entry for *Ihi hankyō kenbunroku* in six volumes, 'published in Ansei 4 (woodblock printing, Takanabe domain).' The edition printed at the Meirindō in Takanabe domain was photolithographically published by Kyūko shoin in 1974 as the first volume in a series entitled *Wakokuhon Min-Shin shiryōshū* (Collection of Documents from the Ming and Qing Dynasties in Japanese Woodblock Editions) (Tokyo: Koten kenkyūkai, 1974); it was based on the text held in the library of the late Obama Toshie.

m. (Tokyo: Seikadō bunko, 1930); (Taibei reprint: Guting shuwu, 1969).

CHAPTER TEN

1. In *Shōin zenshū* (Complete Works of [Yoshida] Shōin) (Tokyo: Iwanami shoten, 1935), volume 9.

2. Yoshida Shōin copied out separately the 'introductory comments' and bibliography from this book.

a. Published by the Iwase bunko, Nishio city, Aichi prefecture, 1936.

b. Printed by the Kokō shokyokuzō in the Kaei period in one stringbound volume. There is a reprint of the *Tokushi zeigi*: (Tokyo: Zuiōginsha, 1938). A copy can be found in the Harvard-Yenching Library.
c. In one stringbound volume (Sendai: Ise Yasuemon, 1879).
d. Two stringbound volumes (Sendai: Saitō Daizaburō, 1893).
e. (Tokyo: Rikugōkan, 1927). It was later appended to *Kokusho kaidai* (Japanese Books, Annotated) which was compiled initially by Samura Hachirō (1865–1914) and reprinted several times: (Tokyo: Rikugōkan, 1900, 1926); and (Tokyo: Yoshikawa Hanshichi, 1904). Either it was reprinted again thereafter, or Masuda has confused something, for the *Nihon sōsho mokuroku* only appeared in 1927.
3. The *Ban shi* received a certain amount of attention from scholars concerned with events overseas. Yoshida Shōin, in a letter to his elder brother, Sugiume Tarō, dated the eleventh month of Ansei 1 (1854), wrote: 'I have taken a glance through Saitō Chikudō's *Ban shi* and [Yasuzumi] Gonsai's *Yō shi kiryaku* (Brief Chronicle of Western History). If you have the opportunity, I would gladly offer them to you.' Yasuzumi's work, correctly titled *Yōgai kiryaku* (Brief Chronicle of the West) (preface dated Kaei 1 [1848], written in Kanbun) circulated widely in manuscript form. I have two such copies: one in one stringbound volume; another in three stringbound volumes but dated Genji 1 (1864).

CHAPTER ELEVEN

a. The Chinese characters given for these biblical and post-biblical proper nouns are given in the glossary under their English spelling.
b. Noah 'walked with God' (Genesis 5:9).
c. 'Noah was a just man and perfect in his generations' (Genesis 6:9).
d. Edited by Kaikoku hyakunen kinen bunka jigyōkai, this volume is the work of both Ōkubo and Ayusawa Shintarō, each authoring discrete sections of the text. It was reprinted unchanged by Hara shobō (Tokyo) in 1978.
e. The Masuda Bunko does have a copy of the *Yōgai tsūran* but not of the *Seiyō shōshi*; thus, Masuda or his editor may have meant the reverse of what appears in this text here.
f. This work by You Tong appears in volume 18 of his *Xitang quanji* (Collected Works of Xitang [You Tong]) (Changzhou, Kangxi era). The Japanese edition referred to here was published in Ōsaka by Yoshino Rokubee et al.
g. Printed in Ise by Matsuura Hiroshi. The original Chinese text is the work of Chen Zhaokui etal.
h. Written by Hayano Kei (Edo, 1850), five volumes; a copy of this rare work can be found in Harvard-Yenching Library.

CHAPTER TWELVE

1. There are biographies of Huang Juezi in *Qing shi gao* (Draft History of the Qing Dynasty), 'liezhuan' (biographies), 165; and *Qing shi liezhuan* (Biographies in Qing History), *zhuan* 41, 'Dachen zhuan xu' (Biographies of high officials, continued), section 6.
2. Yasuzu Motohiko, 'Kaisetsu' (Explanatory Essays), in *Satō Nobuhiro shū*, in *Kokugaku taikei* (Compendium on Nativism) (Tokyo: Chiheisha, 1943).
3. Mori Senzō, *Satō Nobuhiro, gimon no jinbutsu* (Satō Nobuhiro, Dubious Personage) (Tokyo: Konnichi no mondaisha, 1942).
a. Respectively: (Tokyo: Iwanami shoten, 1927), edited by Takimoto Seiichi (1857–1932); in *Nihon bugaku taikei 22* (Collection on Japanese Military Science, Volume 22) (Tokyo: Iwanami shoten, 1942).

4. Perhaps, because many of Satō's writings were published during the Meiji period, little detail is now known about them. I have a manuscript copy of this work which I believe is from the *bakumatsu* era. It is printed on Mino paper in eight *kan* and four stringbound volumes, and it covers the Opium War in considerable detail. It has a preface dated the second month of Kōka 2 (1845) and the final *kan* includes both 'military strategy at sea' and 'military strategy on land.' At the very end, it reads: 'Fifth day, fifth month, first year of Kaei [1848]. Chin'en Satō Nobuhiro.' Thus, it would seem that the work was completed in 1848. It has been reprinted in the *Satō Nobuhiro bugaku shū*, ed. Nihon bugaku kenkyūjo, *Nihon bugaku taikei 23* (Tokyo: Iwanami shoten, 1943).

In comparing the *Kairiku senbō roku* which is included in *Kaikoku kigen* with *Suiriku senpō roku*, one can readily see that the gist of the former has been condensed in the latter. However, *Suiriku senpō roku* contains rather long commentaries under the aegis of 'Chin'en shi iwaku' (Mr. Chin'en's [i.e., Satō Nobuhiro's] remarks) at the end of each section of the text; these are comments of a 'military strategic' nature. All of these commentaries are absent in the *Kairiku senbō roku*.

The *Kairiku senbō roku* is missing from the list of Satō's writings. This would seem to indicate that it was composed by someone else extracting the essentials of the *Suiriku senpō roku* and taking out the commentary passages.

b. Edited by Yasuzu Motohiko, in the *Kokugaku taikei* (Compendium on Nativism) (Tokyo: Chiheisha, 1943).

c. (Tokyo: Hokkai shuppansha, 1941).

d. (Tokyo: Iwanami shoten, 1976), p. 2289.

CHAPTER THIRTEEN

a. The editor of the original is given as the proprietor of the 'Xiaoheng xiangshi' (Shanghai: Zhonghua yuanyin sanbanben, 1917); (Shanghai reprint: Zhonghua shuju, 1921); (Shanghai reprint: Shanghai shudian, 1981, three volumes). Masuda cites the second of these three and the Masuda Bunko has the seventh edition (Shanghai: Zhonghua shuju, 1936); Harvard-Yenching Library has the 1917 and 1981 editions in its collection.

b. In addition to the 1868 edition cited by Masuda, Harvard-Yenching Library also has two Taibei reprints by Wenhai chubanshe (1962 and 1967). Xia Xie wrote under the pseudonym Jiangshang Jiansou.

c. The full title of Duncan MacPherson's work is: *Two Years in China, Narrative of the Chinese Expedition, from its formation in April, 1840, to Aug., 1842. With an appendix, containing the most important of the general orders and despatches published...* (London: Sauders and Otle, 1843).

d. Respectively: (Tokyo: Bessho heishichi, 1887) and (Kōfu: Naitō Tsutauemon, 1881). Both can be found in the collection of the Harvard-Yenching Library.

e. Rev. ed. (Tokyo: Shun'yōdō shoten, 1936, 1944).

f. The author's name is given as Tokai Gyojin or Fisherman of the Eastern Sea, certainly a pseudonym.

g. (Tokyo: Hakubunkan, 1894), one stringbound volume.

1. In this connection, let me note in advance that the *Ei-Shin ahen sen shi* was translated in an abridged edition and published by the Datong yishuju in Shanghai in lithograph form by Tang Rui (Juedun, a man from Fanyu, Guangdong) in eight *juan* during the Guangxu era; it appeared with the title *Yingren qiangmai yapian ji* (Account of the Forced Sale of Opium by the English). I have not seen the work myself, but it is held in the Guangdong Provincial Library according to a note in volume six of *Yapian zhanzheng*, ed. Zhongguo shixuehui which transcribes the text. Except for the notice 'written by a Japanese,' there is no mention that the author was Matsui Kōkichi. When

we compare the translation with the *Ei-Shin ahen sen shi*, we can see that it was a translation of this work into Chinese.

An explanatory note in the *Yingren qiangmai yapian ji* [p. 513] reads as follows: This work was originally written by a Japanese whose name is now unknown. The translation is extremely poor. In particular, the names of foreigners were first translated from English into Japanese and then from Japanese into Chinese; as such, they have traveled from their original pronunciation and in many cases cases may be unrecognizable. For example, [the Chinese translator] rendered the English King Kyōchi [Ch., Qiaozhi, or George] as Qiyaoqi; and the English Consul Giritsu [Ch., Yilü, or Elliott) as Xianliyazi. In content, it makes use of English accounts, and thus there is considerable detail on the actions of the English side. The assistance rendered to the Chinese in the war by the Russians, which is described in this work, is material not to be found in other books. There are numerous errors in the chronicling in this work. One especially egregious [error], for example, can be found in the reference to the fact that the Daoguang Emperor took refuge in Fengtian because he was defeated in the war. My view of the author's argument is that it demonstrates the attitudes of one group of Japanese in the late Qing who worked with great intensity to bring about the reform [of China] as early as possible.

h. (Edo, Kaei 3 [1850]).
i. (Shusai ō, Kaei 2 [1849]).
j. (Tokyo: Rikugōkan, 1900).
k. (Ōsaka: Oshimaya Ihee, Ansei 2 [1855]). The *Kaigai shinwa* (Edo, 1849), the *Kaigai shinwa shūi* (1949), the *Kaigai yowa* (n.p., Ansei 2 [1855]), and the *Kaigai jitsuroku* (1854 preface) can all be found in the collection of Harvard-Yenching Library. Only the *Kaigai yowa* is a different edition than that mentioned by Masuda whose copy predates the Harvard-Yenching edition.

CHAPTER FOURTEEN

(Concerning this chapter, see Bob T. Wakabayashi's article, 'Opium, Expulsion, Sovereignty: China's Lessons for Bakumatsu Japan,' *Monumenta Nipponica* 47.1 [Spring 1992], pp. 1–25, which offers a fine analysis of Mineta Fūkō's work – JAF)

a. The following can all be found in the collection of Harvard-Yenching Library: *Kaigai shinwa* (Edo: n.p., 1849); Shusai ō, *Kaigai shinwa shūi* (Edo: n.p., 1849); *Kaigai jitsuroku* (Edo: Suharaya Mohee, 1854), five *kan*, with other editions published under the title *Kaigai jitsuwa* (True Stories from Overseas); and *Kaigai yowa* (n.p.: Kōyodō zōshi, 1855). A copy of the *Kaigai shinwa* can also be found at UCLA.
b. (Tokyo: Asakaya shoten, 1926); revised and enlarged edition (Seikōkan shuppanbu, 1929).
c. Copy in the Harvard-Yenching Library and in the collection of the Hoover Institution, Stanford University: (Tokyo: Kokusho kankōkai, 1910–11), five volumes.
d. (Tokyo: Iguchi shoten, 1943).
e. (Chiba: Chiba Yajiuma, 1919).

CHAPTER FIFTEEN

a. Respectively: (Tokyo: Tōhō jironsha, 1917); (Tokyo: Min'yūsha, 1931); (Tokyo: Dokuga shoin, 1915–16), two volumes; and (Tokyo: Dokuga shoin, 1919).
b. (Tokyo: Dai Nihon tosho, 1914; Kyoto reprint: Shibunkaku, 1971).
1. See 'Shotoku zasshū' (Collections of Letters), in Yoshida Kurazō, ed., *Shōin sensei icho* (The Posthumous Works of Yoshida Shōin), volume 2 (Tokyo: Min'yūsha, 1909).

c. A copy of this edition can be found in the collection of Harvard-Yenching Library.
d. Ed. Ishin shiryō hensan jimukyoku (Tokyo: Meguro shoten, 1937).
e. (Tokyo: Shun'yōdō, 1926).
f. (Tokyo: Fuzanbō, 1939).

CHAPTER SIXTEEN

a. This may be a misprint or a transription error. The text in the Masuda Bunko gives 'Tōdo haiya no hanashi' (Story of a Chinese ashman) as its subtitle.
b. A copy of this edition of *Shin Min gundan* can be found at Harvard-Yenching Library. Franz Michael lists the five-volume woodblock-printed edition of this work, published by the Aoe juku in 1854: *The Taiping Rebellion: History and Documents* (Seattle: University of Washington Press, 1971), vol. III, p. 1764.
c. A copy of these editions of both the *Man-Shin kiji* and the *Shin zoku ibun* may be found in the collection of Harvard-Yenching Library. Michael (vol. III, p. 1764) lists a five-volume woodblock edition of the latter work, published by Tenjikurō in 1855.
1. They took the Susong Circuit Intendant Wu Jianzhang prisoner and put to death the Shanghai County Magistrate Yuan Shide.
2. They seized and occupied in rapid succession the county of Shanghai and five more in its immediate vicinity: Jiading, Baoshan, Nanhui, Chuansha, and Qingpu. They then proceeded to the west and attacked nearby Taicang.
d. In *Shanghai zhanggu congshu* (Collection of Records of Shanghai) (Shanghai: Shanghai tongshe, 1935).
3. *Yi jing* 26 (March 1937). In addition, historical material on the Small Sword Society has been gathered from many directions (including documents of foreigners, such as the articles in the *North China Herald*) and published in *Shanghai Xiaodaohui qiyi shiliao huibian* (Collection of Historical Materials on the Uprising of the Small Sword Society in Shanghai), ed. Institute of History, Shanghai Academy of Social Sciences (Shanghai: Shanghai renmin chubanshe, 1964). This work is in excess of 1000 pages, but its third volume, entitled 'Shanghai Xiaodaohui qiyi zongxu' (General Account of the Uprising of the Small Sword Society in Shanghai), provides a comprehensive discussion of the activities of the Small Sword Society and its historical background.

CHAPTER SEVENTEEN

a. (Tokyo: self-published, 1883). This work in seventeen traditional volumes was reprinted by Gannandō shoten (Tokyo) in 1968. This edition can be found in the Masuda Bunko.
b. Franz Michael lists a work in fifteen volumes with this (romanized) title, giving an estimated date of 1855 for publication by Kinseikaku. *The Taiping Rebellion*, vol. III, p. 1763. Given the great difference in size of these two works, though, it is extremely unlikely that they represent the same texts.

CHAPTER EIGHTEEN

a. This is a reference to *Shiji* 7: 'Xiang Yu benji' (The Basic Annals of Xiang Yu): 'Hsiang Yü led his entire forces across the river. Once across, he sank all his boats, smashed the cooking pots and vessels, and set fire to his huts, taking three days' rations, to make clear to his soldiers that they must fight to the death, for he had no intention of returning.' *Records of the Grand Historian: Chapters from the Shih Chi of Ssu-ma Ch'ien*, trans. Burton Watson (New York: Columbia University Press, 1969), p. 77. For an extremely useful, annotated edition of much of the *Shiji*, see Tanaka

Kenji and Ikkai Tomoyoshi, trans. and annot., *Shiki, So-Kan hen* (Records of the Grand Historian, Chu and Han Sections) (Tokyo: Asahi shinbunsha, 1974). The reference here appears on p. 34 of this edition.

1. In Yoshida Kurazō, ed., *Shōin sensei icho* (The Posthumous Works of Yoshida Shōin) (Tokyo: Min'yūsha, 1909), volume 2; and in *Yoshida Shōin zenshū*, volume 2, pp. 93–121. The latter of these couplets did in fact appear at the beginning of a section of documents on the Triads in the Chinese work, *Taiping tianguo shiliao* (Historical Documents on the Taiping Rebellion) (Beijing reprint: Zhonghua shuju, 1959); in the last form, the expression of 'proceeding immediately to cleanse' has been changed to 'proceeding immediately ahead.'

b. Printed in Japan with Japanese reading punctuation: (Nagasaki: Ryokuten sanbō, Ansei 1 [1854]). Another edition of this work, dated Ansei 2 (1855), is also to be found in the Masuda Bunko. The text has been reprinted as well in the *Wakokuhon Min-Shin shiryōshū*, volume 2.

2. See *Taiping tianguo shiliao congbian jianji* (Collection of Historical Documents on the Taiping Rebellion, Abridged Edition), ed. Taiping tianguo lishi bowuguan (Historical Museum of the Taiping Rebellion) (Beijing: Zhonghua shuju, 1961–1963), 6 volumes.

3. (Beijing: Kaiming shudian, 1950; reprinted, Beijing: Zhonghua shuju, 1955). The latter is edited by Jin Yufu and Tian Yuqing, et al.

4. (Tokyo: Shiryō hensanjo, Tokyo University, 1922). The text notes that they could not 'now obtain an original edition' of the *Xiaer guanzhen*.

c. Reprinted together with another work by Kawaji, *Nagasaki nikki* (Nagasaki Diary) (Tokyo: Heibonsha, Tōyō bunko series #124, 1970), ed. Fujii Sadafumi and Kawata Sadao.

5. In Appendix One, 'Bakumatsu gaikoku kankei monjo,' in *Dai Nihon komonjo*.

d. *Yoshida Shōin zenshū*, volume 2, p. 99.

e. (Shanghai: Guangzhi shuju, 1911). According to Kawabata Genji, this work was entitled *Jindai Zhongguo bishi* (Secret History of Modern China) and published in 1904; it was a collection of documents concerning the revival of the Han people. See Kawabata, 'Kindai Chūgoku hishi,' in *Ajia rekishi jiten* (Historical Encyclopedia of Asia) (Tokyo: Heibonsha, 1960), vol. 3, p. 21b.

6. For example, the name 'Wan Da Hong' in a placard of a Triad group appears changed in *Zhongguo jinshi bishi* as 'Wan Sui Hong,' and 'Wan Sui Hong' refers to Heavenly King Hong Xiuquan of the Taipings.

7. In *Torii Hisayasu sensei kakō kinen ronshū: Chūgoku no gengo to bungaku*.

CHAPTER NINETEEN

a. Michael (p. 1763) has similar, though less detailed, information, except that he lists the publisher as Sanpōken.

b. Michael (p. 1753) lists a woodblock print work which may be the same as this one: *Shin Min kassen senki*, five volumes, published by the Sanpōken in 1854.

c. (Liulichang, Beijing: Bansong jushi).

1. Before this work appeared, the *Taiwan waiji* (External Chronicle of Taiwan) by Jiang Risheng (30 volumes, with a preface dated Kangxi 43 [1704] by Chen Qi) was a novel that took the form of a historical biography; it cited the *Xiaotian jinian fukao* as a reference (see below). In Jiang's work, Gan Hui's name appears as 甘輝 (the two characters 輝 and 煇 are effectively the same), and the points where he is reviling the last Qing commander whom he encounters and is then killed are practically identical prose passages in the two works. In the *Taiwan waiji*, though, Gan Hui is captured and dies at Chongming after the defeat at Nanjing.

d. This work can be found in the collection of Harvard-Yenching Library, where the author is given as Ukai Sekisai and publication information: (Edo: Nakamura Shinshichi, 1725). The Masuda Bunko text contains the same publication information.

e. Zheng Juzhong (Yizou), *jinshi* of 1700, published *Zheng Chenggong zhuan* in 1702; a copy can be found in the collection of the Harvard-Yenching Library. A Japanese edition (dated Ansei 3 [1856]), published in Ōsaka, can also be found in this same collection.

f. *Qing su jiwen* (Tokyo: Suharaya Mohee, 1876), six stringbound volumes, ed. Nakagawa Chūei; (Tokyo reprint: Heibonsha, 1965), ed. Nakagawa Chūei, Son Hakujun, and Muramatsu Kazuya, two volumes. Liang Zonglin, *Jingchu suishiji* (Ōsaka: Kitada Kiyozaemon, [Genbun 2] 1737).

CHAPTER TWENTY

1. Later reprinted in *Kokushijō gimon no jinbutsu, chūshin ka gyakushin ka jitsuzai ka densetsu ka* (Mysterious Figures in Japanese History: Loyal Retainers? Rebellious Servants? Really Existed? Rumors?), ed. Kokushi kōshūkai (Tokyo: Yūzankaku, 1926).

a. (Ōsaka: Ōsaka shi sanjikai, 1911), six volumes.

b. (Tō-A shobō, 1910); later revised and published in 1942 by Sōgensha in Ōsaka, in the *Nihon bunka meicho* series.

2. In *Ōgai zenshū* (Collected Works of [Mori] Ōgai) (Tokyo: Chikuma shobō, 1973), volume 15, pp. 1–79. [Masuda used an earlier edition of this work].

c. Discussion of the *Ōsaka Ōshio Heihachirō bankiroku* appears in Ōgai's appendix, in *Ōgai zenshū*, 15:59–60; the chronological biography appears on pp. 62–69. Ōgai's account of Heihachirō was first published in 1914.

3. Inoue Tetsujirō, *Nihon Yōmeigakuha no tetsugaku* (The Philosophy of the Wang Yangming School in Japan) (Tokyo: Fuzanbō, 1900). Reprinted by Fuzanbō in 1903 and 1913.

d. The *Senshindō sakki* has been published in many editions. The Masuda Bunko has three editions: preface dated 1835, published by the Seigidō, on thin paper in two stringbound volumes; Yoshikawa Nobutarō, ed. (Ōsaka: Mitamura Kōji, 1939); and Yamada Jun, ed. (Tokyo: Iwanami shoten, 1941). An 1833 edition in three stringbound volumes is held in the collection of Harvard-Yenching Library. I have also located reprints of 1910, 1913, and, most recently, 1978 by Chūō kōron sha.

e. (Tokyo: Fuzanbō, 1924–25).

4. For example, under the entry for Tenpō 8/7/19 in *Bakin nikki shō* (Selections from the Diary of [Takizawa] Bakin), ed. Aeba Kōson (Tokyo: Bunkaidō shoten, 1911), where it reads 'the incident involving Ōshio is said to be under careful scrutiny in Edo,' Haga Yaichi (1867–1927) adds a detailed explanation: 'Although there are numerous facts that can be related concerning this case, we already have a number of accounts, including *Ōsaka ikki roku* (Account of the Osaka Uprising), *Tenpō nikki* (Tenpō Diary), *Jitsuji dan* (Story of the Truth), and *Seiten hekireki* (A Bolt from the Blue).... In addition, [the evidence] has been most carefully investigated and corroborated in a fine work recently published, Ōshio Heihachirō, by Kōda Shigetomo.'

f. (Tokyo: Taitōkaku, 1920).

g. Included in *Hyakka setsurin* (Views of Various Thinkers) (Tokyo: Yoshikawa kōbunkan, 1906), supplemental volume.

5. *Egawa Tan'an zenshū* (Collected Works of Egawa Tan'an [Tarōzaemon]), ed. Tobayama Kan (Tokyo reprint: Gannandō shoten, 1972), two volumes. The duplicates of Kazan's letters can be found as well in *Kazan zenshū* (Collected Works of

[Watanabe] Kazan), ed. Suzuki Kiyofushi (Toyohashi: Kazan sōsho shuppankai, 1941).

h. See *Gaikō shi kō* (Draft Chronicle of Foreign Affairs) (Tokyo: Gaimushō, 1884), two volumes.

6. Hayakawa Kōtarō, *Ōkura Nagatsune* (Tokyo: Yamaoka shoten, 1943).

7. Fujita Tōko, *Naniwa sōdō kiji*, in *Tōko zenshū* (Collected Works of [Fujita] Tōko), ed. Kikuchi Kenjirō (Tokyo: Hakubunkan, 1909), pp. 641–50.

8. In Furumi Kazuo, *Egawa Tarōzaemon* (Tokyo: Kokumin bungaku sha, 1930), we read: 'When stories to the effect that remnants of those who had assisted Ōshio Heihachirō in Ōsaka had filtered into the domain of Kai, which was terrain under his control, he [i.e., Egawa] together with shop employee Saitō Yakurō dressed in the garb impersonating a sword dealer and personally made a round of inspection.'

CHAPTER TWENTY-ONE

1. In eighteen *juan*, with four *juan* of 'Supplementary Records,' woodblock printed in Tongzhi 9 (1870). Later, the title was changed to *Pingding Yuekou jilüe* (Brief Record of the Quelling of the Bandits of Guangdong and Guangxi), the language of the contents was somewhat edited, and it was reprinted [by the Jiaojingtang] in Guangxu 1 (1875).

a. Harvard-Yenching Library has an edition of this work dated Tongzhi 10 (1871) in eight stringbound volumes, eighteen *juan* and four additional *juan*. It also has a Taibei reprint by Wenhai chubanshe of 1967. Franz Michael lists editions of 1869, 1871, and 1888; see Michael, vol. III, p. 1639.

2. The *Yuekou jilüe* has an expression here meaning 'form.'

3. The *Yuekou jilüe* uses a slightly different expression here and elsewhere.

4. Hamberg: (Hong Kong: China Mail, 1854); also published serially in the *North China Herald*. The Chinese translation by Jian Youwen appears in Jian, *Taiping tianguo zaji diyiji* (Various Accounts of the Taipings, First Collection) (Shanghai: Commercial Press, 1935).

b. (Beijing: Yanjing daxue tushuguan).

c. (Tokyo: Seikatsusha, 1941).

d. *Yi jing* 2 (1936).

e. *Guangzhou xuebao* 1.2 (1937).

f. (Chongqing and Shanghai: Commercial Press, 1946), 2 volumes.

g. Revised and enlarged edition (Beijing: Zhonghua shuju, 1957).

h. Revised and enlarged edition (Hong Kong: Jianshi mengjin shuwu, 1967).

i. (Hong Kong: Jianshi mengjin shuwu, 1962).

j. (Kōfu: Naitō Tsutauemon, 1881), twelve stringbound volumes.

5. In the passage represented here by the elipses, the author inserted wording drawn from the *Dunbi suiwen lu*, as will be discussed in the next chapter.

6. The Three Dots Society or Sandianhui was affiliated with the Triads.

k. (Tokyo: Hayashi Heijirō, 1898), four stringbound volumes.

l. It runs to 242 pages and is printed from movable type with Western binding (Tokyo: Nisshūsha, 1879 [printed by Katō Kurō]).

7. See Tao Chengzhang, 'Jiaohui yuanliu kao' (A Study of the Origins of [Triad] Religious Society), in Luo Ergang, ed., *Tiandihui wenxian lu* (Studies of Documents on the Triads) (Hong Kong: Shiyong shuju, 1942); (Shanghai: Zhengzhong shuju, 1943).

8. *Zhongshan wenhua jiaoyuguan jikan* II.3 (1935). Also in *Jindai mimi shehui shiliao* (Historical Materials on Modern Secret Societies), ed. Xiao Yishan (Beiping: Guoli Beiping yanjiuyuan zongbian shichu chubanke, 1935), vol. 1. [The Masuda Bunko also contains another, reprint edition of this work: (Taibei: Wenhai chubanshe, 1965)].

9. *Lishi jiaoxue* 37–39 (1954). Also included in his *Taiping tianguo shishi kao* (A Study of the History of the Taiping Rebellion) (Beijing: Sanlian shudian, 1955; 1979 reprint).
10. *Guowen zhoubao* XIII.17 (1936); reprinted in *Taiping tianguo congshu shisan zhong* (Thirteen Works in a Collection on the Taipings) (Beiping: n.p., 1938; Taibei reprint: Wenhai chubanshe, 1968).
m. In *Taiping tianguo shi jizai dingmiu ji* (Collection of Critical Essays on the History of the Taiping Rebellion) (Beijing: Sanlian shudian, 1955).
n. (Tokyo: Bessho heishichi, 1877), six volumes.
o. (1880), two volumes.
p. (Tokyo: Higashinari Kamejirō, 1877), five stringbound volumes.
q. Masuda gives Han instead of Wang for the surname here and later in the text, but this contradicts every other source and must be an error.

CHAPTER TWENTY-TWO

a. There is a 1968 reprint of the *Dunbi suiwen lu* (Taibei: Wenhai chubanshe, Jindai Zhongguo shiliao congkan 298), copy in the collection of Harvard-Yenching Library.
b. In *Tōkō sensei ibun*; reprinted in *Takasugi Shinsaku zenshū* (Collected Works of Takahashi Shinsaku), ed. Hori Tetsusaburō (Tokyo: Shin jinbutsu ōraisha, 1974), 2:141–216.
c. (Tokyo: Nakamuda Takenobu, 1919).
d. In *Bunkyū ninen Shanhai nikki*.
e. All of these texts are translated in Michael, volumes II and III.
f. In his extensive, multilingual bibliography, Franz Michael (vol. III, p. 1751) gives another Japanese edition of this book: Sha Hei, *Kinryō kikō sekidan* (Ōsaka: Kawachiya, 1869), 2 volumes. The publisher's full name should read Kawachiya Shinshichi. Harvard-Yenching Library holds a copy of a similarly titled work by Xie Jiehe (with the final character of his name read by its alternate reading of 'hao').
g. (Ōsaka: Ōsaka tosho shuppangyō kumiai, 1936); (Ōsaka reprint: Seibundō, 1964).
h. (Beiping: Beijing yaozhai congke, 1938); (Taibei reprint: Wenhai chubanshe, 1968). Originally appeared in *Yi jing* 2 (1936).
i. Appended to *Taiping tianguo* (The Taiping Rebellion) (Shanghai: Shanghai renmin chubanshe, 1957), by Zhang Xiumin and Yu Hui'an.
j. There are many Chinese editions of this work. The following four are held in Harvard-Yenching Library: (Shanghai: Commercial Press, 1898); (n.p.: Haishang wuyuan, 1937); (Taibei: Guangwen shuju, 1969); (Taibei: Tailian guofeng chubanshe, 1969).
k. (Tokyo: Tōyō Bunko, 1930).
l. *Juan* 3, 'Dunbi suiwen lu danghui' (Destruction by Fire of the *Dunbi suiwen lu*) (1902). There are two editions of Xue's work, both in six stringbound volumes, in the Masuda Bunko: (Xiaoshan Chenshi, 1897); (Shanghai reprint: Commercial Press, 1937). Masuda's date of 1902, given in the text, may be a misprint or error.
m. In *Taiping tianguo shiliao bianwei ji* (Essays Distinguishing Forgeries of Historical Documents of the Taiping Rebellion) (Beijing: Sanlian shudian, 1955).
n. There are three editions of this large collection listed in the catalogue of the Harvard-Yenching Library: (Tokyo: Kondō kappanjo, 1882–83); rev. ed. (Tokyo: Kondō kappanjo, 1900–03); (Tokyo: Rinsen shoten, 1967–68). All edited by Kondō Heijō, and the last edition which appeared well after Kondō's death also gives as co-editors Tsunoda Bun'ei and Gorai Shigeru. The Masuda Bunka has an edition (Tokyo:Kondō kappanjo, 1881–85) in 47 stringbound volumes.
1. Luo Ergang, *Taiping tianguo shigao* (Draft History of the Taiping Rebellion), revised and enlarged edition (Beijing: Zhonghua shuju, 1957), citing C. A. Tesns, 'Historic Shanghai' [which I have been unable to locate – JAF].

2. Luo Ergang, *Taiping tianguo shigao*.
o. (Hong Kong: Jianshi mengjin shuwu, 1958).
p. Translation based closely on Michael, vol. III, pp. 1404, 1406.
3. Emphasis Masuda's. To the end he maintained this strained explanation of trying to pass Hong Xiuquan off as a Japanese (namely, Ōshio Heihachirō). After the original leaders of the rebellion had departed, Hong's two elder brothers held power, although, as concerns these two elder brothers, Ishizaki does nothing whatsoever to resolve the question of whether they were Japanese or of mixed Sino-Japanese blood. Thus, this is undoubtedly the reason that the *Yuefei jilüe* and the Japanese histories of China of the time that relied on it do not even mention the two older brothers.
q. Jing-Chu: A reference to the ancient state of Chu which comprised Hunan, much of Hubei, some of Guizhou, and portions of Anhui, Jiangxi, Jiangsu, and Henan; ca. B.C.E. 740–330. Qing-Qi: Eastern and northern Shandong.

CHAPTER TWENTY-THREE

a. In *Zoku shiseki shūran* (Collection of Historical Documents, Continued) (Tokyo: Kondō shuppanbu, 1893). There is also an edition of this work in six stringbound volumes, edited by Kondō Heijō and with the same publication information, that appeared in 1917. It is held in the collection of Harvard-Yenching Library and elsewhere. The Masuda Bunko has the same text with a 1912 date of publication.
b. (Edo: Tsuruya Kiuemon), three stringbound volumes. There is a Taibei reprint of this work by the Bank of Taiwan (1958, Taiwan wenxian congkan 5).
c. In volume 40 of *Kokushi taikei* (Great Compedium of Japanese History), revised edition) (Tokyo: Keizai shinbunsha, 1901).
d. (Tokyo: Waseda University Press, 1914), chapter 28, pp. 430–52. This is the seventh printing held in the Masuda Bunko. There is also a Chinese translation of this work by Dan Dao (Shanghai: Zhonghua shuju, 1921), III:35–53.
e. Issue 2.15, pp. 125–33. This journal later changed its name to the much more well known *Shigaku zasshi*.
f. (Tokyo: Naigai shoseki, 1930). The Masuda Bunko has the fifth printing from 1942 of this edition.
g. Part of this document, as well as certain details of this tale, have been closely examined in Ronald P. Toby, *State and Diplomacy in Early Modern Japan: Asia in the Development of the Tokugawa Bakufu* (Stanford: Stanford University Press, 1991), esp. p. 125. The names in this list of daimyōs include titles (only some of which are translated *inter alia*); such titles only extremely rarely indicate an actual job one performed.
h. Editions of these works, most of them held in the collection of Harvard-Yenching Library, include the following:

Huang Zongxi, *Xingchao lu*, in Xu Youlan, comp., *Shaoxing xianzheng yishu* (Literary Remains of Scholars from Shaoxing) (Zhejiang, 1895), volumes 47–48; (Taibei reprint: Wenhai chubanshe, 1969?).
——, *Lizhou yizhu huikan*, comp. Xue Fengchang (Shanghai: Zhonghua shuju, 1910), 20 stringbound volumes; (Taibei reprint: Longyan chubanshe, 1969), two volumes; (Taibei reprint: Wenhai chubanshe, 1969), two volumes.
——, *Jingtuo yishi*, comp. Chenhu Yishi (n.p.: Jinzhang tushuju, n.d.), 24 stringbound volumes. It should be noted that the *Riben qishi ji* is not to be found in the list of texts given for this collection in the Harvard-Yenching catalogue.

i. The following bibliographical citations for editions of works mentioned in this paragraph can (also) be found in the collection of Harvard-Yenching Library:

Xu Zi, *Xiaotian jinian fukao* (1861, 20 *juan*); Wang Chongwu, annot. (Shanghai reprint: Zhonghua shuju, 1957), 2 volumes; (Taibei reprint: Bank of Taiwan, 1962, Taiwan wenxian congkan 134), five volumes; (Beijing: Zhonghua shuju, 1967), 20 *juan*.

——, *Xiaotian jizhuan* (Jinling, 1887); (Beijing reprint: Zhonghua shuju, 1958), 65 *juan*; appended to Xu Zi, *Xiaotian jinian* (Taibei reprint: Bank of Taiwan, 1963, Taiwan wenxian congkan 138), 65 *juan*; (Taibei reprint: Wenhai chubanshe, 1969?), 4 volumes; (Taibei reprint: Taiwan xuesheng shuju, 1977), 2 volumes.

Wen Ruilin, *Nanjiang yishi* (Shanghai reprint: Zhonghua shuju, 1959), 52 *juan*; (Taibei reprint: Bank of Taiwan, 1962, Taiwan wenxian congkan 132), 1830 edition in six stringbound volumes; (Tokyo reprint: Daiyasu, 1967, in a volume entitled *Ban-Min shiryō sōsho* [Collection of Documents on the Late Ming]).

Wengzhou Laomin, *Haidong yishi* (Taibei reprint: Bank of Taiwan, 1961, Taiwan wenxian congkan 99), 18 *juan*.

Shao Tingcai, *Dongnan jishi* (Taibei reprint: Bank of Taiwan, 1961, Taiwan wenxian congkan 96), 12 *juan*.

Zha Jizuo, *Lu chunqiu* (Taibei reprint: Bank of Taiwan, 1961, Taiwan wenxian congkan 118).

j. The Zhonghua shuju edition in four *juan* of this work (mentioned in the next paragraph) appeared in 1959 (Beijing). There is an earlier edition in nine *juan* that appeared in *Siming congshu*, ed. Zhang Shouyong (preface dated 1934), *ji* (collection) 2, volumes 30–37. Both are held at the Harvard-Yenching Library.

k. Edited by Zhang Shouyong (1934).

l. Many editions of this collection have been published, such as the following: (Shanghai: Commercial Press, 1929), 38 *juan*; (Shanghai: Commercial Press, 1936), 15 *juan*; Taibei: Wenhai chubanshe, 1969?), three volumes.

CHAPTER TWENTY-FOUR

a. 'Biography' 37, *juan* 24 (postface dated Tongzhi reign, printed in Guangxu 2 [1876]). Reprints: (Shanghai: Fugushe, 1910), 6 volumes; (Taibei: Bank of Taiwan, 1960), 26 *juan*; the former is in the Masuda Bunko.

b. 'Biography' 49, *juan* 53 (Shanghai reprint based on a manuscript held in the Shanghai Library: Zhonghua shuju, 1957); (Taibei reprint: Bank of Taiwan, 1962, Taiwan wenxian congkan no. 132), 1830 edition in six stringbound volumes; (Tokyo reprint: Daiyasu, 1967, in *Ban-Min shiryō sōsho*). The last of these, based on the Zhonghua shuju edition, can be found in the Masuda Bunko.

c. Compiled by Hayashi Shunshō and Hayashi Nobuatsu (Tokyo reprint: Tōyō bunko, 1958); (Tokyo reprint: n. p., 1964).

d. *Zoku zenrin kokuhō ki* and *Zoku zenrin kokuhō gaiki* are both included in Fujita Tokutarō, ed., *Shiryō shūsei: Yoshino Muromachi jidai gaikan* (Collection of Historical Materials: An Overview of the Yoshino Muromachi Period) (Tokyo, 1935); the edition of *Shiseki shūran* cited here, the revised edition, was edited by Kondō Heijō (Tokyo: Kondō kappanjo, 1900–03), 10 volumes; and *Zoku gunsho ruijū* (Tokyo: Keizai zasshisha, 1893–1902), nineteen volumes.

1. There is a two-year discrepancy here with the *Ka-i hentai*. Is this Lin Gao 林皋 the same as the aforementioned Lin Gao 林高? The two characters of the given names are pronounced in the first tone and are used, on occasion, interchangeably.

2. In the biography of Zhou Hezhi, number 49, *juan* 53 in the *Nanjiang yishi*, it is Feng Jingdi who was sent at this time to Japan, with Ruan Mei as assistant envoy.

3. It would appear from this that after requesting 3000 men, he sought an additional 5000, but the letter is no longer extant.
e. By Guan Ming (Taibei reprint: Bank of Taiwan, 1961), 8 *juan*.
f. (Beiping: Guoli Beiping tushuguan, 1932), twenty *juan*. Revised edition: (Shanghai: Guji chubanshe, 1981).
g. (Taibei: Shijie shuju, 1971).
h. Within the biography of Chen Zilong, no. 165 in 'liezhuan' (biographies), *juan* 277.
i. By Cha Jizuo, 1 *juan*, in *Shiyuan congshu* (Shiyuan Collection) compiled by Zhang Junheng (1916).
j. The characters given here are 長吉, but this may be a transcription error.

CHAPTER TWENTY-FIVE

a. (Beiping: Hafo-Yanjing xueshe, 1934). This was issued initially as a special number of the journal *Yanjing xuebao*. Also: (Beijing reprint: Renmin chubanshe, 1957). Both editions can be found in the Masuda Bunko.
b. 1939 edition, five *juan*, photolithographic reprint of the original manuscript; no place of publication or publisher noted.
c. Xu Xueju, *Jiajing dongnan pingwo tonglu* (Nanjing: Jiangsu shengli guoxue tushuguan, 1932); *Guochao dianhui* (Taibei reprint: Xuesheng shuju, 1965), 4 volumes.
d. Postface dated Kanbun 3 (1663), in *Shiseki shūran* (1881–85 edition), in the Masuda Bunko; (Tokyo reprint: Kyōikusha, 1981).
1. The text gives the term *sanshi* for what had been translated here as 'emissary.' In the *Riben yijian*, Zheng Shungong referred to himself as *tianshi* (J., *tenshi*), and *san* may be a mistranscription for *ten*.
2. The text gives the character *jiang* (river), though this is probably an error for *kou* (mouth, port).
e. It is included in Zheng Ruoceng, *Zheng Kaiyang zazhu* (Miscellaneous Writings of Zheng Kaiyang [Ruoceng]) (Nanjing reprint: Jiangsu shengli guoxue tushuguan, 1932), eleven *juan*.
f. (Tokyo: Heibonsha, 1926).
g. *Tokugawa shoki no kaigai bōekika* (Ōsaka: Asahi shinbunsha, 1916); *Shuinsen bōeki shi* (Kyoto: Naigai shuppan, 1921), (Ōsaka reprint: Kōjinsha, 1940).
h. In Fujita Tokutarō, ed., *Shiryō shusei: Yoshino Muromachi jidai gaikan* (Tokyo, 1935).
3. The copy of this work in my possession is a fine copy in three stringbound volumes of the Keian edition and bears the library imprint of 'Watanabe Chiaki.' It is also included in the *Satsu han sōsho* (Collection on Satsuma Domain) (1906), two stringbound volumes.
i. (Tokyo: Seikidō, 1918).
j. Masuda incorrectly transcribes the second character of Sach'ŏn in the text.
k. Masuda here makes the common error of attributing authorship of the *Chouhai tubian* to Hu Zongxian. It was really the work of Zheng Ruozeng. This has been demonstrated now by several scholars, including Tanaka Takeo and Wang Xiangrong. See, for example, Tanaka Takeo, 'Chūkai zuhen no seiritsu' (The Formation of the *Chouhai tubian*), in his *Chūsei kaigai kōshō shi no kenkyū* (Studies in the History of Overseas Relations in the Medieval Period) (Tokyo: Tokyo University Press, 1981), pp. 215–26, a reprinting of his 1953 article which appeared in *Nihon rekishi*; Wang Xiangrong, 'Guanyu *Chouhai tubian*' (On the *Chouhai tubian*), in his *Zhong-Ri guanxi shi wenxian lunkao* (Essays on Materials in the History of Sino-Japanese Relations) (Changsha: Yuelu shusha, 1985), pp. 159–217: and Stanley Y. C. Huang, 'Cheng Jo-tseng,' in

Dictionary of Ming Biography, ed. L. Carrington Goodrich and Chaoying Fang (New York and London: Columbia University Press, 1976), pp. 204–08.

CHAPTER TWENTY-SIX

a. (Tokyo: Jinbutsu ōraisha, 1966–67), section 2: 'Sengoku shiryō sōsho' (Collection of Historical Materials of the Warring States Era), part 6.

b. (Taibei reprint of Wanli 34 edition: Xuesheng shuju, 1969), five *juan*.

c. Masuda has 'Eiroku 2' (1559) here, but this is clearly a misprint for Bunroku 2. You Qimin and Zhou Qiqian also caught this error in their Chinese translation, p. 165. Masuda also gives 錄 as the character for 'roku'; it should be 禄.

d. Masuda makes the same apparent error as noted in note c, confusing Bunroku for Eiroku.

e. The Harvard-Yenching Library has a copy of this work: (Ōsaka: Eibunken kankō, 1693). The Masuda Bunko has a manuscript edition of this work in two stringbound volumes dated Genbun 5 (1740) and three reprints: (Tokyo: Kōbunko kankōkai, 1927); (Tokyo: Kondō shuppanbu, 1936); and (Tokyo: Kokusho kankōkai, 1975).

f. (Taibei reprint of edition with preface dated Wanli 44: Xuesheng shuju, 1966), 124 *juan*.

g. The University of California at Berkeley has two reprint editions of this, both in 291 *kan*: (Tokyo: Yoshikawa kōbunkan, 1904–5), 30 volumes; and (Tokyo: Nihon zuihitsu taisei kankōkai, 1929–30), six volumes. The latter can also be found at the Harvard-Yenching Library. The Masuda Bunko has a Yoshikawa kōbunkan reprint of 1906.

h. See *Guochao xianzheng lu*, 57:48. Citation given in You and Zhou, p. 167.

i. (Tokyo: Sōsandō shoten, 1883), six stringbound volumes. There is a copy of this work in the Harvard-Yenching Library: (Tokyo: Kitashima Shigebee, 1884).

j. There are at least three editions of this work, all in the Harvard-Yenching Library: (Edo: Mankyūdō Hokurindō, 1845), five stringbound volumes; *Hyakka setsurin* (Writings of 100 Authors) (Tokyo: Yoshikawa kōbunkan, 1905–7); and *Nihon zuihitsu zenshū* (Collected Japanese Random Notes) (Tokyo: Kokumin tosho, 1927–30).

k. (Tokyo: Kōbunko kankōkai, 1927–31), 12 volumes. A copy may be found in the Harvard-Yenching Library.

CHAPTER TWENTY-SEVEN

a. The Masuda Bunko holds the following editions of these four texts: Gu Yingtai, *Ming shi jishi benmo* (Shanghai: Commercial Press, 1938); Wang Hongxu, *Ming shi gao* (Taibei reprint: Wenhai chubanshe, 1963); Xia Xie, *Ming tongjian* (Taibei: Hongye shuju, 1974); Chen Hao and Chen Kejia, *Ming ji* (Guoxue zhenglishe, 1935). The Harvard-Yenching Library has the following editions: Gu Yingtai, *Ming shi jishi benmo* (Guangya shuju, 1887); (Shanghai reprint: Shangwu qianyin, 1934); (Taibei reprint: Taiwan shangwu, 1983); Wang Hongxu, *Ming shi gao* (1723; Taibei reprint: Wenhai chubanshe, 1963); Xia Xie, *Ming tongjian* (Beijing reprints: Zhonghua shuju, 1950, 1983), 8 volumes; Chen Hao and Chen Kejia, *Ming ji* (Jiangsu shuju, 1871; Shanghai reprint: Zhonghua qianyinben, 1930).

b. The character used for the surname in this instance, 毛, is pronounced the same as the one ordinarily used, 茅.

c. 'Si yi' (Four Barbarians) 17: 'Chaoxian kao.'

d. (Academia Sinica, Institute of Historical Linguistics, 1967), in six stringbound volumes.

e. (Tokyo: Yao shoten, 1892; reprinted in 1902) (Tokyo reprints: Iwanami shoten, 1940, 1943).

f. (Edo: Yamashiroya Sahee, 1850), one stringbound volume.

g. 'Kaisetsu' (explanatory note) to *Kokusen'ya kassen*, in volume 3 of *Dai Chikamatsu zenshū* (Complete Works of the Great Chikamatsu) (Tokyo: Dai Chikamatsu zenshū kankōkai, 1922).

h. The characters *keisei* (lit. "courtesan") in this and many other titles were a way of placing a story in the 'demi-monde.' See Donald Keene, *The Battles of Coxinga* (London: Taylor's Foreign Press, 1951), pp. 80, 201. There is information on the *Min Shin tōki* in this work by Keene, pp. 76–80.

i. As Donald Keene (p. 176) notes, this title is untranslatable because of several internal puns.

j. By Wu Zhenfang (1705, reprint 1868), volume 14.

k. Ten *juan*. There is also a Japanese edition, *Bukyō kaisō*, in the Masuda Bunko: (Kyoto: Chōshiya Tōkichirō, n.d.). A copy of the Chinese edition can be found at the Harvard-Yenching Library, dated 1636; a Japanese edition can also be found there: Yamanaka Shōan, ed. (Kyoto: Nakano Ichizaemon, 1661), fourteen *kan*.

l. (Tokyo: Kokusho kankōkai, 1917–18), three stringbound volumes.

m. 30 *juan* (1833 edition); ten *juan*, ed. Fang Hao (Taibei reprint: Bank of Taiwan, 1960). Both can be found at the Harvard-Yenching Library. The Masuda Bunko has an edition of 1878 published by Shenbaoguan.

n. The Chinese translators of Masuda's book, having access to the original source under discussion, note that in their edition it is the preface by Jiang Risheng that makes this reference and that there is no preface by Chen Zheyong.

o. A copy of the Japanese edition, *Tei Seikō den* (Ōsaka, 1856), 2 volumes, can also be found in the Harvard-Yenching Library.

p. It appears as volume six of *Nishikawa Joken isho* (The Works of Nishikawa Joken) (1898).

q. (Shanghai reprint: Commercial Press, 1957). The Masuda Bunko has a Taibei reprint by Shijie shuju of 1965.

r. As You Qimin and Zhou Qiqian note (p. 180), Xie Guozhen only wrote that 'those who studied there came from far away.' 'Japan' is not mentioned. See the 1981 revised edition (Shanghai: Guji chubanshe), p. 474.

CHAPTER TWENTY-EIGHT

a. Eleven volumes, with numerous charts and maps (Ōsaka: Kawachiya Shigebee).

b. By Ji Luqi (18 *juan*), four editions of this work can be found in the Harvard-Yenching Library: (Beijing: Liulichang bansong jushi, 1671); (Shanghai reprint: Commercial Press, 1936), three stringbound volumes; (Taibei reprints: Wenhai chubanshe, 1969?), two volumes; (Bank of Taiwan, 1963, 3 volumes).

c. (Taibei: Taiwan wenxian congkan, 1962, no. 62).

d. Respectively: (Tokyo: Ōhata shoten, 1931) and (Taibei: Taiwan keisei shinpōsha, 1929).

e. Included in *Zheng Chenggong danchen jinian teji* (Special Issue Commemorating the Birth of Zheng Chenggong), in *Wenxian zhuankan* 1.3 (1950).

1. The meaning of the character given here, 屋, is unclear, but it may be a misprint for a similarly drawn character, 危 "in danger" or "humiliated."

2. Edited by Feng Menglong in one stringbound volume. This book was reprinted and published in Japan in Shōhō 3 [1646], namely some fifteen years earlier. It will be discussed below.

f. By Ro Takeshi (Bunsei 2 [1819]), two volumes.

g. (Edo: Eiheikichi, Bunka 8 [1811]), five stringbound volumes. An edition of this work published in Edo by the Bankyūdō and dated Tenpō 7 (1836) can be found in the Harvard-Yenching Library.

h. (Tokyo: Ida shoten, 1943); (Kawasaki reprint: Rinkyūkaku shoten, 1966). Both of these editions can be found in the Harvard-Yenching Library.

3. 'Nihon ryūgū no Minmatsu shoshi' (Various Late-Ming Scholars Who Wandered to Japan), in *Kindai Shina no gakugei* (Letters and Science in Modern China) (Tokyo: Min'yūsha, 1931).

4. Komatsubara Tō, *Chin Genpin no kenkyū* (Studies on Chen Yuanbin [yun]) (Tokyo: Yūzankaku, 1962).

i. This is apparently the same edition that can be found in the Harvard-Yenching Library. The Masuda Bunko has a text with a preface dated 1885.

j. (Tokyo: Daigakukan, 1903).

k. (Taibei: Wenhai chubanshe, 1971).

l. Included in volume three of his *Geming yishi* (Unofficial History of the Revolution) (Taibei reprint: Taiwan shangwu, 1965).

m. (n.p., 1902).

n. (Tokyo: Sanshōdō, 1942).

o. (Mitt. der Deutschen Geschichte für Natur- und Völkerkunde Ostasiens, 1897); translated into Japanese as *Taiwan tō shi* by Yoshikuni Tōkichi (1898). A Chinese translation appears in *Taiwan jingji shi* (Taiwan: Bank of Taiwan, 1956); another is by Wei Ruizheng and Lai Yongxiang, 'Ming Zheng zili shiqi zhi Taiwan' (Taiwan in the Period of Zheng [Chenggong]'s Independence during the Ming), *Taiwan fengwu* 6.2 (1956).

p. (Shanghai: Commercial Press, 1937), in the series 'Shidi xiao congshu' (Small Series on History and Geography). There is also: (Taibei reprint: Taiwan shangwu, 1955).

q. (Taibei: Taiwan shangwu, 1975), in series 'Renren wenku' (People's archive).

r. (Taibei: Zhengzhong shuju, 1973).

s. (Hong Kong: Qishi niandai zazhishe, 1976).

t. There are two Japanese and two Chinese translations: Tanigawa Umeto, trans., *Kankyaku saretaru Taiwan* (Neglected Taiwan) (Taibei: Taiwan nichinichi shinpōsha, 1930); Hirayama Kaoru, trans., *Tōkan ni fukuseraretaru Forumosa* (Neglected Formosa), in *Taiwan shakai keizai shi zenshū* (Complete Works of Social and Economic History of Taiwan) (1934); Wei Qingde, trans., *Bei jianque zhi Taiwan* (Neglected Taiwan), in *Taiwan sheng tongzhiguan kan* 1–2 (1948); and Li Xinyang and Li Zhenhua, trans., *Zheng Chenggong fu Tai waiji* (An Account of Zheng Chenggong's Recovery of Taiwan), 'Xiandai guomin jiben congshu' (Basic Collection of Contemporary Personages), no. 3 (Zhonghua wenhua chuban shiye weiyuanhui, 1955).

u. Edited by Zhang Bingnan and Li Ruhe (Taibei: Taiwan sheng wenxian weiyuanhui, 1970).

v. (Taibei: Bank of Taiwan, 1962–63).

w. (Taibei: Institute of Historical Linguistics, Academia Sinica, 1957), originally from government archives; (Taibei reprint: Weixin shuju, 1972).

APPENDIX

a. (Ōsaka: Kansai University, 1956).

b. (Ōsaka: En'ya Yoshihyōe, 1879).

c. By Kuzuu Yoshihisa (Tokyo: Kokuryūkai shuppanbu, 1936), volume 3.

d. Many editions of this work have been published. It was most recently published with Japanese translation and notes by Maeno Naoaki as *Bunshō kihan* (Tokyo: Meiji shoin, 1996).

e. The *Zizhi tongjian* was a comprehensive history of China by Sima Guang (1019–86), covering through the first reign of the Northern Song dynasty.

f. The number of histories included in this comprehensive term vary. The 'Seventeen Dynastic Histories' include: *Shi ji*, *Han shu* (History of the Han Dynsty), *Hou Han shu* (History of the Later Han Dynasty), *Sanguo zhi* (Chronicle of the Three Kingdoms), *Jin shu* (History of the Jin), *Song shu* (History of the Liu-Song), *Nan Qi shu* (History of the Southern Qi), *Liang shu* (History of the Liang), *Chen shu* (History of the Chen), *Hou Wei Shu* (History of the Later Wei), *Bei Qi shu* (History of the Northern Qi), *Zhou shu* (History of the [Later] Zhou), *Sui shu* (History of the Sui), *Nan shi* (History of the Southern Dynasties), *Bei shi* (History of the Northern Dynasties), *Tang shi* (History of the Tang), and *Wudai shi* (History of the Five Dynasties). For the 'Twenty-One Dynastic Histories,' add *Liao shi* (History of the Liao), *Jin shi* (History of the Jin), *Song shi* (History of the Song), and *Yuan shi* (History of the Yuan). For the 'Twenty-Two Dynastic Histories,' add *Ming shi* (History of the Ming). For the 'Twenty-Four Dynastic Histories,' add *Jiu Tang shi* (Old History of the Tang) and *Jiu Wudai shi* (Old History of the Five Dynasties).

g. See immediately preceding note.

h. Edited by the Okayama Prefectural Library.

i. I am not sure of the spelling of this Dutch name inasmuch as the text gives it only in *katakana* as *raihe*.

j. For the information in this parenthetical note, I would like to thank the Chinese translators of Masuda's book, You Qimin and particularly Zhou Qiqian, p. 232.

k. Included in *Tōsai minken shi* (History of Popular People's Rights along the Eastern Shore), ed. Sekido Kakuzō (Ibaraki: Yōyūkan, 1903; 1973 reprint by Ryūzanron shobō).

l. (Tokyo: Goshorō, 1910; Tokyo repr.: Iwanami shoten, 1957–58), final volume, Chapter 8, 'Handō no higeki' (The Tragedy of Reaction).

m. First volume, section entitled 'Ōi Kentarō ippa no Ōsaka jiken' (The Ōsaka Incident of Ōi Kentarō and His Group).

n. For more in English on the Yokohama Datong School, see Jung-pang Lo, trans. and ed., *K'ang Yu-wei: A Biography and Symposium* (Tucson: The University of Arizona Press, 1967), pp. 178, 253–54.

o. (Changsha: Commercial Press, 1939).

p. Respectively: Printed in 1893 by Kubo Zaisaburō; and printed in 1929 by Watanabe Tokujirō, one volume.

Glossary

Abe Ise no kami 阿部伊勢守
Abe Masahiro 阿部正弘
Abe Tsushima no kami 阿部對馬守
Adam 亞當
Aeba Kōson 饗庭篁
'Afeilijia zhi' 阿非利加志
'Ahen en ryūdoku, fuku Kō Shakushi
　　jōsho ji'
　　鴉片煙流毒，附黃爵茲上書事
Ahen fūsetsugaki 阿片風說書
Ahen ibun 阿芙蓉彙聞
ahen no hen 鴉片之變
Ahen shimatsu 阿片始末
Aikoku shinbun 愛國新聞
Airulüe 艾儒略
Aizawa Seishisai 會澤正志齋
Ajia rekishi jiten アジア歷史事典
Akashi Kichigorō 明石吉五郎
Akishino Teruashi 秋篠昭足
Akitsuki Taneki 秋月種殷
Akutagawa Kan 芥川煥
'Amerika shisetsu mōshitateru sho'
　　亞墨利加使節申立書
Amerika shisetsu taiwasho
　　墨夷使節對話書
Anchang wang 安昌王
Andes 安日
Andō Kiichi 安藤紀一
Anotsu 洞津
Aoe juku 青衛塾
Aoe Sannin 青衛山人
Aoe Shujin 青衛主人
Aoki Shūzō 青木周蔵
Aoki Tomitarō 青木富太郎
Aoyama Daizennosuke 青山大膳亮
Arai Hakuseki 新井白石

Arai Kōri 荒井公履
Arai Shōgo 新井章吾
Arima Chūmu no shōsuke Tadayori
　　有馬中務少輔忠賴
Asakawa Dōsai 朝川同齋
Asakawa Zen'an (Kanae) 朝川善庵 (鼎)
Asakusa bunko 淺草文庫
Asano 淺野
Asō Tomotoshi 麻生知俊
Atai 阿
Atobe Yamashiro no kami 跡部山城守
Ayusawa Shintarō 鮎澤信太郎

Babylonia 罷鼻落你亞
Baien nikki 梅園日記
Baigai sensei nenpu 梅崖先生年譜
Baikon 賣柑
Baiseisho 梅清所
Baiseisho eishi 梅清所詠史
Bakin nikki shō 馬琴日記鈔
Bakufu suibō ron 幕府衰亡論
Bakumatsu gaikoku kankei monjo
　　幕末外國關係文書
Bakumatsu Ishin gaikō shiryō shūsei
　　幕末維新外交史料集成
Bakumatsu Meiji Yasokyō shi kenkyū
　　幕末明治耶蘇教史研究
Bakumatsu seijika 幕末政治家
Bakuten 幕天
Ban Gu 班古
Banjōken shujin 磐上軒主人
bankan 蕃官
Bankoku kōhō reikan 萬國公法蠡管
Bankoku kōhō shakugi 萬國公法釋義
'Bankoku kōhō shisō no inyū'
　　萬國公法思想の移入

254

'Bankoku kōhō to Meiji ishin'
萬國公法と明治維新
Bankoku kōkan roku wage
萬國綱鑑錄和解
Bankoku zushi 萬國圖誌
Ban-Min shiryō sōsho 晚明史料叢書
Ban shi 蕃史
Bansho shirabesho 蕃書調所
Bansong jushi 半松居士
Batabiya shinbun バタビヤ新聞
'Batsu Isabo yugen' 跋伊莎菩喻言
'Beijing cheng' 北京城
Beijing yaozhai congke 北京瑤齋叢刻
'Beilu' 被虜
'Bei Zhili tu' 北直隸圖
'Bekka setchi no jijō' 別科設置の
   事情
Bessho heishichi 別所平七
betsudan fūsetsugaki 別段風說書
bian 變
bianfa 變法
Biaozhong chongyi ji (Hyōchū sūgi shū)
   表忠崇義集
Bichū no kami 備中守
Biming yinde 筆名引得
'Bingbu' 兵部
Bingo 備後
'Bōbyō hen' 防苗篇
Bohu tong 白虎通
Bōkai yoron 防海餘論
Bokuteisha 墨堤舍
Bokutei Yukimaro 墨亭雪
Bomai 伯麥
Bōshū 房州
Bōnotsu 坊津
Bōsō 房總
Bowu xinbian 博物新編
'Bō Yōshi' 茫洋子
bugyō 奉行
buhaole 不好了
'Buji yoki (gibu gohen)'
   武事餘記議武五篇
'Buji yoki (heisei heishō)'
   武事餘記兵制兵餉
'Buji yoki (jikō, zatsujustu)'
   武事餘記事功雜述
'Buji yoki (shōko, kōshō)'
   武事餘記掌故考證
Bukka yoron 物價余論
Bulun 步倫
bumen 部門
Bungaku 文學

Bunkyū ninen Shanhai nikki
   文久二年上海日記
Bunmei genryū sōsho 文明源流叢書
Bunmei tōzen shi 文明東漸史
Bunshi 文之
Bunshō kihan 文章軌範
bunyabushi 文彌節
Butoku hennen shūsei 武德編年集成
Butoku taisei ki 武德大成記

Cain 加印
Cai Shanji 蔡善繼
Caomu lun 草木論
'Caomu zonglun' 草木總論
'Cao zhong' 操塚
Changqi wang 長崎王
Chaobao suiwen lu 鈔報隨聞錄
'Chaoxian kao' 朝鮮考
chaoxun suiyue lun 潮汐隨月論
Chen Dong 陳東
Chen Hao 陳鶴
Chen Hewu 陳和吾
Chen Huacheng 陳化成
Chenhu Yishi 陳湖逸士
Chen Kejia 陳克家
Chen Lin 陳璘
Chen Lunjiong 陳倫炯
Chen Mouheng 陳懋恆
Chen Qi 陳祈
Chen Shiqing 陳世慶
Chen Shiyi 陳世宜
Chen Shouqi 陳壽祺
Chen Yuanyun (Yuanbin) 陳元贇
Chen Yucheng 陳玉成
Chen Zhaokui 陳兆奎
Chen Zheyong 陳折永
Chen Zilong 陳子龍
Chiba Yajiuma 千葉彌次馬
Chigaku seisō 地學正宗
Chigo shinbun 稚兒新聞
Chihoku gūdan 地北寓談
Chikamatsu Monzaemon 近松門左衛門
Chikan keimō jukka shobu
   智環啓蒙塾課初部
'*Chikan keimō* to Yasokyō'
   「智環啓蒙」と耶蘇教
Chikudō bunshō 竹堂文鈔
Chikudō Saitō kun nenpu
   竹堂齋藤君年譜
Chikudō shishō 竹堂詩鈔
'Chin'en shi iwaku' 椿園氏曰
Chin Genpin no kenkyū 陳元贇の研究

dingben 定本
Ding Jinhu 丁金虎
Ding Lüjin 丁履進
Ding Weiliang 丁韙良
diqi lun 地氣論
'Diqiu fenyu lun' 地球分域論
Diqiu lun 地球論
Diqiu shuolüe 地球說略
Diqiu tu shuo 地球圖說
Diqiu yi xingxing lun 地球亦行星論
'Dishi lun' (Historical Geography)
　地史論
'Dishi lun' (Topography) 地勢論
'Diwen zonglun' 地文總論
'Dizhi lun' 地質論
Dokuga shoin 讀畫書院
Dong Huaniang 東花孃
Dongnan jishi (Accounts of the Southeast)
　東南紀事
Dongnan jishi (Records of the Southeast)
　東南記事
Dong Shutang 董樹棠
Dong Xun 董恂
Dongyue rulin houzhuan 東越儒林後傳
donkaku 鈍角
Dunbi suiwen lu 盾鼻隨聞錄
'*Dunbi suiwen lu* ba' 盾鼻隨聞錄跋
'Dunbi suiwen lu danghui'
　盾鼻隨聞錄當燬
'Duojiashagu dao tu' 多伽沙古島圖
Du shi jizhu 杜詩集註
Du Wenlan 杜文瀾

Eden 厄典
*Edo jidai ni okeru Tōsen mochiwatari sho
　no kenkyū* 江戸時代における
　唐船持渡書の研究
Egawa Tan'an zenshū 江川坦庵全集
Egawa Tarōzaemon 江川太郎左衛門
Eiheikichi 英平吉
Eihitsu 永弼
Eikadō 盈科堂
eikaku 銳角
'Eikoku taigunsen zu' 英國大軍船圖
Ei-Shin ahen sen shi 英清鴉片戰史
'Eishō jūsō zu' 英將戎裝圖
engi 演義
'Enkai zu' 沿海圖
Enka manroku 煙霞漫錄
Enkōji 圓光寺
En'ya Yoshihyōe 鹽冶芳兵衛
Enzan sosui kiyū 燕山楚水紀游

'Erchen zhuan' 貳臣傳
Etō Shinpei 江藤新平
Euphrates 歐法臘得
Eve 厄韈
'Ezo chikushi' 蝦夷竹枝

Fang Hao 方豪
Fangshi 方氏
Fang Xiaoru 方孝孺
Fan Liande 范蓮德
Fan Wenhu 范文虎
Fanyu 番禺
Feihong 飛虹
Feihuang 飛黃
'Feihuang shimo' 飛黃始末
'Feiqin lun' 飛禽論
Feng Jingdi 馮京第
Feng Jingru 馮鏡如
Feng Menlong 馮夢龍
Feng shilang yishu 馮侍郎遺書
Fengsu tongyi 風俗通義
Feng Taoshan 馮濤山
'Fengtu' 風土
Feng Youlan 馮友蘭
Feng Yunshan 馮雲山
'Feng Wang liang shilang mulu'
　馮王兩侍郎目錄
Feng Ziyou 馮自由
fu 府
Fu 福
Fugushe 復古社
Fuhai ji 浮海記
'Fuji' 附記
'Fujian sheng tu' 福建省圖
'Fujian sheng Zheng Zhilong xitu'
　福建省鄭芝龍系圖
Fujian tongzhi 福建通志
Fujii Sadafumi 藤井貞文
Fujimori Tenzan (Kōan) 藤森天山
　(弘庵)
Fujita bunko mokuroku 藤田文庫目錄
Fujita Mokichi 藤田茂吉
Fujita Tōko 藤田東湖
Fujita Tokutarō 藤田德太郎
Fujita Toyohachi (Kenpō) 藤田豊八
　(劍峰)
Fujiwara Ietaka 藤原家孝
Fujiwara Nangaku 藤原南岳
Fukken zassan 復軒雜纂
Fūkō Gyochō Mineta shun shōden
　楓江漁長嶺田俊小傳
Fūkō ibun 楓江遺文

257

'Fūkō Mineta ō juhimei'
　楓江嶺田翁壽碑銘
Fukuda Izumi 福田泉
Fukuchi Ōchi (Gen'ichirō) 福地櫻痴
　(源一郎)
Fukuyama 福山
'Fulu Aomen yuebao' 附錄澳門月報
Funai 府内
Funyō Shigeuemon 汾陽茂右衞門
Furansu bunten フランス文典
Furumi Kazuo 古見一夫
Fūryū Keiseiya gundan
　風流傾城爺群談
fūsetsugaki 風説書
fushō 副將
Fuying xinshuo 婦嬰新說
Fuzanbō 富山房

Gaihō taihei ki 外邦太平記
Gaii chinsetsu zakki 外夷珍説雜記
Gaiken 鎧軒
'Gaikoku' 外國
'Gaikoku den (Min jō)' 外國傳 (明上)
Gaikō shi kō 外交志稿
Gaimushō 外務省
Gakushikai 學士會
gan 桿
Gan Hui 甘輝 (甘煇)
Gan Zhao 甘照
Gao Qi 高齊
Gaotang 高唐
Gao You 高誘
Geertun 格爾屯
Ge Gongzhen 戈公振
Geming yishi 革命逸史
'Geming zhi' 革命志
Genji seisui ki 源氏盛衰記
Genkaimaru 玄海丸
Gen Min Shin shiryaku 元明清史略
Genna shōsetsu 元和小説
Gewu qiongli wenda 格物窮理問答
Gewu rumen 格物入門
Gewu tanyuan 格物探原
gimu 義務
Giritsu (Yilü) 義律
Gi shi no sho 魏氏の書
Godai Saisuke (Tomoatsu) 五代才助
　(友厚)
goki shichidō 五畿七道
Gokyū Hisabumi (Sessō) 五弓久文
　(雪窗)
Gongfa bianlan 公法便覽

Gongfa huitong 公法會通
Gorai Shigeru 五來重
Gorōbee 五郎兵衛
Gosharō 五車樓
Gotō 五島
Gotō Shōjirō 後藤象次郎
Greece 厄勒祭亞
guang lun 光論
'Guang lun' 光論
'Guangdong sheng tu' 廣東省圖
Guangdong tongzhi 廣東通志
Guangming ribao 光明日報
Guangwu 光武
'Guangxi sheng tu' 廣西省圖
Guangyu 光禹
Guangzhou xuebao 廣州學報
Guanlubu 官祿㘪
Guan Ming 關明
Guanwen 官文
'Guanyu *Chouhai tubian*'
　关於筹海图编
'Guanyu '*Daoguang yangsao zhengfu ji*'
　de zuozhe wenti'
　關於「道光洋艘征撫記」的作者
　問題
'Guanyu '*Yangwu quanyu*' yishu'
　關於「洋務權輿」一書
Guan Zhong 管仲
'Guizhou tu' 貴州圖
'Gujin mingjiang' 古今名將
Gujin wanguo gangjian lu
　古今萬國綱鑑錄
'Guncho hen' 軍儲篇
'Gunsei hen' 軍政篇
guo 國
Guochao dianhui 國朝典彙
'Guochao fusui Xizang ji'
　國朝撫綏西藏記
Guochao xianzheng lu 國朝獻徵錄
Guo Guoan (Lixin) 郭國安 (理心)
Guo Moruo 郭沫若
Guo Tingyi 郭廷以
Guowen zhoubao 國聞周報
guoxing 國姓 (national name); 國性
Guoyou 國游
'Guozheng lun' 國政論
Guweitang neiji 古微堂内集
Gu Yingtai 谷應泰
gyōyū zetsurin 驍勇絕倫

Hachimojiya Jishō 八文字屋自笑
Haga Yaichi 芳賀矢一

hai 海
Haidong yishi 海東逸史
Haiguo tuzhi 海國圖志
Haiguo wenjian lu 海國聞見錄
Hai lu 海錄
Hakatanotsu 花旭塔津
hakkō ichiu 八紘一宇
Hakkō shorin 發弘書林
Hakkō tsūshi 八紘通誌
Hakodate igakujo 箱館醫學所
Hakubunkan 博文館
Hakubutsu shinpen yakkai
　博物新編譯解
Hakuen 泊園
hakurai shoseki 舶來書籍
Hakuryū 白龍
Hamada Yahee 濱田彌兵衛
Hamano Tomosaburō 濱野知三郎
'Handō no higeki' 反動の悲劇
Han Hui 函輝
Hanjōken shujin 磐上軒主人
Han Shanwen 韓山文
Hantarō 繁太郎
Han wen 韓文
Hara Nensai 原念齋
Hara shobō 原書房
Harimaya Shōgorō 播磨屋勝五郎
Hashimoto Keigaku zenshū
　橋本景岳全集
Hashimoto Sanai 橋本左内
Hattori Unokichi 服部宇之吉
Hayakawa Kōtarō 早川孝太郎
Hayama Sanai 葉山佐内
Hayama Takayuki (Gaiken) 葉山高行
　(鎧軒)
Hayano Kei 早野惠
Hayashi Akira 林煒
Hayashi Dōshun (Razan) 林道春 (羅山)
Hayashi Fukusai 林復齋
Hayashi Heijirō 林平次郎
Hayashi Nobuatsu (Hōkō) 林信篤
　(鳳岡)
Hayashi Shihei 林子平
Hayashi Shunsai 林春齋
Hayashi Shunshō (Shunsai) 林春勝
　(春齋)
He Changling 賀長齡
He Guiqing 何桂清
Heikei 平啓
heikōsen 平行線
'Henan sheng tu' 河南省圖
henseikyoku 編成局

'Hensha atogaki' 編者あとがき
'Henshin no rekishi dorama'
　變身の歷史ドラマ
He Qiaoyuan 何喬遠
He Shaoji 何紹基
Hexin 合信
Hezha congtan 荷㯹叢談
Hibino Teruhiro 日比野輝寬
Hidaka Seijitsu 日高誠實
Hido 彼土
Higashinari Kamejirō 東生龜次郎
Higashi Seijun (Takusha) 東正純 (澤瀉)
Higuchi Tatarō 樋口多太郎
Hikka shi 筆禍史
Hine Oribemasa 日根織部正
Hirado 平戶
Hirado bōeki shi 平戶貿易史
Hirado Ikkan 平戶一官
Hirado Rōikkan 平戶老一官
Hiratsuka 平塚
Hirayama Kenjirō 平山謙二郎
Hirayama Shū 平山周
hirei 比例
Hirose 廣瀨
Hirose Motoyasu 光瀨元恭
Hiseki 匪石
Hitotsubashi gakumonjo 一橋學問所
Ho 甫
Hōan jūshu 匏庵十鍾
Hōchi shinbun 報知新聞
Hōka shuchi 砲家須知
Hōkō gikai 報效議會
Hokuchi kigen 北地危言
Hokuchō 北廳
Hokuriku jiyū shinbun 北陸自由新聞
Honda Tamesuke 本多爲助
Hong 洪
Hong Deyuan 洪德元
honglu si qing 鴻臚寺卿
Hongmaofan Yingjili kaolüe
　紅毛番嗫吉利考略
Hong Quanzhong 洪全忠
Hong Renda 洪仁發
Hong Renfa 洪仁達
Hong Ren'gan 洪仁玕
Hongwu 洪武
Hong Wulong 洪武龍
Hong Xiuquan 洪秀全
Hong Xiuquan 洪秀泉
Hongye shuju 宏業書局
Honkoku chikan keimō 翻刻智環啓蒙
Honma 本間

Honyaku no shisō 翻訳の思想
Hori Iga no kami 堀伊賀守
Horio Mosuke 堀尾茂助
Hori Tetsaburō 堀哲三郎
Hōsei 法政
Hoshi Tōru 星亨
Hosokawa Higo no kami Mitsunao
　細川肥後守光尚
'Hosotsu gunsō sokumen' 歩卒軍装側面
'Hosotsu gunsō zenmen' 歩卒軍装前面
Hotei shujin 穂停主人
Hotta Masayoshi 堀田正睦
Houguan 侯官
Hou Jigao 侯繼高
Hou-Ming 後明
Houshile 侯失勒
Hou Wailu 侯外盧
Hua 華
huache 滑車
Huacun kanxing shizhe 花村看行侍者
Huainan honglie jie 准南鴻烈解
Huang Binqing 黄斌卿
Huangchao jingshi wenbian
　皇朝經世文編
Huang Cheng 黄澄
Huang Dianquan 黄典權
'Huangdi zunqin zhi bao' 黄帝尊親之寶
Huanghuaguan 黄華關
Huang Juezhi 黄爵之
Huang Juewen 黄爵文
Huang Juezi 黄爵滋
'Huang Ming dixi' 皇明帝系
Huang Ming jishi benmo 皇明紀事本末
Huang Ming zhifang ditu
　皇明職方地圖
Huang Quan 黄詮
Huang Xianchen 黄獻臣
Huang Xiaoqing 黄孝卿
Huang Zhengming 黄徵明
Huang Zonghan 黄宗漢
Huang Zongxi (Lizhou) 黄宗羲 (梨洲)
Huang Zunxian 黄遵憲
huaqi 花旗
Hu gong Zongxian jiao Xu Hai benmo
　胡公宗憲剿徐海本末
'Huguang sheng tu' 湖廣省圖
Hui'ai yiguan 惠愛醫館
Huidun 惠頓
huixing lun 慧星論
Huoxing lun 火星論
Hu Yiguang (huang) 胡以洸 (晃)
Hu Zongxian 胡宗憲

Hyakka setsurin 百家說林
Hyakka zuihitsu 百家隨筆
hyōchū 標注
'Hyō sei-Kan eki' 評征韓役
'Hyō Shinkoku kakumei' 評清國革命
'Hyō Tōbu hōchū' 評湯武放誅
'Hyō tōsō' 評黨爭
'Hyō Yasukyō' 評耶蘇教

Iba Kashō 伊庭可笑
Ichimei haiya no hanashi
　一名はいやのはなし
Ichimei Tōdo haiya no hanashi
　一名唐土はいやのはなし
Iehisa 家久
Iguchi shoten 井口書店
Iguchi Toraji 井口寅次
Ihi hankyō bunkenroku
　夷匪犯境聞見錄
Ihi hankyō kenbunroku
　夷匪犯境見聞錄
Iida Tadahiko 飯田忠彦
Iijima Seiken 飯島靜謙
Ii Kamonnosuke Naotaka
　井伊掃部頭直孝
Ii Naosuke 井伊直弼
Ikkai Tomoyoshi 一海知義
Ikuei 育英
Imaizumi Mine 今泉みね
imashime no kagami 戒めの鑑
Ima Watōnai Tōdo bune
　今和藤内唐土船
Imazeki Tenpō 今關天彭
Inaba Kunzan (Iwakichi) 稻葉君山
　(岩吉)
Inagaki Magohee (Kigai) 稻垣孫兵衞
　(其外)
Indus 印度
'Ingirisu kokki ryaku' 英吉利國紀略
Ingirisu nichiyō tsūgo
　インギリス日用通語
Inoue Kiyonao (Shinano no kami)
　井上清直 (信濃守)
Inoue Misao 井上操
Inoue Shun'yō 井上春洋
Inoue Tetsujirō 井上哲次郎
Inō Yoshinori 伊能嘉矩
Inukai Ki 犬養毅
In'yū roku 陰憂錄
Irisawa Tatsukichi 入澤達吉
Ise Saisuke 伊勢齋助
Ise Yasuemon 伊勢安右衛門

Ishibashi Jojūrō 石橋助十郎
Ishida Gyokusan 石田玉山
Ishida Mitsunari 石田三成
Ishihara Michihiro 石原道博
Ishii 石井
Ishii Kendō 石井研堂
Ishimura Teiichi 石村貞一
Ishin shiryō kōyō 維新史料綱要
Ishin shi sōsetsu 維新史叢說
Ishizaki Tōgoku 石崎東國
Ishō Nihon den 異稱日本傳
Isoyama Seibee 磯山清兵衛
Isumi-gun 夷隅郡
Itagaki Taisuke 板垣退助
Itakura Shigemune 板倉重宗
Itazawa Takeo 板澤武雄
Itō Yukimiki 伊藤之幹
Itsuzon shomoku 佚存書目
Iwase bunko tosho mokuroku
　岩瀬文庫圖書目錄
Iwase Higo no kami (Tadanori)
　岩瀬肥後守 (忠震)
'Iwase Higo no kami to jireki'
　岩瀬肥後守と事歷
'Iwayuru Chōhatsuzoku no shinsō'
　所謂長髮賊の眞相
Izumida Jirō 泉田次郎

Jagarata no kashirayaku no mono kara
　mōshitsukete kita kara 咬嚼吧の頭
役の者から申しつけて來たから
ji 集
Jiajing dongnan pingwo tonglu
　嘉靖東南平倭通錄
Jiang Min shilüe 江閩事略
Jiang Risheng (Dongxu) 江日昇 (東旭)
Jiangshang Jiansou 江上蹇叟
Jiang Shixing 蔣式惺
'Jianguo ji' 監國紀
Jiang Xingqin (yu) 江星禽 (畬)
'Jiangxi sheng tu' 江西省圖
Jiang Youren 蔣友仁
Jian Youwen (Jen Yu-wen) 簡又文
Jiao Hong 焦竑
'Jiaohui yuanliu kao' 教會源流考
'Jiaoxue lun' 教學論
Jiao Xun 焦循
'Jiaqing dongnan jinghai ji'
　嘉慶東南靖海記
jichi 自治
Jidu shilu 基督實錄
'Jieli jiangqi lun' 借力匠器論

Jieqi ting ji 鮚埼停集
Jieyu hui lu 劫餘灰錄
jihe (kika) 幾何
Jihe yuanben 幾何原本
Jijitsu bunpen 事實文編
Ji [Li] Zhou 季(李)州
Ji Kan 嵇侃
Ji Luqi 計六奇
'Jinbao Wo jing' 近報倭警
Jin Chengfu 金成福
Jindai mimi shehui shiliao
　近代秘密社會史料
Jing-Chu 荊楚
Jingchu suishiji 荊楚歲時記
Jingguo xionglüe 經國雄略
jingji 經紀
Jingshi daxuetang 京市大學堂
Jingtuo yishi 荊駝逸史
Jingyang 鏡揚
Jinling guijia zhitan 金陵癸甲摭談
'Jinling jinshi' 金陵金事
Jinpingmei 金瓶梅
Jin Shengtan 金聖嘆
Jin Shengwu 金省吾
jinshi 進士
Jintian 金田
Jinxing lun 金星論
Jin Xueceng 金學曾
'Jinyao' 津要
Jin Yufu 金毓黻
jishu 自主
Jitsuji dan 實事譚
'Jiu bian tu' 九邊圖
Jiujing 九京
Jiyūtō 自由黨
Jiyūtō shi 自由黨史
Jizhong 躋仲
jōi 攘夷
'Jōiron to kaikokuron'
　攘夷論と開國論
'Jōkisen zu' 蒸氣船圖
'Jōshu hen' 城守篇
Judea 如德亞
junkan shōsū 循環少數
Juntendō 順天堂
'Ju-Qing pian' 拒清篇
juren 舉人
Jūsen kidan 銃戰紀談
'Jusuo lun' 居所論

Kaei Meiji nenkan roku
　嘉永明治年間錄

Kafuseisha 何不成社
Kageyama Eiko 景山英子
Kaibōbi ron 海防備論
Kaibō okusoku 海防臆測
Kaibō shigi 海防私議
Kaibō shigi hoi 海防私議補遺
Kaibō shiryō sōsho 海防史料叢書
Kaihan shishin 開板指針
Ka-i hentai 華夷變態
'Kaigai chishiki' 海外知識
Kaigai iden 海外異傳
Kaigai jitsuroku 海外實錄
Kaigai shinwa 海外新話
Kaigai shinwa shūi 海外新話拾遺
Kaigai yowa 海外餘話
'Kaiguo qian haineiwai geming shubao
　yilan' 開國前海内外革命書報
　一覽
kaihei 開平
Ka'i hentai 華夷變態
Kaikoku kigen 開國起原
Kaikoku kigen Ansei kiji
　開國起原安政紀事
Kaikoku taisei shi 開國大勢史
Kairiku senbō roku 海陸戰防錄
Kaisei gakkō 開成學校
Kaiseijo 開成所
Kaiseikan 開成館
'Kaisetsu' 解說
Kaishintō 改進黨
Kaishū sensei: Hikawa seiwa
　海舟先生：冰川清話
Kaitai shinsho 解體新書
Kaizō 改造
Kajima Nobushige 加嶋信成
Kakken bosu 活賢勃斯
Kakka ron 隔靴論
Kaku 恪
Kakubutsu nyūmon wage 格物入門和解
Kakujirō 恪二郎
kakumei 革命
Kakunosuke 格之助
Kakuyama Rikichirō 隔山利吉郎
Kamon 掃部
kan 貫
Kanagawa yūki 金川游記
Kanamori Shintoku 金森慎德
Kanaya Sōshirō 錢屋惣四朗
kanban 官板
Kanda 神田
Kanda Mitsuru 神田充
Kanda Kiichirō 神田喜一郎

Kan'ei 觀永
Kan'ei shōsetsu 觀永小說
Kangakusha 漢學者
Kang Changsu 康長素
Kang Guangren 康廣仁
Kang Mengqing 康孟卿
Kang Tongwen 康同文
kangun 官軍
Kang Youwei 康有爲
'Kangxi Qianlong Eluosi mengpin ji'
　康熙乾隆俄羅斯盟聘記
kanjō bugyō 勘定奉行
kanjō ginmiyaku 勘定吟味役
Kano Sōtoku 狩野宗得
kanpaku 關白
'Kanpōtei kōkyū Ryū Ki'
　咸豐帝后宮劉輝
Kansai daigaku nenshi kiyō
　關西大學年史紀要
Kansai daigaku shichijū nen shi
　關西大學七十年史
*Kansai daigaku shozō Masuda bunko
　mokuroku*
　関西大学所蔵増田文庫目録
Kanseki kaidai 漢籍解題
Kanseki mokuroku 漢籍目錄
Kanshi 漢詩
Kanshi enryaku 漢詩沿略
Kanton nikki 廣東日記
Kariganaya Seikichi 鴈金屋清吉
'Karinsen zu' 火輪船圖
Kasai Shigesuke 香西成資
Kasai Sukeji 笠井助治
Kashiwabara Buntarō 柏原文太郎
Kataoka Kenkichi 片岡健吉
Katayama Kenzan 片山兼山
Katayama Tomoyuki 片山智行
Katō 加藤
Katō Kiyomasa 加藤清正
Katō Kurō 加藤九郎
Katō Shūichi 加藤周一
Katsu Kaishū 勝海舟
Katsuragawa Hoshū 桂川甫周
Katsura Isoo (Koson) 桂五十郎 (湖村)
Kawabata Genji 河鰭源治
Kawachiya Shigebee 河内屋茂兵衛
Kawachiya Shinshichi 河内屋眞七
Kawaguchi Chōju 川口長孺
Kawaji Toshiakira 川路聖謨
Kawashima Genjirō 川島元次郎
Kawata Sadao 川田貞夫
Kazan zenshū 崋山全集

ke 課

Keichō shōsetsu 慶長小說

Keigaku shibun shū 景岳詩文集

Keimō chie no tamaki 啓蒙智慧乃環

keisei 傾城

Keisei bunpen shō 經世文編抄

Keisei Kokusen'ya 傾城國性爺

Keizai yōroku 經濟要錄

Kenkadō zōsho in 蒹葭堂藏書印

kenrei 縣令

kenri 權利

Ken shuroku 憲手錄

kibyōshi 黄表紙

Kidō 毅堂

kikagaku (jihexue) 幾何學

'Kikka rō shin rokurokubu shū'
喫霞樓新六々部集

Kikka senkaku 喫霞仙客

Kikuchi Kenjirō 菊池謙二郎

Kikuma gakkō meishinkan
菊間學校明親館

Kim Ok-kyun 金玉均

Kimura Kaishū 木村芥舟

Kimura Kenkadō (Kōkyō)
木村蒹葭堂 (孔恭)

Kimura Junyū 木村淳邑

Kimura Nagato no kami 木村長門守

Kimura Shigenari 木村重成

Kinaishō 宮内省

'Kindai Chūgoku hishi' 近代中國秘史

Kindai meika chojutsu mokuroku
近代名家著述目錄

Kindai Shina no gakugei
近代支那の學藝

Ki no Kaion 紀海音

Kinryō kikō sekidan 金陵癸甲摭談

Kinryū Dōjin 金龍道人

*Kinsei hankō ni okeru shuppansho no
kenkyū*
近世藩校にをける出版書の研究

Kinsei Kangakusha denki chosaku daijiten
近世漢學者傳記著作大事典

Kinsei meika bunshō 近世名家文鈔

*Kinsei Nihon no kokusai kannen no
hattatsu*
近世日本の國際觀念の發達

'Kinsei Shina yori Ishin zengo no Nihon ni
oyobashitaru shoshu no eikyō'
近世支那より維新前後の日本に
及ばしたる諸種の影響

Kinsei sōdan 近世叢談

'Kinsho' 禁書

Kinshōjo 錦祥女

kinshu 今主

Kirishitan 切支丹

Kirishitan kyō jahōsha keizaisei sho
切支丹行邪法者刑罪制書

Kiseki 其磧

Kishida Ginkō 岸田吟香

Kitabatake Mohee 北畠茂兵衛

Kitada Kiyozaemon 北田清左衛門

Kitani Hōgin 木谷逢吟

Kita Shingen (Seiro) 北慎言 (靜盧)

Kiuemon 喜右衛門

Kiyō ki 崎陽記

Kiyomasa 清正

Kō-A in 興亞院

Kobayashi Eichi 小林營智

Kobayashi Kuzuo 小林樟雄

Kōda Shigetomo 幸田成友

Kōdō 皇道

Koga Dōan 古賀侗庵

Kōgai yūkoku ron 慷慨憂國論

Kōgaku sōsho 皇學叢書

kōgi 講義

kōgi (protest) 抗議

Kōgyokujuku 攻玉塾

Koike Yōjirō 小池洋二郎

'Kōin Rondon hyōban ki o yomu'
讀「甲寅嘯頓評判記」

Kōjien 廣辭苑

Kojima Korekata 兒島惟謙

Kojō Teikichi 古城貞吉

Kōjunsha 交詢社

Kōkaen 黄花園

Kokkai kisei dōmeikai
國會期成同盟會

Kokō shokyokuzō 古香書局藏

koku 石

Kokubo Kishichi 小久保喜七

Kokugaku taikei 國學大係

Kokusen'ya chūgi den 國性爺忠義傳

Kokusen'ya gonichi no kassen
國性爺後日合戰

Kokusen'ya gozen gundan
國性爺御前軍談

Kokusen'ya hanjō 石千屋繁昌

Kokusen'ya kassen 國性爺合戰

Kokusen'ya kassen (by Bokutei Yukimaru)
國性谷合戰

Kokusen'ya kassen (picture book)
こく情や合戰

Kokusen'ya Minchō taiheiki
國性爺明朝太平記

263

Liu Mingchuan 劉銘傳
Liu Tianchong 柳天寵
Liu wen 柳文
Liu Yizheng 柳詒徵
Liu Yuanlin 劉元霖
Li Xiucheng 李秀成
lixue (rikigaku) 力學
Liyage 理雅各
Li Zhizao 李之藻
'Lizhou xiansheng shendao beiwen'
　梨洲先生神道碑文
Lizhou yizhu huikan 梨洲遺著彙刊
Li Zicheng 李自成
Li Zongtong 李宗侗
Longwu 隆武
Long Ya 龍涯
Lu 魯
Lü Bi 呂芘
Lu chunqiu 魯春秋
'Lun Dongya shiyi' 論東亞事宜
'Lun Zhongguo xueshu sixiang zhi
　bianqian dashi'
　論中國學術思想之變遷大勢
lunzhu 輪軸
Luo Ergang 羅爾綱
Luo Sen 羅森
Luo Xianglin 羅香林
Luo Xiaoquan 羅孝全
luoxuan 螺旋
Luo Yawang 羅亞旺
Luo Zhenyu 羅振玉
Lushuang 露霜
Lu Xun 魯迅
Lu Xun de yinxiang 魯迅的印象

Maeno Naoaki 前野直彬
Maezono Sōbu 前園嘈武
Makino 牧野
Maki Tsuneharu 牧常春
Man-Shin kiji 滿清紀事
'*Man-Shin kiji* to sono hissha, waga kuni ni
　tsutaerareta 'Taihei tengoku' ni tsuite'
　『滿清紀事』とその筆者，わが國に
　傳えられた「太平田國」について
Man-Shin shiryaku 滿清史略
Mao Dun 茅盾
Mao Guoke 茅國科
Mao Guoqi 茅國器，毛國器
Mao Kun (Lumen) 茅坤 (鹿門)
maomei 冒昧
Mao Yibo 毛一波
Mao Yuanyi 茅元儀

Mao Zedong 毛澤東
Maruyama Kunio 丸山国雄
Maruyama Masahiko 丸山正彦
Maruyama Masao 丸山真男
Masanori 正則
Masuda Bunko 增田文庫
Masuda Mitsugu (Gakuyō) 增田貢
　(岳陽)
Masuda Wataru 增田涉
'Masuda Wataru san no omoide arekore'
　增田涉さんの思い出あれこれ
Masuya-chō 升屋町
matou 馬頭
Matsudaira Aki no kami Mitsuage
　松平安藝守光晟
Matsudaira Awa no kami Tadahide
　松平阿波守忠英
Matsudaira Chikanao (Kawachi no kami)
　松平近直 (河内守)
Matsudaira Dewa no kami Naomasa
　松平出羽守直政
Matsudaira Echigo no kami Mitsunaga
　松平越後守光長
Matsudaira Iga no kami 松平伊賀守
Matsudaira Izu no kami Nobutsuna
　松平伊豆守信綱
Matsudaira Nagato no kami Hidenori
　松平長門守秀就
Matsudaira Satsuma no kami Mitsuhisa
　松平薩摩守光久
Matsudaira Shintarō Mitsumasa
　松平新太郎光政
Matsudaira Shungaku (Yoshinaga)
　松平春嶽 (慶永)
Matsudaira Ukyōdaifu Yorishige
　松平右京大夫賴重
Matsuda Tarōzaemon 松田太郎左衛門
Matsueda Shigeo 松枝茂夫
Matsui Kōkichi (Hakken) 松井廣吉
　(柏軒)
Matsushiro 松代
Matsushita Kenrin (Seihō) 松下見林
　(西峰)
Matsuura 松浦
Matsuura Hiroshi 松浦弘
Matsuura Shijū 松浦子重
Meihuasuo 梅花所
Meiji bunka zenshū 明治文化全集
Meiji bunken mokuroku 明治文獻目錄
Meiji ishin 明治維新
Meiji Ishin shi kenkyū 明治維新史研究
Meiji jibutsu kigen 明治事物起原

men 面

Menshitanghuge 捫蝨談虎客

Mikuni sha みくに社

Mianning 綿寧

Minamoto 源

Mindai wokou kaolüe 明代倭寇考略

Mineta Fūkō 嶺田楓江

Mineta Noritoshi 嶺田矩俊

Mineta Ugorō 嶺田右五郎

Mingchao xiao shi 明朝小史

Ming ji 明紀

Mingji bianwu 明季辨誤

Mingji nanlüe 明季南略

Mingji suizhi lu 明季遂志錄

Ming Qing shiliao 明清史料

Ming Shenzong shilu 明神宗實錄

Ming Shenzong shilu jiaokan ji
  明神宗實錄校勘記

Ming shi 明史

Ming shi jishi benmo 明史紀事本末

Ming shi gao 明史稿

Ming shilu 明史錄

Ming tongjian 明通鑑

Ming Yanping wang Taiwan haiguo ji
  明延平王台灣海國記

Ming yimin lu 明遺民錄

Ming yu xingguo lu 明餘行國錄

Minmatsu gunki 明末群記

'Minmatsu Shinsho ni okeru Nihon no
  ichi' 明末清初における日本の
  位置

'Minmatsu no yūshin Kan Kō'
  明末ノ勇臣函光

Minogami 美濃紙

Min Shin gundan Kokusen'ya chūgi den
  明清軍談國性爺忠義傳

Min Shin tō ki 明清鬬記

Mitamura Kōji 三田村高治

Mitsukuri Genpo 箕作阮甫

Mitsukuri Keigo 箕作奎五

Mitsukuri Shōgo 箕作省吾

Miyajima Yaisaemon 宮嶋屋伊佐衛門

Miyake 三宅

Miyatake Gaikotsu 宮武外骨

Miyazaki Raijō 宮崎來城

Miyazaki Torazō 宮崎寅藏

Miyoshiya 美吉屋

Mizuno Isanori 水野軍記

Mizuno Tadanori (Chikugo no kami)
  水野忠德（筑後守）

Mochizuki Kotarō 望月小太郎

'Mogu' 默觚

Molisong 莫利宋

Momijiyama gakumonjo 紅葉山學問所

Mondo no suke 主水祐

monme 匁

Mōri Jōsai 毛利貞齋

Mori Keizō (Taikyō) 森慶造（大狂）

Mori Naiki Nagatsugu 森內記長繼

Mori Ōgai 森鷗外

Moriogi Sonosa no kami Ryūho
  森荻園三守柳圃

Mori Sakutarō 森作太郎

Mori Senzō 森銑三

Morita Tetsugorō 森田鐵五郎

Motoya Keitarō 本屋啓太郎

Motoyama Zenkichi 本山全吉

Mozume Takami 物集高見

Mumei sannin 無明散人

Muramatsu Kazuya 村松一稱

Murase Shū 村瀨栞

Muweilian 慕維廉

Muxing lun 木星論

Muze Kōshi 無是公子

Myōjin 明神

Nabeshima Shinano no kami Katsushige
  鍋島信濃守勝茂

Nagahara Takeshi 長原武

Nagai Hisayuki 永井尚志

Nagai Hyūga no kami 永井日向守

Nagai Kafū 永井荷風

Nagai Nogihara 永井禾原

Nagamochi Kōjirō 永持享次郎

Nagaoka Kōnosuke 長岡行之助

Nagasaki nikki 長崎日記

Nagasaki senmin den 長崎先民傳

Nagasaki yawa sō 長崎夜話草

Nagasawa Kikuya 長澤規矩也

Nagata 長田

Nagayama Nuki (Kan) 長山貫

Nagori no yume 名ごりの夢

na huar 那話兒

Naikaku bunko 內閣文庫

Naikaku bunko Kanseki bunrui mokuroku
  內閣文庫漢籍分類目錄

*Naikaku bunko tosho dainibu Kansho
  mokuroku* 內閣文庫圖書第二部漢
  書目錄

Naitō Chisō 內藤耻叟

Naitō Hida no kami 內藤飛彈守

Naitō Shōhei 內藤庄兵衛

Naitō Tsutauemon 內藤傳右衛門

Nakae Chōmin 中江兆民

Nakagawa Chūei 中川忠英
Nakagawa Kiyohide 中川清秀
Nakajima Kurō 中島久郎
Nakajirō 半次郎
Nakamuda Kuranosuke 中牟田倉之助
Nakamuda Kuranosuke den
　中牟田倉之助傳
Nakamuda Takenobu 中牟田武信
Nakamura Keiu 中村敬宇
Nakamura Kōya 中村孝也
Nakamura Masanao 中村正直
Nakamura Shinshichi 中村進七
Nakane Yukie 中根雪江
Nakanishi Masaki 中西正樹
Nakao Shinsuke 中尾新助
Nakayama Kyūshirō 中山九四郎
Nakayama Sakusaburō 中山作三郎
Nakayori 乃隔依理
Namura Hanamichi 名村花蹊
'Nanbei Zhi[li] tu' 南北直(隸)圖
Nanbing Wenshe 南屏文社
nandao . . . bucheng 難道 . . . 不成
Nanhai 南海
Naniwa ashi 浪花蘆
Naniwa Ōshio sōdō ki 浪花大鹽騒動記
Naniwa sōjō kiji 浪花騒擾記事
Nanjiang yishi 南疆逸史
'Nanjing cheng' 南京城
Nanjuku shū 南塾集
Nankai chiran ki 南海治亂記
Nankin hishi 南京秘史
Nankoku shiwa 南國史話
Nanpo Bunshi ōshō 南浦文之和尚
Nanpo bunshū 南浦文集
Nanryū kō furyaku 南龍公譜略
Nanryū kun iji 南龍君遺事
Nansui man'yū shūi 南水漫游拾遺
Nan tian hen 南天痕
'Nan Zhili tu' 南直隸圖
Napoleon 那波列翁
Narahara Nobumasa 楢原陳政
Narushima Motonao 成島司直
Narushima Ryūhoku 成島柳北
Nawa Nagatoshi 名和長年
neige 那個
Neike xinshuo 内科新說
niaoshou lüelun 鳥獣略論
'Nichen zhuan' 逆臣傳
Nichi-Ran bunka kōshō shi no kenkyū
　日蘭文化交渉史の研究
Nihon bugaku kenkyūjo
　日本武學研究所

Nihon bunka meicho 日本文化名著
Nihon gaishi 日本外史
Nihon kindai shisō taikei
　日本近代思想大系
Nihon kobunka kenkyūjo hōkoku
　日本古文化研究所報告
Nihon kōra 日本甲螺
Nihon Kirisuto kyōkai shi
　日本基督教會史
Nihon rekishi 日本歴史
'Nihon ryūgū no Minmatsu shoshi'
　日本流寓の明末諸士
Nihon shiseki kyōkai 日本史籍協會
Nihon shinbun rekishi 日本新聞歴史
Nihon sōsho mokuroku 日本叢書目録
Nihon Yōgaku hennen shi
　日本洋學編年史
Nihon Yōmeigakuha no tetsugaku
　日本陽明學派の哲學
Nihon zuihitsu zenshū 日本隨筆全集
Nimrod 泥摸路多
Ninggudao 寧古島
Ningguta 寧古塔
Ninnaji 仁和寺
Nishi Amane 西周
Nishikawa Joken 西川如見
Nishikawa Joken isho 西川如見遺書
Nishiki Bunryū 錦文流
Nishikitani rōjin 錦溪老人
Nis-Shin kyōwakai 日清協和會
Noah 諾厄
Nongxue bao 農學報
Nōtomi Kaijirō 納富介次郎
Noyama goku bunkō 野山獄文稿
Numazu 沼津
Nuttari 沼垂

Obama Toshie 小汀利得
Ōba Osamu 大庭脩
ōbun 横文
Ochi 越智
Ochiguri monogatari 落栗物語
Ōgai zenshū 鷗外全集
Ogawa Gihei 小川儀平
Ogura Hidenuki 小倉秀管
Ogura Naofusa 小倉正房
Ōhara Sakingo (Donkyō) 大原左金吾
　(呑響)
Ōi Kentarō 大井憲太郎
'Ōi Kentarō ippa no Ōsaka jiken'
　大井憲太郎一派の大阪事件
Okahashi Kiyoshi 岡橋清

reigen 例言
re lun 熱論
Ren 璉
Renda 仁達
Renfa 仁發
Renji yiguan 仁濟醫館
'Renlei lun' 人類論
'Renlei zonglun' 人類總論
'Renren wenku' 人人文庫
Ren Ruitu 任瑞圖
Renshen gaishuo 人身概說
'Rensheng huiju tongju dengshi lun'
　人生會聚同居等事論
Renyin Zhapu xunnan lu
　壬寅乍浦殉難錄
'Riben' 日本
Riben guo zhi 日本國志
'Riben kao' 日本考
Riben qishi ji 日本乞師紀
Riben riji 日本日記
'Riben rukou tu' 日本入寇圖
Riben tuzuan 日本圖纂
Riben wendian 日本文典
Riben yijian 日本一鑑
Rigaku teiyō 理學提要
Rikken seitō 立憲政黨
Rikken seitō shinbun 立憲政黨新聞
rippōtai 立方體
Risshisha 立志社
Ro Jin annai 魯迅案内
Ro Jin den 魯迅傳
Ro Jin no inshō 魯迅の印象
Ro Jin no kotoba 魯迅の言葉
Ro Jin senshū 魯迅選集
Rōjū 老中
Rome 邏馬
Rōmon 樓門
ron 論
Rong Mengyuan 榮孟源
Rongo shiken 論語私見
Rongo shikō 論語私考
Rōsōkan 老皂館
Ro Takeshi 盧驤
Ruan Jin 阮進
Ruan Mei 阮美
Ruan Yuan 阮元
'Rulin' 儒林
'Ru Mian lucheng' 入緬路程
Rusui 留守居
'Ryōgun waboku, fuku wayaku jōmoku'
　兩軍和睦，附和約條目
Ryokuten sanbō 綠天山房

Ryūhaku 龍伯
Ryūhoku ikō 柳北遺稿
'Ryūkyū chikushi' 琉球竹枝
Ryūkyū shiryaku 琉球志略

Sach'ŏn 泗川
Saigō Takamori 喜鄉隆盛
Saikin Shina shi 最近支那史
Saint Mary 撒多私馬利牙
Sairan igen 釆覽異言
Sairensha サイレン社
Saitō Chikudō 齋藤竹堂
Saitō Daizaburō 齋藤大三郎
Saitō Kaoru (Shitoku) 齋藤聲 (子德)
Saitō Setsudō (Masanori) 齋藤拙堂 (正謙)
Saitō Yakurō 齋藤彌九郎
Sakamoto Ryōma 坂本龍馬
Sakaya Yutaka 昌谷碩
Sakoku jidai Nihonjin no kaigai chishiki:
　sekai chiri, Seiyō shi ni kansuru bunken
　kaidai 鎖國時代日本人の海外知識:
　世界地理，西洋史に關する文獻
　解題
Sakuma 佐久間
Sakuma Morimasa 佐久間盛政
Sakuma Shōzan 佐久間象山
Sakumu kiji 昨夢記事
sama 樣
Samura Hachirō 佐村八郎
Sanada Kōkan 眞田幸貫
Sandianhui 三點會
San'gan 山顏
Sanhai サンハイ
Sanjū nen shi 三十年史
sanshi 三使
santo kamae 三都構へ
Sanyō ikō 山陽遺稿
Satō Chin'en 佐藤椿園
Satō Eishichi 佐藤榮七
Satō Haruo 佐藤春夫
Satō Issai 佐藤一齋
Satō Issai to sono monjin
　佐藤一齋とその門人
Satō Motokura 佐藤元晦
Satō Nobuhiro 佐藤信淵
Satō Nobuhiro bugaku shū, Nihon bugaku
　taikei 佐藤信淵武學集，日本武學
　大係
Satō Nobuhiro, gimon no jinbutsu
　佐藤信淵，疑問の人物
Satō Nobuhiro kagaku zenshū
　佐藤信淵家學全集

Shigakkai 史學會

Shigakkai zasshi 史學會雜誌

Shigaku zasshi 史學雜誌

Shigenori 重矩

Shigeno Seisai 重野成齋

Shigeno Yasutsugu 重野安繹

Shiichi 子一

Shi ji 史記

Shijing 詩經

shijō 市場

Shi Jun 史峻

Shiki, So-Kan hen 史記，楚漢篇

Shimabara Eiji 島原英治

Shimabara Kammonosuke 島原掃部助

Shimabara Kiuemon 島原喜右衞門

Shimai Kiyomitsu 島居清滿

Shimazu 島津，石曼子

Shimazu Hisamitsu 島津久光

Shimazu Hisatoshi 島津久通

Shimazu Narioki 島津齊興

Shimazu shi keifu ryaku 島津氏系譜略

Shimazu shiryō shū 島津史料集

Shimazu Yoshihiro 島津義弘

Shimazu Yoshihisa 島津義久

Shimizu Ichijirō 清水市次郎

Shimoda nikki 下田日記

Shina gikyoku shū 支那戲曲集

Shinai torishimari ruishū 市内取締類集

Shina jinbun kōwa 支那人文講話

Shina koku 支那國

'Shina zairyū Yasokyō senkyōshi no Nihon bunka ni oyoboseru eikyō' 支那在留耶蘇教宣教師の日本文化に及ぼせる影響

Shinbon honkoku 清本翻刻

Shinbunshi jitsureki 新聞紙實歷

Shinbun zasshi no sōshisha Yanagawa Shunsan 新聞雜誌の創始者柳河春三

Shinchō jōran fūsetsugaki 清朝擾亂風説書

Shinchō shiryaku 清朝史略

Shinchō zenshi 清朝全史

Shin-Ei ahen no sōran 清英阿片の騷亂

'Shin-Ei kassen no koto' 清英合戰の事

Shin-Ei kinsei dan 清唭近世談

Shin-Ei sen ki 清英戰記

Shinkoku Kanpō ran ki 清國咸豐亂記

Shinkoku kinsei ran shi 清國近世亂誌

'Shinkoku ryakuzu' 清國略圖

'Shinkoku ryūgakusei kaikan' 清國留學生會館

shinko ryō Kapitan 新古兩かぴたん

Shinkyanfuoi シンキャンフヲイ

Shin Min gundan 清明軍談

Shinonome shinbun 東雲新聞

Shinozaki Shōchiku 篠崎小竹

Shinron 新論

shinpan 親藩

Shinpan jiryaku 侵犯事略

shin sekai 新世界

Shinsetsu Min Shin kassen ki 新說明清合戰記

Shinshi ranyō 清史攬要

Shinshū 信州

Shin Tōkyōmaru 新東京丸

Shin zoku ibun 清賊異聞

Shionoya On 鹽谷溫

Shionoya Tōin (Seikō) 鹽谷宕陰 (世弘)

Shionoya Tokitoshi (Seizan) 鹽谷時敏 (青山)

shi o okashite 死を冒して

Shiping 石屏

Shi Qi 石器

Shiqi shiji zhi shijiu shiji sishi niandai 十七世紀至十九世紀四十年代

Shiryō shūsei: Yoshino Muromachi jidai gaikan 史料集成：吉野室町時代概觀

'Shiryō sōsho' 史料叢書

Shisei 子成

Shiseki shūran 史籍集覽

Shi Shiyong 史世用

Shitaya sōwa 下谷叢話

shitensei 司天生

Shitoku 士德

Shiwu bao 時務報

Shiyuan congshu 適園叢書

Shōdō 聖堂

Shōei-chō 松永町

Shoga kaisui 書畫薈粹

Shōheikō 昌平黌

Shōheizaka gakumonjo 昌平坂學問所

Shōin sensei icho 松陰先生遺著

Shōkyo 正教

'Shōkyō' 尚志

'Shoshū shishi, Ryohaku no chishin Shu I, nochi ni Shōtōkai no gunshi to naru' 處州刺史，呂伯ノ智臣・朱韋，後ニ小刀會ノ軍師ト成ル

'Shōtōkai daini no tōryo Yō Shūei' 小刀會第二ノ棟梁・楊秀榮

'Shōtōkai hanashi' 小刀會話

'Shōtōkai no chōhon So I'
小刀會ノ張本・蘇意
'Shōtōkai sōtaishō Kō Shūsen'
小刀會總大將・洪秀泉
'Shotoku zasshū' 書牘雜輯
shou (kami) 守
Shōzaemon 庄左衛門
shu 樞
Shū Bunjizaemon 周文二左衛門
Shuihu zhuan 水滸傳
'Shui lun' 水論
Shuinsen bōeki shi 朱印船貿易史
Shuixing lun 水星論
shuizhi lun 水質論
Shujing 書經
shuken 主權
Shundairō 駿台樓
Shuo ling 說鈴
Shuping 書評
Shusaiō 種菜翁
Shuyuan Tuisou 檟園退叟
Shuxue qimeng 數學啓蒙
Sibu beiyao 四部備要
Sibu congkan 四部叢刊
'Sichuan sheng tu' 四川省圖
Siku quanshu zongmu tiyao
　四庫全書總目提要
Sima Guang 司馬光
Siming congshu 四明叢書
Simingzhou 思明州
Sishu daquan 四書大全
Siwen 思文
Siwen daji 思文大紀
'Si yi' 四夷
Sizhou zhi 四洲志
Sō 宗
Soejima Taneomi 副島種臣
Sōkikan 相輝館
Sokuja manroku 息邪漫錄
sokuryōgaku 測量學
Sone Toshitora 曾根俊虎
'Song Huang Jinwu [Xiaoqing] Feng
　Shiyu [Jingdi] qishi Riben'
　送黃金吾 [孝卿] 馮侍御 [京第]
　乞師日本
Song Shu 宋恕
Son Jirō 孫次郎
Son-Ka zateki ron 存華挫狄論
Sonkeikaku bunko 尊經閣文庫
soshiki 組織
soshiki teki 組織的

Suganuma Teifū 菅沼貞風
Suga Tatehiko 菅楯彦
Sugawara no Michizane 菅原道眞
Sugita Genpaku 杉田玄白
Sugita Teiichi 杉田定一
Sugiume Tarō 杉梅太郎
Suharaya Mohee 須原屋茂兵衛
Suimu chijin 醉夢痴人
Suiriku senpō roku 水陸戰法錄
'Suishu hen' 水守篇
Suitō hiroku 垂統秘錄
Sunagawa Yūshun 砂川雄峻
Sun Yaoqing 孫耀卿
Sun Zhongshan 孫中山
Sunzi 孫子
Suō 周防
suojian suowen 所見所聞
Suozhi lu 所知錄
Suruga 駿河
Su Yi 蘇意
Suzuki Kiyofushi 鈴木清節
Suzuki Shōtō 鈴木松塘
Suzunari 鈴成

Tachibana Sakon no shōgen Tadashige
　立花左近將監忠茂
Tagawa 田川
Tagawa Shichizaemon sojō
　田川七左衛門訴狀
Taibikaku 對嵋閣
Taihei isshi 太平逸士
Taihei ki 太平記
taikakusen 對角線
taiko 太古
Taiping lizhi 太平禮制
Taiping tianguo 太平天國
Taiping tianguo congshu shisan zhong
　太平天國叢書十三種
Taiping tianguo dianzhi tongkao
　太平天國典制通考
'Taiping tianguo Hong Tianwang jiashi
　kaozheng'
　太平天國洪天王家世攷證
Taiping tianguo lishi bowuguan
　太平天國歷史博物館
'Taiping tianguo qiyi ji'
　太平天國起義記
Taiping tianguo quanshi 太平天國全史
Taiping tianguo shigao 太平天國史稿
Taiping tianguo shi jizai dingmiu ji
　太平天國史記載訂謬集
Taiping tianguo shiliao 太平天國史料

Taiping tianguo shiliao bianwei ji
太平天國史料辨偽集
Taiping tianguo shiliao congbian jianji
太平天國史料叢編簡集
Taiping tianguo shishi kao
太平天國史事考
Taiping tianguo shishi rizhi
太平天國史事日誌
'Taiping tianguo yu Tiandihui guanxi de
wenti'
太平天國與天地會關係的問題
Taiping tianguo zaji diyiji
太平天國雜記第一輯
Taiping tianguo ziliao mulu
太平天國資料目錄
Taiping zhaoshu 太平詔書
taiseki 體積
taisū 對數
Taitōkaku 大鐙閣
Taiwan lishi zhaji 台灣歷史札記
Taiwan sheng tongzhi 台灣省通志
Taiwan shi 台灣誌
Taiwan tō shi 台灣島史
Taiwan waiji 台灣外記
Taiwan Teishi kiji 台灣鄭氏記事
'Taixi jinshi jiyao' 泰西近事紀要
Taizu zuxun 太祖祖訓
Takaichi Yoshio 高市慶雄
Takami Inosuke 高見猪之介
Takanabe 高鍋
Takano Chōei 高野長英
'Takasago no koto narabete Kokusen'ya
monogatari'
塔伽沙谷之事并國姓爺物語
Takasu 高洲 (太佳自)
Takasugi Shinsaku 高杉晉作
Takasugi Shinsaku zenshū
高杉晉作全集
Takata Sanae 高田早苗
Takaya Ryūshū 高谷龍州
Takebe Seian 建部清庵
Takeda Taijun 武田泰淳
Takekura 武庫
Takemoto Chikugo no jō 竹本筑後掾
Takemoto Gidayū 竹本義太夫
Takemura Shōrei 竹村勝禮
Takenaka Kuniyoshi 竹中邦香
Takeuchi Yoshimi 竹内好
Takimoto Seiichi 瀧本誠一
Taki Seiichi 瀧精一
Takishirō 多氣志樓
Tamada Onkichi 玉田音吉

Tamaki Bunnoshin 玉木文之進
Tamiya Yukiharu 田宮之春
Tamura Hisatsune 田村久常
Tanabe 田邊
Tanaka 田中
Tanaka Kenji 田中謙二
Tanaka Shōhee 田中庄兵衛
Tanaka Takeo 田中健夫
Tang 唐
Tangren 唐人
Tang Rui (Juedun) 湯叡 (覺頓)
Tan Sitong 譚嗣同
Tan tian 談天
Tan wang 談往
Tao Chengzhang 陶成章
Tatemori Kō (Shūkai) 館森鴻 (袖海)
Tazan no ishi 他山之石
Tei Enpei jiryaku 鄭延平事略
teihen 底邊
'Teikai ken zu' 定海縣圖
Teikoku chihō gyōsei gakkai
帝國地方行政學會
Teinhei テインヘイ
Tei Seikō 鄭成功
Tei Seikō den 鄭成功傳
'Teishi enpeigan ra fuku fūsetsu'
鄭氏援兵願等附風說
Tei shōgun Seikō den 鄭將軍成功傳
'Tei Shun kō' 鄭舜侯
teki (de) 的
ten 點
Tenchū ki 天柱記
Tenjinmaru 天神丸
Tenkōdō 天香堂
Tenkōrō sōsho 天香樓叢書
Tennōjiya Ichirōhee 天王寺屋市郎兵衛
Tenpō ran ki 天保亂記
Tenryūji 天龍寺
Tenpō nikki 天保日記
Tenshōsha kaiwa 天香社會話
Tentei Nyorai 天帝如來
Teramachi 寺町
Terusawa Shima no kami 寺澤志摩守
Tezuka Ritsu 手塚律
Tiande 天德
'Tiandihui qiyuan kao' 天地會起源考
Tiandihui wenxian lu 天地會文獻錄
Tiandinghui 添丁會
tianguo 天國
Tianli 天理
Tianli yaolun 天理要論
Tianming zhaozhi shu 天命詔旨書

'Tianqi zhutian lun' 天氣諸天論
tianshi 天使
'Tianwang Hong Xiuquan zhi chushen'
　天王洪秀全之出身
'Tianwen chandu tu' 天文纏度圖
Tian Yuqing 田余慶
'Tianxia zongtu' 天下總圖
Tianxue chuhan 天學初函
tianwen lüelun 天文略論
'Tianzi zhi bao' 天子之寶
Tigris 知幾里斯
Tō-A senkaku shishi kiden
　東亞先覺志士記傳
Tobayama Kan 戶羽山瀚
Tōbun 東文
Tōda 遠田
Toda Yamashiro no kami 戶田山城守
Tōdo 唐土
'Tōdo haiya no hanashi'
　唐土はいやのはなし
Tōdō Izumi no kami 藤堂和泉守
'Tōdo kōyo no zenzu' 唐土皇輿之全圖
'Tōetsu ken no shu Tō [Tō] Jun, nochi ni
　Shōtōkai no gun ni kuwawaru'
　騰越縣ノ主剗[鄧]順，後ニ小刀
　會ノ群ニ加ハル
Tōin sonkō 宕陰存稿
Tōin sensei nenpū 宕陰先生年譜
Tōjō Kindai (Nobuyasu)
　東條琴台（信耕）
Tōjō shoten 東城書店
Tōjuen 桃樹園
Tōkai Gyojin 東海漁人
Toki Yorimune (Tanba no kami)
　土岐賴旨（丹波守）
Tōkoku 唐國
'Tōkoku bu' 唐國部
Tōkō sensei ibun 東行先生遺文
Tōko zenshū 東湖全集
'Toku Fushimi sen ki' 讀伏見戰記
Tokugawa Iemitsu 德川家光
'Tokugawa Iemitsu no Shina shinryaku no
　kito' 德川家光の支那侵略の企圖
Tokugawa Ieyasu 德川家康
Tokugawa shoki no kaigai bōekika
　德川初期の海外貿易家
Tokugawa Yorinobu 德川賴宣
Tokugawa Yoshikatsu 德川慶勝
Tokugawa Yoshinobu 德川慶喜
'Toku Hōjō kyūsei shi' 讀北條九世史
'Toku kagaku jigen' 讀下學邇言
Tokunō Michiaki 得能通昭

'Toku Saden' 讀左傳
'Toku Sanyō gaishi' 讀山陽外史
Tokushi zeigi 讀史贅議
Tōkyō nichinichi shinbun 東京日日新聞
Tōkyō shihan gakkō 東京師範學校
Tomita monjo 富田文書
Tomita Takahiro 富田等弘
'Tongshang maoyi lun' 通商貿易論
Tongwenguan 同文館
Tongzhi Shanghai xian zhi 同治上海縣志
Tōō 唐王
Torii Hisayasu sensei kakō kinen ronshū:
　Chūgoku no gengo to bungaku
　鳥居久靖先生華甲記念論集：
　中國の言語と文學
Toriya Gisaburō 鳥屋儀三郎
Tōsai minken shi 東陲民權史
Tōsen banashi ima Kokusen'ya
　唐船噺今國性爺
'Tōsen ni karamaru Bōnotsu no seisui'
　唐船に絡まる坊津の盛衰
Tōsō 唐僧
totokushoku no mono 都督職の者
Totsukawa 十津川
Tōyama Saemon no jō 遠山左衛門尉
Tōyama Unjo 遠山雲如
Tōyō bunko 東洋文庫
Tōyō garon shūsei 東洋畫論集成
Tōyō gyosha 東洋漁舍
Toyoda Mitsugi 豐田貢
Toyotomi Hideyoshi 豐臣秀吉
Tōzaian Nanboku 東西庵南北
'Tōzai honzō rokuyō' 東西本草錄要
Tsêkê ツェーケー
tsūbun 通分
Tsuitōji 追悼辭
Tsuji Zennosuke 辻善之助
Tsukamoto Ki 塚本毅
Tsūkō ichiran 通航一覽
Tsumagi 妻木
Tsune 恆
Tsunoda Bun'ei 角田文衞
Tsuruya Kiuemon 鶴屋喜右衛門
Tsutsui Kii no kami 筒井紀伊守
Tsutsumi Asakaze 堤潮風
Tsutsumi Kōshishi 堤轂士志
Tsutsumi Seiji 堤精二
Tsūzoku Kokusen'ya chūgi den
　通俗國姓爺忠義傳
Tsūzoku zentai shinron 通俗全體新論
Turks 都爾格
Tuxing lun 土星論

Udagawa Kaien (Genzui) 宇田川槐園
　（玄隋）
Udai kindō hisaku 宇内混同秘策
Udono Chōei 鵜殿長鋭
Ueki Emori 植木枝盛
Uemura Masahisa 植村正久
Ukai Nobuyuki (Sekisai) 鵜飼信之
　（石齋）
U kō shūran 禹貢集覽
Umeda Unpin 梅田雲濱
Unebi shobō 畝傍書房
Unko shinbun ki 溫古新聞記
Unnan shinwa 雲南新話
Unsō zuihitsu 雲莊隨筆
'Unryōsan no gōtō Chō Kaku, nochi ni
　Shōtōkai no gun ni kuwararu'
　雲龍山ノ剛盜・趙角，後ノ小刀
　會ノ群ニ加ハル
Uryū Tora 瓜生寅
Ushigome-dōri 牛込道

'Waiguo' 外國
'Waiguo zhuan (Chaoxian)' 外國傳
　（朝鮮）
Waiguo zhuzhi ci 外國竹枝詞
Waiyi xiao shi 外夷小史
Wakagi bunko 若樹文庫
wakō (wokou) 倭寇
Wakokuhon Min-Shin shiryōshū
　和刻本明清資料集
Wan Da Hong 萬大洪
Wang (wang) 王
Wang Chongwu 王崇武
Wang Hongxu 王鴻緒
Wang Kangnian (Rangqing) 汪康年
　（穰卿）
Wang Kun 汪堃
Wang Lipei 王禮培
Wang Shouyun 王少雲
Wang Shuming 汪叔明
Wang Tao 王韜
Wanguo gangjian lu 萬國綱鑑錄
Wanguo gongfa 萬國公法
Wang Wentai 汪文泰
Wang Xiangrong 王向荣
Wang Xianqian 王先謙
Wang Xiqi 王錫祺
Wang Yangming 王陽明
Wang Yi 王翊
Wang Youling 汪有齡
Wang Zhao 王照
Wang Zhi 王直

Wan Ming shiji kao 晚明史籍考
Wan Sui Hong 萬歲洪
Wanxing tongpu 萬姓統譜
Washizu Ikutarō 鷲津郁太郎
Washizu Kan 鷲津監
Watanabe Chiaki 渡邊千秋
Watanabe Kazan 渡邊崋山
*Watanabe Kazan, Takano Chōei, Kudō
　Heisuke, Honda Toshiaki*
　渡邊崋山，高野長英，工藤平助
　，本田利明
Watanabe Kōhei 渡邊公平
Watanabe Shūjirō 渡邊修次郎
Watanabe Tokujirō 渡邊得次郎
Watanabe Yakurō 渡邊約郎
Watōnai 和藤内
Wayaku bankoku kōhō 和譯萬國公法
Weibin 渭濱
Wei Changhui 韋昌輝
Weilianchen 韋廉臣
Weilieyali 偉烈亞力
Wei Moshen 魏默深
weixin 維新
Weixin shuju 維新書局
Wei Yuan 魏源
'Wei Yuan de sixiang' 魏源底思想
Wei Zheng 韋正
Wei Zheng jishi 僞鄭記事
wen 文
Wengzhou Laomin 翁州老民
Wen Ruilin 溫睿臨
Wen Tianxiang 文天祥
Wenxian zhuankan 文獻專刊
'wenyuan' 文苑
'Wenyuan zhuan' 文苑傳
Wenzhang guifan 文章軌範
Wubei zhi 武備志
Wuerxi 吳爾璽
Wu Fa 吳法
'Wuguan lun' 五官論
Wu Jianzhang 吳健彰
Wujing kaizong (Bukyō kaisō) 武經開宗
Wu Zhenfang 吳震方
'Wushi yuji' 武事餘記
'Wuzhi ji yidong deng lun'
　物質及移動等論
Wu Zhongluan 吳鍾欒

Xiaer guanzhen 遐邇貫珍
Xianfeng donghua lu 咸豐東華錄
Xianggang xinwen 香港新聞
'Xiangheng xiangshi' 小橫香室

Yang Xiurong 楊秀榮
Yang Yi 楊宜
Yangzijiang 揚子江
Yanjing xuebao 燕京學報
Yan Matai 晏瑪太
Yanping 延平
Yanping shijia 延平世家
Yansêkian ヤンセーキアン
Yan Siqi 顏思齊
Yan Zhenguan 顏振泉
Yao Jiyun 姚際雲
Yao shoten 八尾書店
Yao Weiyuan 姚薇元
Yapian zhanzheng 鴉片戰爭
*Yapian zhanzheng shiqi sixiang shi ziliao
xuanji*
鴉片戰爭時期思想史資料選輯
Yapian zhanzheng shishi kao
鴉片戰爭史實考
'Yapian zhanzheng shumu jieti'
鴉片戰爭書目解題
Ya shi 野史
Yassekian ヤッセキアン
Yasuzumi Gonsai 安積艮齋
Yasuzu Motohiko 安津素彥
'Yaxiya zhi' 亞西亞志
ye (ya) 爺
Ye Ma 葉麻
Ye Shanji 葉善繼
Yi 李
'Yibu Taiping tianguo de jinshu'
一部太平天國的禁書
*Yifei fanjing lu (Ihi hankyō
roku)* 夷匪犯境錄
Yifen wen ji 夷氛聞記
Yi jing (journal title) 逸經
Yijing (Classic of Changes) 易經
'Yikuan' 議款
Yilibu 伊里布
Yinbingshi wenji 飲冰室文集
'Yindu jinshi' 印度近事
Yinghuan zhi lüe 瀛環志略
Ying-Hua shuyuan 英華書院
'Yingjili yichuan rukou ji'
英吉利夷船入寇記
'Ying nü beiqin' 英女被擒
Yingren qiangmai yapian ji
英人強賣鴉片記
Ying Shao 應邵
'Yinshi lun' 飲食論
Yinyou lu 隱憂錄
'Yishou' 議守

Yi Tuho 李斗搞
Yi Wuzi 奕吾子
Yi Yin 伊尹
'Yi zhan' 議戰
'Yochi ryakuzu' 輿地略圖
Yōgai kiryaku 洋外紀略
Yōgai tsūran 洋外通覽
Yōgaku benran 洋學便覽
Yokohama hanjō ki 橫濱繁昌記
Yongan biji 庸庵筆記
Yongli 永曆
Yongzheng 雍正
'Yoroppa bu' 歐羅巴部
Yorozuya Hyōshirō 萬屋兵四郎
Yoshida Kurazō 吉田庫三
Yoshida Shōin 吉田松陰
Yoshida Shōin zenshū 吉田松陰全集
Yoshikawa Nobutarō 吉川延太郎
Yōshi kiryaku 洋史紀略
Yoshikuni Tōkichi 吉國藤吉
Yoshimoto Noboru 吉本襄
Yoshino Maho 吉野眞保
Yoshino Rokubee 良野六兵衛
Yoshino Sakuzō 吉野作造
Yoshiteru 義輝
'Yoshū Nojima-shi shin tai Minkoku ki'
預州能島氏侵大明國記
'You Hong Xiuquan guxiang suo dedao de
Taiping tianguo xin shiliao'
游洪秀全故鄉所得到的太平天國
新史料
You Ming 右命
You Qimin 由其民
You Tong 尤洞
Youyi 有儀
Yōzō kaiku ron 鎔造化育論
Yuan Shide 袁視德
yuanxu 原序
Yu Dafu 郁達夫
'Yudi beikao' 輿地備考
Yuefei dalüe (Etsuhi tairyaku) 粵匪大略
'Yuekou jilüe' 粵寇紀略
yuelun yuanque lun 月輪圓缺論
Yuelu shusha 岳麓书社
'Yuesheng jinshi shulüe' 粵省近事述略
yueshi dingli lun 月蝕定例論
Yuexi Guilin shoucheng ji
粵西桂林守城記
Yūgei en zuihitsu 游藝園隨筆
'Yu gong' 禹貢
Yu Hui'an 玉會庵
Yui Shōsetsu 由井正雪

Zhongguo sixiang tongshi
　中國思想通史
Zhongguo zaoqi qimeng sixiang shi
　中國早期啓蒙思想史
Zhongguo zhexue shi ziliao xuanji, jindai zhi bu
　中國哲學史資料選輯，近代之部
Zhong Jingwen 鐘敬文
*Zhong-Ri guanxi shi wenxian lunkao*中日关系史文献论考
Zhongshan wenhua jiaoyuguan jikan
　中山文化教育館季刊
zhongtang 中堂
Zhongwai xinbao 中外新報
Zhongwai zazhi 中外雜誌
Zhong-Xi jishi 中西紀事
Zhongxing weilüe 中興偉略
zhongxue 重學
Zhongxue qianshuo (Jūgaku sensetsu)
　重學淺說
Zhou 周
Zhou Cuizhi 周崔芝
Zhou Hezhi 周鶴芝
Zhou Qiqian 周啓乾
zhouye lun 晝夜論
Zhou Yunshan 周雲山
Zhou Zuoren 周作人
Zhu 朱
'Zhuge Kongming bazhen tu'
　諸葛孔明八陣圖
Zhuge Liang 諸葛亮
'Zhuge Liang bazhen tu' 諸葛亮八陣圖
Zhuge Xiu 諸葛繡

Zhuge Yuansheng 諸葛元聲
Zhu Hua 朱華
Zhu Jiutao 朱九濤
'Zhu Jiutao kao' 朱九濤考
Zhu Junwang 朱均旺
Zhuoru 卓如
Zhu Tiande 朱天德
Zhu Yuanye 朱元曄
Zhu Yuanzhang 朱元璋
Zhu Wu 朱烏
'Zhu wuzhi ti lun' 諸物質體論
Zhuzi yulei daquan 朱子語類大全
Zhu？朱熹
Ziye 子夜
Zizheng xinpian 資政新篇
Zizhi tongjian 資治通鑑
Zoku gunsho ruiju 續群書類從
Zoku Shiseki shūran 續史籍集覽
Zoku zenrin kokuhō ki 續善鄰國寶記
Zoku zenrin kokuhō gaiki
　續善鄰國寶外記
'Zongjiao kao' 宗教考
Zōsho mokuroku 藏書目錄
Zōtei kaigai kyōtsū shiwa
　增訂海外交通史話
Zōtei sairan igen 增訂采覽異言
Zuguan 祖官
Zuoyin Feiren 左尹非人
Zuozhuan 左傳
Zuo Zongtang 左宗棠

Index